Bow Church.

Cheape Crosse

S Laurens

Gut

The Stilliarde

Cole harb

lly fuste

The Globe

# THE TIMES

# HISTORY
OF
# LONDON

NEW EDITION

# THE TIMES

# HISTORY
## OF
# LONDON

### NEW EDITION

## EDITED BY HUGH CLOUT

**TIMES BOOKS**

# CONTENTS

Fourth Edition
Published in 2004 by
TIMES BOOKS
HarperCollins*Publishers*
77-85 Fulham Palace Road
London W6 8JB

The Collins website address is:
**www.collins.co.uk**

First published by Times Books in 1991
Reprinted in 1994
Second edition published in 1997
Third edition published in 1999
Copyright © Times Books 1991, 1997, 1999 and
2004

*Artwork and typesetting*
Swanston Graphics, Derby
Ralph Orme
Andrew Bright
Advanced Illustration

*Colour processing*
Colourscan, Singapore

*Design*
Ivan Dodd
Tracey Enever
Mabel Chan
Martin Brown

*Editorial direction*
Elizabeth Wyse
Malcolm Swanston
Isobel Willetts
Caroline Lucas
Ailsa Heritage
Sarah Allen
Philip Parker

*Picture research*
Jane Parsons

*Place names consultant, Index*
P J M Geelan

*Chronology*
Sid Holyland and Len Phillips

*Endpapers*
Map of London by Nicholas John Visscher,
published in Amsterdam in 1616

The publisher wishes to thank Gavin Morgan of
the Museum of London, Marrianne Behm, Ian Smith
and Lesley Branscombe

Printed and bound in Italy by Rotolito Lombarda, SpA

British Library Cataloguing in Publication Data
A catalogue record for this book is available from the
British Library

**ISBN 0 00 716653 2**

# CONTRIBUTORS

## GENERAL EDITOR:
Dr Hugh Clout FBA, Professor of Geography, University College
London, Dean of Social and Historical Sciences

## CONTRIBUTORS:
John Clark, Curator, Medieval Collections, Museum of London

Jonathan Cotton, Curator, Prehistory, Museum of London

Dr Richard Dennis, Reader in Geography, University College
London

Jenny M N Hall, Curator, Roman Collections,
Museum of London

Dr Vanessa Harding, Lecturer in London History, Birkbeck College,
University of London

Gustav Milne, Department of Urban Archaeology,
Museum of London and University College London

Dr Richard Overy, Professor of Modern History, Kings College London

Dr Michael Power, Lecturer in Economic and Social History,
University of Liverpool

Dr Hugh Prince, Reader Emeritus in Geography,
University College London

Dr Eric Robinson, President of The Geologists' Association,
London and University College London

Dr John Schofield, Archaeology Officer (City of London),
Museum of London

Dr Peter Wood, Professor of Geography, University College London

## CONSULTANTS:
Dr John Adams, Professor Emeritus of Geography, University
College London

Dr Clive Agnew, Professor of Geography, University of Manchester

Dr Andrew Gurr, Professor of English, University of Reading

Dr Carolyn Harrison, Professor of Geography, University College
London

Dr Ted Hollis, Late Reader in Geography, University College
London

Dr Peter Jackson, Professor of Geography, University of Sheffield

Dr John Salt, Professor of Geography, University College London

## ETYMOLOGY COMPILED BY:
Dr Robert Ilson, Honorary Research Fellow, University College
London

## HUGH CLOUT WISHES TO THANK:
Anne Oxenham MBE of the Department of Geography,
University College London, for help in exploring many
cartographic sources

Michael Jahn of the London History Library,
University College London, for identifying many historic maps
and books on London

Malcolm Ward for help in checking many details of London's
history on the ground

# INTRODUCTION

THIS BOOK is a visual celebration of two thousand years of urban settlement. The history of London is traced from Roman times, through many centuries of political and commercial greatness, reaching their pinnacle in the Victorian era, to the present when London is confronted by new challenges in a rapidly changing world. After an introduction on the physical resources of the London region, successive chapters are arranged in a conventional chronological way, with the exception of the last two, which concentrate on themes and places in the metropolis. Our interpretation of 'history' is liberal, encompassing social and economic conditions and the processes that led to the formation of London's landscape, as well as key events in the city's past. Great buildings have their place, but so do the poor and deprived whose plight so shocked Victorian observers. Urban history is viewed in a comprehensive way, complemented by the special perspectives of the archaeologists, geologists, geographers and professional historians who have contributed to the book. New evidence on the pattern of London in Roman and medieval times is converted into maps, while images of the city in later periods are created from contemporary statistics and other records.

The book contains not only specially-drawn maps and diagrams but also many reproductions of paintings, facsimiles of historic maps, engravings and photographs. Meticulous reconstructions of parts of London at various times in the past form a unique element. A great deal of imagination and draughtsman's skill have gone into interpreting fragmentary historic records in order to produce convincng and visually attractive images. Last but by no means least are the texts and captions which complement the hundreds of illustrations. These essays provide a succinct digest of our knowledge of the metropolis in successive periods and raise questions about London in the future.

The Museum of London, located in the Barbican, offers a superb series of displays on the capital's social, economic and political life from the earliest days of settlement to present times. London's many specialist museums and local history collections provide an unrivalled range of information on particular topics and neighbourhoods. But urban history is not just about books and museums. It is to be found in the streets we walk, the trains we take and the buildings we use every day. Indeed, the best way to study London's past is to interrogate its present with an inquisitive eye, armed with a detailed map and a good guidebook. Every building, square, street and monument was created at some time past, often according to a logic that was different from our own. Ancient property boundaries are reflected in the alignment of roads and in differences in house type, long-lost trades and activities are recorded in street names, ancient villages form the cores of sprawling suburbs, while historic churches recall the past vibrancy of community life in parts of the city that are now depopulated. The list is endless. A lifetime spent exploring the metropolis convinces me that there is always another street corner to be turned and a fresh townscape to interpret. Continuity and change are vital themes in urban history. New forces have transformed the size, shape, appearance and functioning of our city, but the legacy of the past remains. An appreciation of history helps us understand landscape features that may seem odd or illogical. As Italo Calvino argues: 'the city … does not tell its past, but contains it like the lines of a hand, written in the corners of the streets.'

But what of the future? Controversy rages every time historic features are threatened with demolition to make way for a new building or a motorway. Some battles for conservation are won and others lost, but every excavation offers the chance of unearthing new evidence of London's past. Sadder still are the hundreds of listed buildings in Greater London that are literally crumbling away through neglect and lack of capital investment. Most of those at risk are in inner boroughs and include warehouses, redundant churches, hospitals and neglected public monuments. In recent years 'gentrification' has saved many of London's Georgian terraced houses, albeit at the cost of social change. Many more are in a dilapidated state. Saving the city's crumbling buildings will cost vast sums and raises important questions about the wisest use of scarce public resources in a city where public transport, housing, schools and so many other facilities need massive investment if they are to remain viable in the future.

I was born in what is now called the 'inner city' and London is my home town. My life-long fascination with London remains and has been strengthened each weekend over recent years as I have 'checked out' information and visited (and revisited) places that appear in the book. I can do no better than quote Dr Johnson's assertion: 'when a man is tired of London, he is tired of life.' I hope this book will help preserve and extend the reader's fascination with our great city.

I am delighted to have had the opportunity of producing a new edition, which allows new information to be included on the prehistory of the London area and on the capital in the new century, as well as some minor modifications.

*Hugh Clout*

# History, Politics and Society

**AD**
**43** Romans invade England.
**50** Foundation of *Londinium*.
**60** Sack of *Londinium* by Boudicca.
**61** *Londinium* rebuilt and designated capital of province.
**125** *Londinium* destroyed by fire.
**200** *Londinium* designated as capital of Britannia Superior.

**457** Britons defeated by mercenaries. *Londinium* disappears from historical record.
**604** Mellitus appointed Bishop of London.

**842** Viking attack on London: 'Great Slaughter'.
**c.871** Danes occupy London. Recaptured by King Alfred (878).
**911** Edward takes control of London after Alfred's death.
**1016** Cnut captures London, becomes king.
**1042** Edward the Confessor becomes king. London made capital of England.
**1066** Harold killed at Hastings; William crowned at Westminster Abbey.
**1085** Population c. 10-15,000.

**1180** Population inside walls c.40,000.

**1192** Permission granted for mayor and aldermen with own court.
**1207** Archbishop of Canterbury takes up residence at Lambeth.
**1215** Magna Carta: Mayor of London one of signatories.

**1290** Expulsion of Jews from London ghetto in Old Jewry.

**1327** First Common Council of City of London.
**1348-9** Black Death epidemic: c.10,000 buried at West Smithfield.

**1377** Population c.40,000.
**1381** Peasants revolt led by Wat Tyler.

**1397** First of Richard Whittington's four terms as Lord Mayor.

# Commerce, Industry and Infrastructure

**AD**
**50** Road network begun; Thames bridged; provision of port facilities.

**125** New waterfront built.

**c.290** London Mint established.

**c.640** Gold coins minted in London: the first since Roman times.

**899** First mention of Queenhithe.
**949** First mention of Billingsgate.

**1066** William grants London Charter.

**c.1130** Charters establishing liberties.

**c.1155** Vintner's Company granted Charter.
**1170** Weekly horse fair at Smithfield.
**1180** First mention of Goldsmith's Company.

**c.1199** First building regulations introduced in the City.

**1214** City Charter awarded by King John.

**1272** First Craft Guild.
**1274** First mention of 'Flete Strete'.
**c.1290** The Hop and Grapes in Aldgate High St: London's oldest Licensed House.

**1358** 138 shops on London Bridge.
**1358** First Goldsmith's Hall.

**1380** First Skinner's Hall.

**1382** First Custom House.

**1389** River wall built at Tower.
**1394** Farringdon wards formed outside the wall.

# Building and Architecture

**BC**
**600** Middle Iron Age domestic sites at Rainham, Dawley, Bedfont, Heathrow.

**AD**
**80-125** Building of basilica and forum, governor's palace, public baths, fort.

**200** City wall built.
**240** Mithraic temple built

**c.600** Saxon London built mainly outside walls.
**604** St Paul's Cathedral built.
**606** St Mary Overie Nunnery established on the site of present Southwark Cathedral.

**898** Conference of King's Council re restoration of London.

**c.1000** Earliest reference to London Bridge.

**1067** Building of Tower of London and other castles began.

**1089** Bermondsey Abbey founded.
**1123** Building of St Bartholomew's Priory and Hospital begun.
**1140** Priory of St John established at Clerkenwell.
**1140** Nunnery of St Mary's established at Clerkenwell.

**1176** Old London Bridge begun

**1185** Temple Church consecrated.
**1205** St Helen's Nunnery, Bishopsgate.

**1212** Southwark Cathedral.
**1220** Wakefield Tower at Tower of London begun.
**1250** First Gothic arch (at St Bartholomew the Great).
**1256** St Paul's Cathedral extended in Gothic style.

**1290** Wall extended from Ludgate to Fleet River.

**1375** First mention of Staple Inn.

# Institutions and Popular Culture

**c.1050** St James's Leper Hospital.

**1148** St Katharine's Hospital founded by Queen Matilda.

**1180** Leisure activities include cock fights, archery, wrestling, skating on Thames when frozen.

**1213** St Thomas's Hospital established at Southwark.
**1247** Bethlem Hospital for insane established.
**1253** Elephant given to King and kept in Tower of London.
**1272** Baynard's Castle handed over to Dominican Friars.

**1297** Pig-styes banned from streets.

**1371** Foundation of Charterhouse at Clerkenwell.

# Science and the Arts

**c.1173** Fitz Stephen, London historian, gave first description of the city.
**1180** 'Miracle Plays' performed at Clerkenwell.

**1245** Westminster Abbey began to acquire art treasures.
**1253** Sculptured bosses carved in Westminster Abbey.

**1349-52** Stained glass windows made for St Stephen's Chapel, Westminster Palace.

**1377** Effigy of Edward III by John Orchard placed in Westminster Abbey.

**1396** Portrait of Richard II painted for Westminster Abbey.

## History, Politics and Society

**1415** Henry V leads victory parade after Agincourt (London Bridge to St Paul's).
**1422** First records of the Honourable Society of Lincoln's Inn.

**1440** First reference to the Honourable Society of the Inner Temple.

**1535** Sir Thomas Moore executed at the Tower of London.

**1550** Population c.80,000.

**1580** Proclamation forbidding housebuilding within three miles of any London gate.
**1583** Population c.120,000.

**1603** Outbreak of plague: c.25,000 deaths.
**1605** Guy Fawkes' 'Gunpowder Plot'.

**1630** Population c.200,000.

**1642** Royalist Army defeated at Turnham Green.
**1649-60** Charles I executed in Whitehall; the Commonwealth declared.
**1662** Royal Society founded.
**1665** Bubonic Plague: c.70,000 deaths.
**1666** Great Fire of London.

**1700** Population over 500,000.
**1702-5** Buckingham House built.

## Commerce, Industry and Infrastructure

**1400** Billingsgate Market granted its charter.

**1422** 111 crafts recorded in London.
**1425** First Draper's Company Hall.

**1479** Billingsgate Market rebuilt by Hanseatic merchants.
**1501** First printing press set up in Fleet Street.

**1513** Foundation of Royal Dockyard at Woolwich and Deptford.

**1554** First mention of The George Inn, Southwark.
**1566** Royal Exchange instituted by Thomas Gresham.

**1584** First mention of Ye Old Cheshire Cheese Inn, Fleet St.
**1593** Horse-driven water pump installed near Queenhithe.
**1599** First dry dock built at Rotherhithe.

**1613** Opening of 38-mile canal (from Herts to Clerkenwell) – London's main water supply.
**1614** East India Docks built at Blackwall.

**1651** Hay's Wharf opened.
**1656** 1,153 taverns in the city.
**1663** First toll roads.

**1667** Fleet Canal and Thames Quay project.
**1669** Regular 'Flying Coaches' – London-Oxford-Cambridge.

**1680** 'Penny Post' introduced.

**1694** Foundation of the Bank of England.

## Building and Architecture

**1411** First Guildhall built.
**1414** Sheen Palace built by Henry V.

**1490** Gatehouse, Lambeth Palace.

**1512-19** Henry VII Chapel at Westminster Abbey.
**1523** Bridewell Palace.

**1547** Somerset Palace begun.

**1571** Middle Temple Hall.

**1616-35** Queen's House, Greenwich.
**1619-25** Banqueting House, Whitehall.
**1631** Kew Palace.
**1635** Piazza, Covent Garden.

**1665** Southampton Square, now Bloomsbury Square.

**1670-7** College of Arms.
**1670-1700** Rebuilding of City churches: 50 by Wren, one by Hawksmoor.
**1671-77** The Monument.
**1675-1711** St Paul's Cathedral rebuilt.

**1698** Berkeley Square.
**c.1700** Bedford Row.
**1701** The Synagogue of Spanish and Portuguese Jews.
**1711** Marlborough House.
**1712** St Paul's Chapter House.
**1714** St Alphage, Greenwich.

## Institutions and Popular Culture

**1509** St Paul's School founded by John Colet.

**1539** St Bartholomew Hospital refounded after dissolution of monasteries.
**c.1550** First use of private coaches.
**1552** Christ's Hospital founded.
**1558** First proper map of London by Ralph Agas.

**1572** Harrow School founded.

**1579** Gresham College founded.

**1598** John Stow complains of 'terrible number of coaches, world run on wheels'.
**1608** Great Frost Fair on Thames; taverns and football.

**1611** Charterhouse School founded by Thomas Sutton.

**1625** First Hackney carriages permitted to ply for hire.
**1634** Sedan chairs for hire.
**1637** Hyde Park opened for public use.
**1637** 50 licensed coaches (by 1652, 200).
**1648-9** Frost Fair on Thames; printing press set up on ice.

**1676** Foundation of Chelsea Physic Garden.

**1682** Foundation of Royal Hospital, Chelsea (Wren).
**c.1685** Sadler's Music House Theatre (now Sadler's Wells).

## Science and the Arts

**1476** First printing press set up in Westminster by William Caxton.

**1510** Birth of Thomas Tallis, composer (died 1585).

**1552** Birth of Edmund Spencer, poet and writer (died 1599).
**1564** Birth of William Shakespeare, poet and dramatist (died 1616).
**1573** Birth of John Dunne, poet and Dean of St Paul's (died 1631).
**1577** First London theatre built at Shoreditch by James Burbage.
**1587** Rose Theatre built in Southwark.
**1598** John Stow's 'Survey of London' published.
**1599** Globe Theatre built in Southwark.

**1620** Birth of John Evelyn, diarist and writer (died 1706).

**1633** Birth of Samuel Pepys, civil servant and diarist (died 1703).

**1658** Birth of Henry Purcell, musician (died 1695).

**1675-6** Foundation of the Royal Observatory, Greenwich.

**1685** Birth of George Frederick Handel, composer (died 1759).
**1697** Birth of William Hogarth, artist (died 1764).

**1705** Her Majesty's Theatre.

# History, Politics and Society

**1720** The 'South Sea Bubble'.

**1732** Sir Robert Walpole offered 10 Downing St as official residence.

**1751** Licensing Act.

**1762** Westminster Paving and Lighting Act.
**1767** Houses in city numbered for first time.

**1780** Gordon Riots: c.850 killed.

**1811** Population c.1,000,000.
**1812** Prime Minister Spencer Perceval assassinated at House of Commons.

**1825** Gallows and turnpike removed from Tyburn.

**1829** Metropolitan Police Act.

# Commerce, Industry and Infrastructure

**1720** Charters granted to the Royal Exchange Assurance and London Assurance companies.
**1729** 2,484 private coaches, and 1,100 coaches for hire; 22,636 horses in London.

**1734** *Lloyd's List* established as regular weekly publication.

**1747** Coal Exchange opened.

**1756** 600 stage coaches licensed to towns within 19 miles of London; fixed routes from 123 stations in London.
**1761** New Road from Paddington to Islington (first London bypass).

**1780** London bankers issued their own notes.
**1785** First publication of *The Times*.

**1794** Grand-Junction Canal opened.

**1798** 7,000 watchmakers listed in Clerkenwell.
**1802** West India Docks opened.
**1802** Stock Exchange opened on new site.
**1803** Surrey Iron Railway (Wandsworth-Croydon, horse-drawn): first public railway.
**1803** Dickens and Jones department store.
**1803** Commercial Road opened: improved access to docks.
**1807** Installation of gas lighting in Pall Mall.
**1807-9** Royal Mint opened.

**1815** First steamboat service on Thames.
**1817** New Custom House.

**1819** Burlington shopping arcade, Piccadilly.
**1820** Regent's Canal opened.

**1827** First publication of *Evening Standard*.

**1828** Covent Garden Market.

**1829** General Post Office opened.
**1829** First omnibus service: Paddington-City.

# Building and Architecture

**1717** Cavendish Square.

**1720** Hanover Square.

**1729** Chiswick House.
**1729** Marble Hill House, Twickenham.
**1730** St George, Bloomsbury.
**1730** St Paul's, Deptford.
**1735** The Treasury.
**1739-53** The Mansion House.

**1750-8** Horse Guards.
**1750** Westminster Bridge.

**1758** Kew Palace.
**1758** Horse Guards, Whitehall.

**1766** City Wall demolished and removal of gates begun.
**1769** Kenwood House.
**1772-4** Royal Society of Arts.
**1775** Boodle's Club, St James's.
**1776-86** Somerset House.

**1778** Brook's Club, St James's

**1786** Osterley Park House.
**1788** White's Club, St. James's.
**1789** The facade of Guildhall.

**1802-3** Albany Chambers, Piccadilly.

**1804** Russell Square.
**1806** Sir John Soane's House, Lincoln's Inn Fields.

**1824** Royal College of Physicians.
**1824-31** London Bridge rebuilt.
**1825** All Soul's, Langham Place.
**1827-33** Carlton House Terrace.

**1828** Marble Arch.

**1829** Constitution Arch.
**1829** Travellers' Club.

# Institutions and Popular Culture

**1715** Geffrye Museum (built as almshouses)
**1718** Maypole removed from front of Somerset House.
**1720** Westminster Hospital opened.
**1722** Guy's Hospital founded.

**1733** The Serpentine created in Hyde Park.
**1739** Foundling Hospital, founded by Thomas Coram.
**1741** London Hospital founded.

**1759** The Royal Botanic Gardens, Kew founded.

**1784** Balloon ascent from Artillery Ground, Finsbury.

**1805** Moorfields Eye Hospital founded.

**1818** Charing Cross Hospital founded.
**1819** Brixton Prison opened.
**1819** Bedford College for Women founded.

**1828** University College, Gower Street founded.

# Science and the Arts

**1717** Birth of David Garrick, actor (died 1779).

**1720** Theatre Royal, Haymarket.

**1728** Birth of Oliver Goldsmith, writer (died 1774).

**1732** Covent Garden Theatre (destroyed by fire 1808).

**1746** Visit of Antonio Canaletto, Italian artist and painter of London views.
**1755** Dr Samuel Johnson published his 'Great Dictionary'.
**1757** Birth of William Blake, poet and mystic (died 1827).
**1759** British Museum opened.
**1763** James Boswell, biographer, meets Dr Johnson.
**1768** Foundation of Royal Academy.

**1776** Birth of John Constable, artist (buried Hampstead 1837).
**1778** Birth of William Hazlitt, writer (died 1830).
**1784** Birth of James Leigh Hunt, poet (died 1859).

**1792** Birth of George Cruickshank, engraver for Charles Dickens (died 1878).
**1795** Birth of Thomas Carlyle, writer (died 1881).
**1802** 'On Westminster Bridge' sonnet by William Wordsworth.

**1806** Birth of John Stuart Mill, philosopher (died 1873).

**1809** Covent Garden Theatre rebuilt after fire (Smirke).

**1816** Keats' house built, Hampstead.

**1821** Haymarket Theatre opened.

**1823** Royal Academy of Music opened.
**1824** National Gallery founded.

**1827-8** Zoological Gardens in Regent's Park opened.

**1829** Cruickshank's 'March of Bricks' cartoon illustrates London's growth.

## History, Politics and Society

**1832** Cholera epidemic.

**1835** Animal fighting made illegal.

**1837** Buckingham Palace becomes permanent London residence of the Court.
**1837** Typhus epidemic.

**1845** Mass meeting of Chartists on Kennington Common.
**1848-9** Major cholera epidemic.

**1850** Board of Health report on cholera epidemic of 1848-9 and supply of water to metropolis.
**1853** Smoke Abatement Act.
**1853-4** Cholera epidemic.

**1857** Thames Conservancy Act.

**1858** 'The Great Stink': pollution on the Thames.
**1859** Metropolitan Drinking Fountain Association founded.
**1860** Metropolis Gas Act.
**1860** London Trades Council founded.

**1865** Foundation of the Salvation Army in East End.
**1866** Last major outbreak of cholera, 5,915 deaths in Poplar.
**1866** Sanitation Act.

**1868** Toll gates abolished.
**1868** Last public execution at Newgate Prison.

**1870** School Board of London established.

**1878** Epping Forest acquired by City of London Corporation.

**1885** Highgate Woods acquired by City of London Corporation.

**1888** London County Council created.
**1890** Housing Act enabling the LCC to clear slums.

## Commerce, Industry and Infrastructure

**1834** Hansom Cabs introduced.

**1836** First passenger railway in London: London-Greenwich.
**1837** Euston Railway Station opened.

**1838** Paddington Railway Station opened.
**1840** Penny Post introduced.
**1841** Fenchurch Street Railway Station opened.
**1843** Thames Tunnel opened.

**1848** Waterloo Railway Station opened.
**1851-2** King's Cross Railway Station opened.
**1852** Poplar Docks opened.
**1853** Harrod's store opened.

**1855** Royal Victoria Docks opened.
**1855** Metropolitan board of Works created.

**1863** Metropolitan Railway opened first Underground.
**1863-9** Holborn Viaduct.
**1864** First London bus with stairs.
**1864** Charing Cross Station opened.
**1864-70** Victoria Embankment.

**1866** Cannon St Railway Station opened.

**1867-72** St Pancras Station.
**1868** Millwall Docks opened.
**1868** New Smithfield Market opened.
**1868** Abbey Mills Pumping Station opened (Bazalgette).
**1869** First Sainsbury's opened in Drury Lane.
**1869** Last warship built at Royal Navy Dockyard, Woolwich.
**1871** Lloyds Incorporated by Act of Parliament.
**1874** Liverpool Street Railway Station opened.
**1876** First arrival of refrigerated meat from abroad (America).
**1879** First Telephone Exchange, Lombard St (ten subscribers).
**1880** Royal Albert Docks opened.

**1886** Tilbury Docks opened.
**1886** Shaftesbury Avenue opened.
**1888** First issue of the *Financial Times*.
**1890** First 'Tube' railway: City and South London.

## Building and Architecture

**1837-52** Houses of Parliament rebuilt after fire.

**1841** St George, Roman Catholic Cathedral, Southwark.
**1843** Trafalgar Square.

**1848-51** Army and Navy Club.

**1851-96** Public Record Office.

**1853** Brompton Oratory.

**1859** Floral Hall Covent Garden.

**1862-4** First Peabody Trust buildings erected.

**1866** Leighton House.

**1868** Royal Albert Hall.

**1871-82** Royal Courts of Justice, Strand.
**1875-81** Bedford Park Garden Suburb.

**1878** 'Cleopatra's Needle' erected on Victoria Embankment.

## Institutions and Popular Culture

**1831** King's College founded.
**1833** London Fire Brigade established.
**1834** University College hospital founded.
**1835** Madam Tussaud's Waxworks opened.
**1836** University of London founded.
**1837** King's College Hospital founded.

**1839** River Police formed.
**1839** Highgate Cemetery opened.
**1841** Last frost fair on Thames.
**1842** Pentonville Prison opened.

**1845** Victoria Park opened.
**1845** Surrey County Cricket Club founded.
**1849** Wandsworth Prison opened.

**1852** Holloway Prison opened.
**1853** Battersea Park opened.

**1860** Battersea Dogs Home founded.
**1863** Middlesex County Cricket Club formed.

**1865** Metropolitan Fire Brigade formed.

**1869** Southwark Park and Finsbury Park opened.

**1873** Alexandra Palace opened.

**1874** Wormwood Scrubs Prison opened.

**1877** First Wimbledon Tennis tournament.

**1880** First ever Cricket Test, England v. Australia, at the Oval.

**1882** Central London Polytechnic, Regent St founded.

## Science and the Arts

**1833** Soane Museum founded.

**1834** Birth of William Morris, artist, writer, designer (died 1896).

**1836** Birth of Walter Besant, London historian (died 1901).
**1837** Royal College of Art founded.

**1838** National Gallery completed (Wilkins).

**1842** British Museum new building begun (opened 1847).

**1851** Great Exhibition held in the 'Crystal Palace', Hyde Park.

**1858** Alhambra Theatre opened.

**1859** National Portrait Gallery opened.

**1866** Birth of H G Wells, writer (died 1946).

**1867** Birth of John Galsworthy, writer (died 1933).

**1870** Royal Albert Hall opened.

**1875** Bethnal Green Museum opened.
**1876** Albert Memorial completed.

**1881** Greenwich recognised as meridian.
**1881** Natural History Museum opened (Waterhouse).
**1883** Royal College of Music founded.

**1888** Shaftesbury Theatre opened.

# History, Politics and Society

**1899** London Government Act: 28 new metropolitan boroughs created.

**1902** Metropolitan Water Board created.

**1908-33** London County Hall built.
**1908** Port of London Authority created.

**1911** Population of Greater London c.7,252,000.

**1915-18** German zeppelins bomb London.
**1919** 'The Cenotaph' war memorial unveiled in Whitehall.
**1920** 'Unknown soldier' buried in Westminster Abbey.
**1922** First Queen Charlotte Ball for debutantes.

**1926** The General Strike.

**1929** Local Government Act: LCC takes over hospitals and schools.

**1931** Population of Greater London c.8,203,000.

**1933** London Transport Act (Board formed).

**1935** 'Greenbelt' established by LCC.
**1936** Jarrow unemployed march to London.

**1939** Population of Greater London c.8.700,000.

# Commerce, Industry and Infrastructure

**1897** Queen Victoria's Diamond Jubilee procession.
**1899** Savoy Hotel and Theatre built.
**1901** First electric trams in London.
**1902** Spitalfields Market rebuilt.

**1904** First double decker bus running in London.

**1905** First telephone box in London.

**1906** Bakerloo Line opened.
**1906** Piccadilly Line opened.
**1907** Northern Line opened.
**1907** First Taxicabs in London.
**1908** Kingsway Tram Tunnel opened.
**1908** Rotherhithe Rd Tunnel opened.
**1909** Selfridge's department store, Oxford St opened.

**1911-22** Port of London Authority Headquarters erected (Cooper).
**1912** Whiteley's department store, Bayswater, opened.

**1921** King George V Docks opened.

**1924** First Woolworths store in London, Oxford St.
**1924** British Empire Exhibition at Wembley.
**1925** Great West Rd opened.
**1926** London's first traffic roundabout at Parliament Square.
**1927** Park Lane Hotel opened.

**1930** Dorchester Hotel, Park Lane opened.
**1930-4** Battersea Power Station.

**1931** Liberty's department store, Regent St opened.
**1931** Shell Mex Offices, Strand.
**1932** Cockfosters, Arnos Grove, and Manor House Underground Stations (Holden).

**1937** Earls Court Exhibition Hall.

# Building and Architecture

**1891** New Scotland Yard.

**1899-1906** The War Office, Whitehall.

**1903** Westminster Cathedral.

**1905** Kingsway & Aldwych opened.
**1905-8** The Quadrant, Regent St.

**1907** Central Criminal Court (The Old Bailey).
**1908** Rhodesia House, Strand.

**c.1910** Ducane Housing Estate, Hammersmith (LCC).
**1910** Admiralty Arch.

**1930** Y.W.C.A. Hostel, Great Russell St.

**1931** *Daily Express* Offices, Fleet St.

**1932** R.I.B.A., Portland Place.

**1935** South Africa House, Trafalgar Square.
**1936** Senate House, University of London.
**1937** Bow Street Police Court.
**1937** LCC Fire Brigade Headquarters.

# Institutions and Popular Culture

**1895** First motor bus in London.
**1897** Blackwall Tunnel opened.

**1904** London Fire Brigade formed.

**1908** Twickenham Stadium opened.
**1908** Olympic Games held at Shepherds Bush.

**1910** London Palladium, Argyll St opened.
**1911** 'Pearly King' Association formed.

**1914** Cinemas in LCC area total 266.

**1921** Last horse-drawn fire engine in London.
**1922** BBC begins broadcasting from Savoy Hill.
**1923** First F.A. Cup Final at Wembley Stadium.

**1927** First London greyhound track, White City Stadium.
**1929** Dominion Theatre opened (became cinema in 1932).
**1929** Tower Pier opened.
**1930** FInsbury Park Astoria Cinema opened.
**1930** First Chelsea Flower Show.
**1930** Leicester Square Theatre opened (became cinema 1968).
**1931** London public buildings floodlit for first time.
**1932** Arsenal Stadium, Highbury, built.
**1932** BBC moved to new offices in Portland Place.

**1937** Empress Hall Ice Rink opened.

# Science and the Arts

**1893** Statue of Eros unveiled at Piccadilly Circus.
**1895** First Promenade concert.
**1897** Tate Gallery opened.

**1900** Wallace Collection opened.
**1901** Horniman Museum, Forest Hill opened.
**1902** Life and Labour of People of London published by Charles Booth.
**1904** London Symphony Orchestra founded.
**1904** London Coliseum Theatre opened.
**1905** Strand Theatre opened.
**1905** Aldwych Theatre opened.

**1907** Queen's Theatre opened.

**1909** Science Museum founded.

**1911** Queen Victoria Memorial unveiled by George V in the Mall.
**1911** London Museum founded.
**1914** Opening of King Edward VII Galleries at British Museum.

**1926** J C Baird gave first demonstration of television in Frith Street, Soho.

**1928** Discovery of penicillin by Alexander Fleming at St Mary's Hospital, Paddington.
**1930** Whitehall Theatre opened.

**1931** Windmill Theatre opened.

**1932** London Philharmonic Orchestra founded by Sir Thomas Beecham.
**1933** Open-air theatre, Regent's Park opened.
**1934** National Maritime Museum, Greenwich founded.

**1935** Geological Museum, South Kensington founded.
**1936** First regular television service from Alexander Palace.

## History, Politics and Society

**1940** Air attacks on London docks.
**1940** Second great fire of London: 30,000 incendiary bombs.
**1941** National Fire Service formed.
**1944** First flying bomb hits London.
**1946** New Towns Act: eight new towns around London.

**1948** First immigrants arrive from Jamaica.

**1951** King George VI opens Festival of Britain.
**1952** 4,000 deaths attributed to 'smog' lasting several days.
**1953** Coronation of Elizabeth II at Westminster.

**1955** City of London declared 'smokeless zone'.

**1957** Survey shows no fish in Thames from Richmond toTilbury (40 miles).

**1962** Commonwealth Institute, Kensington opened.
**1965** Formation of Greater London Council to replace LCC.

**1968** Large anti-Vietnam war demonstration in London.

**1973** Statue of Sir Winston Churchill unveiled.
**1974** First salmon caught in Thames for 100 years.
**1976** Population of Greater London c.7,000,000.

**1981** London Docklands Development Corporation formed.
**1981** London Wildlife Trust formed.
**1981** Greater London Enterprise Board formed.

**1986** Greater London Council abolished.
**1987** Fire at King's Cross underground station.

**1989** *Marchioness* pleasure boat disaster on Thames.

**1990** Population of Greater London c.6,500,000,

**1992** IRA bombs Baltic Exchange.

**1995** Aldwyich bus bombed by IRA.
**1996** Canary Wharf tower bombed by IRA.

**2002** Funerals of Princess Margaret; Queen Mother. Royal Jubilee of Queen Elizabeth II

## Commerce, Industry and Infrastructure

**1944** Port of London used as base for invasion of Europe.

**1947** Last horse-drawn cab licence given up.
**1947** King George VI Reservoir, Staines inaugurated.

**1951** London Foreign Exchange Market reopened after 12 years.
**1952** Last tram journey in London.
**1953** London Airport, Heathrow, opened.

**1956** London Gold Market reopened after 15 years.

**1960-64** Post Office Tower.
**1961-3** Hilton Hotel, Park Lane, opened.

**1966** Carnaby St Market.

**1968** Closure of London and St Katharine Docks.
**1968** Euston Station opened.
**1968** Victoria Line opened.

**1974** Covent Garden Market moved to Nine Elms.
**1976** Brent Cross Shopping Centre opened.
**1979** Jubilee Line opened.
**1981** Royal Docks closed, last of London's docks to close.
**1982** Enterprise Zone established in London docks.
**1982** Billingsgate Market moved to Isle of Dogs.
**1982** Thames Flood Barrier at Woolwich completed.
**1986** Big Bang in City.
**1986** Terminal Four completed at Heathrow Airport.
**1987** Docklands Light Railway opened.
**1987** London City Airport opened at Docklands.
**1991** Spitalfields Market moved to Leyton.

**1991** Channel Tunnel Rail terminal under construction.
**1991** Queen Elizabeth II Bridge opened.

**1994** Eurostar terminal completed at Waterloo station.

**1999** Jubilee Line extension completed.

## Building and Architecture

**1940** The Citadel, the Mall.

**1955** Trade Union Congress HQ, Great Russell St (sculpture by Epstein)
**1957-79** The Barbican Complex.

**1961** United States Embassy, Grosvenor Square.
**1962** Shell Centre, South Bank.
**1963** Vickers Tower, Millbank.

**1968** 'Ronan Point' Tower Block collapses. Fatalities.

**1978** Central London Mosque, Regent's Park.

**1982** New British Library building founded.

**1986** Lloyd's Building opened.

**1987** Princess of Wales Conservatory, Kew Gardens.
**1988** New Chapter House, Southwark Cathedral.
**1989** Great storm causes much damage in London.
**1990** Canary Wharf tower completed.
**1991** Broadgate Centre completed at Liverpool Street station.

**1995** Conversion of County Hall into flats.

**1999** Ferris wheel built on the South Bank.
**2000** Millennium Dome opened, Greenwich

## Institutions and Popular Culture

**1940** Savoy Cinema, Holloway Road, opened.

**1948** First jazz club opened by Ronnie Scott and John Dankworth.
**1948** Olympic Games held at Wembley Stadium.
**1951** National Film Theatre, South Bank.

**1953** First 'coffee bar', 'the Mika', opened on Frith St.

**1955** 'Bazaar': the first boutique, Kings Rd, Chelsea.

**1958** The London Planetarium opened.

**1961** First Notting Hill Carnival.

**1964** The Beatles recorded at EMI Studios, St John's Wood.

**1968** Rolling Stones gave first open-air concert in Hyde Park
**1968** London Weekend Television started.

**1970** Radio London started.

**1973** LBC began.
**1973** Capital Radio began.

**1985** 'Band Aid' Concert, Wembley Stadium; 72,000 attend.

**1991** Open-air concert at Hyde Park.

## Science and the Arts

**1948** 'Eros' reinstated at Piccadilly Circus.

**1951** Royal Festival Hall, South Bank opened.

**1954** 'Temple of Mithras' excavation at Bucklersbury.
**1955** BBC TV Centre opened at White City.

**1957** Imperial College of Science building, Kensington opened.
**1959** Mermaid Theatre, Puddle Dock opened.
**1961-2** Royal College of Art, Kensington Gore opened.

**1967** Queen Elizabeth Hall, South Bank opened.
**1968** Hayward Gallery, South Bank opened.

**1969** Greenwich Theatre opened.
**1970** The Young Vic Theatre opened.
**1973** British Library formed.

**1975** New Museum of London opened.
**1976** National Theatre, South Bank opened.
**1980** London Transport Museum opened at Covent Garden.

**1982** Barbican Arts Centre opened.

**1988** Museum of the Moving Image opened on South Bank.
**1989** Design Museum opened on Butlers Wharf.

**1990** Courtauld Gallery moved to Somerset House.
**1991** Sainsbury Wing opened at National Gallery.

**1993** Quaglino's opened.
**1993** Buckingham Palace opened to general public.

**1996** Millennium site confirmed at Greenwich.
**1997** New Globe Theatre opened on Bankside.
**1999** New British Library building completed.

# MAPPING AND DEPICTING LONDON

Despite the great wealth and political power of London during many centuries, the first detailed depictions of the city did not appear until the 1550s. At that time intricate panoramic views of the city started to be produced, and in 1559 the first detailed map of London was published, a full century after the earliest European printed maps had been engraved in Italy *(page 142)*. Three quarters of the span of London's history had passed without accurate cartographic record being made. A surge of interest in history and geography took place in the Elizabethan Age and gave rise to numerous county maps and to some London maps, which were then reissued in the early seventeenth century. But at this time the science of map-making was new and survey techniques were poorly understood. In Restoration England growing interest in scientific knowledge encouraged cartographers to produce new maps. This trend was further stimulated by the Great Fire of London (1666), which destroyed supplies of existing charts and maps. Damage to the city was so extensive that publishers were dissuaded from reprinting from out-dated copper plates. New surveys were made to assist reconstruction, with John Ogilby's vast map of 1676 (8 ft x 4 ft) giving a reasonably accurate view of the City. Other late seventeenth-century maps embrace Westminster and Southwark, and were sometimes printed in reduced form as pocket maps for visitors.

By contrast, John Rocque's map of 1746 (16 ft x 6 ft) showed the churches, streets, squares and numerous other features of the capital in enormous detail (26 inches to the mile). It depicted the pattern of urban development across 10,000 acres and displayed 5,000 place names. Despite a lack of absolute mathematical rigour, its 24 sheets provided an unparalleled source for tracing the appearance of the rapidly growing city. Methods of survey improved in the late eighteenth century and were employed by Richard Horwood, whose great map of London (17ft x 7 ft) appeared in the 1790s *(page 75)*. The Ordnance Survey was founded in 1791 with its roots in both military and civilian cartography. It continued to improve map-making techniques during the nineteenth century to produce standard topographic maps (one inch to one mile) and a variety of detailed urban plans which chart the vigorous expansion of Victorian London. Specialized maps were also published in the last century to show land use, canals, roads and railways, and many aspects of social life, including poverty, disease, education and religious observance. Twentieth-century maps have been particularly concerned with matters related to urban planning, especially after the widespread destruction incurred in World War II, and have incorporated data from new sources such as aerial photographs and imagery from earth-observation satellites.

This enormous wealth of historical maps and other information has been used in many ways to produce the plates in this Atlas. The most direct method involves the straightforward reproduction of sections of old maps which show how London was depicted by map-makers in the past. For about three centuries these maps were printed in black, with a small proportion being coloured by hand. Not until the 1860s did maps of London start to be printed in colour. A second approach involves abstracting information on specific themes from historic maps in order to create new specialized images. Contemporary verbal descriptions, censuses and statistical enquiries provide other important evidence which has been converted into maps. The most creative cartography involves making maps to show archaeological and documentary evidence which pre-dates London's first printed maps. Last, but emphatically not least, the most imaginative technique in the Atlas is the combining of cartographic, pictorial, statistical and verbal descriptions in order to "reconstruct" buildings and urban scenes in the past, thereby conveying three-dimensional views of London, in contrast with the two-dimensional images of conventional cartography.

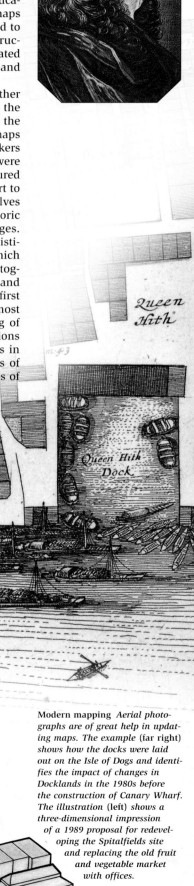

**Modern mapping** *Aerial photographs are of great help in updating maps. The example (far right) shows how the docks were laid out on the Isle of Dogs and identifies the impact of changes in Docklands in the 1980s before the construction of Canary Wharf. The illustration (left) shows a three-dimensional impression of a 1989 proposal for redeveloping the Spitalfields site and replacing the old fruit and vegetable market with offices.*

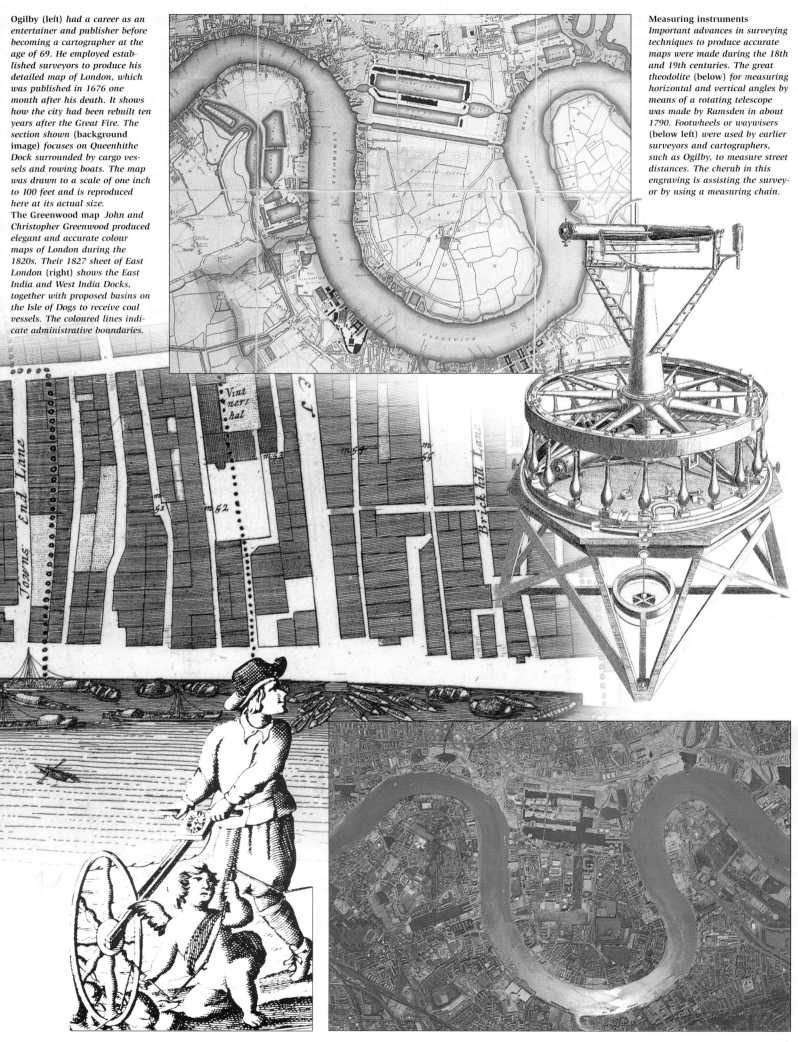

Ogilby (left) *had a career as an entertainer and publisher before becoming a cartographer at the age of 69. He employed established surveyors to produce his detailed map of London, which was published in 1676 one month after his death. It shows how the city had been rebuilt ten years after the Great Fire. The section shown (background image) focuses on Queenhithe Dock surrounded by cargo vessels and rowing boats. The map was drawn to a scale of one inch to 100 feet and is reproduced here at its actual size.*

The Greenwood map *John and Christopher Greenwood produced elegant and accurate colour maps of London during the 1820s. Their 1827 sheet of East London (right) shows the East India and West India Docks, together with proposed basins on the Isle of Dogs to receive coal vessels. The coloured lines indicate administrative boundaries.*

Measuring instruments *Important advances in surveying techniques to produce accurate maps were made during the 18th and 19th centuries. The great theodolite (below) for measuring horizontal and vertical angles by means of a rotating telescope was made by Ramsden in about 1790. Footwheels or waywisers (below left) were used by earlier surveyors and cartographers, such as Ogilby, to measure street distances. The cherub in this engraving is assisting the surveyor by using a measuring chain.*

15

# CHAPTER 1
# LAND UNDER LONDON

*Archaeologists working on a 5-mile stretch of the A13 road scheme between Dagenham and Canning Town have found evidence that the area was exploited intensively during the late Mesolithic/early Neolithic (6500-2500 BC), the Middle Bronze Age (1500-1000 BC), and the Later Bronze Age (1000-500 BC). New information has been discovered on cereal production in Neolithic times, and on weaving. Sea-levels started to rise during the Later Bronze Age, burying this floodplain area of the Thames (and its tributaries the Lea and the Roding) under at least 2 ft of alluvial clay and silt.*

*Rising water levels under London are being tackled by a series of boreholes, each 360 feet deep, that will prevent damage to buildings and the Underground system (60-120 ft beneath the surface). In 1905 the water table was 300 ft below Trafalgar Square; by 1955 it was 240 ft below, and is now only 120 ft under the surface. Up to 50 boreholes have been planned to extract a total of 15 million gallons of water each day in order to lower the water table that is currently rising by up to 10 ft per year. If nothing were to be done, the foundations of some of the city's tallest office blocks and deepest sections of the Underground could be adversely affected within a decade. Already London Underground has invested heavily to secure sections of the Bakerloo and Northern lines, and the new British Library at St. Pancras has had to incorporate reinforced walls in its 100 ft.-deep basement to guard against flood damage. The first phase of drilling has been completed and many more borehole sites have been identified.*

OVER THE CENTURIES, the debris of past generations – known as 'made ground' – and the bricks and mortar of present-day London, have masked the natural land surface. If we are to understand the complete history of the city, then it is with geology that we must begin. Geology is concerned with deposits, such as sands, clays and – further back in time – Chalk, which were laid down by ancient river systems or accumulated on the beds of ancient seas. These sediments consolidated in time to become rocks which were either 'hard' or 'soft'. Erosion by streams fashioned the hills and ridges and hollow plains of the London Basin. 'Deposition' occurred over millions of years; by contrast, the shaping of the present landscape may be measured in mere thousands of years.

London is located in the middle stretch of the Thames valley, near the heart of the London Basin. Moving north from Hyde Park, the suburbs present a switchback of hills before giving way to the slow haul into the Chilterns. These hills are fringed to the north-west by a prominent Chalk scarp edge which overlooks an older plain of clay. Similar changes in topography occur to the west or south of central London. When these traverses are connected together, they constitute the bowl-like shape of the Chalk, known as the London Basin. Clays and sands of younger geological ages – the marine London Clay and the sands of the Bagshot Beds – are found inside the Basin. These materials make up the subsurface geology of the London area.

The Bagshot Beds date back to 40 million years ago. Geologists interpret them as sediments laid down by the flooding of a great river the size of the modern Ganges. Rising in the hills of south-west England, it deposited most of its load of sediment in a broad sheet of sand extending over present-day Middlesex and northern Surrey. 50 million years ago, southern England lay beneath a warm tropical sea which, when it receded, left behind the London Clay which can still be glimpsed in deep excavations at, for instance, building sites. The layer of soft clay facilitated the excavation of the Underground railway, but is notorious for causing the subsidence of housing foundations.

Running water and the sediments it carried, formed the main agent for shaping the natural landscape of south-east England. Early rivers, forerunners of the Thames, steadily removed much of the cover of sand and clay, reducing ancient ridges to the isolated hills of what are now suburban areas. Two or three million years before the present, the early Thames ran through what is now the Vale of Aylesbury, continuing east towards the North Sea. The main river had its source well to the west in Wessex, and was joined by tributaries rising on Chalk slopes to the north and south. At this time, southern tributaries flowed northwards from what is now Surrey, across Middlesex into Hertfordshire. This pattern persisted until 500,000 years ago, when the glaciers of the Ice Age blocked the drainage system, forcing the river to find a route further to the south. In this way the Thames evolved its present course. What were originally floodplain deposits along the Thames were cut into by streams, and deposits of sediment were carved into terraces which flanked the old river courses, the highest terraces being the oldest and the lowest the youngest. Archaeological remains, including the tools of early Man who colonised the area during the past 500,000 years, provide the key to dating these terraces.

The melting of large ice caps during warm climatic periods resulted in a rise in sea level. During cold climatic periods this process was reversed, with vast amounts of water locked up in glaciers. Today, the water levels under London are rising. There are also fears that south-eastern England is sinking in relation to the North Sea. The consequences of economic changes in London itself over the last few decades have also played their part in this process. The decline of manufacturing, especially brewing, in the city means that less groundwater is being pumped up, and hence subsurface water levels have risen. In addition, the land surface is being depressed by new building schemes in what was previously open ground, such as Docklands. The challenges posed by problems of 'global' warming and local concerns over ground stability, all demonstrate the importance of London's geology and topography in the city's past, present and possible future.

| MILLION YEARS | EON | ERA | PERIOD | |
|---|---|---|---|---|
| | | | Quat. | |
| – 1.6 | | | | |
| – 5.3 | | | | Pl |
| | | | | M |
| – 23.7 | | CENOZOIC | Tertiary | |
| | | | | O |
| – 36.8 | | | | |
| – 57.8 | | | | E |
| | | | | Pa |
| – 66.4 | | | | |
| | | | Cretaceous | |
| – 14.4 | | | | |
| | PHANEROZOIC | MESOZOIC | Jurassic | |
| – 208 | | | Triassic | |
| – 245 | | | Permian | |
| – 286 | | | Carboniferous | |
| – 360 | | | Devonian | |
| – 408 | | PALEOZOIC | Silurian | |
| – 438 | | | Ordovician | |
| – 505 | | | Cambrian | |
| – 570 | | | | |
| | PROTEROZOIC | | | |
| – 2500 | ARCHEON | | | |

Pl = Pliocene
M = Miocene
O = Oligocene
E = Eocene
Pa = Paleocene

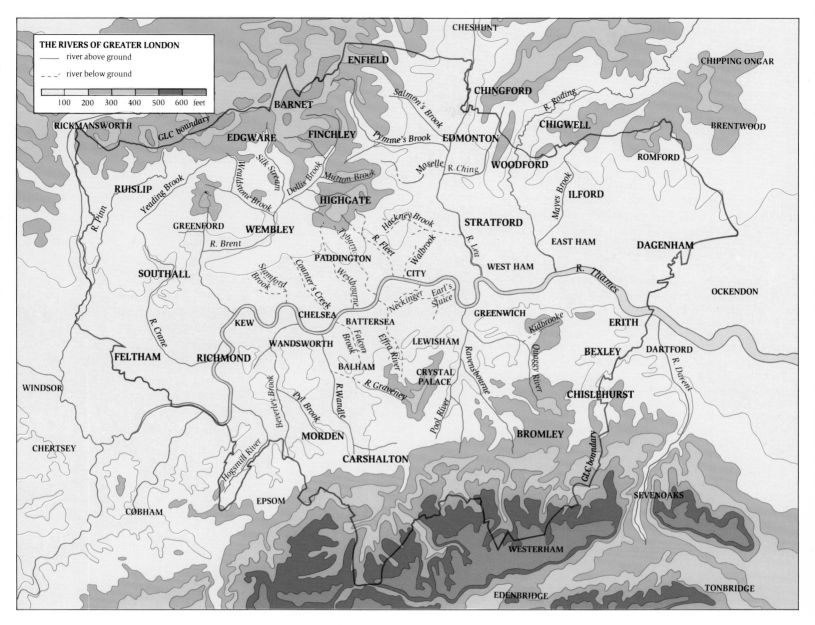

THE RIVERS OF GREATER LONDON

— river above ground
- - - river below ground

100 200 300 400 500 600 feet

## THE THAMES BASIN

In c.120,000 BP sea level and the level of the Thames in London were much higher than they are now (*below left*). For example, the pavement outside the National Gallery in Trafalgar Square would have been lapped by tidal waters, and the junction of Whitehall and Trafalgar Square would have been underwater, even at low tide. The highest points of land were Ludgate Hill and Cornhill. Bones and fossils found in the Trafalgar Square area show that animals such as hippopotamus and elephant thrived in the warm climate.

*The Thames Basin The map (above) traces the drainage pattern of the Thames tributaries formed by the sands and clays of the London Basin. The dotted lines indicate what are often called the 'Lost Rivers of London', now largely converted into the sewer system of drainage. Prolonged or heavy rain can result in the sewers flooding in Gospel Oak, Wandsworth and Battersea.*

By 8,000 BP the level of the Thames was considerably lower than it had been in 120,000 BP (*below right*). At high tide it would have reached the southern end of Northumberland Avenue, some 6½ feet above its present level at the Embankment. Recent development around Upper Thames Street has exposed deposits of alluvium which had built up on the much earlier sands and gravels of the Thames terraces. At this stage, the Fleet River made a significant inlet where it joined the Thames close to Blackfriars. This inlet was an integral part of the port of Roman London.

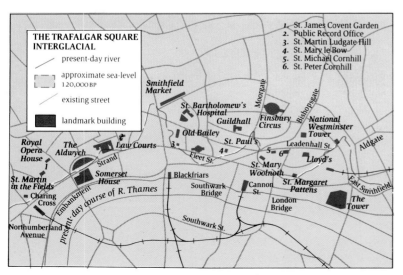

THE TRAFALGAR SQUARE INTERGLACIAL

— present-day river

approximate sea-level 120,000 BP

existing street

landmark building

1. St. James Covent Garden
2. Public Record Office
3. St. Martin Ludgate Hill
4. St. Mary le Bow
5. St. Michael Cornhill
6. St. Peter Cornhill

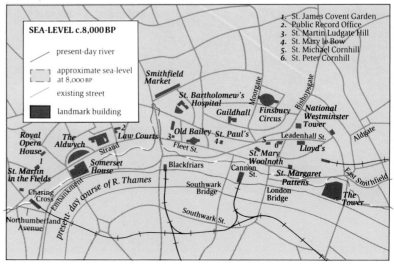

SEA-LEVEL c.8,000 BP

— present-day river

approximate sea-level at 8,000 BP

existing street

landmark building

1. St. James Covent Garden
2. Public Record Office
3. St. Martin Ludgate Hill
4. St. Mary le Bow
5. St. Michael Cornhill
6. St. Peter Cornhill

# LONDON'S GEOLOGY

The geology of the London area can be best understood by the image of a structural basin, with the Chalk forming the rim and the younger Tertiary beds forming the filling. The green strips on the map (*right*), the Chilterns in the top left corner, the North Downs the broader strip to the bottom right, define that basin.

There is, however, an aspect of London geology which is less well-known, yet at the same time, more striking. This is best revealed by any cross-section of the rocks that are found deep beneath the surface. Such probing reveals a structure which is in complete contrast with the structural basin already identified. The oldest rocks (Silurian age, c.425 million years) form a central core with younger beds to north and south – an arrangement which has the structure of an anticline (an arch-shaped fold system) contrasting directly with the higher level basin-shaped fold system, or syncline. From the manner in which the younger rocks wedge against the older core, it is possible to surmise that the older core may have been a shallow ridge, or even dry land until it was overwhelmed by the seas in which the Chalk was formed some 90 million years ago. The wedges – which thin out northwards – are best seen to the south of London beneath the North Downs, and are revealed in the contrasts between the deep boreholes at Warlingham and those which probe below central London.

When we examine the solid geology of the London Basin we find that erosion during glacial periods stripped away younger Tertiary deposits within the ancient drainage system of the Thames. This has left broad tracts where London Clay is exposed at the surface (indicated by the chocolate-brown tone on the map). Only small cappings of Claygate Beds and Bagshot Sands remain on some hills. The map shows that these are the well-known high-points of London: Harrow on the Hill, Hampstead Heath and Shooters Hill are all relics of once continuous layers.

The pale buff tones of river terrace deposits, and alluvium impressed upon the deeper tones of the solid geology, demonstrate the great magnitude of the ancient drainage system of the Thames. During glacial episodes, the volume of river flow fluctuated according to the supply of water from the northern ice sheets that were gradually melting. At times then, the Thames was almost Ganges-like in size; at other times, it shrank considerably. The terrace gravels, referred to below, result from these fluctuations.

**London's geology** *This column (right) attempts to summarise the rock units which might be encountered in a borehole beneath London, listing the names used universally for geological time periods. A distinction is drawn between younger rocks and so-called 'basement' rocks, which make up the deeper structure. The cross-section (below) is taken from the north-west of London to the south-east. The line of the cross-section is annotated on the map (right).*

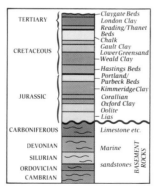

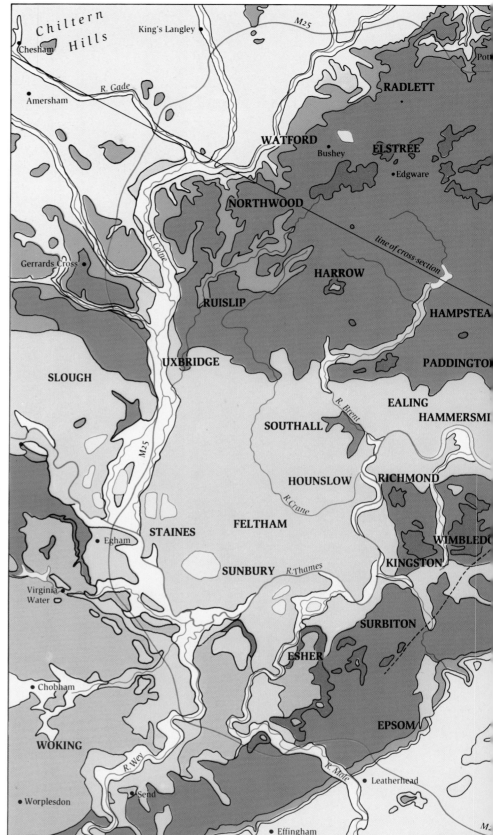

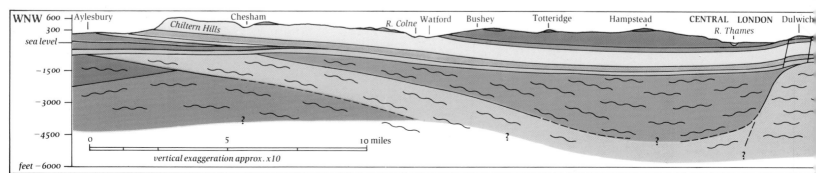

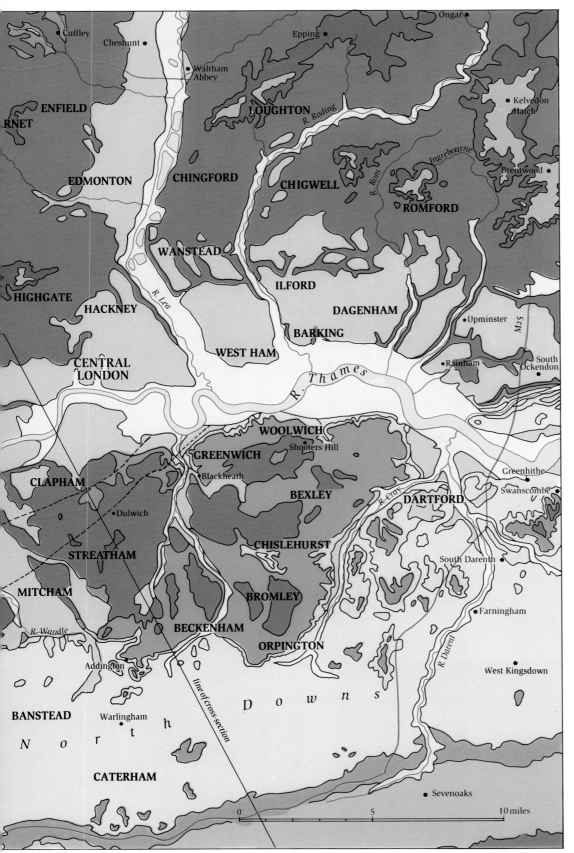

ENFIELD

Cuffley

Cheshunt •

• Waltham Abbey

RNET

LOUGHTON

Epping •

Ongar •

R. Roding

Kelvedon Hatch •

EDMONTON

CHINGFORD

CHIGWELL

R. Rom

Ingrebourne

Brentwood •

WANSTEAD

ROMFORD

HIGHGATE

HACKNEY

R. Lea

ILFORD

DAGENHAM

Upminster •

M25

CENTRAL LONDON

WEST HAM

BARKING

Rainham •

South Ockendon

R. Thames

WOOLWICH

CLAPHAM

GREENWICH

Shooters Hill

Blackheath •

BEXLEY

R. Cray

DARTFORD

Greenhithe •

Swanscombe •

Dulwich •

STREATHAM

CHISLEHURST

South Darenth •

MITCHAM

BROMLEY

R. Wandle

BECKENHAM

ORPINGTON

Farningham •

Addington

line of cross-section

West Kingsdown •

BANSTEAD

Warlingham •

D o w n s

N o r t h

CATERHAM

R. Darent

Sevenoaks •

0          5          10 miles

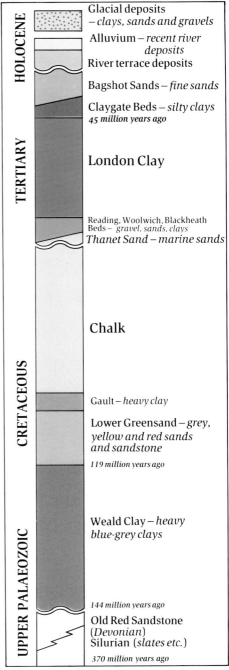

| | | |
|---|---|---|
| HOLOCENE | | Glacial deposits – *clays, sands and gravels* |
| | | Alluvium – *recent river deposits* |
| | | River terrace deposits |
| TERTIARY | | Bagshot Sands – *fine sands* |
| | | Claygate Beds – *silty clays* 45 million years ago |
| | | London Clay |
| | | Reading, Woolwich, Blackheath Beds – *gravel, sands, clays* |
| | | Thanet Sand – *marine sands* |
| CRETACEOUS | | Chalk |
| | | Gault – *heavy clay* |
| | | Lower Greensand – *grey, yellow and red sands and sandstone* 119 million years ago |
| UPPER PALAEOZOIC | | Weald Clay – *heavy blue-grey clays* 144 million years ago |
| | | Old Red Sandstone (*Devonian*) Silurian (*slates etc.*) 370 million years ago |

River terraces *of the ancient Thames create and underlie the slopes of London's streets (for example Haymarket to Piccadilly; Whitehall to Trafalgar Square, below). Older terraces were eaten into by later river flow which always tended to bite down to lower levels. In simple terms, the oldest terraces are highest, and those of most recent date lie close to the present river. In fact, the Thames today occupies a route beneath which a super-deepened channel exists. This has always complicated the excavation of tunnels beneath the Thames. The infilled deep channel provides evidence of rising sea levels over the past 10,000 years* (page 19).

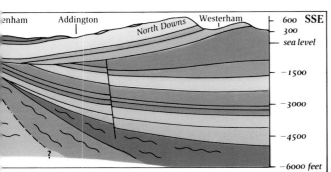

Addington

Westerham

North Downs

SSE

600
300
sea level
−1500
−3000
−4500
−6000 feet

?

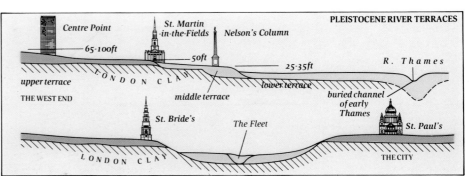

PLEISTOCENE RIVER TERRACES

Centre Point

St. Martin-in-the-Fields

Nelson's Column

65-100ft

50ft

25-35ft

R. Thames

LONDON CLAY

upper terrace

lower terrace

THE WEST END

middle terrace

buried channel of early Thames

St. Bride's

The Fleet

St. Paul's

LONDON CLAY

THE CITY

# PEOPLE BEFORE LONDON

Groups of people belonging to early forms of the genus *Homo* roamed the London area intermittently from around 450,000 years ago. They scavenged, hunted and foraged across the landscape, and learnt to cope with climatic conditions which varied from the warmth of interglacials to the sub-arctic cold of full glacials. They left behind many thousands of flint tools, principally hand axes, swept from long vanished land surfaces by the ancient Thames and redeposited in the gravel terraces which underlie modern London. Finds of later flint tools associated with the remains of mammoth and woolly rhinoceros sealed beneath brickearths at Southall and Crayford mark undisturbed kill sites.

The emergence of biologically modern people in Europe some 40,000 years ago coincided with a phase of particularly severe climate. Our best evidence for their presence in the London area comes from the very end of the last glacial, as the climate began to warm up. Excavations in the Colne valley at Uxbridge and Staines have revealed butchery sites dating to 10,000 BC, where tundra-loving reindeer and horses were killed and their carcasses processed. A later phase of activity at Uxbridge is dominated by woodland species, including red and roe deer, showing that trees had colonised the landscape.

The melting of the ice sheets led to the final separation of Britain from the continent around 6500 BC. Traditional hunting grounds in the lower-lying valleys were flooded and people forced back up the valleys and onto the valley slopes. From 3900 BC scattered communities constructed earthern enclosures in clearings carved out of the lime- and oak-dominated woodlands fringing the west London Thames. Repeated clearances here led to the creation of a locally open landscape dotted with 'ritual' monuments, one of which, an embanked avenue at Stanwell, is nearly four kilometres long. Special offerings, including human and animal remains, pottery vessels and stone and antler tools, were deposited on land and in the Thames.

Major changes occurred after about 1600 BC: large tracts of land were divided up between farming communities, whose dead were buried in small cremation cemeteries; field systems were laid out in areas of suitable subsoil, while traces of criss-cross ploughing have even been found on the valley floor at Bermondsey. Wooden

*Gifts to earth and water Special offerings were frequently deposited on land and in the Thames during later prehistory. The dismembered remains of an early Bronze Age wild cow or aurochs (right), accompanied by six flint arrowheads, were carefully arranged in a deep pit at Harmondsworth, while the splendid bronze oval shield (below), dated to between 400 and 250 BC, was recovered from a former river channel at Chertsey.*

*An Iron Age tribal centre Occupied during the last two centuries BC, Uphall Camp, Ilford (far right) could be a local oppidum. Recent excavations within its 48-acre interior have produced evidence of weaving and metal-working.*

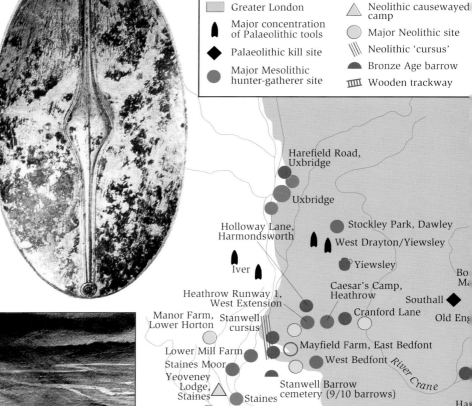

### Prehistoric sites in Greater London

- ▭ Greater London
- ◣ Major concentration of Palaeolithic tools
- ◆ Palaeolithic kill site
- ● Major Mesolithic hunter-gatherer site
- △ Neolithic causewayed camp
- ● Major Neolithic site
- ⫽ Neolithic 'cursus'
- ◗ Bronze Age barrow
- ▥ Wooden trackway

Harefield Road, Uxbridge

Uxbridge

Stockley Park, Dawley

Holloway Lane, Harmondsworth

West Drayton/Yiewsley

Yiewsley

Iver

Caesar's Camp, Heathrow

Bo
M

Heathrow Runway 1, West Extension

Cranford Lane

Southall

Old Eng

Manor Farm, Lower Horton

Stanwell cursus

Mayfield Farm, East Bedfont

Lower Mill Farm

West Bedfont

River Crane

Staines Moor

Yeoveney Lodge, Staines

Stanwell Barrow cemetery (9/10 barrows)

Ha

Staines

Runnymede Bridge

Littleton

Ashford

Sandy L
Tedding

Thorpe Lea

St Ann's Hill, Chertsey

Staines Road Farm, Shepperton

Hurst Park

Muckhatch Farm

*Prehistoric sites in Greater London (c 450,000 BC–AD 43) Despite the obvious difficulties of undertaking fieldwork in the area, excavations across a range of geological strata have revealed much that is new and unexpected (map above right). Work on the free-draining and fertile gravel terraces has been especially productive and has located sites such as the Neolithic circular earthern enclosure at Yeoveney Lodge, Staines (artist's impression, left). More recent has been the realisation that wooden trackways, such as the Bronze Age example from Beckton (far right), survive intact beneath later alluvial deposits on the Thames floodplain.*

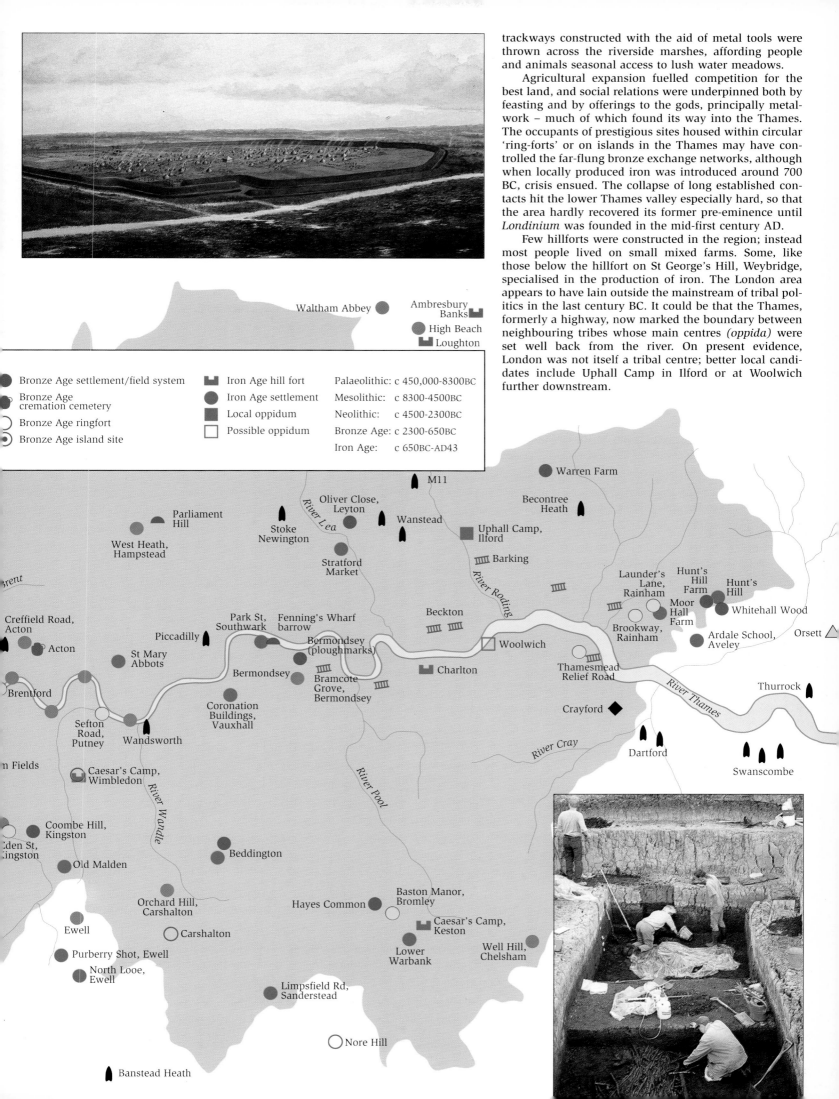

trackways constructed with the aid of metal tools were thrown across the riverside marshes, affording people and animals seasonal access to lush water meadows.

Agricultural expansion fuelled competition for the best land, and social relations were underpinned both by feasting and by offerings to the gods, principally metalwork – much of which found its way into the Thames. The occupants of prestigious sites housed within circular 'ring-forts' or on islands in the Thames may have controlled the far-flung bronze exchange networks, although when locally produced iron was introduced around 700 BC, crisis ensued. The collapse of long established contacts hit the lower Thames valley especially hard, so that the area hardly recovered its former pre-eminence until *Londinium* was founded in the mid-first century AD.

Few hillforts were constructed in the region; instead most people lived on small mixed farms. Some, like those below the hillfort on St George's Hill, Weybridge, specialised in the production of iron. The London area appears to have lain outside the mainstream of tribal politics in the last century BC. It could be that the Thames, formerly a highway, now marked the boundary between neighbouring tribes whose main centres (*oppida*) were set well back from the river. On present evidence, London was not itself a tribal centre; better local candidates include Uphall Camp in Ilford or at Woolwich further downstream.

### Legend

- Bronze Age settlement/field system
- Bronze Age cremation cemetery
- Bronze Age ringfort
- Bronze Age island site
- Iron Age hill fort
- Iron Age settlement
- Local oppidum
- Possible oppidum

Palaeolithic: c 450,000–8300 BC
Mesolithic: c 8300–4500 BC
Neolithic: c 4500–2300 BC
Bronze Age: c 2300–650 BC
Iron Age: c 650 BC–AD 43

### Map labels

Waltham Abbey
Ambresbury Banks
High Beach
Loughton
Warren Farm
M11
Becontree Heath
Parliament Hill
Oliver Close, Leyton
Stoke Newington
Wanstead
Uphall Camp, Ilford
West Heath, Hampstead
Barking
Launder's Lane, Rainham
Hunt's Hill Farm
Hunt's Hill
Stratford Market
River Lea
River Roding
Brent
Moor Hall Farm
Whitehall Wood
Creffield Road, Acton
Park St, Southwark
Fenning's Wharf barrow
Beckton
Brookway, Rainham
Ardale School, Aveley
Orsett
Piccadilly
Acton
St Mary Abbots
Bermondsey (ploughmarks)
Woolwich
Brentford
Bermondsey
Bramcote Grove, Bermondsey
Charlton
Thamesmead Relief Road
Thurrock
River Thames
Coronation Buildings, Vauxhall
Sefton Road, Putney
Wandsworth
Crayford
River Cray
Caesar's Camp, Wimbledon
River Wandle
Dartford
Swanscombe
n Fields
River Pool
Coombe Hill, Kingston
den St, Kingston
Old Malden
Beddington
Orchard Hill, Carshalton
Baston Manor, Bromley
Hayes Common
Caesar's Camp, Keston
Well Hill, Chelsham
Ewell
Carshalton
Purberry Shot, Ewell
Lower Warbank
North Looe, Ewell
Limpsfield Rd, Sanderstead
Nore Hill
Banstead Heath

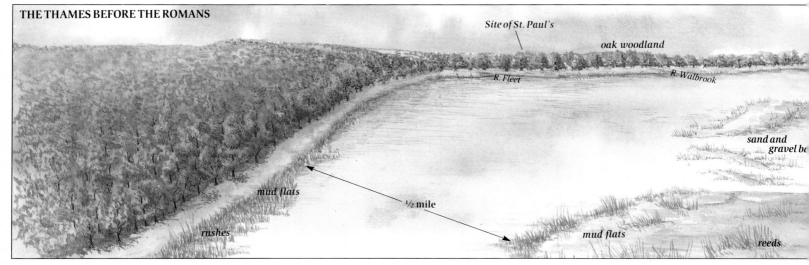

THE THAMES BEFORE THE ROMANS

Site of St. Paul's

oak woodland

R. Fleet

R. Walbrook

sand and gravel be

mud flats

½ mile

rushes

mud flats

reeds

# THE TOWN AND THE THAMES

The 'Thames' is one of the oldest documented place names in British history, for it is recorded in the account of Julius Caesar's invasion of these islands in c. 55 BC. The town of London did not exist then — it made its first entry into the history books in AD 60. The river carved a broad and sinuous route through the fertile lands of south-east England, while its estuary opened out into the North Sea beyond which was the Baltic and the mouth of the River Rhine, one of the great waterways of continental Europe. A town on the Thames would therefore share the twin advantages of a prosperous hinterland and ready access to and from the wider world. London, then, was the gift of the Thames. Londoners drank, washed and fished in it; it powered their mills and provided a ready highway in times when more people owned boats than horses and carts. But above all, London prospered by water-borne trade, by the traffic swept upstream from the estuary on incoming tides, and sent out into the North Sea when the tide turned. However, the Thames was not always a passive, benevolent force; riverside settlements were particularly vulnerable to catastrophic floods and such un-welcome visitations as Viking raiders. Other unwanted imports such as plagues were brought in by foreign merchants and sailors.

Nevertheless, Londoners learned to live with their river and eventually saw their harbour become the busiest in the world. In the process, the townscape was transformed on a spectacular scale. The Romans who built *Londinium* would not recognise the vast conurbation we now call Greater London; nor would they recognise the Thames, for the river they had to cross, with its islands, marshes and mudflats, was much wider than the deeper, dirtier Thames we see today. The level of the sea and the Thames relative to the land has been gradually rising. High tide in the Roman period was some nine feet below the present-day level, and the tidal range (the difference between high and low tides) in the 1st century was only some six feet, compared with over twenty feet today. While the Thames has been rising, its banks have been progressively pushed riverwards, narrowing the channel. In the City, this process began with the Romans, but such reclamation schemes continued throughout the medieval period. In other parts of the Thames valley, the inter-tidal marshes were embanked

LONDON'S ADVANCING WATERFRONT

Thames Street

warehouse  quay

AD 100  AD 125

riverside wall  AD 270  AD 250

AD 1000  AD

AD 150

natural river bank

**The changing river** *The view (top) illustrates the Thames riverscape before the arrival of the Romans. In the foreground is the low-lying Southwark shore; across the untamed Thames is the high ground on the north bank where the Romans were to build* Londinium. *Throughout the city's history, Londoners have changed the shape of the Thames by reclaiming land on the banks of the river. This north-south section (above) shows how the north bank was gradually advanced into the river from c. AD 100 to the present day. In parts of the City, over 110 yards of land were won in this way. The series of plans (right) show the Thames at high tide and low tide in the 1st century AD, compared with today's constricted river. The islands and inter-tidal marshes on the south bank of the Thames in the Roman period are clearly visible – they are now all built over.*

*Not only has the Thames changed: so has the site of London and its port. These plans (right) show the location of the Roman settlement, replaced by a Saxon market town on a new site well to the west. The medieval town shared the Roman wall, and its new bridge effectively prevented most larger ships sailing further upstream. Increased trade saw the port expanding far to the east of London Bridge with the development of the enclosed docks from 1800.*

THE THAMES AT HIGH TIDE c. AD 50

basilica & forum

R. Walbrook  LONDINIUM

bridge

R. Thames

Stane St.  Watling St.

causeway

SOUTHWARK

THE THAMES AT LOW TIDE c. AD 50

bas & f

R. Thames

Stane St.  Watling St.

SOUTHWARK

Roman wall

THE ROMAN PORT

Roman port (site of Medieval & Tudor port)

R. Thames

Roman wall

THE ANGLO-SAXON PORT

'Aldwych', Anglo-Saxon port

R. Thames

Roman wall

THE MODERN PORT

DOCKLANDS  R. Thames

0  4

miles

and drained: for example the monks of Lesnes Abbey were largely responsible for reclaiming the land now occupied by the Thamesmead estate.

The history of the Port of London is a history of four harbours. First, the Roman centre of *Londinium* which was founded in AD 50 at a major junction of road, river and sea-going traffic. Initially, this port prospered, becoming the provincial capital, but then dramatically collapsed and was abandoned by the 5th century. 200 years later, Saxons developed a quite different port on a new site to the west of the old city. The sprawling riverside market town of *Lundenwic* also prospered, but was to attract the attentions of Viking

raiders who sacked it in 842, 851 and 871.

The Londoners then moved inside the area protected by the ancient Roman wall, abandoning the old market (Ald-wych) by c. 900. This new settlement saw slow but sure growth in spite of Viking and Norman invasions. The medieval harbour was well placed to lead the nation's all-important trade in wool and cloth, expanding dramatically in the 16th century. But the 18th century saw it choked with its own success. The length of the legal quays upon which all cargoes had to be discharged was only 470 yards, quite insufficient to accommodate the large contemporary vessels bringing in cargoes from Europe,

Site of Roman City  Site of Tower of London

River Thames

mud flats

**SOUTHWARK**

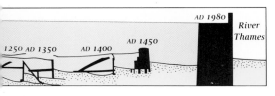

1250 AD 1350  AD 1400  AD 1450  AD 1980  River Thames

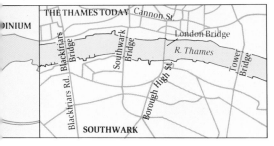

THE THAMES TODAY  Cannon St.

DINIUM

London Bridge

Blackfriars Bridge  Southwark Bridge  R. Thames  Tower Bridge

Blackfriars Rd.  Borough High St.

**SOUTHWARK**

Africa, the Americas and the East. A series of enclosed docks built to the east of the City from 1800 to 1920 remedied the situation. As the Empire grew, so the Port expanded downstream, together with the suburbs and the many industries which relied upon it. London survived the Blitz, and trade reached new records in 1959-62. However, this was the age of supertankers and containerisation and London's docks, some of which were built in the age of sail, were unable to adopt new cargo-handling facilities. From 1967-81, the entire docklands complex from the Tower to Woolwich was closed; the unthinkable had happened — the city was a port no more.

**Flooding and reclamation.**
*Reclamation of land on the Thames banks started with the Roman period and continued in the 19th century with elaborate schemes such as the Victoria Embankment, a broad carriageway incorporating an underground railway line and a new sewer. The map (below left) shows the line of indented waterfront in the Strand area with its projecting river stairs before the scheme began in 1866, and (superimposed) the outline of the new Embankment. The painting (below) shows the view towards the City along the newly-completed Embankment in c. 1873.*

*London has always been vulnerable to flooding, and the low-lying areas to the east and south of the City are particularly at risk (map top right); records of such disasters go back to 1294, when Southwark suffered severe damage. The situation is made more serious by geophysical changes: since all of south-east England is slowly sinking, the level of the highest Thames tides is therefore rising. The £435 million Thames barrier was completed in 1982. Its flood gates are raised 90 degrees from their normal lowered position to hold back incoming tides, forming a steel wall when needed (right).*

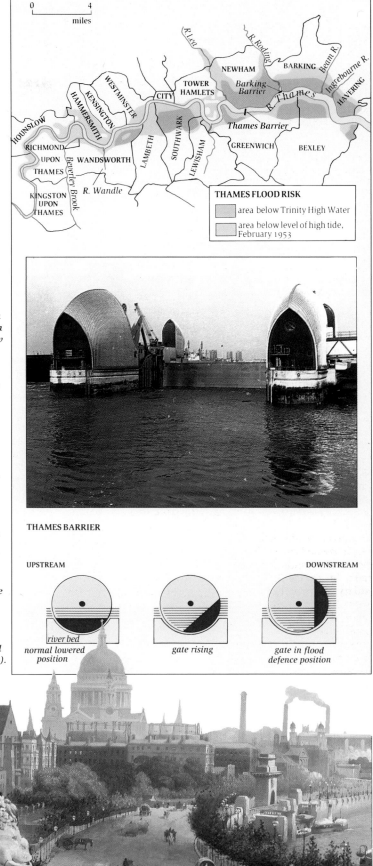

R. Lea  R. Roding  Beam R.

NEWHAM  BARKING

WESTMINSTER  TOWER HAMLETS  Barking Barrier  Ingrebourne R.  HAVERING

CITY  R. Thames

KENSINGTON  HAMMERSMITH

HOUNSLOW  Thames Barrier

RICHMOND  SOUTHWARK  GREENWICH  BEXLEY

UPON  WANDSWORTH  LAMBETH  LEWISHAM

THAMES  Beverley Brook

KINGSTON  R. Wandle
UPON
THAMES

0  4
miles

**THAMES FLOOD RISK**
  area below Trinity High Water
  area below level of high tide, February 1953

**THAMES BARRIER**

UPSTREAM  DOWNSTREAM

river bed
normal lowered position  gate rising  gate in flood defence position

THE BUILDING OF THE
EMBANKMENT 1870
(18th century streets
are shown in grey)

Long Acre

St. Martin's Lane

Strand

Surrey Stairs

Arundel Stairs

Somerset Stairs

Savoy Stairs

Salisbury Stairs

Victoria Embankment

York Buildings Stairs

Trafalgar Square

Charing Cross

Black Lyon Stairs

Hungerford Stairs

Whitehall

Whitehall Stairs

reclaimed land

Privy Garden Stairs

Manchester Stairs

Westminster Bridge

The New Road

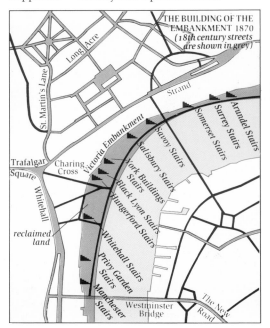

# CHAPTER 2
# ROMAN LONDON

THE THAMES VALLEY has attracted settlers since the time of the first hunter-gatherers, nearly half a million years ago. It provided everything necessary for successful habitation: water, fertile soils and abundant timber. However, there is no evidence as yet for any settlement of importance in the London area before the advent of the Romans, although isolated homesteads existed on the higher ground of Southwark, south of the Thames, and were scattered throughout the Thames area.

The physical geography of the region was a major influence on the origin and development of *Londinium*. The north bank of the Thames was elevated and well-drained, consisting of a gravel terrace capped by brickearth. Although bisected by a stream (later called the Walbrook), it was a relatively flat platform and ideal for building. Protected to the west by the River Fleet, the steep slopes down to the water's edge provided an additional defence. There was a constant fresh water supply provided by the Thames and the Walbrook and by springs at the base of the gravel terrace that could be exploited by shallow wells.

For political reasons the Emperor Claudius needed a conquest to safeguard his position in Rome and to deploy surplus legions throughout the Empire. In Britain, strong native leaders were emerging, uniting the various tribes in lowland Britain, interfering with those tribes who were allied to or had peaceful relations with Rome. As a state of open hostility with Rome was an ever-increasing threat, Claudius decided to dispatch his formidable army to Britain in AD 43. The force, comprising four legions and auxiliary units from Europe, must have totalled some 40,000 men. Under the command of Aulus Plautius, the troops landed at the natural harbour of *Rutupiae* (Richborough), unopposed by the Britons. From this coastal base, the army gained control of much of the south-east of England. A decisive battle with British tribes took place at the River Medway and from that point on only local pockets of resistance were encountered. The invasion force then advanced to the Thames which the troops crossed successfully in two places, probably by means of a floating pontoon bridge constructed by the military engineers and by swimming across. The Britons retreated eastwards and the pursuing Roman army lost many men in the Essex marshes.

After the crossing of the Thames, the campaign halted on the pretext that reinforcements were needed. Word was sent to the Emperor in Rome and after a delay, Claudius took command of his troops near the Thames and took over the campaign. He marched on the tribal centre, *Camulodunum* (Colchester), where he received the surrender of eleven British kings. After a stay of just sixteen days, Claudius returned triumphant to Rome. He left the army behind to establish *Camulodunum* as the capital of the Province of *Britannia*, and to

*For a more detailed discussion of the physical geography of the London region, see Chapter 1 Land under London, pp.18-23.*

*In the late 1990s, archaeologists discovered the remains of a massive oak structure on the Thames foreshore at Vauxhall. This suggested the existence of a bridge, wide enough to allow two carts to pass. It appears to have been installed in the middle Bronze Age long before Roman military engineers built their bridge almost 3 miles downstream. The huge wooden foundation pilings have been carbon-dated to between 1750 and 1285 BC. In prehistoric times the Thames at this site was wider and shallower than today, with many islands. The bridge-like feature may have linked to an island or crossed the whole river, but no remains have been found on its northern shore. The discovery of such a large structure from such an early period means that scholars will have to redraft fundamental aspects of London's history.*

*Remains of a dozen circular houses, some 5 m in diameter, were discovered at Gresham Street. Dating evidence suggests that they were in use from AD 50, just after the Roman invasion of AD 43. They represent a pre-Roman building tradition and were probably occupied by local British people. These remains provide valuable clues toward understanding the transition of settlement from the Iron Age in what would become Londinium.*

**Left** *The Bucklersbury pavement. This large Roman mosaic dates to the 3rd century AD and was discovered in 1869 close to the Mansion House.*

impose a single firm control over the various tribal groups on both sides of the Thames.

The Thames must have been finally crossed by a bridge, although its method of construction and material are uncertain. The new roads made by the Roman army leading from the Kent coast to *Camulodunum* and to the rest of the new province beyond had to converge on this bridge, which became strategically important. The earliest occupation of London, therefore, was probably by Roman soldiers defending the new crossing and consisted of temporary fortified camps. It must have taken some years after the invasion of AD 43 to build the permanent bridge and road network around *Londinium*. Archaeological work in Southwark and on the north bank has uncovered evidence of a bridge which could not have been built earlier than AD 50.

Traces of the earliest phase of occupation have been found most clearly in a small area north of an east-west road running parallel with the river, underlying parts of Lombard Street where a regular lay-out of timber buildings and roads is evident. This first *Londinium* was destroyed by fire in AD 60 by Queen Boudicca (Boadicea), who led her tribe, the Iceni, from East Anglia, joined by the Trinobantes of Essex, in revolt against the Romans. The Roman army at that time was scattered throughout Britain and the Governor of Britain, Suetonius Paulinus, was in Anglesey fighting the Druids with a large part of the army. The Governor was unable to save *Camulodunum*, the first target of Queen Boudicca's army, from destruction but attempted to rescue *Londinium*, reaching it with his cavalry before Boudicca's arrival. There were not enough troops to defend the town and he therefore evacuated anyone willing to leave. The inhabitants who remained were massacred by the rebels and the town destroyed. It is possible that some of the many human skulls since recovered from the stream-bed of the Walbrook were ritually deposited there by the tribesmen, although no human remains can be positively attributed to the massacre. *Verulamium* then met the same fate. Suetonius Paulinus finally confronted Boudicca in the Midlands and, although vastly outnumbered, the Romans proved victorious. For some months after the revolt they inflicted retribution on the native Britons.

Nero sent a new *procurator* to administer the province's financial and economic affairs, Julius Alpinus Classicianus. He was a fair and just administrator, putting right the injustices that had caused the rebellion. The office of *procurator* continued to be based in *Londinium*, emphasising the town's importance. The Governor also had his permanent headquarters in *Londinium*, where he maintained a civil service which kept him in touch with the rest of the province and Rome. *Londinium* arose from the ashes of its destruction and underwent substantial expansion and development. A large public building, probably the first basilica and forum, was built on the high ground to the east of the Walbrook. Tacitus, writing in the early 2nd century, described *Londinium* at the time of the Boudiccan revolt as a place teeming with businessmen and a famous centre of commerce. Surviving wooden writing tablets record financial transactions, the repayment of loans and the selling of commodities such as slaves. The port soon revived after AD 60 and when *Londinium* became the capital of the province there was an upsurge in commercial vitality and much upgrading of the port facilities. Indeed, the port seems to have reached its peak of activity during the late 1st century.

*Londinium*'s street system was laid out and many parts of the city had become densely built up by about AD 100. Shops and commercial buildings had been built along the main road leading from the forum. Residential areas and public baths had been developed away from the main streets and the

**Above** *Head of the Emperor Hadrian. This large bronze head was found in the Thames. He visited London in AD 122.*

*The new town which grew up on the Thames was named* **Londinium** *by the Romans. The name is of pre-Roman origin, possibly connected with the original British name for the area.*

*Excavations at Plantation Place, south-east of the site of the Roman forum, reveal new evidence about the uprising led by Boudica in AD 60–61, when Londinium was destroyed completely. Defensive ditches and a rampart were built directly on the ruins of the devastated city, indicating that the Roman army was closely involved in its reconstruction. Settlement at Plantation Place had begun fewer than ten years after the Roman invasion of AD 43, with the main east-west street of Londinium crossing the site. Boudica's army ransacked mudbrick buildings to the south of that street. Fire debris and abandoned pots and other artefacts indicate the haste with which inhabitants fled the city.*

*In 2000 a hoard of 43 Roman coins was discovered at Plantation Place, to the south-east of the site of the Forum. The coins span over a hundred years, from the reign of Emperor Nero (AD 65–66) to that of Marcus Aurelius (AD 174).*

*For a full reconstruction of the 2nd-century city, see pp. 30-31.*

*For a detailed discussion of the Roman port and London's commercial activities, see pp. 32-33.*

For a reconstruction of Roman fort and detailed map of London's defensive walls, see pp. 34-35.

Remains of the 2nd-century AD Roman fort are preserved beneath the Museum of London. In 1988 archaeologists discovered the Roman amphitheatre beneath Guildhall Yard that was being excavated prior to building the new Guildhall Art Gallery. This important site, where gladiators fought and wild animals were slaughtered to entertain the residents of Londinium, may now be visited.

Excavations during the 1990s have emphasised the importance of Roman settlement on the low sandy islands of Southwark. As early as AD 50–60 settlers built timber-framed buildings along a 'high street' that led to the bridge over the Thames. These contained shops, a smithy and a market hall. Wheat and barley were milled, and beef butchered in large amounts, but virtually no pork or mutton. East of the high street was residential property, with military and perhaps governmental buildings to the west. Londinium, to the north and south of the Thames, covered more than twice the area of any other city in Roman Britain.

Evidence from the west side of Watling Street in Southwark suggests that Roman cemeteries comprised paved streets and small houses built by important families to form 'cities of the dead'. A small temple or mausoleum dates from the 2nd century AD, with important debris from graves and cremation pyres. Later, small walled enclosures were laid out with a tomb or mausoleum between them. Such arrangements are evocative of the great cemeteries still found in Egypt and other parts of the Mediterranean world.

**Right** Statue of British hunter-god found in Southwark, 3rd century AD. Statues and inscriptions of the period indicate **Londinium's** continuing importance.

amphitheatre and fort built to the west of the town. The Emperor Hadrian visited *Londinium* in AD 122 and many public buildings were either built or rebuilt for his visit. However, very soon after, in about AD 125, *Londinium* was again severely damaged by fire, a date fixed by the quantities of burnt pottery found on various sites.

The reigns of the Emperors Antoninus Pius and Marcus Aurelius in the mid-2nd century were not a stable period in general for Roman Britain, and *Londinium* in the mid-2nd century was beginning to undergo changes. Houses and workshops in the Walbrook valley and elsewhere in the city and Southwark were no longer required and were deliberately demolished. In certain areas such as Milk Street and Newgate Street to the west, they were overlaid by a dark earth, which initially must have been brought from outside the town. In addition, the large public baths at Huggin Hill and the smaller baths at Cheapside were demolished towards the end of the 2nd century perhaps because their maintenance for a much reduced population could no longer be justified. Despite this, *Londinium* was still regarded as important by the Roman authorities, and this is testified to by the construction of a new timber waterfront and a massive city wall which enclosed 330 acres, making *Londinium* the largest city in Britain. At a period when the working population seems to have abandoned large areas of the city, the wall extended beyond the existing inhabited areas and stretched from modern-day Blackfriars to the Tower where the ends of the wall must have had special fortifications to prevent attackers reaching the city. The tributaries of the Walbrook were allowed to flow through the wall in brick culverts.

The city wall was perhaps built to protect the capital during the civil wars at the end of the 2nd century. Clodius Albinus, Governor of Britain, had declared himself Emperor in AD 193 and had taken most of Britain's troops to fight on the Continent. He may well have realised the importance of protecting *Londinium* against any advances the true Emperor, Septimius Severus, might have chosen to make. The dating of the wall has been made possible by finds of coins: one coin set a date for its construction not earlier than AD 190; and other coins and clay coin moulds belonging to a forger indicate that it could not have been built later than about AD 210.

In AD 200 Britain was divided into two separate provinces. *Londinium* was made capital of *Britannia Superior* (Upper Britain) and *Eburacum* (York) capital of *Britannia Inferior* (Lower Britain). While large numbers of sculptures and inscriptions belonging to the 3rd century indicate that *Londinium* was still a town of considerable importance and wealth, its population was reduced and large areas within the wall were perhaps used for horticulture. The Walbrook area was re-occupied before the mid-3rd century, and the marshy ground was stabilised and substantial buildings were built, many with finely patterned mosaic floors. A large area in the south-western corner of the walled city was occupied during the 3rd century by a pre-

cinct of public buildings, probably including temples, which was possibly entered by a monumental arch, surviving fragments of which were found re-used in the later riverside wall. The temple of Mithras was built in about AD 240 on the east bank of the Walbrook.

In AD 286 Carausius, the admiral of the Roman fleet based in the English Channel, was accused of taking the treasure of Saxon and Frankish pirates for his own use. Crossing to Britain, he declared himself Emperor and ruled Britain until he was murdered by his financial adviser, Allectus, in AD 293. This was a period of political and economic isolation for Britain. To compensate for the loss of official coinage reaching Britain, Carausius in AD 288 created, for the first time, a coin mint in *Londinium*, which continued to produce coins spasmodically into the 4th century.

In AD 296, the army of the Roman Emperor Constantius Chlorus landed in Hampshire and defeated Allectus near *Calleva* (Silchester). Constantius sailed up the Thames and arrived in time to save *Londinium* from being sacked by rebels from the defeated army of Allectus, restoring Britain to the Empire. In the early 4th century the Emperor Diocletian completely reformed the whole imperial system of government with a policy of devolution which was to alter the political status of *Londinium*, and this move perhaps coincided with the demolition of the forum and basilica complex. Britain was sub-divided into four smaller provinces. Despite this division and the political upheavals, *Londinium* retained its place as capital of the new province of *Maxima Caesariensis*. Following Constantine the Great's conversion to Christianity in the early 4th century, the Christians became powerful in Britain. Records show that a Bishop of *Londinium* went to the Council of Arles in AD 314. The Mithraic temple was attacked on several occasions, and sculptures were broken up and discarded. It seems that the Mithraists forestalled one of the Christian attacks by burying the more precious marble sculptures. The temple was to continue in use for pagan (but not necessarily Mithraic) worship for a few more years until the building finally fell into ruin in the mid-4th century.

Political unrest throughout the Empire was affecting Britain. In AD 350 the usurpers Magnentius and Decentius withdrew troops from Britain but failed in their attempt to win the Empire. When Hadrian's Wall was overrun in AD 367, the Emperor Valentinian sent his general, Theodosius, to regain control of Britain. The little archaeological evidence that there is for *Londinium* at this period shows that the city's defences were improved and strengthened, with a riverside wall completing the defensive circuit. For the last half of the 4th century, the main occupied areas in the city were to the east of the Walbrook. Some areas of the city had not been inhabited since the late 2nd and 3rd centuries.

In AD 410 the Emperor Honorius refused to defend Britain further. Britain was now independent from the rest of the Empire and British towns were forced to recruit mercenaries in order to protect themselves against the threat of increased attacks from Saxon and German tribes. Finds of military buckles and belt sets in burials in the extramural cemeteries testify to a military presence in late-Roman *Londinium*. Such adornments, made in the Rhineland area, would have been worn by government officials and army officers, and may indicate that German mercenaries were employed by the army. Nevertheless, life seems to have continued in much the same way as before for some years. Excavations revealed that a fine 3rd-century house in Lower Thames Street continued in use into the 5th century. A fragment of pottery amphora of that date, imported from the eastern Mediterranean, was found there, indicating that supplies were still reaching the city from some distance. However, when the building slowly fell into disrepair and was eventually demolished in the late 5th century nothing was built to replace it. The Romans had left *Londinium* to its fate but they left strong foundations and traditions that were to leave a lasting impression on the later city.

**Above** *Gold medallion from Arras, France, showing the city of* **Londinium** *welcoming Constantius Chlorus who rescued the city from plunder in AD 296.*

*Londinium required substantial amounts of fresh water, but had no aqueducts. Excavations at Gresham Street have revealed two Roman machines for lifting water from two deep oak-lined wells or cisterns. Tree rings allow one to be dated to AD 63, following the destruction of much of the city by Boudica in AD 60/61. The second well was sturdier and was constructed in AD 108/109 and was probably destroyed by fire. Both machines had bucket-chain mechanisms, possibly powered by human treadmills.*

*At Spitalfields a major excavation took place during the 1990s, revealing a Roman cemetery beneath a medieval priory, hospital and graveyard. An important discovery was the grave of a rich young Roman woman.*

**Map below** *The extent of Roman London at its peak is contrasted to the size of the city in 1820.*

EXTENT OF LONDON 2ND CENTURY AD

LONDON 1820

✢ St. Paul's

✢ Westminster Abbey

LONDON 1820

# THE GROWTH OF LONDINIUM

Road systems, quickly established after the Roman conquest, facilitated the movement of troops, and many road alignments laid out by the Romans are still in use today. Watling Street, leading from the Kent coast, presumably crossed the Thames in the Lambeth/Westminster area, prior to *Londinium*'s foundation, and continued its route to *Verulamium* (St. Alban's) and the north-west. With the building of the bridge across the Thames, most traffic would have passed through *Londinium*, with roads leaving the city for Silchester, York, Colchester and Chichester.

An essential part of the officially organised communication system were posting stations (*mansiones*) along the road network, at set distances apart, where fresh horses were available for the imperial post and inns were provided for refreshments. Several known Romano-British centres near to *Londinium* originated as *mansiones*: Ewell on Stane Street; Crayford and Brockley Hill on Watling Street; and Staines on the Silchester road.

For the ordinary farmer in the countryside around *Londinium* the Roman conquest probably meant little more than exchanging a native, tribal landlord for a foreign Roman tax official. The nearest known villas, or more elaborate farm-houses, lie mainly to the south of *Londinium*, for example at Beddington, Keston and Orpington, and further still in the Darenth valley and beyond Ewell.

Early *Londinium* mainly occupied the area around modern Lombard Street and Gracechurch Street. The majority of the early buildings were constructed of timber, clay and mud brick with thatched roofs, the more important buildings were tiled. Boudicca's total destruction of the town in AD 60 left layers of burnt red clay which are all that remain of the clay and timber houses and give clear evidence of *Londinium*'s size. In about AD 120 *Londinium* was again destroyed by fire. The burnt debris shows that the area of habitation had grown considerably over the intervening years, spreading to the south-east and west of the Walbrook stream with major public buildings (as befitted the capital of the province) now in place. *Londinium* was rebuilt once again and continued to prosper. New waterfronts were constructed, shops were rebuilt and temples built and repaired.

The nature of *Londinium* in the 3rd century, however, was changing. The city wall provided a defensive barrier; large town houses replaced areas of local industry; some areas of the town were deliberately demolished and the population was decreasing. Archaeological evidence shows that in the 4th century the main area of occupation was

*The London area in the Roman period: The natural advantages of the surrounding area helped to determine* Londinium*'s position. The Thames was tidal in the city area and being navigable it enabled ships to travel direct from the heart of Europe via the Rhine. After the conquest in AD 43 the Romans quickly established the road network to allow the army and merchants alike fast passage. Towns grew up along the roadsides either originating as official resting posts or at river-crossing points. Other settlements centred on areas where raw products such as clay for pottery were readily available or where shrines or temple worship were established. Much of the countryside around* Londinium *was thickly wooded, a useful source of timber, and the rural areas probably altered little after the conquest, with many farming communities being subsumed in the Roman villa estates that clustered around* Londinium.

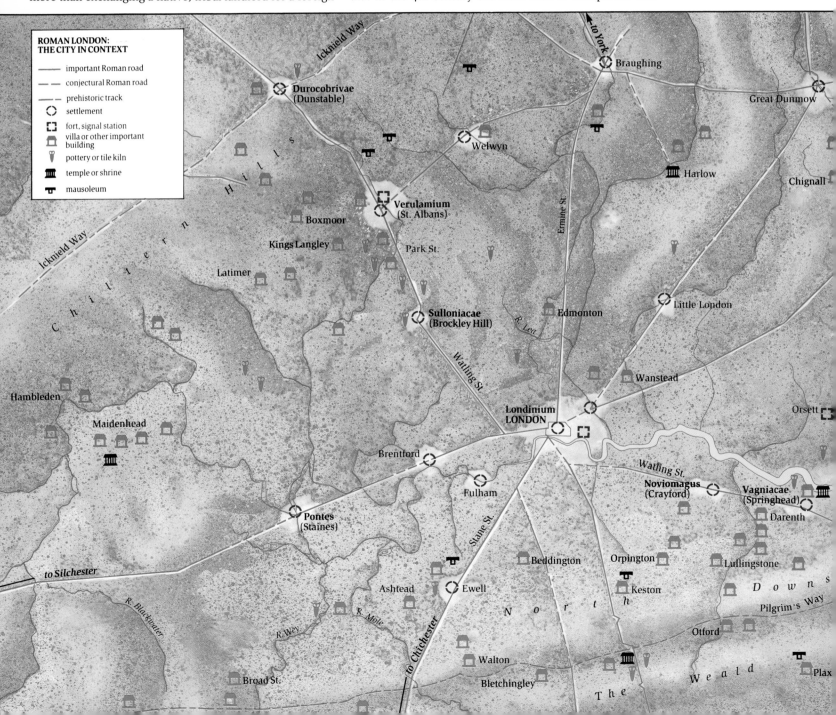

ROMAN LONDON:
THE CITY IN CONTEXT

— important Roman road
-- conjectural Roman road
— prehistoric track
⊂⊃ settlement
⊏⊐ fort, signal station
🏛 villa or other important building
♈ pottery or tile kiln
🏛 temple or shrine
⊓ mausoleum

- area of settlement
- probable road
- probable bridge
- building
- city wall
- gate-house
- bastion
- turret
- quays

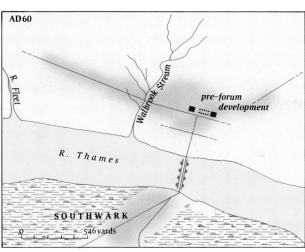

AD 60

R. Fleet

Walbrook Stream

pre-forum
development

R. Thames

0          546 yards

SOUTHWARK

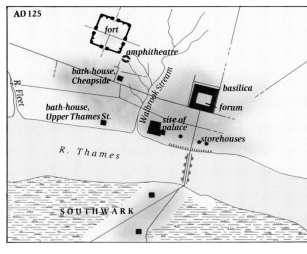

AD 125

fort

amphitheatre

bath-house,
Cheapside

R. Fleet

bath-house,
Upper Thames St.

Walbrook Stream

basilica

site of
palace

forum

storehouses

R. Thames

SOUTHWARK

**The growth of Londinium (maps right)** *Most of the early town lay east of the Walbrook stream. The town was completely destroyed during the Boudiccan rebellion, AD 60/61. The rebuilt town became the thriving provincial capital in the late 1st century AD with many major public buildings. A wall was built around the city c. AD 200 to enclose a dwindling population. Additional fortifications had been added by AD 375 to protect the city from attack.*

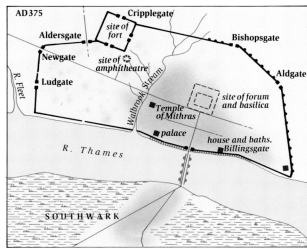

AD 200

Cripplegate

fort

Newgate

amphitheatre

Bishopsgate

bath-house

R. Fleet

Ludgate

Aldgate

Walbrook Stream

basilica

forum

bath-house

palace

R. Thames

SOUTHWARK

AD 375

Cripplegate

Aldersgate

site of
fort

Bishopsgate

Newgate

site of
amphitheatre

Ludgate

Aldgate

R. Fleet

Walbrook Stream

site of forum
and basilica

Temple
of Mithras

palace

house and baths,
Billingsgate

R. Thames

SOUTHWARK

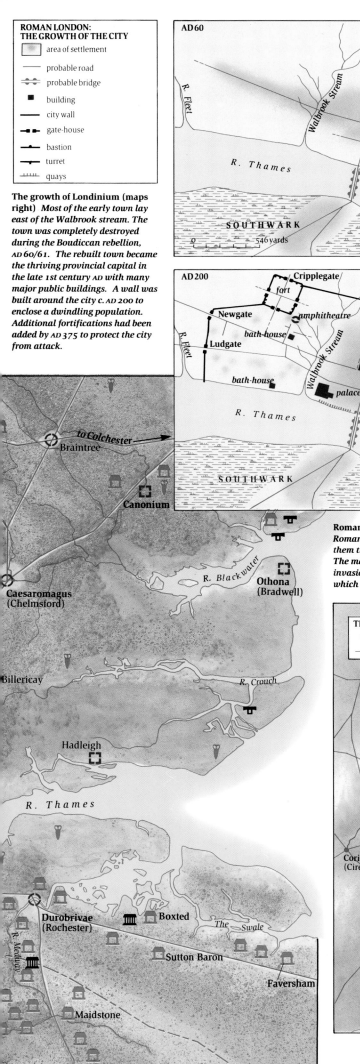

to Colchester
Braintree

Canonium

R. Blackwater

Othona
(Bradwell)

Caesaromagus
(Chelmsford)

Billericay

R. Crouch

Hadleigh

R. Thames

Durobrivae
(Rochester)

Boxted

The Swale

Sutton Baron

Faversham

Maidstone

**Roman invasion AD 43** *When the Romans invaded they brought with them their skill in building roads. The map (below) shows both their invasion routes and the network which began to take shape.*

centred on the east side of the Walbrook. People were still living in *Londinium* in Roman style, but houses were finally abandoned in the early 5th century, coinciding with the refusal of the Emperor Honorius in AD 410 to send more troops to the province to defend Britain.

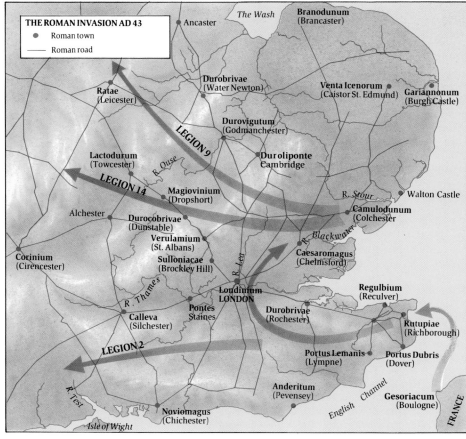

THE ROMAN INVASION AD 43
- Roman town
- Roman road

The Wash

Ancaster

Branodunum
(Brancaster)

Durobrivae
(Water Newton)

Venta Icenorum
(Caistor St. Edmund)

Gariannonum
(Burgh Castle)

Ratae
(Leicester)

LEGION 9

Durovigutum
(Godmanchester)

Lactodurum
(Towcester)

R. Ouse

Duroliponte
Cambridge

LEGION 14

Magiovinium
(Dropshort)

R. Stour

Walton Castle

Alchester

Durocobrivae
(Dunstable)

Camulodunum
(Colchester)

Corinium
(Cirencester)

Verulamium
(St. Albans)

R. Blackwater

Sulloniacae
(Brockley Hill)

Caesaromagus
(Chelmsford)

R. Lea

Londinium
LONDON

Calleva
(Silchester)

Pontes
Staines

R. Thames

Durobrivae
(Rochester)

Regulbium
(Reculver)

LEGION 2

Rutupiae
(Richborough)

Portus Lemanis
(Lympne)

Portus Dubris
(Dover)

R. Test

Anderitum
(Pevensey)

Gesoriacum
(Boulogne)

FRANCE

English Channel

Noviomagus
(Chichester)

Isle of Wight

# LONDINIUM: THE ROMAN CITY

In the last 30 years of the 1st century AD, *Londinium* became the capital of the province and was transformed into a Roman city. The timber-framed houses with their walls of wattle and daub and thatched roofs were upgraded and the walls given coverings of painted plaster. Public buildings were built of Kentish ragstone and flat tile-like bricks. Of *Londinium*'s public buildings, the great *basilica* and *forum* was the most important. Built about AD 120 to 125, and situated on the highest ground in the city, it would have dominated the skyline. The *basilica* served as town hall and law courts, indicating that *Londinium* must have now had a constitution for local government. The new *basilica* was more than 164 yards long, longer than any other north of the Alps. It had a great hall with a nave and northern aisle, with a double row of offices to one side. At the eastern end was a raised platform for judges. The *forum* enclosed a great central courtyard on three sides with the *basilica* on the fourth. Its three wings formed the business centre of the city, containing shops and offices, and the central courtyard provided an open market and assembly area. It seems that the whole complex was demolished in about AD 300.

An imposing residence was also sited at the junction of the Thames and Walbrook. Built between AD 80 and 100, it may have been the governor's headquarters. Areas of the building are now buried under Cannon Street Railway Station and recent excavations there have added more information. The great building covered a wide area of at least three acres and consisted of state rooms, reception halls and offices, as well as baths and living accommodation, all built around a central garden court. To the north was a great hall. The east wing consisted of small rooms and may have been the quarters for visiting officials or administrative offices, while other areas probably contained the residential quarters.

For their entertainment, Roman Londoners would have congregated at the amphitheatre in which animal baiting and possibly gladiatorial combat took place. It may also have served to stage plays, house state ceremonials and as a training ground for the army. It was situated to the south-east of the fort and its site has only recently been uncovered. It consisted of an oval arena of packed sand with an under-floor drainage system. A main entrance-way was discovered with the remains of two ante-rooms on either side suitable as waiting rooms for the participants or combatants in the arena events.

As befits the capital of any Roman province, sanitation and hygiene were given a high priority. The Britons were encouraged to adopt the pleasures of civilisation, including daily bathing. Public bath-houses in Upper Thames Street and Cheapside were built in the late 1st century and enlarged in the 2nd. The Cheapside bath-house was sited near to the Roman fort, and because of its small size, was perhaps intended for the military rather than the public. The baths in Upper Thames Street, however, were built on a grander scale, overlooking the Thames in a position where natural spring water fed the baths. In later Roman times, finer houses also had private bath-houses.

Religion in Roman Britain was a combination of Roman and native Celtic ideas, and cults from the east, such as Mithraism, were also popular. The only temple identified in London is dedicated to the mystery cult of Mithras, the god of heavenly light. Mithraism emphasised honesty, purity and courage and was favoured by soldiers, officials and merchants. The temple, on the east bank of the Walbrook, was built about AD 240 and had a central nave and side aisles. Fine marble sculptures of Mithras and other Roman gods and goddesses were found deliberately hidden. It seems that when Christianity finally overcame Mithraism in the 4th century the sculptures from the temple were buried to protect them from destruction.

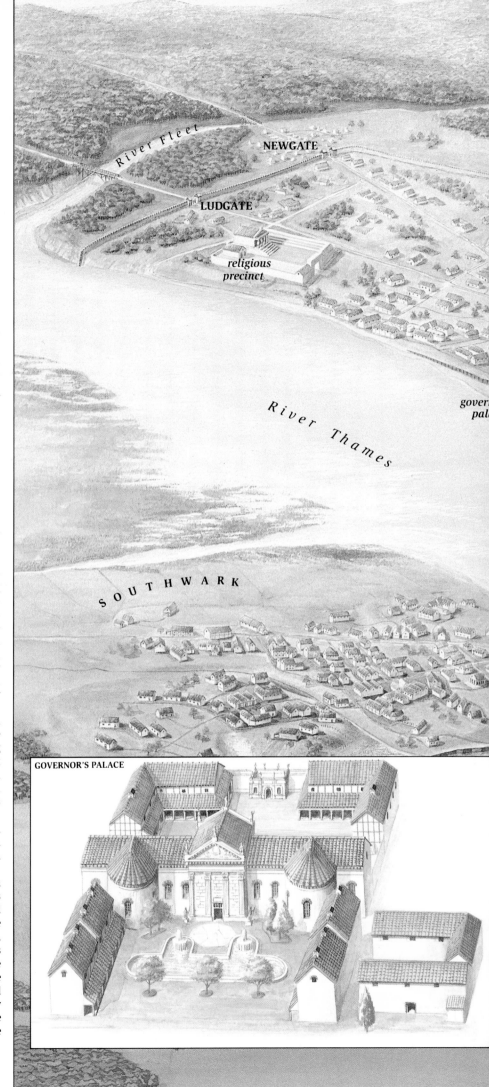

NEWGATE

LUDGATE

*religious precinct*

River Fleet

River Thames

govern palc

SOUTHWARK

GOVERNOR'S PALACE

ALDERSGATE

CRIPPLEGATE

fort

Cheapside Baths

amphitheatre

Walbrook Stream

Temple of Mithras

BISHOPSGATE

cemetery

forum &
basilica

ALDGATE

**CHEAPSIDE BATHS**

# COMMERCIAL LONDINIUM

In the wake of the Roman invasion, merchants and traders followed closely after the army. They exploited the fact that ocean-going ships could reach the city, and the Thames provided deep-water anchorage. The town's commercial vitality and growth after AD 60 depended on the construction of adequate port facilities along the river. In the mid 1st-century AD the riverbank lay to the north of modern Thames Street, and the waterfronts were built out into the river on reclaimed land. Their construction and their successive replacements throughout the Roman and later periods, have resulted in today's river lying about 100 yards or more to the south of its original shoreline. Excavations near Pudding Lane, downstream of the Roman bridge, have revealed a series of timber quays dating from the mid-1st–early 3rd centuries. Here goods were unloaded from ships and moved into rectangular storehouses at the back of the quay.

Trade flourished in Roman London, where a prosperous community of differing nationalities demanded the same goods as the rest of the Empire. Many of *Londinium*'s inhabitants would have been British or Gaulish in origin; others came from Germany, Greece and beyond. Although *Londinium* was politically and culturally Roman it must have been a constantly changing racial mixture. While the province was developing, imports were essential, since there were not the native craftsmen to produce the high-quality goods required. However, in time, British goods were also to flood into *Londinium* and the province gradually became self-sufficient. The cosmopolitan population of *Londinium* also had a taste for Mediterranean foods such as olives, olive oil, wine, grape juice, dates, figs and salted fish products, which were imported in large pottery containers (*amphorae*) to meet this demand. Glossy red pottery (samian), standard Roman tableware, was imported in great quantities from regions of France. Bronze tableware, glass and lamps came from Italy; bronze, pottery, glass, millstones and wine from Germany and fish sauce and olive oil from Spain.

The archaeological evidence for shops in *Londinium* is limited, restricted to surviving ground plans or occupational debris. Carbonized grain recovered from Pudding Lane and Fenchurch Street suggests a bakery or mill was sited there, and part of a donkey-driven mill found in Princes Street suggests that the milling of flour on a large-scale must have taken place there. Few traces have survived of the numerous merchants of Roman London, apart from the balances and steelyards which were probably used for weighing out foodstuffs in their shops.

*Londinium's commercial vitality and growth depended on the rapidly expanding port situated to the west of The Tower (right). New quays were constantly being built out into the river, using varying methods of construction: the 3rd-century quays (below right) used small timbers in complicated box-like structures. The busy waterfronts received sea-going ships laden with imports from all over the empire (map below). Amphorae were used as containers for olive oil, wine or fish products. The example (below left) comes from Southwark and bears an ink inscription testifying to the fish sauce's quality. Emeralds were imported from Egypt, and were used in this emerald and gold necklace found in Cannon Street. Lamps, such as the example (below centre) found on the bank of the Thames, were imported from Gaul. The bustling port supplied the town's needs through shops and workshops. Excavations in Newgate Street revealed two such buildings of 2nd-century date (plan left), while this reconstruction of a cutler's stall (left), gives a vivid impression of the appearance of a Roman shop. During the late 3rd century, Londinium produced minted coins, and this bronze antoninianus (see obverse and reverse below) of Allectus (AD 293-296) has the mint mark ML (Moneta Londinii).*

**PLAN OF ROMAN SHOPS: NEWGATE STREET 1ST CENTURY AD**

gravel
lane
air vent
?dining room
residential quarters
shop or workshop
hearth
possible lean-to or corridor
residential quarters
alley
shop or workshop
probable line of wall
remains of wall
hearth
hearth

**LONDON'S TRADE WITH THE EMPIRE**

— extent of Roman empire, 2nd century AD

— Roman road

■ provincial capital

commodities imported to London:

- wine (in amphorae)
- pottery
- millstones
- dried fruit (in amphorae)
- sea-food (in amphorae)
- olive-oil (in amphorae)
- brooches
- glassware
- figurines
- amber
- marble
- emeralds
- lamps
- bronze tableware

*multiple-box framework of jointed beams*

*horizontally-laid timbers*

CROSS-SECTION OF 3RD-CENTURY QUAY AT CUSTOM HOUSE SHOWING METHOD OF CONSTRUCTION

THE ROMAN RIVERSIDE

# LONDINIUM'S DEFENCES

The early 2nd-century fort was built away from the centre of the town. It covered an area of nearly 12 acres and was constructed on the standard Roman rectangular pattern, with rounded corners and internal towers. There were also intermediate towers containing stairs to the rampart walk. The fort's function was probably not primarily defensive but to provide a suitable barracks for troops stationed in the capital of the province. Soldiers, who acted as military escorts and performed guard and ceremonial duties, would have been based there. Members of the governor's staff, probably seconded from the legions based in Britain, would have assumed the duties of civil servants. A tombstone of a legionary soldier depicts him in military attire, but also carrying a case of writing tablets, to denote his clerical function.

Up until AD 200, the town boundaries were marked by a bank and ditch, but then

*Londinium* was enclosed by a great wall on the landward side. The wall stretched over two miles from modern Blackfriars to the Tower of London. It was probably at least twenty feet high when built and was nine feet thick on ground level narrowing to eight feet above the sandstone plinth. The wall was made of ragstone quarried at Maidstone and brought, via the River Medway, up the Thames by boat. The outer faces of the city wall, like the fort, were built of squared blocks of ragstone, skilfully cut to shape and the intervening space was filled with irregular lumps of ragstone and mortar. At yard intervals two or three courses of tiles were laid across the wall to provide stability.

The outside of the wall was defended by a ditch about four yards away. The earth dug from both the ditch and the wall's foundation trench formed a great reinforcing bank against the inner face of the wall. Where the existing Roman roads left the city, gate-houses were built, later to be called Aldgate, Bishopsgate, Newgate, Ludgate and in the north of the fort, Cripplegate. The west gate was blocked up in the

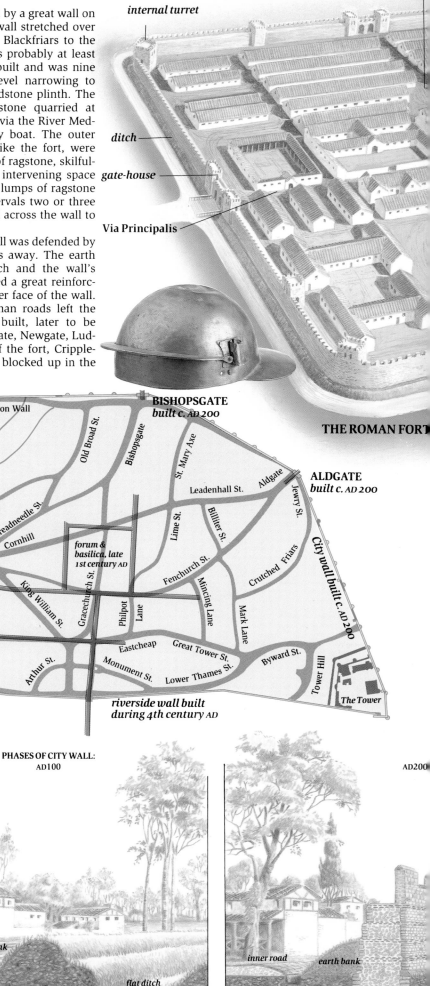

*internal turret*

*ditch*

*gate-house*

*Via Principalis*

Via Decumana

**THE ROMAN FORT**

**The City wall** *was built to a uniform standard in c. AD 200 (below). More than a million ragstone blocks were used for the two faces of the wall, with horizontal tile courses at regular intervals.*

*city wall built c. AD 200*

**fort built** *c. AD 120*

London Wall

London Wall

**BISHOPSGATE** *built c. AD 200*

**ALDERSGATE** *late Roman addition*

**NEWGATE** *built c. AD 200*

**LUDGATE** *built c. AD 200*

**ALDGATE** *built c. AD 200*

Moorgate, Coleman St., Gresham St., Lothbury, Old Broad St., Bishopsgate, St. Mary Axe, Aldgate, Jewry St., Leadenhall St., Lime St., Billiter St., Crutched Friars, Mark Lane, King Edward St., Angel St., St. Martin's Le Grand, Wood St., King St., Princes St., Threadneedle St., Cornhill, Cheapside, forum & basilica, late 1st century AD, Gracechurch St., Fenchurch St., Mincing Lane, Philpot Lane, St Paul's Cathedral, Watling St., Cannon St., St Paul's Church Yard, Godliman St., Queen Victoria St., Walbrook, King William St., Eastcheap, Great Tower St., Byward St., Arthur St., Monument St., Lower Thames St., Tower Hill, Queen St., Warwick Lane

*City wall built c. AD 200*

**The Tower**

*riverside wall built during 4th century AD*

**THE DEFENCES OF ROMAN LONDON**
- ▭ wall
- ▭ bastion
- ▭ gateway
- ▭ turret
- —— presumed
- —— recorded
- —— surviving
- —— Roman road
- —— modern road

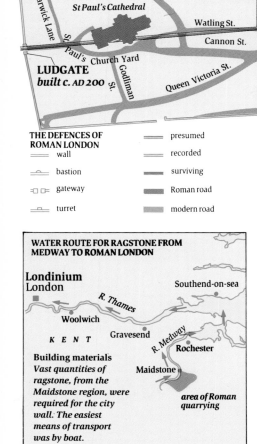

**WATER ROUTE FOR RAGSTONE FROM MEDWAY TO ROMAN LONDON**

**Londinium** London

Southend-on-sea

R. Thames

Woolwich

Gravesend

**KENT**

R. Medway

**Rochester**

Maidstone

*area of Roman quarrying*

**Building materials**
*Vast quantities of ragstone, from the Maidstone region, were required for the city wall. The easiest means of transport was by boat.*

**PHASES OF CITY WALL:**
AD 100

*earth bank*

*flat ditch*

AD 200

*inner road*

*earth bank*

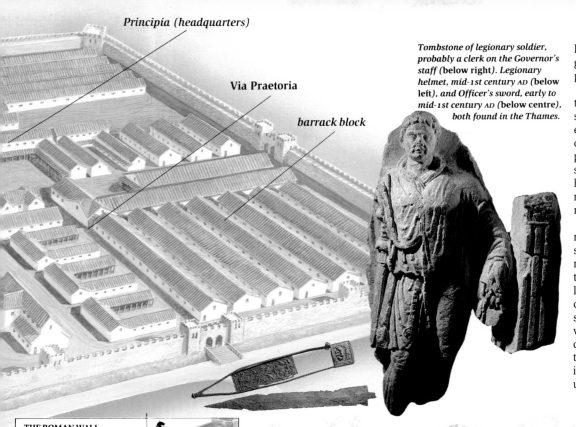

Principia (headquarters)

Via Praetoria

barrack block

*Tombstone of legionary soldier, probably a clerk on the Governor's staff (below right). Legionary helmet, mid-1st century AD (below left), and Officer's sword, early to mid-1st century AD (below centre), both found in the Thames.*

later Roman period and a new gate, Aldersgate, was inserted just beyond the fort's perimeter to allow traffic to by-pass it.

As *Londinium's* fortunes became more troubled in the later 4th century some 20 semi-circular bastions were added to the eastern side of the city wall as platforms for catapult machines. These towers were probably about 26 feet high and regularly spaced. Their outer walls were constructed like the wall itself and the infill consisted of re-used stonework from neighbouring Roman cemeteries.

In the late 3rd and 4th centuries a riverside wall finally completed the defensive circuit. Excavations near Blackfriars revealed varying styles of wall construction, some taking into account the water-logged position, with a wooden pile and chalk-raft foundation. Elsewhere large ragstone blocks, including re-used sculptures, were simply rammed into clay. This lack of consistency in the riverside wall's construction suggests it was built at different times in the 4th century with varying degrees of urgency.

THE LATE ROMAN GATE AT ALDERSGATE

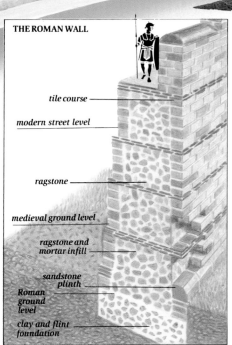

**THE ROMAN WALL**

tile course

modern street level

ragstone

medieval ground level

ragstone and mortar infill

sandstone plinth

Roman ground level

clay and flint foundation

**Londinium's Defences** The city wall, built c. AD 200, was further strengthened by eastern bastions and the riverside wall in the later 3rd and 4th centuries AD when *Londinium* was increasingly subject to attack.

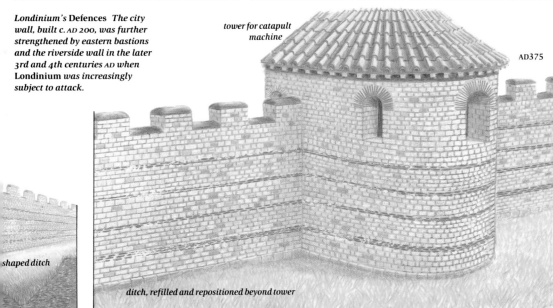

tower for catapult machine

AD375

shaped ditch

ditch, refilled and repositioned beyond tower

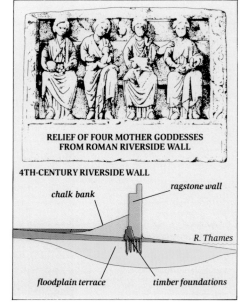

**RELIEF OF FOUR MOTHER GODDESSES FROM ROMAN RIVERSIDE WALL**

**4TH-CENTURY RIVERSIDE WALL**

chalk bank

ragstone wall

R. Thames

floodplain terrace

timber foundations

# CHAPTER 3
# SAXON AND NORMAN LONDON

THE CENTURY IN which Roman Britain was transformed into Anglo-Saxon England and Roman *Londinium* died, remains the most puzzling and hotly-debated period in our history. After AD 410, when the Emperor Honorius instructed the provincial authorities of Britain to look to their own defences, Britain was effectively outside the Roman empire; yet it remained within the Roman sphere of influence. When in 429 Germanus, Bishop of Auxerre, travelled from Gaul to Britain, he found people apparently living a recognisably 'Roman' lifestyle in the south-east of the country, and a flourishing Church. Raids by Picts and Saxons were a problem, but were meeting British resistance. On a second visit a few years later he seems to have found little change.

However, the middle of the 5th century saw dramatic events. In about 446 the Britons sent a vain plea to Rome for support against barbarian invaders. By the end of the 5th century most of the east of Britain was under Anglo-Saxon control. The last evidence for Roman *Londinium* is of a shrunken settlement such as Germanus might have seen in the early 5th century. One site, the Roman bathhouse near Billingsgate, has produced the earliest trace of Saxon presence in the city: a Saxon brooch dropped among the ruins of the abandoned building by a scavenger or squatter. By the end of the 5th century London must have been largely deserted. Whether the inhabitants were British or Saxon is of little account; the place no longer functioned as an urban centre. To the Anglo-Saxon settlers it was irrelevant; as self-sufficient farmers belonging to small family or tribal groupings, they had no use for towns. Few actual habitation sites have been excavated in the London area; the pattern of isolated farmsteads and small village communities seen elsewhere in the country seems to be repeated, some growing up at, or adjacent to, Roman sites, some on new sites – though perhaps farming the old fields.

By the end of the 6th century, the London area was part of the kingdom of the East Saxons which included the later counties of Essex and Middlesex and much, probably originally all, of Hertfordshire, stretching as far as the Chiltern Hills. Even part or all of Surrey ('*Sutherge*', or the 'southern district'), south of the Thames, was at one stage part of the kingdom. No 'princely' burials like those of Sutton Hoo or Taplow (in Buckinghamshire) can confidently be assigned to East Saxon rulers, and they often appear to have been in some sense subordinate to more powerful neighbours. Thus, King Saeberht of Essex was nephew of Ethelbert of Kent and accepted his authority when he received Christian missionaries in 604. He allowed Ethelbert to have a church, dedicated to St.Paul, erected in London as the cathedral of a bishop for the East Saxon people. Other early churches were founded in Roman towns, as at Canterbury and Rochester, and it is likely that it was the former existence of *Londinium*, rather than the presence of any major centre of Saxon population, which ensured the establishment of the church in London. East Saxon conversion to Christianity was, however, only superficial. On the death of Saeberht his people reverted to paganism, and it was the middle of the century before Christianity once more took hold. In the meantime London's function as an '*emporium*' was developing; as early as the 670s a royal charter referred in passing to the 'port of London where

*Saxon settlers moved up the Thames and the valleys leading off it, meeting little resistance from former British landowners. Mitcham cemetery (page 40) close to the River Wandle is evidence of this movement.*

*For a detailed map of the Saxon kingdoms, please see page 40.*

Below *A 13th-century crucifix figure, found at the Cluniac Priory of Bermondsey, founded 1089. It is gilded bronze with enamel decoration.*

**Left** *The first known view of London, a section from a road map (from London to Rome) drawn by the monk, Matthew Paris, in about 1252. The view shows three recognisable monuments: on the left, the Tower, St. Paul's in the centre, and to the right, Westminster Abbey. The wall, with its gates, is visible in the foreground.*

*Until recently, the earliest finds relating to the Middle Saxon trading settlement of Londinium comprised scattered materials from the late 6th and early 7th centuries, located beneath St Martin-in-the-Fields and other sites. Recent discovery of a few sherds of Early Saxon pottery at the west end of Long Acre shows that the first Saxon activity in the area may have been about a hundred years earlier than previously thought. In 2000 a fine Early Saxon brooch was unearthed by archaeologists digging near the Royal Opera House, Covent Garden. It is almost 3 inches in diameter and is made of copper discs, embellished with gold and garnets. It was found in a grave that probably belonged to a lady of noble birth, and dated from between 650 and 700 AD. The find is on the site of mid-Saxon Lundenwic but pre-dates the main phase of urban development*

ships land'. Since 1985, a growing number of sites excavated north of the Strand, between Trafalgar Square and Aldwych, have produced traces of a flourishing settlement of the 7th to early-9th centuries, and work near Charing Cross in 1988 revealed a river embankment which may have served for ships to beach for unloading. In contrast, the area to the east within the Roman city walls remained largely empty, apart from the cathedral and, perhaps, an as yet unlocated royal palace. In contemporary documents, London is referred to as *Lundenwic*; the Old English ending *-wic*, found also in names like Ipswich and Sandwich, usually denotes a port or trading town. International trade in northern Europe depended on a network of such ports, subject to royal control and taxation. Most trade would have been local – the buying and selling of agricultural produce. Yet finds of imported pottery on sites in the Strand area indicate more extensive trade links. Silver coins minted in London found their way to the Continent; the port of London probably handled export of English woollen cloth, famous throughout Europe.

At the end of the 8th century Vikings from Scandinavia began to raid the towns and monasteries of northern Europe. English chroniclers record 'great slaughter' in London in 842, and a force of 350 Viking ships stormed London and Canterbury in 851. Such direct attacks, together with the total disruption of trade, sealed the fate of *Lundenwic*. In 865 a 'great army' of Danes gathered in East Anglia; in a series of summer campaigns they destroyed the power of the Anglo-Saxon kingdoms in the east and north of England. In 871-72 they made London their winter quarters. Effectively, the only Anglo-Saxon kingdom to survive was the Wessex of King Alfred. Alfred was campaigning in the London area in the early 870s, but hard fighting was to follow before he occupied London, probably a town in ruins. In 886 Alfred formally re-established London, the walled Roman city, as a fortified town – a *burgh*.

*Alfred ceded to the Danes the part of England later known as the Danelaw (see map, page 41), which comprised most of the country east and north of London. He was accepted as king by all the English not under Danish rule.*

The site on the Strand was abandoned and reverted to fields, remembered only as Aldwych, the 'old wic', and marked by old churches stretching from St. Bride's westwards to St. Martin in the Fields. Alfred placed London, together with what was left of old Mercia, in the charge of his son-in-law, the Mercian Ealdorman Ethelred. A programme for the defence and resettlement of the town was put in hand. Grids of new streets were laid out in the centre of the Roman walled area, between Cheapside and the Thames to the west of the

Walbrook and around Cannon Street to the east. Massive ruins of Roman buildings must have remained a feature of the townscape. The great Roman amphitheatre to the north of Cheapside survived long enough to influence the layout of later medieval buildings. The presence on this site of the medieval Guildhall, centre of the city's government, inspires the suggestion that the open-air *folkmoot*, at which the business of the Anglo-Saxon town was discussed, had once met on the banked seats of the amphitheatre.

Alfred and his successors established a defensive network of forts and walled towns; an early list of such *burghs* includes Southwark (the 'work of the men of Surrey'), which with London itself could guard the Thames and the Thames crossing. The progress made by Alfred's successors in winning back England from Danish rule culminated in the reign of Athelstan (925-39), who claimed on his coins the title 'King of All Britain'. Athelstan's law-codes reflect the importance of London, assigning to it more royal moneyers (mint-masters) than any other town. Yet London did not yet have the massive pre-eminence over other towns it achieved later, and was in no sense the capital city. Royal councils met in London; equally they could meet in any other royal town or convenient centre.

A new series of attacks from Scandinavia began towards the end of the 10th century. In 994, a joint force led by Swein Forkbeard, son of the king of Denmark, and the Norwegian Olaf Tryggvason attacked London; London held out, and the attackers 'suffered greater loss and injury than they ever expected' – according to the English chronicler. For the next twenty years London was the centre of resistance – 'praise God, still [in 1009] it stands safe and sound' – but also contributed vast sums in silver to the *danegeld* collected to buy off the attackers. By the end of 1016 the English King Ethelred and his eldest son Edmund were dead and Cnut, son of Swein Forkbeard, was accepted as king of all England. When his son died in 1042 there was no obvious Danish successor; by popular decision the crown was offered to Edward, surviving son of the English King Ethelred.

*Edward the Confessor died and was buried at Westminster in January 1066 (see page 42). Below A scene from the 11th-century 231-foot Bayeux Tapestry shows Edward greeting Harold, Earl of Wessex, inside the royal hall at Westminster.*

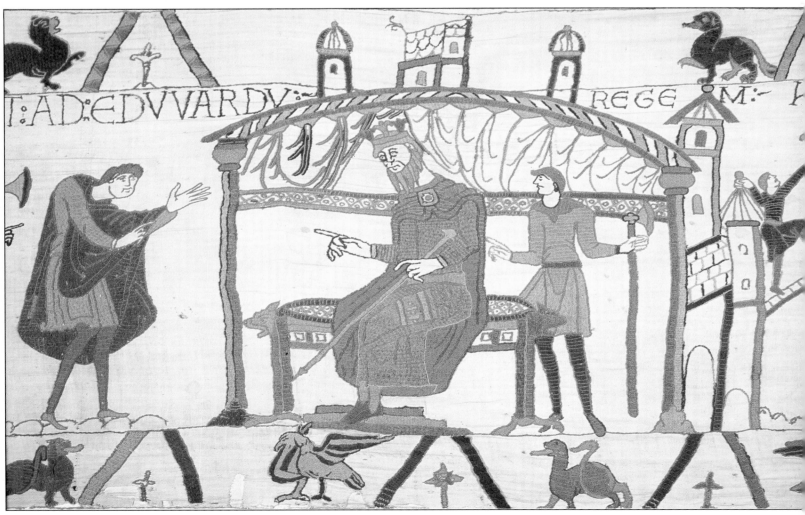

Monasteries were established in the late 11th and early 12th centuries on open land on the fringes of the city (Aldgate and Smithfield) and further out (Southwark, Bermondsey Abbey). Nunneries were founded in Clerkenwell and Shoreditch in the early 12th century. Special hospitals or refuges (for example St. Giles', Bloomsbury) were founded on the roads leading out of London, and sheltered sufferers from leprosy who had been driven out of the town (see map, page 43).

A reconstruction of the Tower of London can be found on page 139.

The period from Alfred's resettlement of London in 886 to the death in 1066 of Edward (nicknamed 'the Confessor') saw major developments in the city. Infilling began in the blocks between the original planned streets; lanes subdivided them, providing access to buildings erected in the formerly open backlands. New streets stretched north from the market place known as 'West Cheap', now Cheapside. Excavation has revealed some of the buildings of the late Saxon town and the activities of its people. They were skilled metalworkers; cloth, leather and bonework were being made and decorated. A new bridge was built to replace the lost Roman river crossing. New quays were erected and gradually enlarged along the riverside at Billingsgate and westward. Much of the trade was local; tolls were levied at Billingsgate on boats carrying timber, fish, chickens, eggs and dairy produce, as well as on larger ships from Normandy, France, Flanders and Germany. Yet from the reign of Cnut, if not before, London seems to have had links with the great northern network of trade-routes opened up by enterprising Scandinavian merchants and colonists.

Many of London's multitude of small parish churches had their origin in the late Saxon period, but it was the favour shown by Edward towards a monastery outside the walls which was to dramatically affect London's future geography. A man of great piety, he donated much of his royal income to the building of an abbey dedicated to St. Peter on an island in the marshes of the River Tyburn – Westminster. Next to his magnificent new church, Edward established a royal hall. Future London was to grow around two locations: the mercantile and industrial centre in the 'City', and the centre of royal law and administration at Westminster. It was at Westminster that Edward died and was buried in January 1066; at Westminster too both Harold of Wessex and William of Normandy were crowned in turn as King of England. Faced with 'the restlessness of its large and fierce population' William built castles to control London; within fifteen years of the Norman Conquest work had started on a fortified palace of stone, the White Tower, which was to develop into the Tower of London. Westminster remained the royal centre; William II had a fine new stone palace built, still standing today as Westminster Hall. Many great buildings of stone were new to the Norman city, but it was massive religious buildings which quickly came to dominate the townscape. The Anglo-Saxon minster church of St. Paul was destroyed by fire in 1087; work began on a magnificent replacement in the new Romanesque style, which was to survive, almost intact, until the Great Fire of 1666.

See reconstruction of St. Paul's, page 43.

The building boom reflected a growth in London's population; the largest town in the kingdom, it may have had 10,000 or even 15,000 inhabitants by 1100, and over 30,000 by 1200, many of whom were newcomers to England. Merchants from the Norman towns of Rouen and Caen settled in London to take advantage of the new market that the Conquest opened up. By 1130 a Jewish community, probably originally immigrants from Rouen, was well established in London, centred on 'Jews' Street' (Old Jewry). Providing essential finance for the activities of kings, nobles and merchants, they nevertheless attracted the envy and suspicion of their neighbours; the London Jewry was burnt down and 30 Jews killed in riots following the coronation of Richard I in 1189.

'Old' London Bridge, begun in 1176, stretched across the river on 19 solid stone piers. Vital to London's communications with the rest of the kingdom, it was an object of wonder to foreign visitors. See page 162 for a reconstruction of London Bridge.

Local administration devolved from the general *folkmoot* to a more select group of leading citizens, dignified by the Old English title 'aldermen', responsible for the 'wards' into which the city was divided. In 1191, Richard I formally recognised the commune of London; henceforth London was a corporate entity which could negotiate directly with the king. By the beginning of the 13th century the future pattern of London's development was well-established and most of its basic institutions already existed. The Londoner William Fitz Stephen, writing in 1173, had no doubt that of all the world London was 'the most noble city'.

Map below The extent of Norman London at its peak is contrasted to the size of the city in 1820.

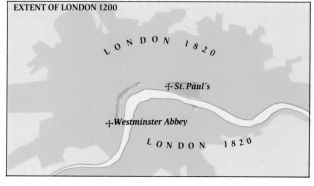

EXTENT OF LONDON 1200

LONDON 1820

+ St. Paul's

+ Westminster Abbey

LONDON 1820

# LUNDENWIC

So far archaeology has revealed little trace of Anglo-Saxon settlement in the inner London area in the century or so after the collapse of the Roman province of Britain. Isolated Saxon huts have been identified in the west of London, and in 1990 a number of buildings were revealed in excavations at Hammersmith, only six miles from Roman *Londinium*. Pagan burials are known further afield; a group of wealthy cemeteries in the Croydon area suggests a concentration of settlement there. But the immediate vicinity of the abandoned Roman city seems to have been largely avoided.

By the end of the 6th century the London area was part of the kingdom of the East Saxons. When Christian missionaries arrived in England in 597, they established the first major churches in old Roman towns: Canterbury, Rochester and London, the seat of the bishop for the East Saxons. Later in the 7th century churches were built elsewhere in the kingdom, at Tilbury and Bradwell-on-Sea, while a nunnery at Barking and a monastery at Chertsey in Surrey (*Suthregeona*), were founded by Erkenwald, who was Bishop of London after 675.

Only in 1985 did excavations in Covent Garden confirm that the 8th-century Saxon trading town, *Lundenwic*, did not lie near St. Paul's Cathedral, within the old Roman city walls, but to the west, along the Strand. Further traces of wooden buildings, rubbish pits, gravelled yards and industry have since come to light in this area. Churches like St Martin-in-the-Fields may have been founded at this time, and the name Aldwych, 'the old port', preserves the memory of the settlement.

*Lundenwic* and other royal 'emporia' were river-ports handling trade among the Anglo-Saxon kingdoms and with Merovingian Europe, where there were major ports at *Quentovic* (a 'lost' site recently rediscovered south of Boulogne) and Dorestad on the Rhine. Fragments of pottery from northern France and pottery and millstones from the Rhineland found in London demonstrate aspects of this trade; excavations near Charing Cross have revealed remains of a reinforced river embankment on which ships could be beached for unloading.

The port of *Lundenwic* was abandoned following Viking raids in the 840s and 850s. After halting the advance of the Danish invaders Alfred, King of Wessex and effectively king of all that remained of 'English' England, re-established London in 886 and encouraged settlement within the Roman city walls. A system of 'burghs', fortified towns, was established to resist further Danish attacks.

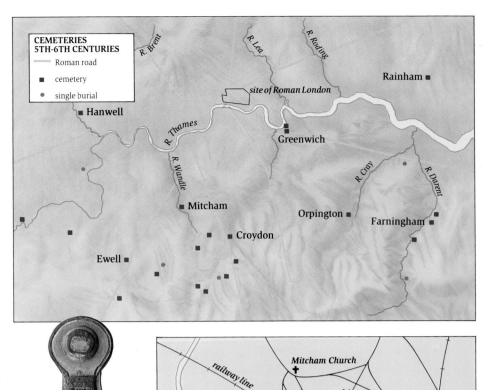

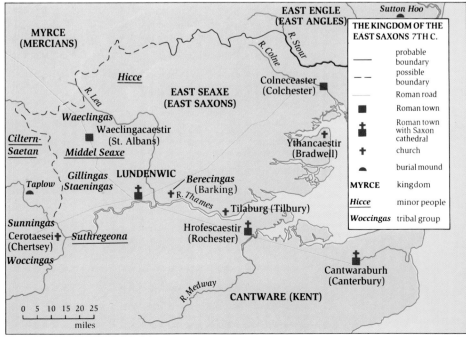

Anglo-Saxon settlement *5th- and 6th-century cemeteries reflect the spread of settlement in the London area (map top), apparently avoiding the vicinity of the old Roman city. The silver-gilt brooch (left) came from burials discovered near Mitcham station, Surrey, between 1888 and 1922 (map above). Few domestic sites from this period have been excavated. At Harmondsworth (lower left), Saxon huts stood in a landscape of Roman and prehistoric fields.*

The East Saxons *The extent of the 7th-century kingdom was largely that of the medieval bishopric of London – Essex, Middlesex and part of Hertfordshire – but included land in the north-west later lost to Mercia (map below). Within the kingdom place-names reveal other smaller groups, perhaps once independent, such as the Gillingas (Ealing), the Berecingas (Barking), the Staeningas (around Staines) and the Waeclingas (around St Albans).*

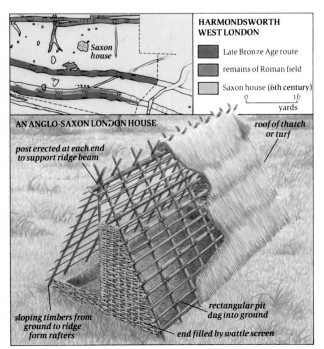

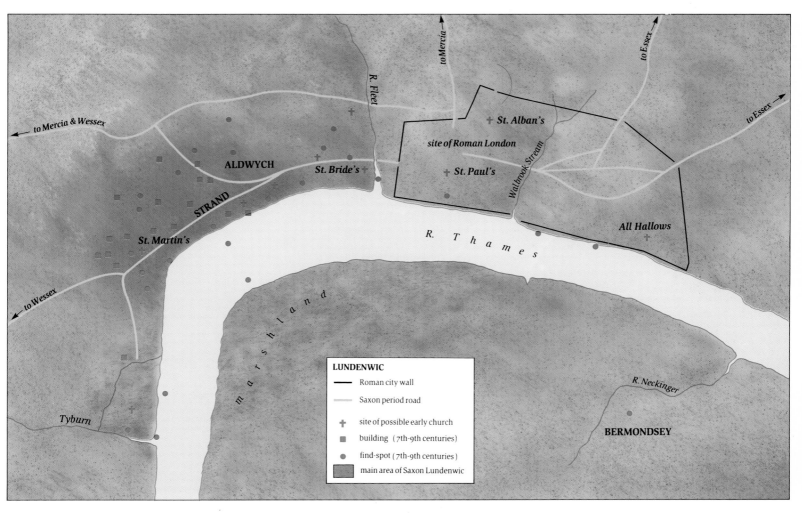

LUNDENWIC

- —— Roman city wall
- —— Saxon period road
- ✝ site of possible early church
- ■ building (7th-9th centuries)
- ● find-spot (7th-9th centuries)
- ▨ main area of Saxon Lundenwic

to Mercia & Wessex

to Wessex

ALDWYCH

STRAND

St. Martin's

Tyburn

R. Fleet

St. Bride's

to Mercia

site of Roman London

✝ St. Alban's

✝ St. Paul's

Walbrook Stream

to Essex

to Essex

All Hallows

R. Thames

m a r s h l a n d

R. Neckinger

BERMONDSEY

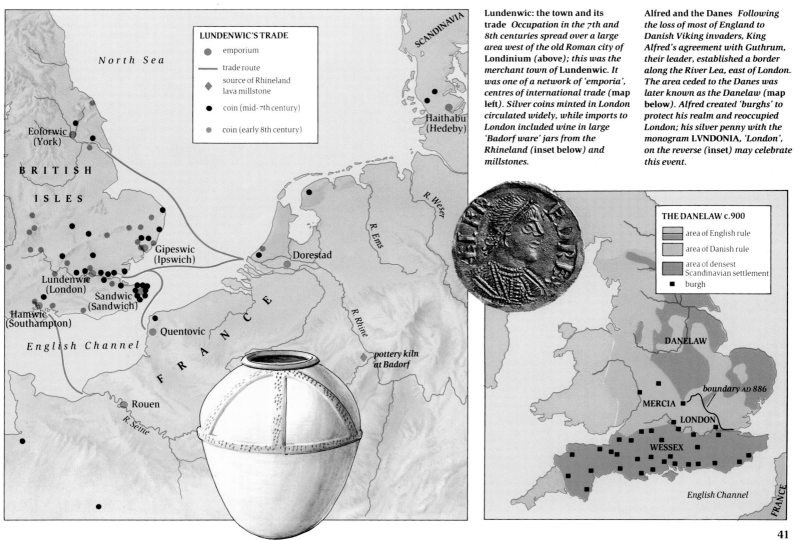

**Lundenwic: the town and its trade** *Occupation in the 7th and 8th centuries spread over a large area west of the old Roman city of Londinium (above); this was the merchant town of* **Lundenwic.** *It was one of a network of 'emporia', centres of international trade (map left). Silver coins minted in London circulated widely, while imports to London included wine in large 'Badorf ware' jars from the Rhineland (inset below) and millstones.*

**Alfred and the Danes** *Following the loss of most of England to Danish Viking invaders, King Alfred's agreement with Guthrum, their leader, established a border along the River Lea, east of London. The area ceded to the Danes was later known as the Danelaw (map below). Alfred created 'burghs' to protect his realm and reoccupied London; his silver penny with the monogram LVNDONIA, 'London', on the reverse (inset) may celebrate this event.*

LUNDENWIC'S TRADE

- ● emporium
- —— trade route
- ◆ source of Rhineland lava millstone
- ● coin (mid-7th century)
- ● coin (early 8th century)

North Sea

SCANDINAVIA

Haithabu (Hedeby)

Eoforwic (York)

BRITISH ISLES

R. Weser

R. Ems

Gipeswic (Ipswich)

Dorestad

Lundenwic (London)

Sandwic (Sandwich)

Hamwic (Southampton)

Quentovic

R. Rhine

pottery kiln at Badorf

English Channel

F R A N C E

Rouen

R. Seine

THE ĐANELAW c.900

- ▨ area of English rule
- ▨ area of Danish rule
- ▨ area of densest Scandinavian settlement
- ■ burgh

DANELAW

boundary AD 886

MERCIA

LONDON

WESSEX

English Channel

FRANCE

41

# SAXON AND NORMAN LONDON

The medieval street-plan of the City of London originated in the Saxon period when the main centre of population of *Lundenwic* lay along the Strand. Long curving streets like Fenchurch and Lombard Street probably developed naturally as routes through the ruins of the Roman city, avoiding obstructions such as the prominent remains of the Roman *basilica*. After 886, when King Alfred initiated settlement within the Roman walls, new streets seem to have been laid out in two areas, some of the blocks being subsequently subdivided by lanes. Roman ruins survived for a long time; a document of 889 relating to a property near Queenhithe refers to 'an old stone building known as *Hwaetmundes stan*' – probably the remains of Roman public baths now known to have stood on the site.

Recent excavations have provided ever-increasing knowledge of the appearance and economy of late Saxon London. Wooden buildings of different types have been discovered, many of them with sunken floors, a feature of much earlier Saxon domestic architecture. Evidence has been recorded of industry – metal-working, boneworking, clothworking – and of trade – new waterfronts at Billingsgate and further west provided berths for cargo vessels. Finds of pottery and millstones from the Rhineland reflect a continuation, or revival, of trade with that area; amber, walrus ivory and whetstones of Norwegian stone demonstrate trade with the north and Scandinavia.

After bearing the brunt of the renewed Danish wars of the late 10th century, London flourished during the 11th century. Developments in the reign of Edward the Confessor, after 1042, were to have a profound long-term effect on its geography. Edward devoted much of his energy, and his finances, to the building of a new monastery dedicated to St. Peter in the west of the city – in the area later known simply as 'the west minster' – with a fine church of Norman style. More important, he established a new royal palace alongside it; an older palace within the city walls, perhaps near Aldersgate, was probably abandoned at this time. Edward's Norman successors continued the development of Westminster as a centre of royal government.

One of the first acts of the new Norman king,

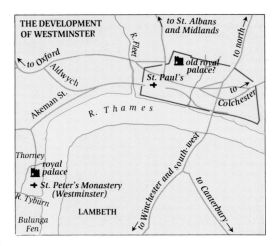

THE DEVELOPMENT OF WESTMINSTER

**London and Westminster** *Edward the Confessor's new London palace stood to the west of the city, adjacent to St. Peter's monastery (the 'west minster') at Thorney ('thorn island'), where the River Tyburn flowed into the Thames (map top). It may have replaced an older palace situated within the city walls. Traces of an earlier monastic church have been found beneath the floor of Westminster Abbey (right). Built for Edward the Confessor, it was inspired by churches he had seen when in exile in Normandy. His funeral, shown in the Bayeux Tapestry (above), took place just a week after the church was consecrated, in January 1066. His tomb became a shrine and place of pilgrimage.*

LATE SAXON LONDON HOUSES

LATE SAXON LONDON
- Roman wall and surviving building
- early routes through city
- possible laid-out street
- later street

BURGH OF SOUTHWARK

**Late Saxon London** *In the late 9th century new streets, flanked by timber houses (above), were laid out in the area of the old Roman city, parts of which were still visible (map above).*
*Viking raiders were followed by settlers and traders (map right) whose trade-routes extended to the Baltic and along the Russian rivers. A runic grave-slab (inset) from St. Paul's commemorates a Scandinavian resident of London in the days of King Cnut.*

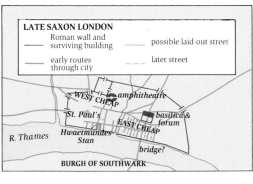

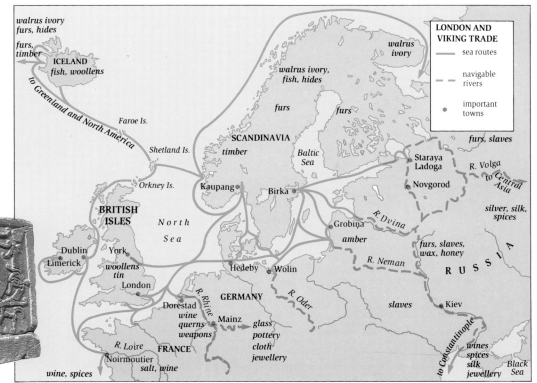

LONDON AND VIKING TRADE
- sea routes
- navigable rivers
- important towns

**London 1200** By 1200 London's suburbs stretched to Southwark and Westminster (map right). There were over 100 parish churches. New features of the Norman city were its castles; great monastic houses; hospitals, including those like St. Giles's and St. James's founded as refuges for lepers expelled from the town; the stone-arched London Bridge, begun in 1176 to replace earlier timber structures; and St. Paul's, the Romanesque cathedral which replaced a Saxon church destroyed by fire in 1087. Shown in an artist's impression (below right), its early 13th-century spire rose some 450 feet over the city.

**The London area in 1086** The Domesday Book compiled for William I in 1085-86 provides a detailed economic survey of the counties around London (map below). Farming settlements bore names which survive today. Fish were netted in the Thames and its tributaries; water mills powered by the same streams ground corn from the openfields.

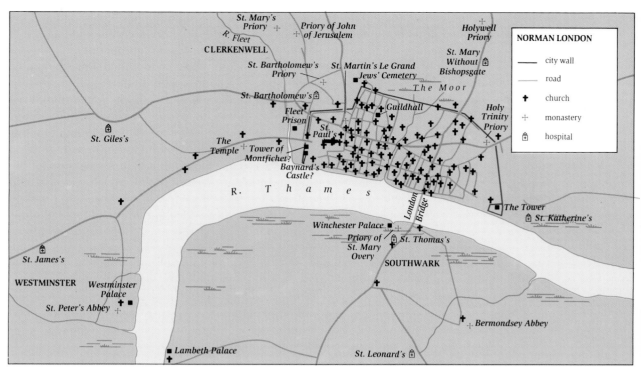

NORMAN LONDON

— city wall
— road
✝ church
✢ monastery
⌂ hospital

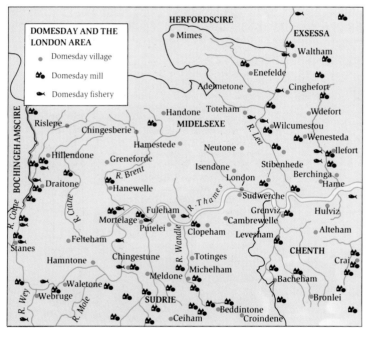

DOMESDAY AND THE LONDON AREA

● Domesday village
⚙ Domesday mill
🐟 Domesday fishery

ST. PAUL'S CATHEDRAL c.1220

William, in 1066 was to establish castles to control London. One, in the east, was the core of the Tower of London (*page 141*). Others, near St. Paul's, seem to have been those later known as Baynard's Castle and the Tower of Montfichet. Both were demolished in the 13th century, and although traces have been found in excavations, their exact sites and layout are still unclear.

The combined evidence of documentary sources and archaeology allows the reconstruction of a much more detailed picture of London at the end of the 12th century than at any earlier period. This is enhanced by William Fitz Stephen's account of the city in about 1173 in which he describes many features: London's walls and gates; its many parish churches and great monasteries, most of them built in the previous 100 years or so; the royal palace to the west and the suburb stretching towards it (recolonising the site of old *Lundenwic*); the weekly horse-fair at Smithfield; the Moor (Moorfields) outside the wall to the north, where Londoners skated in winter. To William Fitz Stephen London was truly 'the most noble city'.

# CHAPTER 4
# MEDIEVAL LONDON

*In 1994 archaeologists discovered the great underground cistern near Old Jewry that received water from springs beside the Tyburn (near Bond Street) that was piped to the City, for the rich and middle classes of medieval London. The lead pipeline was installed in the middle decades of the 13th century. At the end of the 1990s sections of the pipe were found underneath Paternoster Row, north of Saint Paul's Cathedral. (90 mm in diameter, it was installed 2 m beneath the medieval street level, and continued to supply the City until the Great Fire of London.*

*A major archaeological project covering 12 ha on the site of the former Spitalfields Market revealed much of the 12th and 13th-century Priory and Hospital of St. Mary Spital and a cemetery of 10,000 medieval graves. The remains of timber-framed houses, some with fireplaces and possessions dating from the middle ages, have been found within the priory and hospital precincts. In 1538 Henry VIII dissolved this religious foundation. During the reign of Elizabeth I, gentlemen at arms used Spittle Field to practise archery. Trading began here in 1682 when a local silk worker was granted a charter to hold a market in Spittle Square. Huguenot silk merchants settled in surrounding buildings. The fruit and vegetable market was housed in the Horner Buildings in 1856.*

*During the 12th and 13th centuries Westminster became increasingly prominent as a focus of royal government. The centralisation of the justice system and the increased importance of the King's courts at Westminster attracted litigants, petitioners and hangers-on. King Henry III invested in massive building projects. The appearance of medieval Westminster is reconstructed on pages 48-49.*

*After the Norman Conquest a community of Jewish money-lenders and merchants lived between Old Jewry and Milk Street, until their expulsion in 1290. An early 13th-century stone-lined ritual bath (mikveh) has been discovered below floor level on Milk Street. The 3 m x 1.4 m bath (some 1.5 m deep) has been carefully dismantled and will be rebuilt on another site.*

BETWEEN THE 12th century and the end of the 15th London expanded and then contracted in physical size and population, while continuing to increase in political and economic importance. Its appearance undoubtedly changed, though perhaps less markedly than in later centuries. At the end of the period, as at the beginning, it was still shaped by Roman walls and Saxon or early Norman street patterns, and the area of building had not spread far beyond the City itself, except in the two distinct settlements of Westminster and Southwark. The materials of which London was built changed only slowly: some stone was used, especially for churches and public buildings, but timber-framing and plaster predominated. Thatch was banned from the City in the 12th century, and brick was appearing more and more by the 15th century. However, there were considerable changes in London's society and government: a complex and, on the whole, effective system of administration developed, and London law, custom and culture came to be both distinctive and deeply influential on the rest of the country.

It is hard to establish the size of London's medieval population with any precision, but it was clearly substantial by the mid-12th century. There is evidence for continued growth through the later 12th and 13th centuries and it seems probable that the City reached its maximum size, with a population of perhaps 80,000, in the early years of the 14th century. Sustained expansion of the kind London experienced in the 12th and 13th centuries was the result of continued population growth in the rest of the country, and high levels of migration from the country to the capital. Many of the incomers are identified by their surnames – Robert of Clacton, William of Lincoln, Nicholas of Reading. Many foreign settlers in London came from northern France (until 1204 Normandy was under English rule), and the Gascon wine trade also brought a number of merchants. The Norman kings encouraged the settlement of Jews in English cities because of their value as sources of loans and capital. In London the area round the street still known as Old Jewry was the physical centre of the Jewish settlement, and remained so until the decline of the community in the later 13th century and its final expulsion in 1290. Foreign merchants, from Flanders and Italy especially, were present in London to profit from the lucrative export trade in wool as well as government finance.

London's exceptional size and wealth in the middle ages were due to a number of factors: its convenient location at the centre of land and water routes, with easy access to the Continent; the City's long-established role as a port; the growth of Westminster as the focus of government, and the growth of government itself. During the 12th and 13th centuries important government offices either shifted from Winchester to London, like the treasury, or ceased to move round the country with the king and took up permanent headquarters at Westminster. As their business increased, they took on staff and began to accumulate records. Though Westminster and the City remained separate in the medieval period, the presence and activity of the royal court and government offices nearby was a powerful stimulus to London's economy, attracting customers for the City's luxury imports and fine craftsmanship, and increasing the demand for services and supplies of all kinds.

The Black Death, a devastating pandemic, swept Europe and arrived in England in 1348. By 1350, it is possible that half the population of the capital died. Contemporary authors wrote of hundreds of burials a day in the new burial grounds

*The government of the City was clearly an oligarchy, not a democracy: 13th century aldermen were drawn from an elite of mercantile and landowning families with court connections, and held office for long periods. Below This 15th-century manuscript shows Simon Eyre, a City Alderman, in his robes of office. He became Lord Mayor in 1444.*

opened to the east of the Tower and north-west of the City, and it appears that even among the richest in society the death rate was ten times normal. The first plague was followed by others, in 1361, 1369 and 1375; although these had a much smaller impact, plague became established in London and other towns and throughout the 15th century. In 1377 the population of London, including Southwark and Westminster, was probably between 35,000 and 45,000. In the immediate aftermath of the epidemics, the flow of migrants to London may have increased to take up the jobs and opportunities made available, but quite soon the increased attractions of the countryside – where land was now cheaper and the rewards of labour higher – began to take effect. From the late 14th century there is evidence of stagnating or gradually falling population levels in London: rents fell, houses stood unlet and fell into disrepair, vacant lots appeared in the over-crowded City streets. The built-up area may have contracted to a narrow fringe round the walls.

**Above** *Woodcut showing a view of London, from the 'Chronycle of England', published by Wynkyn de Worde in 1497.*

Population decline did not mean economic collapse for London. Living standards for the majority may indeed have improved as the shortage of labour pushed up wages; space and housing were in more generous supply, and the encroachment of the suburbs on the green fields was halted. London in fact increased in importance relative to the rest of England. Though England's involvement in warfare with France, especially in the 1340s and 1350s and from 1415 to 1453, was itself very costly, the financing of warfare and the marshalling of supplies and troops may well have given Londoners some opportunities for profit. Increasingly, from the late 14th century, English overseas trade was channelled through the Port of London, as the London-dominated associations of wool exporters and cloth merchants took control of the country's two main export products. A strong trade axis between London and Antwerp developed in the later 15th century and the City's role as a marketplace for imported goods expanded.

*The trading relationship between London and the Continent is mapped on page 52.*

London's self-government was achieved in the 12th and 13th centuries as a result of strong pressure from the City on the Crown, forcing or buying concessions in times of weakness. Even before the Conquest, London had its own laws, courts and customs, but the drive now was for Londoners to take control of the City as a whole. In the 12th century they won the right to appoint their own sheriffs – hitherto appointed by the Crown – and collectively took on responsibility for the annual payment to the Crown of £300, in exchange for the grant of royal revenues in the City. In the reign of John (1199-1216) they established a commune, a collectivity to which all Londoners swore allegiance, with a leader or mayor, an achievement that was confirmed in Magna Carta. The City's 24 wards were clearly established by 1127. The divisions may originally have been intended to allocate responsibility for the defence of the City, but they also became units of local government. Each was headed by an alderman, at first possibly a hereditary figure and always a man of wealth and importance. He presided over the local forum or wardmote, and in the 13th century and later the mayor and aldermen together formed the principal adminstrative council of the City. While the overall direction of the City was in the hands of the council of aldermen, local custom and law shaped the day-to-day working of the City. A range of civic courts dealt with civil litigation as well as criminal justice, reflecting some of the most important concerns of the citizens. The long-established court of Husting was concerned mostly with property rights, including the recovery of unpaid rents from tenants; the sheriffs' court dealt with minor assault and trespass, while the mayor's court heard cases of commercial debt and contract.

The demographic upheaval of the Black Death and succeeding plagues had a disruptive effect on wages, prices and the expectations of ordinary Londoners; attempts by employers and landlords to hold wages down were bitterly resented. Foreign wars and changes in patterns of trade caused tensions among the mercantile rulers of the City, some of whom were prepared to exploit popular discontents in their struggle for dominance. London's problems interacted with the wider political conflicts of the Good Parliament of 1376, the Peasants' Revolt of 1381, which paralysed the City for several days, and the crisis of the Lords Appellant in 1387-8. In the last of these a former mayor of London, Nicholas Brembre, was impeached and executed. Richard II quarrelled with London in the 1390s, and this probably ensured the City's acquiescence in the usurpation of Henry Bolingbroke (Henry IV) in 1399. Internally, London was more peaceful in the 15th century; the dominance of the great overseas merchants in London politics was confirmed – hardly anyone who was not a member of the half dozen leading City companies reached the Court of Aldermen, let alone the mayoralty.

Throughout the Middle Ages, control of London was crucial to political success, either for the monarch or for a claimant or usurper. In the Wars of the Roses, both sides were anxious to hold on to London, but while the rulers of the City preferred to play a conservative part, tending to support the government in power (to which they were committed in loans and financial support) until the scales were already tipping in the other side's favour, there was probably stronger Yorkist feeling among the people. In 1461, when the City government was prepared to send supplies to Margaret of Anjou, whose army was threatening the City, the people of London shut the gates and turned back the carts: 'the commons of the city and the heads were of two opinions and minds', as a contemporary wrote.

While Westminster was undoubtedly the royal capital, in that the offices of government, royal palace and mausoleum were situated there, the City was used by the Crown as a key element in the presentation of the monarchy to the people. Coronation processions and royal 'entries' used the streets of the City, and indeed the people, as setting and audience for magnificent displays of wealth and power. Richard II's quarrel with London was resolved, not only

*The Priory of the Knights of St John of Jerusalem was one of London's great medieval monasteries, occupying 5 aces in Clerkenwell. Remains have been discovered of what may have been a great barn, in which the priory's own agricultural produce was stored. Like other great medieval monasteries, it was partly self-sufficient, with its own gardens, orchards, and fishponds. The priory was closed in 1540 at the Dissolution of the Monasteries and secular buildings were constructed on its site. Its great Tudor gateway still survives, spanning St John's Street.*

*A recently-discovered sepia drawing of St. Paul's Cathedral by a Dutch artist, Van Overbeck and dating from between 1640 and 1666, shows the medieval structure of the great church after restoration by Inigo Jones (1633-41).*

*If taxation lists of the period are to be believed, only a tiny proportion of London's inhabitants had sufficient goods to be worth taxing, though some of these few were obviously very wealthy indeed. See map of comparative wealth and poverty, assessed by tax, page 52.*

**Right** *The elephant depicted in this manuscript drawing formed part of a royal menagerie at the Tower, which was created in the 13th century. In 1256, King Henry III wrote to the City Sheriffs: 'We command you, that ...ye cause, without delay, to be built at our Tower of London an house of forty feet long, and twenty feet deep, for our Elephant.'*

*In 2001 archaeologists investigated some of the remains of the priory of the Carmelites (or Whitefriars) who settled on the Thames side of Fleet Street in the mid 13th century. Excavations and analysis reveal that during the 1390s the Whitefriars extended their precinct by reclaiming land from the river. A stone wall along this new waterfront had been discovered in 1999. The remains of other walls show that intermediate extensions took place earlier in the 14th century.*

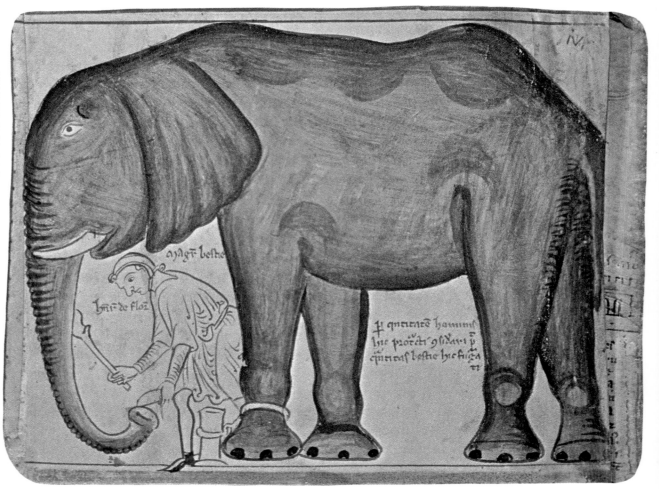

Above *Doorknocker in the form of a grotesque face with a ring in its mouth, late 14th-early 15th century. It was found in Thames Street.*

For a full discussion of London's guilds and livery companies, and a location map, refer to pages 62-63.

by a substantial payment from the City, but with an elaborately-staged procession through the City's streets, emphasising the City's contrition and subordination. Later entries, in which the City was a more equal and perhaps more willing partner, celebrated Henry V's victory at Agincourt, the return of the young Henry VI after his coronation in France, and his marriage to the French princess, Margaret of Anjou. The Tudor dynasty quickly became expert in the construction and presentation of the image of monarchy in this way. Most processions followed the same route, starting with an entry across London Bridge, continuing by way of Gracechurch Street and Cornhill to Cheapside, where pageants were set up at the Conduits and the Eleanor Cross, and terminating at St Paul's.

Ideas of civil rights and responsibilities had been evolving in the 13th century, and with them the definition of citizenship as a specific status, not an automatic right. In return for his civic oath and contribution to civic taxation, the citizen acquired rights to trade retail as well as wholesale, to buy and sell real property and to benefit from the protection of the City's courts. From 1319 new citizens were admitted only with the approval of the men of the trade they intended to practice, effectively giving control of access of citizenship to the emerging associations of traders and craftsmen. It is difficult to estimate the proportion of citizens in London's adult male population in the later Middle Ages, but it seems likely that it was fairly low, probably less than one quarter. Men and women who were not citizens were referred to as 'foreigns', even if London-born; most made their living from unskilled and casual labour, though many illegally practised crafts that were in theory restricted to citizens. One well-recorded feature of medieval London was its guilds and fraternities. We know most about those associated with a particular craft or occupation through their descendants, the Livery Companies, but guilds were formed for many purposes, social, religious, political, as well as economic. In essence they were voluntary associations for mutual support, with a strong emphasis on brotherhood and friendliness; some appear to have been no more than burial clubs and communal chantries, while others evolved into institutions wielding considerable political power. Before 1150 London had guilds of weavers, saddlers and bakers; in 1180 there were at least 19 guilds, including four specifically associated with a trade (goldsmiths, pepperers, clothworkers and butchers). The number of recognised associations seems to have increased continuously, and there were over 100 in the early 15th century. In the 14th and 15th centuries craft groups were obliged to obtain mayoral approval and submit their regulations (often including very detailed descriptions of craft practice) to the City government. The larger companies acquired, through donation and bequest, a considerable amount of real property and with the rent income and members' subscriptions they built halls for their meetings and celebrations, and maintained a lavish communal life. They also devoted money to charitable and pious purposes, especially chantries and commemorations for deceased members.

By 1500, the institutions and bureaucracy of City government had established deep roots, and patterns of social behaviour, focused on household, parish and City company, were also well established. It would be many years before the discovery of the New World in 1492 had an impact on London's economy. However, within the next 50 years the religious ideas proliferating on the continent were, through the process of the Reformation, to have a profound effect on both the City's character and appearance.

For a map of medieval markets see page 148.

*Medieval remains from Plantation Place, not far back from quays along the Thames and near the market of Eastcheap, indicate the city's connections with the Middle East. Drug jars of Syrian or Egyptian origin have been found and were probably used to transport exotic herbs and spices for use by London's apothecaries.*

Map below *The extent of Medieval London at its peak is contrasted to the size of the city in 1820.*

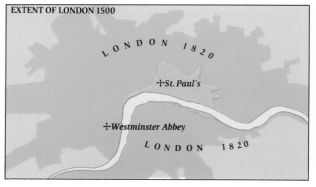

EXTENT OF LONDON 1500

LONDON 1820

+St. Paul's

+Westminster Abbey

LONDON 1820

# THE MEDIEVAL CITY

In 1300, the street-pattern of central London was predominantly influenced by the Roman city wall and the skeleton network of streets laid down from late Saxon and early Norman times. There were certainly some slight alterations in street alignments and building lines, and in the arrangements of houses, yards, gardens and private alleys, but to a great extent the pattern within the walls was already set. Most of the population of perhaps 80,000 was tightly packed within the walls and the nearer suburbs, with only a small proportion living in the outer settlements of Southwark and Westminster.

The most important topographical change in the City between 1100 and 1500 was the reclamation of the waterfront, to the south of both Thames Street and the line of the decayed Roman riverside wall. Much of this reclamation proceeded piecemeal: recent excavations on a number of sites have revealed successive timber and stone quayfronts, as the owners of individual riverfront properties built their wharves further and further south out into the river. The process was all but complete by 1500, by which time a strip of land between 120 and 350 feet in width had been reclaimed. By contrast, the two main public landing places at Queenhithe and Billingsgate remained as inlets in the waterfront, as did the smaller haven of Dowgate. London Bridge (rebuilt in stone in the late 12th and early 13th centuries) remained the only road link between the City and the southern counties, but a number of small landing-places and stairs along the waterfront testify to the importance of river transport for both goods and passengers. The river-front was also affected by the development of the Tower as a concentric fortress, with an enlarged moat and barbican gate. The Walbrook stream had disappeared into a culvert that flowed into the Thames west of Dowgate.

By the early 14th century, thanks to the survival of many records of property transactions, we know the names of almost all of the streets that then existed. Some of these names have since altered, Westcheap becoming Cheapside (while the name Eastcheap survived), and Candlewick Street being simplified to Cannon Street, while the important late medieval estate called Leadenhall did not give its name to the street until the 15th century. Many medieval street and area names (still recognisable today) commemorate trades and activities, though the names sometimes stayed while the trades moved on: Ironmonger Lane was no longer the centre of that trade by 1300, and the bellfounders had moved out from Billiter Lane (the lane of the 'bell-yetteres' or bell-founders) to the suburbs well before 1500.

Westminster (reconstructed below, c.1500) was separate from the City, with its own government and a distinct character. For the whole of the Middle Ages the manor of Westminster belonged to the abbey, and the settlement that grew up there, small by comparison with the City but equal in size to some provincial towns, was dominated by the abbey and the royal palace. Henry III (1216-1272) rebuilt the abbey itself and enlarged the palace, adding St Stephen's chapel. His successors were too often absent on foreign wars to make many changes, but Richard II rebuilt the Norman Westminster Hall, and over a long period accommodation for royal courts and government offices was added. The economy of the Westminster area was shaped by these important neighbours, and came to specialise in lodgings, meals and accommodation, luxury retail and services. The first printing press was established by William Caxton at Westminster, within the abbey close, in 1476, only later moving to the City. Though Westminster and the City were linked by the Strand, it was the river which provided direct and rapid communication.

**MEDIEVAL WESTMINSTER c.1500**

R. Tyburn

St. Stephen's Chapel

Westminster Hall

Westminster Abbey

St. Margaret Westminster

King's Bridge

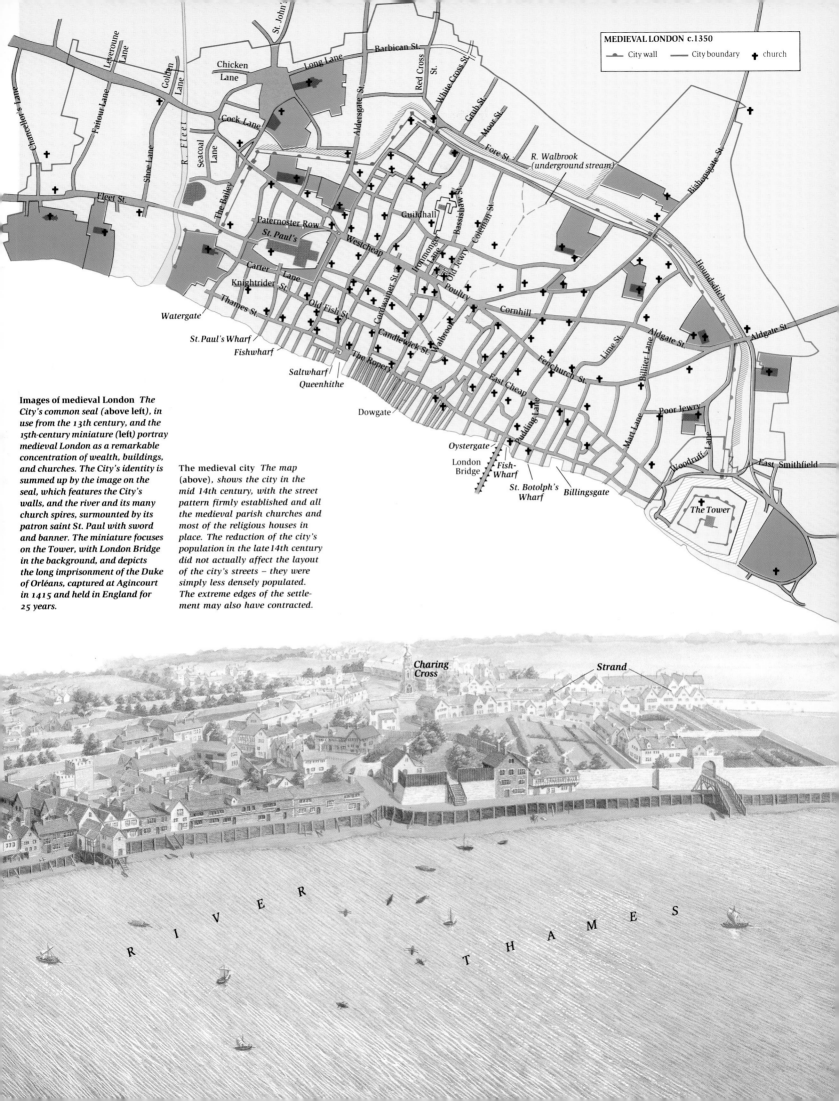

**MEDIEVAL LONDON c.1350**
- City wall
- City boundary
- church

Chancellor's Lane
Leveroune Lane
Fattour Lane
Golden Lane
Shoe Lane
Fleet St.
R. Fleet
Seacoal Lane
The Bailey
Chicken Lane
Cock Lane
Long Lane
Barbican St.
St. John St.
Aldersgate St.
Red Cross St.
White Cross St.
Grub St.
Moor St.
Fore St.
Bishopsgate St.
R. Walbrook (underground stream)
Paternoster Row
St. Paul's
Carter Lane
Knightrider St.
Westcheap
Guildhall
Bassishaw St.
Coleman St.
Ironmonger Lane
Old Jewry
Poultry
Cornhill
Houndsditch
Watergate
Thames St.
St. Paul's Wharf
Fishwharf
Old Fish St.
Cordwainer St.
Walbrook
Candlewick St.
The Ropery
Saltwharf
Queenhithe
Dowgate
East Cheap
Fenchurch St.
Lime St.
Aldgate St.
Billiter Lane
Aldgate St.
Poor Jewry
Mart Lane
Oystergate
London Bridge
Fish-Wharf
Pudding Lane
St. Botolph's Wharf
Billingsgate
Woodruff Lane
East Smithfield
The Tower

**Images of medieval London** *The City's common seal (above left), in use from the 13th century, and the 15th-century miniature (left) portray medieval London as a remarkable concentration of wealth, buildings, and churches. The City's identity is summed up by the image on the seal, which features the City's walls, and the river and its many church spires, surmounted by its patron saint St. Paul with sword and banner. The miniature focuses on the Tower, with London Bridge in the background, and depicts the long imprisonment of the Duke of Orléans, captured at Agincourt in 1415 and held in England for 25 years.*

**The medieval city** *The map (above), shows the city in the mid 14th century, with the street pattern firmly established and all the medieval parish churches and most of the religious houses in place. The reduction of the city's population in the late 14th century did not actually affect the layout of the city's streets – they were simply less densely populated. The extreme edges of the settlement may also have contracted.*

Charing Cross
Strand

R I V E R    T H A M E S

# THE MEDIEVAL CHURCH

The Church played an important role in shaping the appearance and character of medieval London. The City was the seat of an important bishopric and great cathedral; several large and wealthy monasteries, friaries, and nunneries were founded in the City or on its outskirts, and there were over a hundred parish churches in and near the City. The Church's influence permeated everyday life, as people ordered their working day by church bells, made contracts paying 'God's penny', and swore oaths on the gospels.

The Bishop of London was a figure of national importance and close to the top of the ecclesiastical hierarchy. His diocese covered Middlesex, Essex, and part of Hertfordshire, and diocesan courts and officials thus attracted much business from outside the city. Many abbots and bishops from outside London needed to attend Parliament or the monarch, and so found it useful to have a house or inn in the City or nearby in the more spacious western suburbs. The Bishop of

Winchester, whose diocese included Southwark, had a large house there, of which some remains still survive; the locations of others are commemorated by modern place names such as Salisbury Court or Ely Place.

St. Paul's must have been one of the finest and largest of Gothic cathedrals, dating partly from the 12th and partly from the late 13th century. It offered a splendid space both for services and for civic ceremonial. The mayor and aldermen attended mass there on special days, while many civic processions concluded with a service there. St. Paul was regarded as the city's patron saint until the 13th century, when he had to share that position with the murdered Archbishop of Canterbury, Thomas Becket (died 1170), whose cult developed at that time. The citizens founded the Hospital of St. Thomas of the military order of Acre in his honour, on the site of the house in which he had been born in Cheapside.

Most of the big religious houses in London were founded between c. 1100 and 1250, and undoubtedly City wealth contributed to their upkeep, even when the first founder was royal or noble. The monasteries tended to form closed communities, repaying the laity's material gener-

**Churches, saints and pilgrims** *Few medieval churches remain: Austin Friars (right) was destroyed by fire in 1940, while the silver paten (above right) came from St. Michael Crooked Lane, burnt in 1666. The pilgrimage to the shrine of Thomas Becket at Canterbury was immortalised by Geoffrey Chaucer (above) in his Canterbury Tales. Many metal badges (right), showing the saint on horseback, have been found in London, probably pilgrimage souvenirs.*

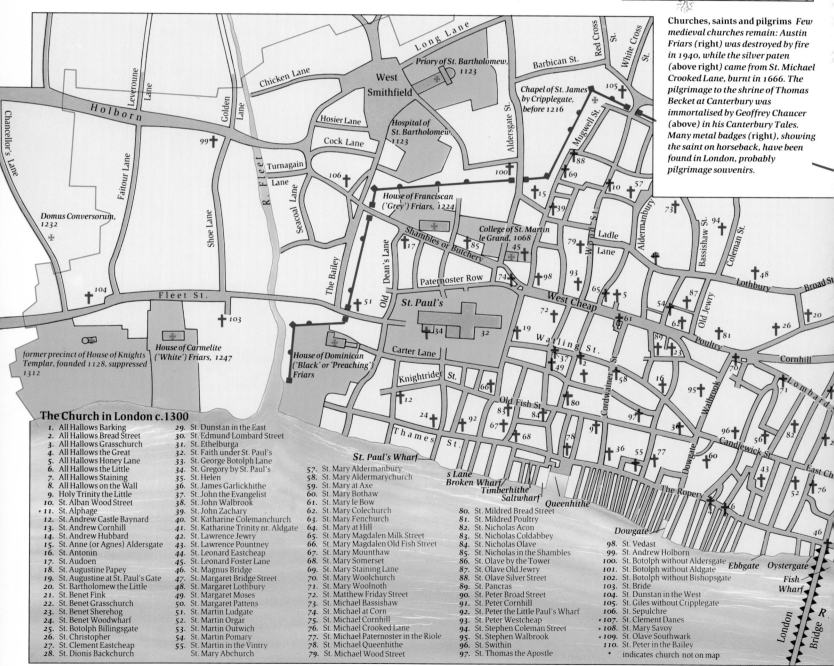

## The Church in London c.1300

1. All Hallows Barking
2. All Hallows Bread Street
3. All Hallows Grasschurch
4. All Hallows the Great
5. All Hallows Honey Lane
6. All Hallows the Little
7. All Hallows Staining
8. All Hallows on the Wall
9. Holy Trinity the Little
10. St. Alban Wood Street
* 11. St. Alphage
12. St. Andrew Castle Baynard
13. St. Andrew Cornhill
14. St. Andrew Hubbard
15. St. Anne (or Agnes) Aldersgate
16. St. Antonin
17. St. Audoen
18. St. Augustine Papey
19. St. Augustine at St. Paul's Gate
20. St. Bartholomew the Little
21. St. Benet Fink
22. St. Benet Grasschurch
23. St. Benet Sherehog
24. St. Benet Woodwharf
25. St. Botolph Billingsgate
26. St. Christopher
27. St. Clement Eastcheap
28. St. Dionis Backchurch

29. St. Dunstan in the East
30. St. Edmund Lombard Street
31. St. Ethelburga
32. St. Faith under St. Paul's
33. St. George Botolph Lane
34. St. Gregory by St. Paul's
35. St. Helen
36. St. James Garlickhithe
37. St. John the Evangelist
38. St. John Walbrook
39. St. John Zachary
40. St. Katharine Colemanchurch
41. St. Katharine Trinity nr. Aldgate
42. St. Lawrence Jewry
43. St. Lawrence Pountney
44. St. Leonard Eastcheap
45. St. Leonard Foster Lane
46. St. Magnus Bridge
47. St. Margaret Bridge Street
48. St. Margaret Lothbury
49. St. Margaret Moses
50. St. Margaret Pattens
51. St. Martin Ludgate
52. St. Martin Orgar
53. St. Martin Outwich
54. St. Martin Pomary
55. St. Martin in the Vintry
     St. Mary Abchurch

57. St. Mary Aldermanbury
58. St. Mary Aldermarychurch
59. St. Mary at Axe
60. St. Mary Bothaw
61. St. Mary le Bow
62. St. Mary Colechurch
63. St. Mary Fenchurch
64. St. Mary at Hill
65. St. Mary Magdalen Milk Street
66. St. Mary Magdalen Old Fish Street
67. St. Mary Mounthaw
68. St. Mary Somerset
69. St. Mary Staining Lane
70. St. Mary Woolchurch
71. St. Mary Woolnoth
72. St. Matthew Friday Street
73. St. Michael Bassishaw
74. St. Michael at Corn
75. St. Michael Cornhill
76. St. Michael Crooked Lane
77. St. Michael Paternoster in the Riole
78. St. Michael Queenhithe
79. St. Michael Wood Street

80. St. Mildred Bread Street
81. St. Mildred Poultry
82. St. Nicholas Acon
83. St. Nicholas Coldabbey
84. St. Nicholas Olave
85. St. Nicholas in the Shambles
86. St. Olave by the Tower
87. St. Olave Old Jewry
88. St. Olave Silver Street
89. St. Pancras
90. St. Peter Broad Street
91. St. Peter Cornhill
92. St. Peter the Little Paul's Wharf
93. St. Peter Westcheap
94. St. Stephen Coleman Street
95. St. Stephen Walbrook
96. St. Swithin
97. St. Thomas the Apostle

98. St. Vedast
99. St. Andrew Holborn
100. St. Botolph without Aldersgate
101. St. Botolph without Aldgate
102. St. Botolph without Bishopsgate
103. St. Bride
104. St. Dunstan in the West
105. St. Giles without Cripplegate
106. Sepulchre
* 107. St. Clement Danes
* 108. St. Mary Savoy
* 109. St. Olave Southwark
110. St. Peter in the Bailey

* indicates church not on map

osity with prayer, though the hospitals offered medical care and shelter. The houses of friars, founded in the 13th century, had a more active role in society, preaching and hearing confessions, although their involvement with the world lowered their reputation with some. Later medieval foundations in and near London included the Cistercian monastery of St. Mary Graces by the Tower, founded by Edward III in 1350, and the Charterhouse to the north west of the city, founded by Sir Walter Manny in 1371: both had their roots in the wealth won from the French wars and in the devastating experience of the Black Death of 1348-9.

It seems to be a characteristic of cities that were large and wealthy in the 11th and 12th centuries, such as Norwich, York and Winchester, that they had a large number of parish churches, which usually survived into the later Middle Ages. London itself had over 100 parish churches by 1200 and their geographical spread indicates the concentration of population and wealth in the City. While the range of church dedications was quite wide, there were many churches which were dedicated to the same saint, and most thus acquired an identifying 'surname', usually indicating their location but sometimes commemorating the founder.

The large number of parish churches in London ensured that most people could belong to a relatively small and intimate group for religious worship. The churches themselves were an important physical focus for parish life, secular as well as religious; many were rebuilt or substantially extended in the later 14th or 15th centuries, largely through the bequests and gifts of parishioners. The comparative wealth of the London livings, and the other attractions of the capital, meant that the City's churches were staffed by churchmen with higher than normal levels of literacy and academic attainment.

The doctrine of Purgatory, which made prayers for the dead a crucially important part of religious observance, took hold in the 14th century, and led to the proliferation of endowments for chantries (prayers for the dead) and anniversary masses in the City churches. Much wealth came to the Church in this way: the churches were adorned with new altars, with lamps and candles, and with subsidiary chapels, and the parish clergy were augmented by an increasing number of chantry priests. Many of the wealthier Londoners set up permanent chantries, usually in their parish churches or St. Paul's, while a very few, including mayor Richard Whittington (died 1423) were able to found colleges of priests to pray for their souls. Poorer individuals, without the resources to pay for prayers in perpetuity, joined small local fraternities which acted as collective chantries, guaranteeing a proper burial and prayers for members when they died. Charity and care for the living went along with this concern for the dead: Whittington's college included an almshouse for thirteen 'poor folk', and many fraternities helped members in sickness and trouble. The City companies played a part in this, administering chantries and bequests for the poor and running almshouses and schools.

Although the evidence of wills and endowments suggests that most Londoners were firmly committed to the rituals and beliefs of the

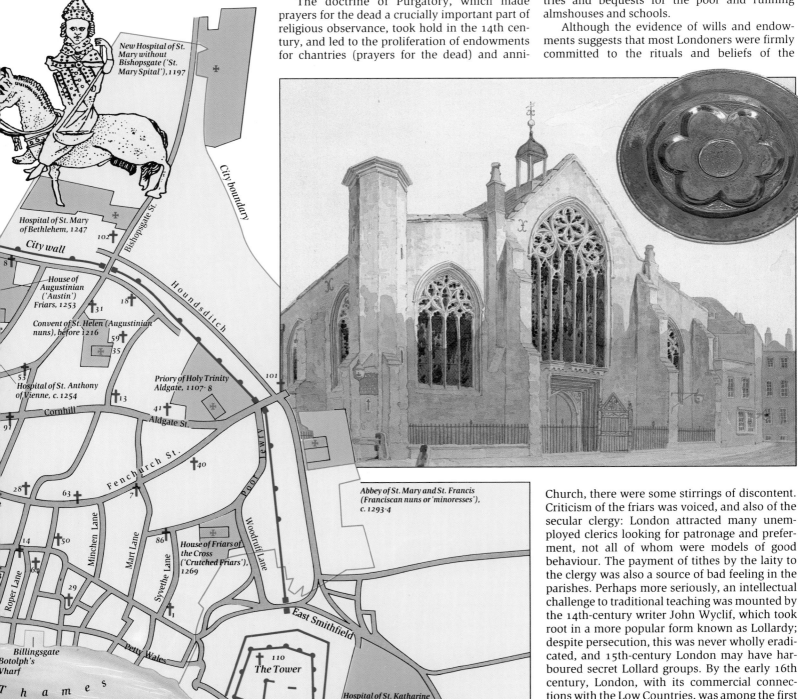

New Hospital of St. Mary without Bishopsgate ('St. Mary Spital'), 1197

Hospital of St. Mary of Bethlehem, 1247

City wall

House of Augustinian ('Austin') Friars, 1253

Convent of St. Helen (Augustinian nuns), before 1216

Hospital of St. Anthony of Vienne, c. 1254

Cornhill

Bishopsgate St.

Houndsditch

Priory of Holy Trinity Aldgate, 1107-8

Aldgate St.

Fenchurch St.

Minchen Lane

Mart Lane

Syrethe Lane

Woodruff Lane

Poor Pewty

City boundary

House of Friars of the Cross ('Crutched Friars'), 1269

Roper Lane

Billingsgate
Botolph's Wharf

Petty Wales

Thames

East Smithfield

The Tower

Abbey of St. Mary and St. Francis (Franciscan nuns or 'minoresses'), c. 1293-4

Hospital of St. Katharine by the Tower, 1148

Church, there were some stirrings of discontent. Criticism of the friars was voiced, and also of the secular clergy: London attracted many unemployed clerics looking for patronage and preferment, not all of whom were models of good behaviour. The payment of tithes by the laity to the clergy was also a source of bad feeling in the parishes. Perhaps more seriously, an intellectual challenge to traditional teaching was mounted by the 14th-century writer John Wyclif, which took root in a more popular form known as Lollardy; despite persecution, this was never wholly eradicated, and 15th-century London may have harboured secret Lollard groups. By the early 16th century, London, with its commercial connections with the Low Countries, was among the first to receive the new Protestant doctrines being preached and published on the Continent.

# TRADE AND TRADERS

Early medieval England largely produced raw materials for export. Its principal product was wool; other exports included Cornish tin, hides, sheepskins, and some foodstuffs. Many English ports on the east and south coasts flourished as centres for the export of wool to the clothmaking cities of the Low Countries and Italy. London was certainly a major wool export centre, and in the early 14th century about one third of the national total was shipped from the city's wharves. More than half of this was in the hands of foreign merchants: many Flemings and Italians used their greater capital resources and financial skills to organise the English trade.

Even more important for the city's economy, however, was London's role as a marketplace for imported goods – fine textiles, spices, furs, small manufactured goods, and especially wine, imported from the English territories in Gascony via Bordeaux and La Rochelle, and stored and sold from cellars in the Vintry. As the great fairs of the 13th century declined, nobles, leading ecclesiastics, and the royal household turned to London for all the luxuries their lifestyle demanded, and London merchants and craftsmen profited from supplying these needs. Many of these imports – French wine excepted – came to England not directly from their country of origin, but via the markets of the Low Countries, especially Bruges.

The start of the Hundred Years' War (c. 1337-1453) between England and France severely damaged the Bordeaux wine trade and led to trade embargoes with the Low Countries, and very large duties on the export of unprocessed wool. This gave English cloth manufacturing a chance to develop, and by the early 15th century cloth, rather than wool, was becoming the dominant export, and London was

*Wealth and Trade London was one of the centres of a complex network of European trade and distribution routes (below left). Overseas trade was concentrated on the waterfront below the Bridge, where the first customs house was built in the late 14th century, but wine was landed upstream at the Vintry, and Baltic trading focused on the Steelyard. Goods were carried up the steep city lanes from the river to the merchants' houses and shops in Westcheap (modern Cheapside), where there were specialist retail areas (map below). Commerce and trade were the source of medieval London's prosperity, as is clearly shown by the map of wealth distribution in the early 14th century (below): the richest areas are the centre and waterfront.*

increasing its advantage over other English ports. Political tension increased the risks of trade, while population loss had had an important impact on the economy. In these more difficult times, the larger merchant had the advantage over the smaller, and London merchants individually, and through the associations of the Staple (for wool exports) and the Merchants Adventurers (for cloth export), were able to take a leading position.

After a period of stagnation in the mid-15th century, there seems to have been a general recovery in European trade. The French wine trade grew again with the ending of hostilities, and English cloth exports began to expand rapidly from the 1470s. English trade was increasingly channelled through London: by 1500 about 45 per cent of England's wool exports and 70 per cent of its cloth were passing through the port of London, much of this then going on to Antwerp or Calais. Antwerp and its hinterland also offered high-quality cloth-finishing skills, so London merchants developed an easy and profitable business exporting

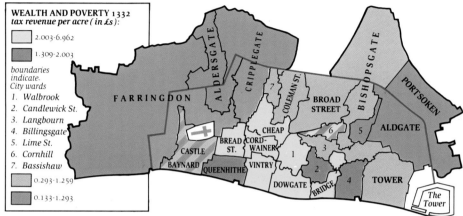

**WEALTH AND POVERTY 1332**
*tax revenue per acre ( in £s ):*

- 2.003-6.962
- 1.309-2.003

*boundaries indicate. City wards*
1. Walbrook
2. Candlewick St.
3. Langbourn
4. Billingsgate
5. Lime St.
6. Cornhill
7. Bassishaw

- 0.293-1.259
- 0.133-1.293

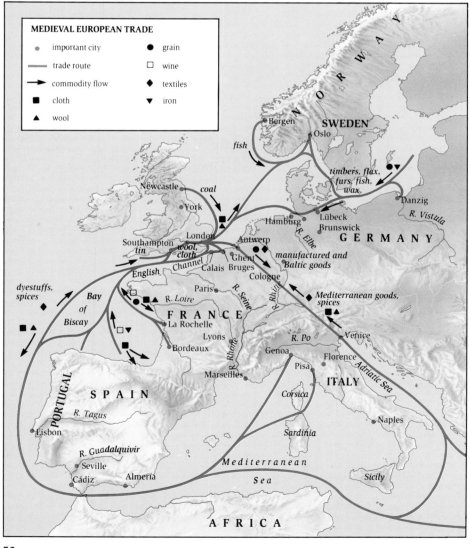

**MEDIEVAL EUROPEAN TRADE**

- important city
- trade route
- commodity flow
- cloth
- wool
- grain
- wine
- textiles
- iron

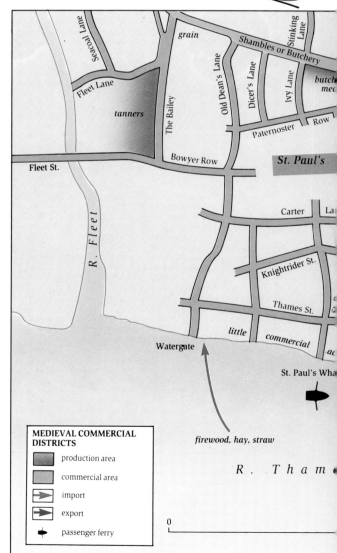

**MEDIEVAL COMMERCIAL DISTRICTS**

- production area
- commercial area
- import
- export
- passenger ferry

undyed, unfinished woollen broadcloths, to the dismay of English clothworkers.

Imports into London in the late 15th century were made up of some raw materials (dyestuffs, spices, fruits, and fish) and a wide range of manufactures, from knives, armour, and weapons, to threads, textiles (especially linen) and haberdashery. Soap, glassware, cheap jewellery, mirrors, spectacles, paper and printed books ('diverse histories') are among the imports listed in a customs account from the 1480s. English craftsmen, including Londoners, objected to this flood of imports which threatened their livelihood, but even Acts of Parliament were powerless to stop it. The evidence suggests that the late 15th-century trade expansion was of greatest benefit to merchants and perhaps also to retailers, but provided little stimulus to London's manufacturing and finishing industries. However, the boom in the import of cheap goods is evidence of high consumer demand in the lower levels of society, which can be attributed to the better standards of living they were then enjoying.

**A medieval shop** *Westcheap (modern Cheapside), the retailing centre of the city, was lined with shops, some less than 8 or 10 feet square. There were also several larger buildings called selds, in which traders owned or rented space for a bench or table, much like an eastern bazaar or a covered market. There may have been 400 retail units in Westcheap in 1300. The drawing (right) reconstructs a mercer's shop on Soper Lane and Westcheap. Mercers sold mostly linen and imported silk textiles, and perhaps also ribbons, kerchiefs, and trimmings. The goods were displayed outside the shop.*

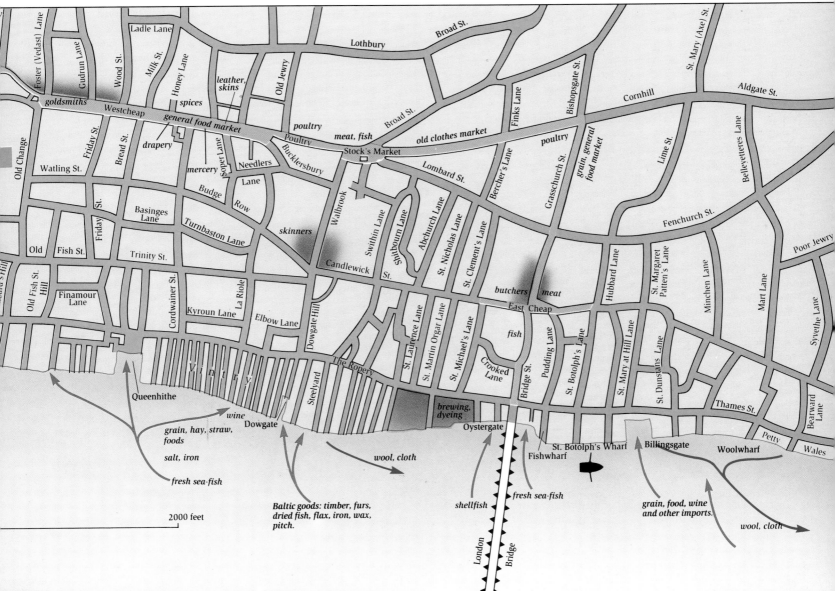

# CHAPTER 5
# TUDOR AND STUART LONDON

WHILE, IN 1500, the topography of London reflected its history of gradual development over the previous three centuries, it was to undergo rapid and violent changes during the second half of the 16th century, the principal change being the Dissolution of the Monasteries (1536). One amongst many of the causes for the Dissolution was the widely-held view that the monasteries were out-of-date, stifling, degenerate institutions. In addition, this was a highly materialistic age, the aim of ambitious men being the acquisition of land and rank. Shrinking government revenues, Henry VIII's extravagance in building his palaces, and troubles overseas, had all contributed to an urgent need for cash.

Three groups were the principal beneficiaries of the sales or grants of monastic lands resulting from the Dissolution: local landowners who were often tenants of the former houses; courtiers in favour at Court and government agents and officials of the Court of Augmentations which handled the transfers. Thus, Blackfriars passed to Sir Thomas Cawarden, Master of the Revels; Austin Friars to Sir William Paulet, Lord Treasurer. In the countryside outside London a ring of rural mansions sprang up within monastic houses, such as at Bermondsey Abbey which was granted to Sir Thomas Pope, Treasurer of the Court of Augmentations. Urban property owned by the monasteries or by former chantries (endowments of parish churches, confiscated by the Crown at the Reformation, and resold or given away) were released onto the market; in certain areas of the city as much as 60% of the property may have been in ecclesiastical ownership before the Dissolution. Colonisation of the former religious precincts, especially by aliens or foreigners, was common. In about 1586 a survey of the shell of the church of Holy Trinity Priory, Aldgate, found houses sprouting from above the Romanesque arches of the roofless choir. This precinct was inhabited by a number of

*Please refer to pages 50-51 for a map of the pre-Dissolution churches and monastic precincts of London.*

**Right** *The painting depicts the coronation procession of King Edward VI in 1547. A traditional route was followed, from the Tower of London to Westminster, and the way was lined with specially-constructed viewing stands from which City Liverymen viewed the procession. Landmarks passed on the way – St. Mary le-Bow, St. Paul's, Ludgate and Charing Cross are all clearly visible. The rural suburb of Southwark on the south bank of the river forms the background.*

Dutchmen, probably refugees, some of whom were making their characteristic Delftware vessels and tiles. Stone monastery buildings were much sought after by craftsmen who used fire in the manufacture of their products, such as glass-makers.

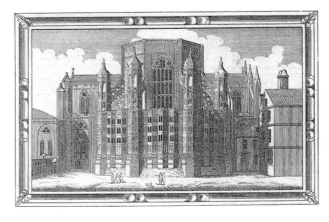

Before 1563, a contemporary historian wrote: '... fair houses in London were plenteous, and very easy to be had at low and small rents, and by reason of the late dissolution of religious houses, many houses in London stood vacant, and not any man desirous to take them.' Between 1550 and 1700 the population of London grew from 80,000 to over half a million. In 1500 it was a national capital inhabited by only four per cent of the English population; by 1700 it had become a major metropolis with almost ten per cent. The resultant pressure on housing in the already overcrowded medieval city necessitated massive building in areas such as the West End – within easy reach of the royal court at Whitehall – and outwards into the suburbs. Buildings and alleys covered a wide area of former fields east of the city, fanning out from the existing ribbon developments on the approach roads and rural hamlets.

*Please refer to pages 64-65 for a map of London's expansion in the 17th century.*

This growth is even more remarkable because it was frequently checked by the ravages of plague. Nearly a quarter of the city's inhabitants died of plague in 1563; in 1665 more than 80,000 people died (a figure equivalent to the combined 17th-century populations of Norwich, Bristol, Newcastle, York and Exeter). Plague was concentrated both socially and geographically. Rats and fleas spread the disease throughout overcrowded alleys, shacks and tenements. Graveyards were soon overflowing and new burial grounds had to be established to take the strain. Though the City authorities had attempted to

*Above An engraving of Henry VII's chapel at Westminster Abbey. The foundation stone was laid in January 1503, and it was still unfinished when Henry died in 1509, although he was buried under the chapel floor. The task of completing the chapel fell to his successor, Henry VIII. The chapel, with its magnificent fan-vaulted ceiling which contrasts with sculptural decorations of extraordinary intricacy, is considered to be one of the great masterpieces of medieval architecture.*

*The present building of Somerset House in the Strand dates from 1776 and was, in effect, the first purpose-built set of government offices. Until 1999 it was assumed that nothing remained of the original palace built in 1547 by Edward Seymour, Duke of Somerset and guardian of King Edward VI. An excavation has revealed walls and masonry structures that formed parts of the palace's guard chamber, kitchen, and chapel. When the old palace was demolished in 1776 the lower rooms were filled with rubble and used to retain the foundations of the present buildings. Some of that rubble contained medieval remains that may have originated from inns and a church demolished in the 16th century on the instructions of Seymour.*

The EXECUTION of KING CHARLES the FIRST before the Banqueting House Whitehall, January 30.16

introduce special measures during the plague of 1518 (such as the isolation of those infected), their response was usually too little and too late.

John Stow's *Survey of London* (1598) is a major starting-point for any understanding of London's medieval and Tudor topography, social history and customs. Stow saw the city spreading in every direction, and lamented the speed and brutality of the many changes during his lifetime, though he took pride in the increased prosperity of the Elizabethan city and the newer buildings which reflected that wealth. He walked round every ward and looked into every church recording what the Reformation had left in its destructive wake. His view of London was imbued with a love of the past and the already vanished or fast-disappearing city of his youth.

*A series of maps based on John Stow's Survey can be seen on pages 60-61.*

By the end of the 16th century, many of the City's older noble houses, arranged around a courtyard with a lofty hall, no longer existed, or were barely recognisable. The Inn (town house) of the Earl of Oxford had been let to poulterers for the stabling of horses and housing of poultry. The hall of the Earls of Norfolk at Brokenwharf was a brewery; several town-houses of monasteries outside London had become taverns, even before 1535. Apart from company halls, houses with courtyards were still rare; they had either been built over or encroached upon. Set back from the street behind rows of smaller dwellings, they were sometimes only one room deep but up to five storeys high.

*See page 63 for a reconstruction of a Tudor house based on a Survey by Ralph Treswell.*

By 1600 a certain zoning of the better residences was becoming apparent. Stow and his near-contemporary, the playwright Dekker, both noticed that certain streets were favoured by the 'worthiest citizens' for their large houses: St Mary Axe, Lime Street, Milk Street and Bread Street for example, all quiet enclaves close to, but sufficiently separated from, Cheapside. The growth of

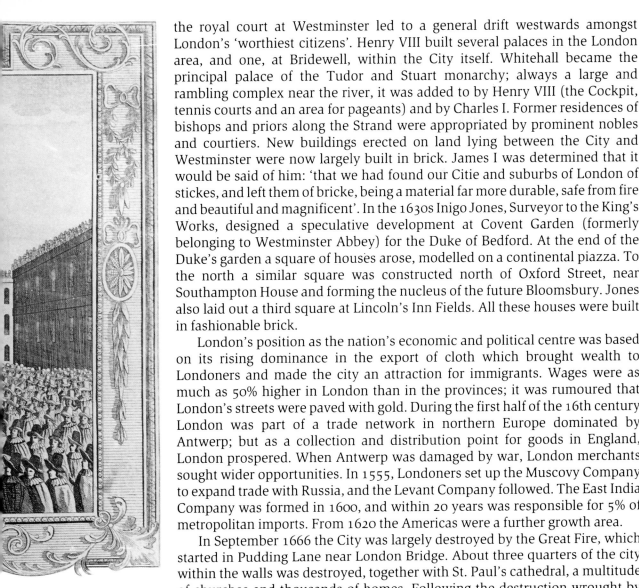

the royal court at Westminster led to a general drift westwards amongst London's 'worthiest citizens'. Henry VIII built several palaces in the London area, and one, at Bridewell, within the City itself. Whitehall became the principal palace of the Tudor and Stuart monarchy; always a large and rambling complex near the river, it was added to by Henry VIII (the Cockpit, tennis courts and an area for pageants) and by Charles I. Former residences of bishops and priors along the Strand were appropriated by prominent nobles and courtiers. New buildings erected on land lying between the City and Westminster were now largely built in brick. James I was determined that it would be said of him: 'that we had found our Citie and suburbs of London of stickes, and left them of bricke, being a material far more durable, safe from fire and beautiful and magnificent'. In the 1630s Inigo Jones, Surveyor to the King's Works, designed a speculative development at Covent Garden (formerly belonging to Westminster Abbey) for the Duke of Bedford. At the end of the Duke's garden a square of houses arose, modelled on a continental piazza. To the north a similar square was constructed north of Oxford Street, near Southampton House and forming the nucleus of the future Bloomsbury. Jones also laid out a third square at Lincoln's Inn Fields. All these houses were built in fashionable brick.

London's position as the nation's economic and political centre was based on its rising dominance in the export of cloth which brought wealth to Londoners and made the city an attraction for immigrants. Wages were as much as 50% higher in London than in the provinces; it was rumoured that London's streets were paved with gold. During the first half of the 16th century London was part of a trade network in northern Europe dominated by Antwerp; but as a collection and distribution point for goods in England, London prospered. When Antwerp was damaged by war, London merchants sought wider opportunities. In 1555, Londoners set up the Muscovy Company to expand trade with Russia, and the Levant Company followed. The East India Company was formed in 1600, and within 20 years was responsible for 5% of metropolitan imports. From 1620 the Americas were a further growth area.

In September 1666 the City was largely destroyed by the Great Fire, which started in Pudding Lane near London Bridge. About three quarters of the city within the walls was destroyed, together with St. Paul's cathedral, a multitude of churches and thousands of homes. Following the destruction wrought by the fire, the opportunity was taken to widen many streets, removing obstructions such as markets and churches. Apart from considerable widening of the quay sides, the only new street actually constructed in the city was King St. and its continuation, Queen St., which led from Guildhall to the wharf. The erection of a flamboyant Monument to the Fire (1677), and the laying out of these streets was the only tangible evidence of a short-lived desire to rebuild London in the style of the Paris of Louis XIV. Up to 1666 the city was largely timber-framed, with few stone buildings and a sprinkling of brick. After 1666 the city must have presented a remarkable contrast, with three quarters of the area within the walls rebuilt almost totally in brick, bordered (at least to the north and east) by older timber-framed buildings. The 1667 Act for rebuilding the City classified buildings into four groups with standards for each group, which brought about a uniformity of street frontage which could already be seen in Bloomsbury. In total, Sir Christopher Wren designed 51 post-fire parish churches in the city, of which 23 remain. The variety of Wren's church steeples was soon to become one of the architectural attractions for foreign visitors to London. Undoubtedly his greatest work is the rebuilding of St. Paul's Cathedral (1675-1711). Wren intended to give the London skyline a dome equal to those in Rome and Paris, and the city has been proud of its most important building ever since. Even today, planning legislation requires that uninterrupted views of Wren's masterpiece are retained from several points outside the City.

*A full reconstruction of Sir Christopher Wren's vision of the rebuilt city can be seen on pages 168-169.*

*Excavations at Spitalfields along the line of Steward Street have revealed the remains of two dozen houses, built in the 1680s and 1690s when the Old Artillery Ground was sold for development. Large quantities of pottery and glass have been found in cellars and cesspits. Wealthy Huguenot silk merchants, such as the Delamare and Beuzeville families, rebuilt many of these houses in the 18th century for occupation.*

*See Hollar's engraving of Covent Garden, page 65.*

*Recent excavations on the eastern bank of the Fleet reveal that reclamation of floodable land took place in the early middle ages prior to extensive urbanisation. The filthy 'Fleet ditch' was canalised in the late 17th century following proposals by Sir Christopher Wren. The wharves he envisaged were not a great success, and the canal became a common sewer that was covered over in 1733, and over which Farringdon Market was held. In the mid 19th century the Fleet was enclosed in a culvert and disappeared from view, but differences in slope and level allow walkers to trace its course easily.*

*See page 68 for a map tracing the progress of the Great Fire, and page 69 for a discussion of post-Fire building regulations, and a map of the Sir Christopher Wren's churches.*

*Map below The extent of Stuart London at its peak is contrasted to the size of the city in 1820.*

EXTENT OF LONDON 1680

LONDON 1820

+ St. Paul's

+ Westminster Abbey

LONDON 1820

# THE TUDOR CITY

Based on the Agas panorama (c. 1559), the reconstruction of Tudor London (*below*) shows a residential city of gabled houses, royal palaces, law courts, markets, walled gardens and innumerable churches. The north and south banks of the city are linked by the single thread of London Bridge, still surviving from the 12th century. London was poised on the brink of change: although it was still essentially a medieval city, the Dissolution of the Monasteries and its aftermath were to have profound consequences.

As in previous centuries, the underlying natural contours of the city continued to be smoothed out and valleys filled in or encroached upon. The part of the River Walbrook which flowed within the City walls had already been embanked by 1500, and was largely covered over by 1600. Concern with the polluted state of the Fleet, and attempts to deepen it and remove wharves and privies, continued throughout the 16th century. The ditch surrounding the City walls was also filled in over much of its length by the encroachment of new buildings and streets.

London still had a noble skyline of church spires, though the greatest of all at St. Paul's had been removed after being hit by lightning in 1561. The city was studded with fine buildings: royal palaces, civic halls and parish churches. Besides the Tower of London, there were two royal palaces in London in the Tudor and Stuart period. Baynard's Castle, on the waterfront between Queenhithe and the Fleet, was rebuilt in 1501 by Henry VII as a royal residence in the City. The ambitions of Henry VIII went much further, for his apartments at the Tower and at Westminster had both been destroyed by fire early in his reign, and he was therefore looking for a site on which to build a palace fit for a European prince. Bridewell Palace was built between 1515 and about 1523. Though positioned in the middle of a built-up area south of Fleet Street, its site was of a suitable size because the buildings were raised largely on reclaimed land at the confluence of the Fleet and Thames. Like the contemporary palace at Hampton Court in Middlesex, it was meant to be approached principally from the river.

London's civic buildings and amenities were constantly being improved. During the 16th and early 17th centuries several gates were rebuilt: Ludgate (1586), Aldgate (1608) and Aldersgate (1610). The last two were in solid Renaissance style, like many in towns in continental Europe. Buildings attached to Ludgate and Newgate continued to be used as prisons, and during the 16th century ward prisons were established in Bread Street, the Poultry, Wood Street and in Southwark. The Guildhall chapel and college buildings were lost at the Reformation, but the chapel was restored for civic religious services. Several medieval hospitals were dissolved in 1538-47 but others survived: St. Bartholomew's Hospital was refounded in 1544.

**THE SURVIVING BUILDINGS OF PRE-FIRE LONDON**
*(dates indicate earliest building, or fragment of building, on site)*

1. Staple Inn (1580)
2. Lincoln's Inn (1490)
3. Middle Temple Hall (1571)
4. Temple (church, 12th century)
5. Inner Temple Gateway (1610-11)
6. St. Dunstan's Porch (1586)
7. Barnard's Hall (early 15th century)
8. Britton's Court (14th century)
9. St. Bride's (Saxon)
10. Apothecaries' Hall (medieval)
11. St. Sepulchre (15th century)
12. Giltspur St. (medieval wall)
13. Gray's Inn (1560)
14. St. Etheldreda's (1290)
15. St. John (12th century)
16. Charterhouse (14th-century)
17. St. Bartholomew the Less (15th century)
18. St. Bartholomew the Great (12th century)
19. St. Paul's Chapter-house (1336)
20. Barbican (city wall)
21. St. Giles Cripplegate (1545-50)
22. London Wall (14th-15th century)
23. Guildhall (late 13th century)
24. St. Mary Le Bow (late 11th century)
25. St. Mary Aldermary (tower, 1511)
26. 34 Watling St. (14th-century undercroft)
27. Abchurch Lane (14th-century undercroft)
28. Merchant Taylor's Hall (14th century)
29. St. Ethelburga (14th century)
30. St. Helen's Bishopsgate (12th century)
31. St. Andrew Undershaft (1520-32)
32. All Hallows Staining (15th-century tower)
33. St. Katherine Kree (1628-31)
34. St. Olave (15th century)
35. All Hallows Barking (Saxon)
36. Mitre Street (14th or 15th-century arch)
37. St. Mary Overie (12th century)
38. Clink Street (west gable of Bishop of Winchester's hall, c.1330)

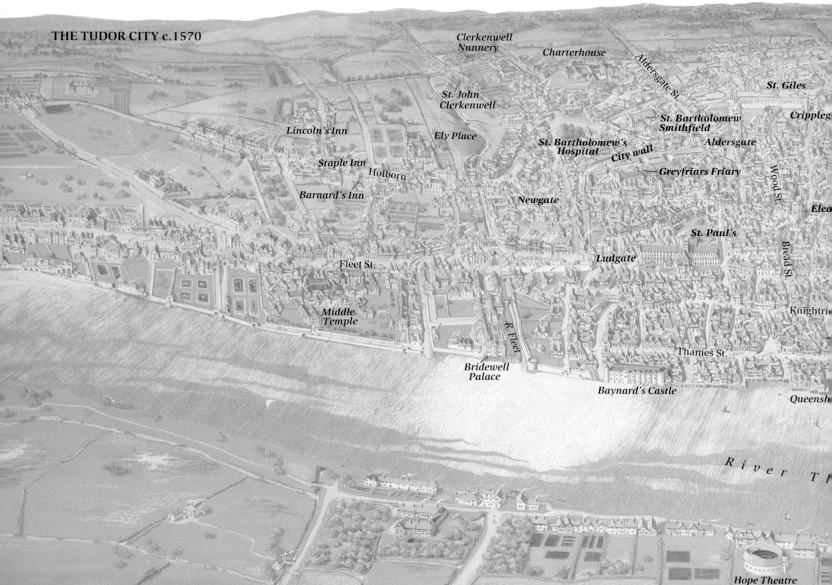

**THE TUDOR CITY c.1570**

Clerkenwell Nunnery

Charterhouse

Aldersgate St.

St. Giles

St. John Clerkenwell

St. Bartholomew Smithfield

Cripplegate

Lincoln's Inn

Ely Place

St. Bartholomew's Hospital

Aldersgate

Staple Inn

Holborn

City wall

Greyfriars Friary

Wood St.

Barnard's Inn

Newgate

Fleet St.

St. Paul's

Elea

St. Paul's

Ludgate

Bread St.

Middle Temple

Knightri

R. Fleet

Thames St.

Bridewell Palace

Baynard's Castle

Queensh

River Th

Hope Theatre

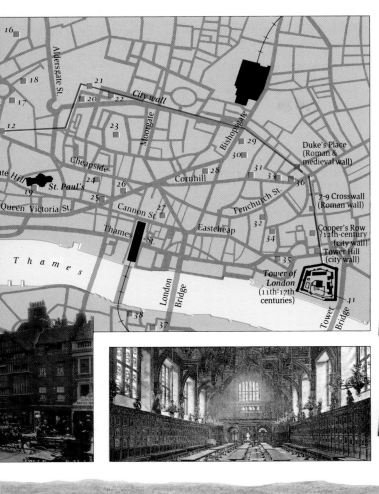

Surviving fragments *of the late medieval and Tudor city can still be seen today* (map left). *They include* (below, from left to right) *the frontage of Staple Inn, Holborn* (1580); *Middle Temple Hall* (1571). *The church of St. Helen Bishopsgate, contains medieval and Tudor monuments to the city's prominent inhabitants.*

*The reconstructed view* (c. 1570, below), *is simplified. In reality there were many more buildings packed in the narrow streets. As the following pages show, historians and archaeologists are now filling out the details of this broad impression.*

Conduits can be identified from early 16th-century documents as being sited near the main City gates. Water was brought to the City from Hertfordshire and from springs in Islington and Bloomsbury by extensions to the water supply system. The New River was constructed by Hugh Middleton in 1609-13, and augmented by water from the Lea in 1618; it entered the City in wooden pipes, and was distributed to houses.

In 1606-16 the moor on the north side of the City was finally drained and laid out as public gardens, a feature of other major European cities later in the century. Bowling alleys are known within the City walls during the later 16th century, as are tennis courts – both on private properties and in dissolved monastic buildings (such as the former nave of Blackfriars). Cockpits and theatres were mostly situated in the suburbs outside the main City (Shoreditch and Southwark), except for the Fortune Theatre in Golden Lane (1600) and private theatres such as Burbage's, also in Blackfriars.

London was already the national centre for legal education: the Inns of Court and Chancery were all to the west of the City. Some of their surviving buildings date from this period: Middle Temple (Hall of 1571, Middle Temple Gateway 1684, New Court of 1676); Inner Temple (Prince Henry's Room or Inner Temple Gateway, 1611); Lincoln's Inn, Staple Inn and Gray's Inn possess halls of 1492, 1581 and 1560 respectively. Other professions, such as the physicians, also established colleges in London at this time.

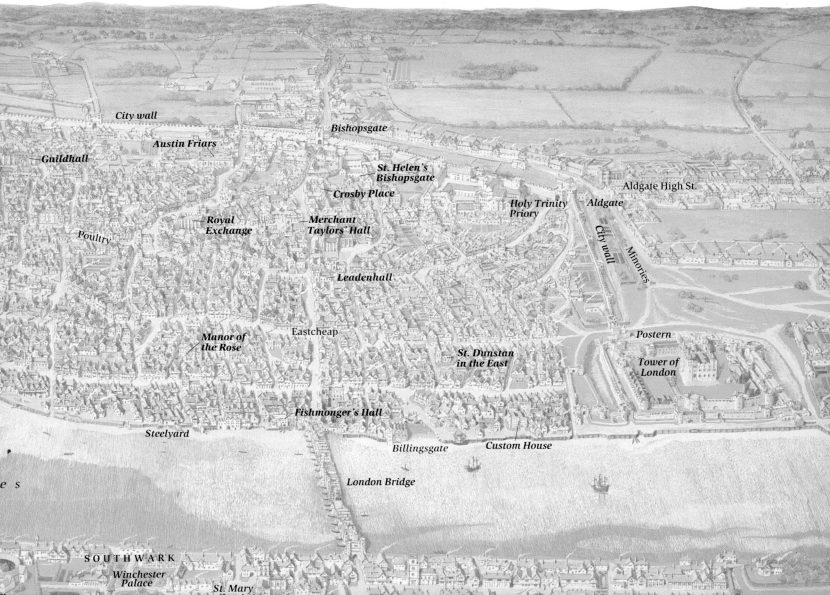

# JOHN STOW'S LONDON

John Stow was born in London in 1525, son of a tallow chandler of Throgmorton Street. He became a merchant tailor, and lived for the whole of his life in the City inside Aldgate. A fascination with history and an observant eye encouraged him to write a *Survey of London*. In this he describes the City's churches and institutions, houses and workshops, people and their customs, and the history of each parish in great detail. He alludes often to his own experience of London life, describing the farm just outside Aldgate where he bought milk as a boy, lamenting the spread of 'mean cottages and tenements' out into the surrounding countryside and mentioning the developers of the Tudor city as men he himself knew and had observed. He is, in turn enthusiastic about the vitality of the growing city, and censorious of the commercial ethic of those developers whose wealth was built on the exploitation of poor tenants bewildered by the pace of change. Stow writes as though he were conducting a tour of his native city and from his unique description we can gain a rare insight into its character and development at that time.

London emerges as a tripartite capital. The City at its centre, most of it enclosed by a wall, was its commercial and industrial heart, densely populated, prosperous and busy. It was the historic core of the capital and Stow was fascinated by its complex history and contemporary vitality. Though already built-up, it continued to change in the 16th century, with much rebuilding on old sites, and new building in monastic precincts after the Dissolution of the monasteries. Its many churches and Company halls were augmented by great 16th-century institutions such as the Royal Exchange and it retained a typical medieval mix of inhabitants, from alder-

**LONDON OCCUPATIONS**

| | | | |
|---|---|---|---|
| 1. Apothecaries | 18. Cutlers | 35. Heralds | 52. Skinners |
| 2. Armourers | 19. Curriers | 36. Ironmongers | 53. Saddlers |
| 3. Butchers | 20. Cordwainers | 37. Innholders | 54. Shipwrights |
| 4. Bakers | 21. Clergy | 38. Joiners | 55. Silversmiths |
| 5. Brickmakers | 22. Drapers | 39. Leathersellers | 56. Salters |
| 6. Brokers | 23. Dyers | 40. Lawyers | 57. Spurriers |
| 7. Blacksmiths | 24. Embroiderers | 41. Mercers | 58. Stationers |
| 8. Basketmakers | 25. Fletchers | 42. Masons | 59. Sailor's Victuallers |
| 9. Brewers | 26. Fishmongers | 43. Mariners | 60. Tenter Stretchers |
| 10. Barber surgeons | 27. Founders | 44. Merchant Tailors | 61. Tallow Chandlers |
| 11. Bowyers | 28. Fruiterers | 45. Pewterers | 62. Upholsterers |
| 12. Clothworkers | 29. Grocers | 46. Painter Stainers | 63. Vintners |
| 13. Carpenters | 30. Girdlers | 47. Parish Clerks | 64. Weavers |
| 14. Clerks | 31. Glaziers | 48. Physicians | 65. Wiredrawers |
| 15. Cheesemongers | 32. Glassmakers | 49. Plumbers | 66. Woodmongers |
| 16. Cooks | 33. Goldsmiths | 50. Printers | 67. Wax Chandlers |
| 17. Corn-millers | 34. Haberdashers | 51. Plasterers | |

• *indicates Company hall*

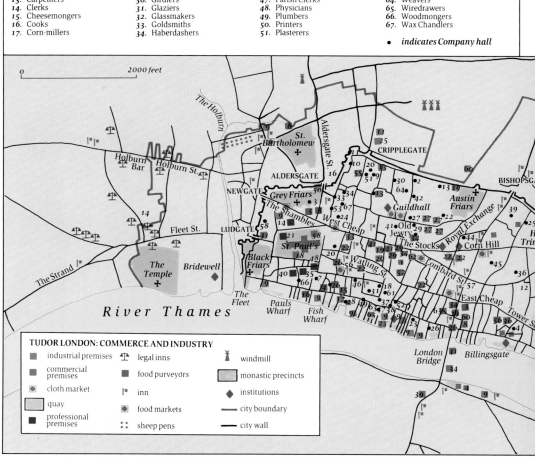

**TUDOR LONDON: COMMERCE AND INDUSTRY**

- ▪ industrial premises
- ▪ commercial premises
- ◉ cloth market
- quay
- ■ professional premises
- ⚖ legal inns
- ▪ food purveyors
- ◉ food markets
- ⁞ sheep pens
- ♙ windmill
- monastic precincts
- ◆ institutions
- — city boundary
- — city wall

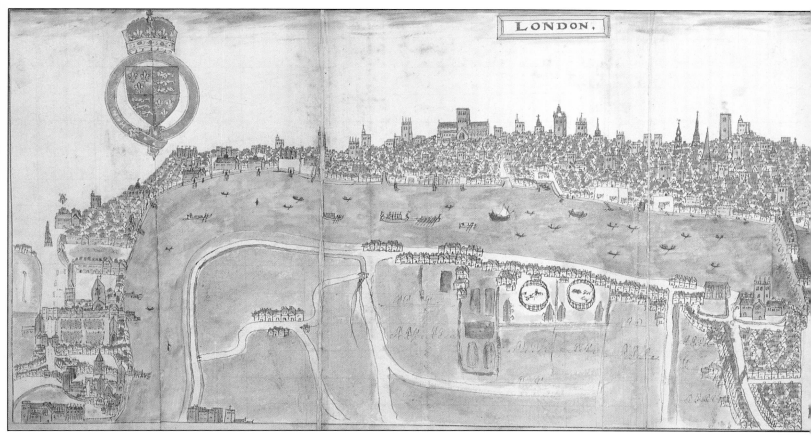

man to pauper, rich and poor living cheek by jowl in a tangle of streets, alleys and courts.

To the west of the City a second area, an exclusive suburb stretching along the Strand towards Westminster, was developing. The landed elite, government servants and lawyers lived in gracious houses along the Thames bank, or in the legal quarter around Fleet Street. It is of particular interest because it heralds a new kind of suburban environment. Unlike the City, with its mixture of rich and poor, craftsmen and merchants, the West End was economically and socially more homogeneous, built for, and inhabited by, political and professional groups.

The third area, a more diffuse suburban growth to the north and east, and in Southwark and its environs, provided a counterbalance to the West End. It housed a growing army of craftsmen and semi-skilled workers who serviced the trade and wealthy population of the capital. Living in an altogether shabbier area dominated by manual work, and with few residential amenities, such workers grew rapidly in numbers and helped increase London's population threefold in the course of the century. It was here that the shipwrights and sailors settled who made London's growth as a centre of overseas trade possible. The social tone of the area was very different to that in the west.

At the time Stow wrote his *Survey*, London was undergoing momentous change. The capital was bursting its medieval bounds and, impelled by the growth of capitalist enterprise and supported by large-scale immigration from the rest of England, the expansion which was to transform the old City into a metropolis had already begun.

**Commerce and industry** *The map (left) shows that commerce and shops tended to be concentrated in the centre, and industry around the city walls, especially in the east.*
**London Housing** *The map (top right) shows a clear pattern: an exclusive West End, a prosperous but mixed centre, and a much poorer suburban sprawl, especially towards the East End.*
**Residents and Social Institutions (right, centre)** *Landed gentry, the governing elite and professionals were based in the West End and Westminster, close to the centre of national government (map centre). Aldermen lived in the city, emphasising its business orientation. Hospitals are near the city wall, within ex-monastic precincts.*
**16th-century Tudor development (below right)** *The 16th-century witnessed the erection of eight great buildings, 21 new churches, much industrial and commercial development, especially towards the east, and the provision of many amenities, especially within the city.*
**Map below** *Bird's eye view of London from the* **Particular Description of England,** *William Smith, 1588.*

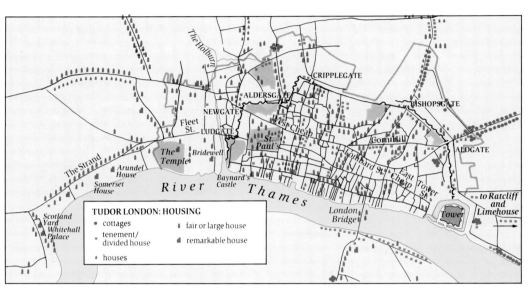

TUDOR LONDON: HOUSING

- cottages
- tenement/ divided house
- houses
- fair or large house
- remarkable house

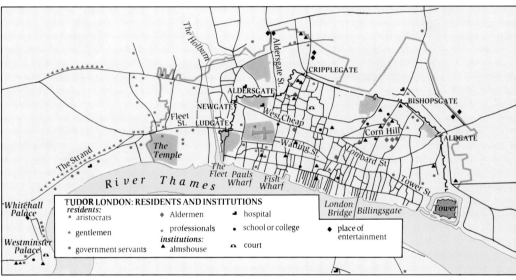

TUDOR LONDON: RESIDENTS AND INSTITUTIONS

**residents:**
- aristocrats
- gentlemen
- government servants
- Aldermen
- professionals
- hospital
- school or college
- place of entertainment

**institutions:**
- almshouse
- court

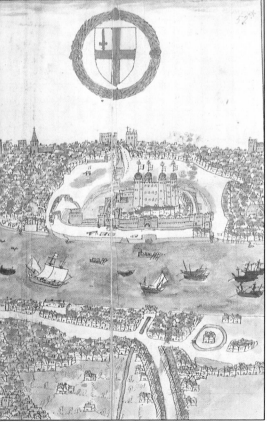

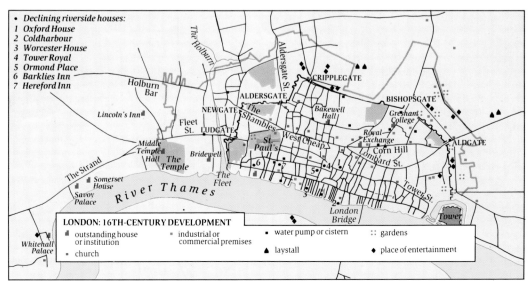

- **Declining riverside houses:**
1 Oxford House
2 Coldharbour
3 Worcester House
4 Tower Royal
5 Ormond Place
6 Barklies Inn
7 Hereford Inn

LONDON: 16TH-CENTURY DEVELOPMENT

- outstanding house or institution
- church
- industrial or commercial premises
- laystall
- water pump or cistern
- gardens
- place of entertainment

# TUDOR TRADE AND COMMERCE

London's status as Britain's largest port was firmly established during the 16th and 17th centuries. In 1559, certain landing places along the quayside, major alleys and watergates of the medieval period, were designated official quays by statute. The chief 16th century quays were still Queenshithe and Billingsgate, but by 1600 ships were setting out on international voyages from the new suburbs downstream of the City: Deptford, Wapping and Ratcliffe. The monopoly of the old-established medieval inlets had been superseded. During this period, companies of merchants were also founded to widen London's international trade. One of the most prominent was the East India Company (founded 1600), although it had no buildings of its own until the 18th century. The Royal Exchange (1571) also helped to stimulate international trade. Duties were levied on merchants at the Custom House, rebuilt in 1559 after being destroyed by fire. It was destroyed again by the Great Fire, and rebuilt by Wren.

Several company halls, the headquarters of the guilds and livery companies, were rebuilt or augmented during the 16th and 17th centuries. Companies took advantage of the Dissolution of the Monasteries and the Reformation: the Leathersellers acquired the large dormitory of the former nunnery of St. Helen Bishopsgate in 1542, and the Butchers acquired the parsonage of the suppressed parish of St. Nicholas Shambles in 1549. Many smaller companies (such as the Embroiderers, Fletchers, or Innholders) now had halls: at least 47 are known by 1600. Taverns were used by some companies as an alternative to their halls. The Weavers, for instance, had a hall but dined in taverns. The Cheapside area was thick with taverns which must have had a regular trade in company meetings and feasts.

The houses and shops of London before the Great Fire can be reconstructed from plans, documents and later engravings. The wealth of the Tudor capital was displayed to the world in large shops on its principal streets. Houses of prominent tradesmen incorporated both cellars and warehouses for merchandise, while well-appointed rooms above the shop provided the living quarters. A typical household would have been crowded; replete with extended family, apprentices and servants.

**A mercantile capital** The map (bottom) shows the location of the Tudor company halls, now situated in all parts of the City, although only two were outside the walls. By 1600 the guildhalls were no longer at the centre of their specialist retail areas, as they had been in the 13th and 14th centuries. The shields of the 12 greater Livery Companies are depicted (below) in their order of precedence at the Mayor's Feast at Guildhall every year.

The composition of London's imports (above right), showing the relative amounts of manufacturers' foodstuffs and raw materials imported. The number of ships entering London from foreign ports (below right) shows a great increase over the period. By 1686, trade across the Atlantic and with the Far East also played an important role in London's commerce.

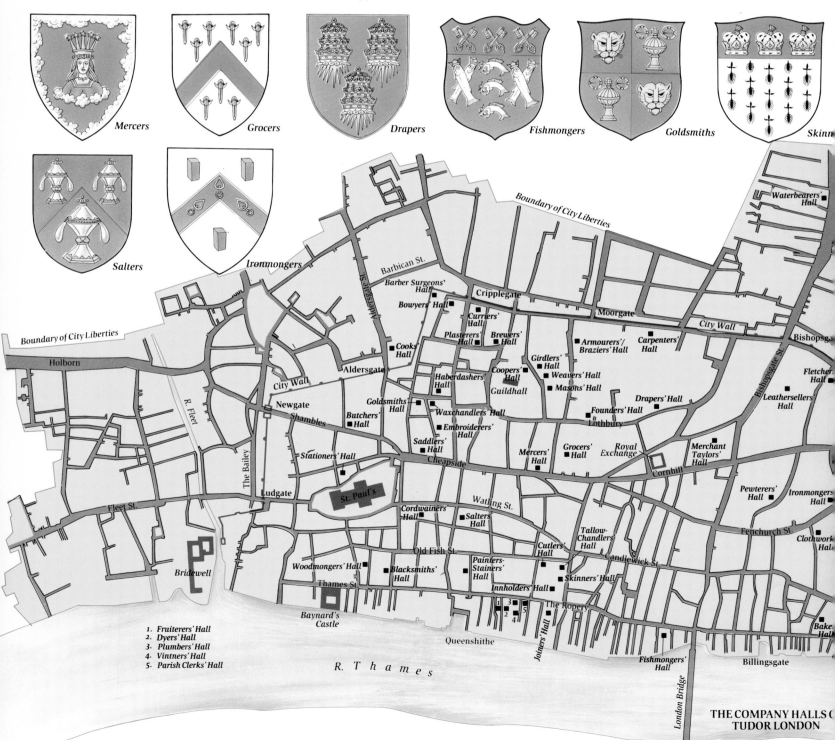

*Mercers* *Grocers* *Drapers* *Fishmongers* *Goldsmiths* *Skinners*

*Salters* *Ironmongers*

1. Fruiterers' Hall
2. Dyers' Hall
3. Plumbers' Hall
4. Vintners' Hall
5. Parish Clerks' Hall

**THE COMPANY HALLS OF TUDOR LONDON**

## COMPOSITION OF LONDON'S IMPORT TRADE
(percentage)

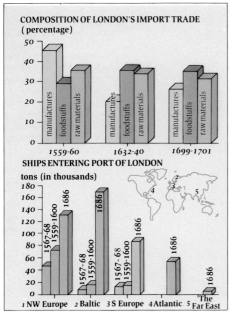

## SHIPS ENTERING PORT OF LONDON
tons (in thousands)

*Byrsa Londinensis vulgo the Royal Exchange*

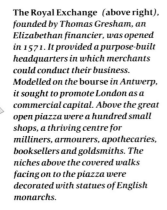

Merchant Taylors

Haberdashers

Vintners

Clothworkers

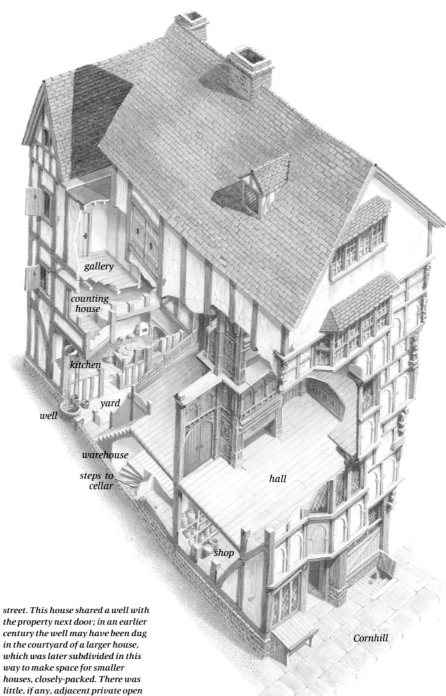

gallery

counting house

kitchen

well

yard

warehouse

steps to cellar

hall

shop

Cornhill

Aldgate

Poor Jewry

Tower of London

**The Royal Exchange** *(above right)*, founded by Thomas Gresham, an Elizabethan financier, was opened in 1571. It provided a purpose-built headquarters in which merchants could conduct their business. Modelled on the bourse in Antwerp, it sought to promote London as a commercial capital. Above the great open piazza were a hundred small shops, a thriving centre for milliners, armourers, apothecaries, booksellers and goldsmiths. The niches above the covered walks facing on to the piazza were decorated with statues of English monarchs.

**A Pre-Fire house in Cornhill,** *facing the Royal Exchange, was surveyed in 1612 by Ralph Treswell for the Clothworkers' Company which owned it. The details have been reconstructed* **(right)** *from engravings of other London houses. The Tudor house was a compact domestic unit; at the ground floor street front there was a shop, with a warehouse behind. Living quarters were on the first floor and above. A fine hall graced the front of the house, while a gallery led to further rooms over the rear kitchen. Merchandise was stored below in large cellars with an entrance to the* street. This house shared a well with the property next door; in an earlier century the well may have been dug in the courtyard of a larger house, which was later subdivided in this way to make space for smaller houses, closely-packed. There was little, if any, adjacent private open space in the city centre.

# THE GROWTH OF LONDON AND THE NEW SQUARES

London in the 16th century saw very marked population growth in the parishes which fell outside the City walls. The pressure on existing housing which this created resulted in the appearance of a new generation of buildings and alleys which were spread over a wide area of former fields to the east of the City, fanning out from the ribbon-developments which already flanked the approach roads into London. Much of this building took place in previously 'rural' hamlets, especially Ratcliffe, Limehouse, Shoreditch, Whitechapel and around St. Katharine's Hospital. In this piecemeal way, the East End of London was born.

Although open space to the north and west of the City was still being used for animal grazing and cultivation, these activities were also being gradually forced out to Islington and surrounding villages, as development began to fill in the fields and open spaces which lay outside the City walls. The village of Clerkenwell, for instance, was absorbed by the northern spread of the City. By the end of the 16th century, in the wake of the dissolution of the monasteries, bishops and priors had been ejected from their fashionable mansions along the Strand. A string of residences built for nobles and courtiers such as Essex House, Arundel House and Salisbury House, replaced them. By the 1630s, the Crown had abandoned its attempts to prevent expansion and now sought to limit growth by allowing only those developments

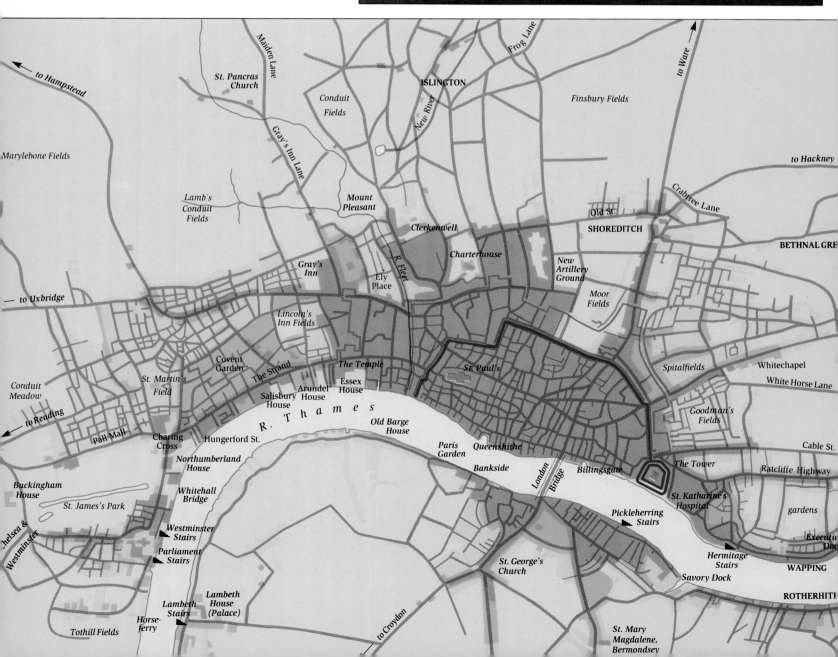

17th-century expansion *The painting (left), by John Collet, shows Covent Garden c.1770-1780, many years after it was built in the 1630s. By this time it had come to be used as a general market – the centre of fashion had by then moved further west to Westminster and St. James's. Originally, the Third Duke of Bedford's garden bordered the piazza on the south (left of painting) – it was his cousin and successor who secured a licence for building gentlemanly residences to the north of his garden.*

*The map (below left) graphically illustrates the spread of London in the first part of the 17th century. Areas of the City, both inside and outside the walls, grew at different rates, and in 1640 certain trades could be identified with certain locations (graphs right). Merchants and officials lived and worked in the old City; but those concerned with distribution, victuals and labouring were found largely in the new suburbs. Hollar's view of west central London in the 1650s (below right) shows a bird's eye view of Covent Garden and many of the surrounding developments. Bedford House is clearly visible to the south of the square.*

which reached certain standards. In this way areas such as Covent Garden and Lincoln's Inn – spacious squares flanked by elegant houses for gentlemen and aristocrats – came to be built. The principal architect of this revolutionary new look was Inigo Jones, a Londoner by birth, but heavily influenced by the Italian Renaissance and the architecture of Palladio. Over the next 27 years he not only designed certain specific buildings, such as the Banqueting Hall in Whitehall, but was influential in the layout of many other schemes. Spacious squares, surrounded by well-appointed houses with uniform Italianate facades began to extend westwards toward Royal Westminster. No shops or other signs of commerce were allowed.

The East End, on the other hand, was fast becoming a mixture of houses and small industrial concerns: bell-founding, glass-making, ivory and horn working and, later, silk-weaving and paper-making. These industries flourished outside the City because of several factors: the lower cost of rents; the exclusion of certain trades from practising within the walls; the failure of the City authorities to control the industries springing up in these areas. Within the City itself, traditional small-scale industry and manufacturing continued to thrive: carpenters, cobblers, tailors and printers were all still based within the walls. However, by the 17th century a division between the East and West End was emerging which was to have profound long-term consequences on the geography of London – government and service industries were based to the west of the City, financial services were located in the City itself, and manufacturing spread out to the east.

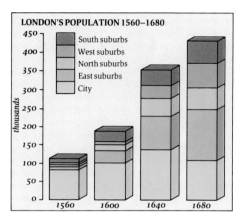

**LONDON'S POPULATION 1560–1680**

Legend:
- South suburbs
- West suburbs
- North suburbs
- East suburbs
- City

thousands: 0, 50, 100, 150, 200, 250, 300, 350, 400, 450

Years: 1560, 1600, 1640, 1680

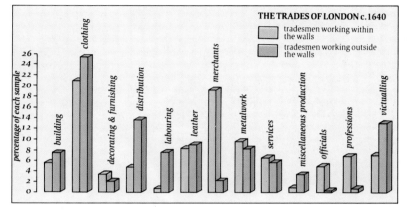

**THE TRADES OF LONDON c.1640**

- tradesmen working within the walls
- tradesmen working outside the walls

percentage of each sample: 0, 2, 4, 6, 8, 10, 12, 14, 16, 18, 20, 22, 24, 26

Trades: building, clothing, decorating & furnishing, distribution, labouring, leather, merchants, metalwork, services, miscellaneous production, officials, professions, victualling

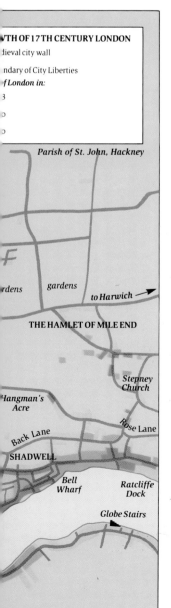

GROWTH OF 17TH CENTURY LONDON

medieval city wall

boundary of City Liberties

of London in:

Parish of St. John, Hackney

gardens

to Harwich →

THE HAMLET OF MILE END

Stepney Church

Hangman's Acre

Rose Lane

Back Lane

SHADWELL

Bell Wharf

Ratcliffe Dock

Globe Stairs

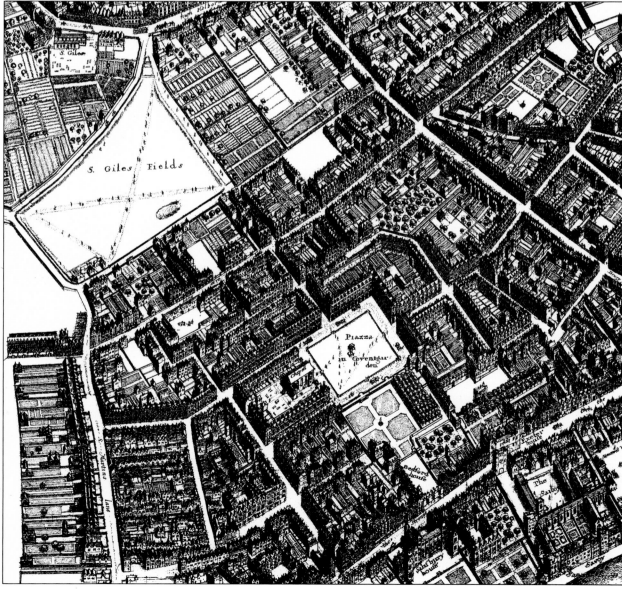

S. Giles

S. Giles Fields

Piazza in Coventgarden

Bedford House

# LONDON BEFORE THE GREAT FIRE

The 17th-century City lived through the Civil War in the 1640s, the Great Plague of 1665, the Great Fire of 1666, and the subsequent Great Rebuilding: as a consequence, London in 1700 bore little resemblance to the town in 1600. When the century opened, London lay cramped and crowded within its medieval walls with open fields to north and east, and a rich suburb expanding westwards towards Westminster. Within the City, surrounding some 100 churches, company halls and other public buildings were streets, lanes and alleys cluttered with tall timber-framed buildings. Rich and poor lived side by side, although the wealthier inhabitants often occupied secluded and more spacious sites set back from the street frontage. Houses of artisans and shopkeepers opened directly onto the road, with little space for a yard behind. The poorest inhabitants lived in single rooms, usually in an upper storey.

Commercial life was in the hands of some 100 companies whose halls were a noteworthy feature of the City. These guilds exercised control over all aspects of trading and manufacture through such measures as their insistence upon a seven-year apprenticeship before granting the freedom to ply a particular trade in London. As a direct result of such restrictions, new businesses often set up outside the walls where the long arm of the guilds could not always reach them. These suburbs developed dramatically as the population rose from 200,000 in 1600 to 375,000 by 1650, an increase due almost entirely to an influx of migrants from the poorer

**The Civil War Defences of London 16413-7** (below left) *During the Civil War, London was protected by the largest circuit of town defences in Europe. It incorporated an earthen bank and ditch running between a series of forts and batteries. This map shows the approximate position of the defences, but includes alternative alignments (as between Hyde Park Corner and Millbank) where the actual line is in doubt.*

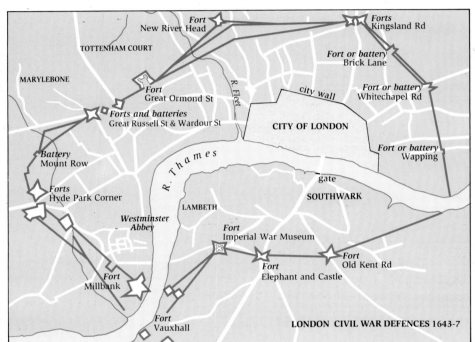

LONDON CIVIL WAR DEFENCES 1643-7

rural areas of England. In the early 17th century the northern and eastern suburbs grew fastest and were filled with artisans and small industries. The western suburb began expanding slightly later, providing services and luxury goods for the capital.

However, this was a century remembered more for its upheavals than for prosperous expansion. In December 1641, following the ousting of the pro-Royalist regime at the election to the Common Council, London became the capital and chief port for the Parliamentarians against the King. The Royalist army was repulsed at Turnham Green in November 1642, after which work began on a massive project to defend the City and its new suburbs. Comparison of the area enclosed by the medieval town wall with that enclosed by the 17th-century work shows how much larger London had become, although extensive areas of open ground were deliberately included within the Civil War circuit. The eleven mile-long defence was a costly

undertaking beset with difficulties, highlighted by the fact that strict Puritans were obliged to countenance Sunday working to get the job done. At the close of the Civil War, London was on the winning side, which did not endear its citizens to later Stuart kings. However, the new defences were never attacked, and were so thoroughly dismantled after 1647 that little trace remains today.

London was rich, powerful and a fortress of Protestant interest but it was also noted for its dirt, overcrowding and squalor. Plague, most unwelcome of all imports brought into this prosperous port, thrived in such conditions, killing over 25,000 Londoners in both 1603 and 1625, and 10,000 in 1636. But the worst and last visitation was in 1665, when over 70,000 citizens died. Large communal graves were dug outside the City, for the churchyards were full: these grim statistics were conscientiously compiled by the parish clerks in the Bills of Mortality, weekly lists of deaths and their cause.

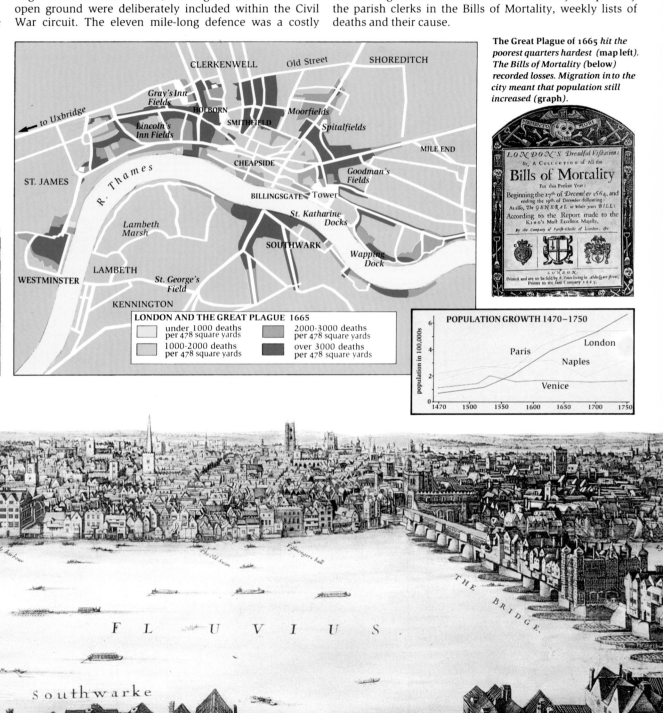

*The Great Plague of 1665 hit the poorest quarters hardest (map left). The Bills of Mortality (below) recorded losses. Migration in to the city meant that population still increased (graph).*

**LONDON AND THE GREAT PLAGUE 1665**

- under 1000 deaths per 478 square yards
- 1000-2000 deaths per 478 square yards
- 2000-3000 deaths per 478 square yards
- over 3000 deaths per 478 square yards

**POPULATION GROWTH 1470–1750**

# THE GREAT FIRE AND THE GREAT REBUILDING

London, like any ancient town, was prey to fire, and had suffered from many conflagrations. What made the disaster of 1666 different from the rest was its sheer scale. It all began by accident or negligence, in Thomas Faryner's bakehouse in Pudding Lane. The City was tinder-dry after a long hot summer. It was early on Sunday morning, the 2nd September, and by the time Londoners were awake to the danger, the fire was already out of hand. With hindsight it is easy to blame Londoners for not acting faster on that first morning. Many citizens understandably refused to allow their houses to be pulled down to create adequate fire breaks; others, like Samuel Pepys, simply thought the fire a long way off and of little consequence, and went back to bed. They had seen fires before, and this one looked no different. They were soon proved to be wrong. Fanned by a driving east wind, it jumped whatever firebreaks had been created. In spite of the best endeavours of parish and ward officials, and even of the Lord Mayor, Sir Thomas Bludworth, the fire moved faster than the firefighters: the City could not save itself. Charles II, arriving from Whitehall to inspect the damage, could do little more. The fire raced west along the waterfront, which was packed with combustibles such as timber, pitch and oil, reaching Three Cranes (present-day Southwark Bridge) by the afternoon. The Londoners gathered up their possessions and fled by foot, road and river.

The fire burnt all night and gained momentum throughout Monday. By order of the King, the Duke of York (later James II) was placed in control of the city, and his guards tried to prevent disorder and looting. Firebreaks at Queenhithe were ineffective, and the fire advanced west towards the River Fleet, and north beyond Cornhill and the Royal Exchange. Belated arrangements were made to check its progress on the northern and western sides of the City with the establishment of Fire Posts, each manned by 130 men with orders to create firebreaks. Had such a system been used earlier, much might have been saved.

By Tuesday morning, even these measures seemed inadequate, and the militia from Middlesex, Hertfordshire and Kent were ordered into the City to prevent riots and fight the fire. But not even the Fleet River served as an effective firebreak: later that day, having destroyed St. Paul's, the Guildhall, Custom House, and much else, the flames burst out of the City gates, leapt the Fleet, and attacked Fleet Street, threatening, for the first time, Whitehall and the Royal residences. Gunpowder was used to clear firebreaks and save the Tower of London.

On Tuesday night all seemed lost, for the Fire was advancing in a vast arc that stretched from Temple church in the west, to Smithfield and St. Giles Cripplegate in the north, to Leadenhall Market and All-Hallows by the Tower in the east. At this point the wind dropped, allowing the tired fire-fighters to check, control and dowse the flames, which they did throughout Wednesday and Thursday. By Friday, they had succeeded and, exhausted, could stop and count the cost. The devastation which confronted them was horrific. London was a vast, unrecognisable blackened ruin. The destruction within the walled area was worse than that suffered by the City in the Blitz: the Great Fire destroyed over 13,000 houses, 87 churches, 52 company halls, and much more besides. The total loss was estimated at £10,000,000 at a time when the City's annual income was £12,000. Could the City ever be rebuilt? Some contemporaries thought not.

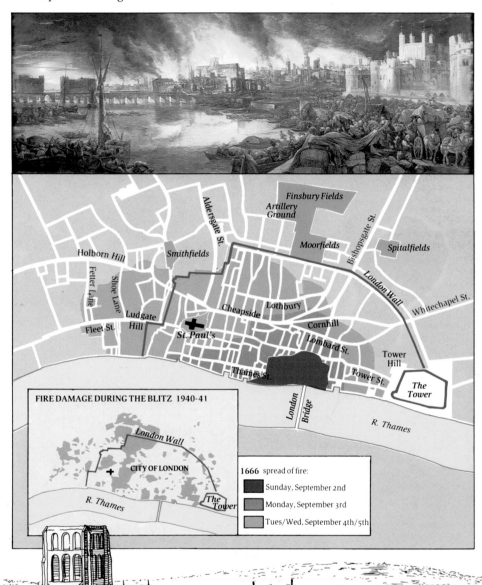

**The Great Fire** *A contemporary painting by an unidentified Dutch artist (below), shows the fire raging uncontrollably. The map (below) plots the daily progress of the fire. The total area devastated in September 1666 was greater than the extent of the city destroyed during 1940-1 (inset map). Wenceslaus Hollar drew St. Paul's after the fire in 1666 (bottom). The burning roof had crashed into the crypt, destroying thousands of pounds worth of books and other goods stored there.*

Finsbury Fields
Artillery Ground
Aldersgate St.
Moorfields
Bishopsgate St.
Spitalfields
Holborn Hill
Smithfields
London Wall
Fetter Lane
Whitechapel St.
Shoe Lane
Lothbury
Cheapside
Ludgate Hill
Fleet St.
St. Paul's
Cornhill
Lombard St.
Tower Hill
Thames St.
Tower St.
The Tower
London Bridge
R. Thames

FIRE DAMAGE DURING THE BLITZ 1940-41
London Wall
CITY OF LONDON
R. Thames
The Tower

**1666** spread of fire:
- Sunday, September 2nd
- Monday, September 3rd
- Tues/Wed, September 4th/5th

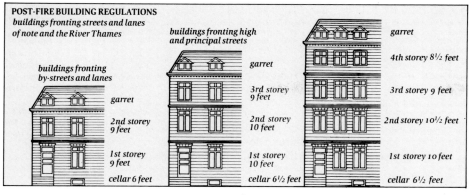

**POST-FIRE BUILDING REGULATIONS**
*buildings fronting streets and lanes of note and the River Thames*

*buildings fronting by-streets and lanes*

garret

2nd storey 9 feet

1st storey 9 feet

cellar 6 feet

*buildings fronting high and principal streets*

garret

3rd storey 9 feet

2nd storey 10 feet

1st storey 10 feet

cellar 6½ feet

garret

4th storey 8½ feet

3rd storey 9 feet

2nd storey 10½ feet

1st storey 10 feet

cellar 6½ feet

**Rebuilding the City** *The 1667 Rebuilding Act decreed that terraced brick buildings of uniform design would replace timber-framed houses (diagram). New buildings in back streets were two-storeyed; those on other streets, three-storeyed; those on main roads, four-storeyed. (Right) John Evelyn's (rejected) plan for a redesigned City, incorporating a radically new pattern of roads and roundabouts. 51 of the 87 City churches destroyed in the fire were rebuilt (map below), all of them designed by Sir Christopher Wren. About 25 survive today. The rebuilding programme culminated in the building of Wren's masterpiece, St. Paul's Cathedral, which was completed in 1711 (below right).*

## THE GREAT REBUILDING

There were many who saw London as an inelegant and insanitary city; the aftermath of the fire presented an opportunity to create a radically new town. The rebuilding plan had to reconcile general improvements to the City with the rights of individual property owners. The proposals promptly submitted by men such as John Evelyn and Christopher Wren (*page 168/9*) were superficially attractive, but incorporated street plans at variance with the medieval pattern and complexities of property ownership. Such bold schemes were rejected by the Corporation in favour of a more practical plan. The six commissioners appointed to

redesign the City drew up the most comprehensive town-planning legislation ever seen in England. Over 100 streets and lanes were widened, gradients diminished and two new streets, King Street and Queen Street, laid out. Timber was banned and the majority of the new buildings were of a uniform red brick design. The rebuilding of all private houses and company halls had to be financed from whatever funds individuals had saved from the flames, whereas a tax on coal raised £736,000 for the public works programme. This included the canalisation of the Fleet River, extensions to the Thames Quay, and the rebuilding of the parish churches, St. Paul's and public buildings such as the Guildhall.

The speed of the recovery was as remarkable as the results: by 1671, 9,000 houses and several major public buildings were complete. Work then began on rebuilding some 50 churches, and finally St. Paul's, which was built between 1675 and 1711. By that date, London was a cleaner, safer city with well-ordered streets of red brick and white stone buildings. All this work was achieved in spite of wars against the Dutch which saw an enemy fleet in the Thames in 1667, the Monmouth Rebellion in 1685, the Glorious Revolution in 1688, and some of the hardest winters on record. The Great Fire was a tragedy, but the Great Rebuilding was a triumph: London now presented as elegant a facade to the 18th century as any of Europe's capital cities.

**WREN'S SURVIVING CHURCHES**
(*'s indicate only tower or shell survives*)

1. St. Paul's
2. St. (Anne and St.) Agnes
3. St. Andrew Castle Baynard (by the wardrobe)
4. St. Benet on Thames
5. St. Clement Candlewick Street (Eastcheap)
6. St. Edmund
7. St. James Garlickhithe
8. St. Lawrence Jewry
9. St. Magnus the Martyr
10. St. Margaret Lothbury
11. St. Margaret Pattens
12. St. Martin Ludgate
13. St. Mary Abchurch
14. St. Mary Aldermary
15. St. Mary-le-Bow
16. St. Mary at Hill
17. St. Mary Woolnoth
18. St. Michael Cornhill
19. St. Michael Paternoster
20. St. Nicholas West Fishmarket (Cold-abbey)
21. St. Peter Cornhill
22. St. Sepulchre (Newgate)
23. St. Stephen Walbrook
24. St. Vedast
25. St. Alban Wood Street*
26. St. Augustine by St. Paul*
27. St. Dunstan towards the Tower (in the East)*
28. St. Mary Somerset*
29. Christchurch*
30. St. Olaf Jewry*
31. St. Brides
32. St. Mary Aldermanbury (rebuilt in Fulton, USA)

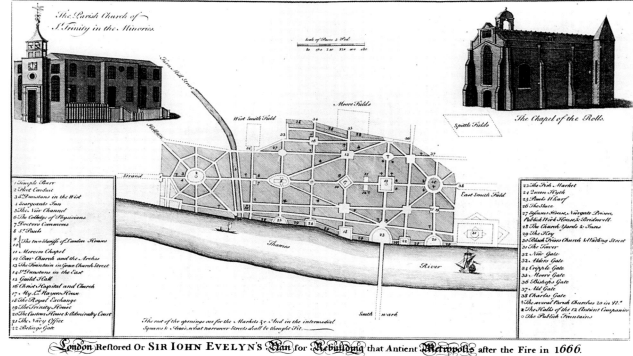

**London Restored Or SIR IOHN EVELYN'S Plan for Rebuilding that Antient Metropolis after the Fire in 1666.**

**POST-FIRE CHURCHES**

✝ churches destroyed, not rebuilt
✣ churches which survived the Fire
✝ churches rebuilt after Fire, still surviving
✝ churches rebuilt, tower or shell surviving
✝ churches rebuilt, subsequently destroyed

# CHAPTER 6
# GEORGIAN LONDON

*Christ Church, designed by Nicholas Hawksmoor, was begun in 1715 and completed fifteen years later. It remains the architectural jewel of Spitalfields. Nearby Fournier Street, Artillery Passage and Elder Street still have many impressive examples of town houses dating from the 17th and 18th centuries. As well as offering refuge for generations of immigrants, Spitalfields also accommodated brewers and other tradesmen who were banned from working within the limits of the City of London.*

*As the West End was developed, so the rent rolls of the great estates increased (see map page 75). The Duke of Bedford's estate, for example, yielded £3700 in 1732 and over £8000 in 1771.*

*From its initial development in 1671 to closure in 1994, Britain's main arsenal and armaments factory was at Woolwich. During the First World War the Arsenal covered 1,200 acres and employed 80,000 workers. Recent excavations have focused on the sites of the Royal Laboratories (1696–97) for ammunition production, and 'The Great Pile' (1717–20) built for boring cannon. Both structures were adapted to a suite of new processes and technologies, including steam power after horse power, and the subsequent installation of hydraulic power, gas and electricity. Beneath a wealth of industrial remains, archaeologists have found traces of a late Roman cemetery containing 140 graves.*

*For a map of Huguenot churches, please refer to page 136.*

IN 1700 LONDON was not only abominably insanitary, having no main drainage, no publicly provided collections of household refuse and utterly inadequate supplies of clean water, but it lacked many other basic services. It had no public transport, no street lighting, no minimum standards of paving, no paid police force, no fire brigade and no restrictions on the sale of liquor, tobacco or dangerous drugs. During the course of the 18th century, City merchants, shipowners and bankers gained large fortunes from maritime trade and the acquisition of new colonies in North America, the West Indies, the Indian Ocean, the Pacific and Africa. Some of this wealth was spent on fine architecture, some found its way into metropolitan improvements and a great deal was invested in suburban development. By the end of the Napoleonic Wars, steps had been taken to improve sanitation, street lighting, paving, policing and public open spaces. Elegant residential suburbs had arisen in the West End and manufacturing districts had expanded in the east. Outlying villages such as Islington, Blackheath and Twickenham had been transformed into satellite towns. Had a citizen of 1700 returned to London and its environs in 1815, he would not have recognised more than one street in ten, or one building in a hundred.

This period saw the growing prosperity of urban landowners and the rise of the newly enriched middle classes. Many aristocrats enjoyed rich pickings from the fruits of offices of state, as well as income from investments in joint stock companies, banks, insurance companies and overseas commerce. Large fortunes made out of trading ventures and commercial activities established many new families among the residents of fine houses in Mayfair and rapidly expanding estates north of Oxford Street. The expansion of the Bank of England, the opening of the new Stock Exchange, the founding of many private banks, the establishment of almost all the leading insurance companies and a consolidation of the wealth of the livery companies secured the preeminence of the City among financial capitals at the beginning of the 19th century.

The ranks of the newly enriched middle classes were swollen not only by financiers but by a throng of manufacturers and tradesmen. Much industrial activity was situated on the fringes of the built-up area as noxious and dangerous industries were forbidden to locate within the boundaries of the City of London. The insanitary, water-polluting business of dressing and tanning leather was concentrated south of the Thames on the banks of the River Wandle. Foul-smelling glue making, soap boiling, tallow candle-making works were located a little further downstream along the Thames in Rotherhithe and Blackwall. Woodworking industries were kept out of the City because of the dangers of fire; the furniture industry was gradually forced to leave Shoreditch for Camden Town and other places at a safe distance from the City. Sawmills, wheelwrights' shops and cooperages making wooden barrels were situated in Deptford and Greenwich. Small foundries in Poplar, Wapping and Limehouse were connected with trades directly serving shipbuilding and ship repairing yards along the Thames. The docks were beginning to attract their own processing industries, such as sugar refining. Further afield at Stratford in Essex were large flour mills and substantial breweries were established at Greenwich, Hammersmith and Chiswick. The advancing edge of the built-up area closed over a multitude of brick and tile works whose smoking kilns blackened the air in Marylebone, Paddington and Kensington.

The silk weavers of Spitalfields were located closer to the City and nearer to retail shops in the West End. Huguenot refugees had settled there in 1685 and in 1745 no fewer than 133 master weavers employed thousands of journeymen and apprentices. The twisting lanes and alleys of Clerkenwell were crowded with hundreds of watch- and clock-makers, cutlers, surgical instrument-makers, jewellers, diamond-cutters, coach-makers, upholsterers, locksmiths and many other craftsmen. In Westminster in 1749 a directory of trades listed dozens of victuallers, tailors, dressmakers, peruke makers, shoemakers, carpenters, butchers, chandlers, bakers and distillers. It was a royal village, supporting a multitude of tradesmen who catered for the luxurious tastes of the ruling elite.

Georgian London generated a prospering middle range of people, whose incomes were derived from shrewd investments overseas, holdings in government stock, rents from urban property, earnings from professions as varied as acting, portrait painting, publishing, preaching, advocacy, medicine, underwriting, stock-broking, merchanting, shopkeeping, building and catering. Parts of London took on the character of specialised business districts. The Inns of Court provided chambers for lawyers, hospitals were adjoined by consulting rooms for physicians and surgeons, St Paul's Cathedral and Westminster Abbey provided quarters for clergy and also premises for robemakers, printers, publishers, booksellers and journalists. Drury Lane and the Haymarket attracted theatres; St Martin's Lane furnished studios for painters and shops for artists' suppliers. A large number of coffee houses and clubs served as meeting places and centres for gathering and passing on news and views on professional, social and political matters. The places that catered for these transactions spread over much of the West End during the Georgian era. By 1815 the centre of London's clubland had shifted decisively westwards to St James's Street and the most prestigious clubs were housed in elegant architect-designed buildings.

*A map showing the location of the Georgian clubs of St. James's, and their dates of opening, can be found on pages 76-77.*

While the rich and the moderately well-to-do gained enormously in numbers, power and wealth during the 18th century, those who earned wages were less favoured. Wages persistently lagged behind the price of bread and household necessities. Poor accommodation and exorbitant rents were causes of far more serious grievance and discontent throughout the century and housing problems grew steadily worse as time passed by. Appalling conditions prevailed in the dilapidated courts and alleys and crumbling tenements that sheltered many wage-earning families. Such was the press of people coming to London in search of employment that modest houses took in more lodgers

**Below  The Thames from Somerset House Terrace towards Westminster**, *by Canaletto, 1750-51. His portrayal of the Thames, like the Grand Canal in Venice crowded with brightly coloured barges and ferries, hardly exaggerates the amount of traffic on the waterway, but his depiction of scores of baroque churches and Palladian palaces built in gleaming white Portland stone gives a heightened impression of the grandeur and urbanity of the city.*

than they could decently accommodate, and stables and sheds were converted into makeshift dormitories. But almost as fast as new rooms were occupied old ruinous buildings collapsed. In 1738, Samuel Johnson remarked that London was a place 'where falling houses thunder on your head'. Leaking roofs, damp walls, floors awash with effluent from impeded drains, bad ventilation, infestation with vermin, darkness, cramped, evil-smelling garrets and basements were just some of the problems that had to be contended with. Death rates continued to exceed birth rates and infant mortality was particularly high in all districts where poorer families were concentrated. Consumption and dysentery were endemic. Smallpox was not brought under control until the end of the 18th century. Periodic visitations of typhus and cholera killed off large numbers and cold, wet winters took a heavy toll of the most vulnerable age groups. Only continual replacement by a massive influx of young men and women from the countryside ensured an overall increase in the population.

In 18th-century London, drunkenness, prostitution, pickpocketing and personal assaults were rife, scarcely to be brought under control as long as the number of very poor people continued to increase and the gap between rich and poor widened. In 1797, Patrick Colquhoun, a magistrate in Tower Hamlets, estimated that London's criminal underworld still numbered 115,000, about one in eight of the population, and many of these people were concentrated in the old rookeries of Seven Dials, Chick Lane and Field Lane, Bethnal Green, Petticoat Lane, Houndsditch and Southwark. The containment of crime was assisted by the introduction of street lighting in the City in 1736. A Watching and Lighting Act for Spitalfields in 1738 contributed to an appreciable reduction in street robberies, burglaries and other offences.

In 1700 an observer who climbed to the gallery around the dome of St Paul's Cathedral would have been able to view London in its entirety. Pastures and scattered farms extended from Lamb's Conduit Fields to the distant hilltop hamlets of Hampstead and Highgate; isolated clusters of buildings at Covent Garden, Lincoln's Inn and Leicester Fields stood in the midst of fields; Hyde Park and St James's Park were surrounded by open countryside. An insistent impression of London at this time would have been its rusticity. Within the City itself gardens and orchards lay behind taverns and City company halls, in the Inns of Court and around hospitals, schools and almshouses. Chestnut trees and planes spread their shade over the city squares and fragrant lavender and rose bushes bloomed in private gardens off the Strand. Every Monday morning Londoners were awakened by a cacophony of animal sounds

Left *Vauxhall Gardens, by Thomas Rowlandson, (1756-1827). Originally called Spring Gardens (see map, page 142), they opened just after the Restoration in 1660. Admission was free, and the gardens appealed to all classes of society. In the 18th century the Gardens were greatly elaborated. Supper boxes, Gothic ruins, Chinese pavilions, cascades and many other attractions were added. In the words of a contemporary ballad: 'Here they drink, and there they cram/ Chicken, pasty, beef and ham,/ Women squeak and men drunk fall,/ Sweet enjoyment of Vauxhall.*

See page 79 for a contemporary illustration of Smithfield market and a map of Georgian markets.

*Between 1720 and 1750 there were no restraints on gin drinking, greatly increasing death rates amongst London's poor. A measure of restraint was imposed by the Gin Act of 1751, which required retailers to obtain licences and pay considerably higher excise duties on the spirits they sold. Above Beer Street and Gin Lane by H. Adlard, from the original design by Hogarth.*

announcing the opening of Smithfield market, and throughout the week the clatter of horses' hoofs echoed from cobbled streets. At midsummer the air was laden with the scent of new-mown hay brought daily to markets at Smithfield, Whitechapel, the Borough and Haymarket itself. London looked as if it were made up of 150 villages each centred upon its own church, inn, market place, great house and rows of cottages. Above all, every village or district contained a social mixture of masters and servants, learned men and labourers, gentlemen and shop-keepers. High and low attended church, drank in the same hostelries, mingled at Ranelagh or Vaux-hall Gardens and all joined Lord Mayor's proces-sions or other public assemblies.

By the end of the 18th century the built-up area covered more than twice as much land as at the beginning, and social segregation had advanced to an even greater extent. Surveying a panorama from the dome of St Paul's in the early 19th century, it would have been difficult to discern the edge of the urban area. Not only had fog and smoke impaired visibility but ribbons of houses and inns stretched along many roads to the far horizon. Everywhere fields were marked out as building plots and new pits were dug for gravel and brick-earth. Daniel Defoe recalled a time when Brick Lane, in Spitalfields, 'had been a deep dirty road, frequented by Carts fetching Bricks that way from Brick-kilns' in fields at Whitechapel. Like hundreds of other country lanes it became a well-paved city street. The New Road, constructed in the middle of the 18th century to by-pass the northern fringes of the built-up area, was reported fifty years later to be 'skirted on both sides with houses' for much of its length. To the South, St George's Fields were rapidly being covered with buildings.

For a discussion on brickmaking see page 133.

The most remarkable changes that came over London during the 18th century were the planning and building of separate residential districts for the rich in the West End and an exodus of middle-class residents from much of the City and from the East End. From the Strand north to Holborn, respectable families were moving out. By the beginning of the 19th century premises in Tottenham Court and mews on the Brewers' Company estate, had begun to be taken over by knife grinders, cab drivers, hawkers of fruit and vegetables, rag and bone collectors and dustmen. Around the Polygon in Somers Town, a shanty town of do-it-yourself houses was springing up. By this time, the middle classes had mostly left the City and its immediate environs east of Aldgate and on the south bank, and their houses were subdivided into tenements; colonies of moderately affluent people had retreated to Blackheath, Dulwich, Brixton, Putney, Kew and Richmond.

The layout of John Nash's scheme in Regent's Park and the building of Regent's Street completed the segregation of upper class neighbourhoods to the west from inferior quarters to the east. The exclusiveness of the West End was sealed by putting up a continuous line of shops along the east side of Regent's Street and by closing entries and alley-ways into Soho (see map page 76).

However deep its social divisions had grown, Londoners still managed to stick together. The royal family continued to live in St James's or at Carlton House. They did not move to a British Versailles. Rioting mobs that rampaged through the streets in 1780 (the anti-Catholic Gordon riots) did not storm the Tower of London or massacre aristocrats. Victories against the French were still occasions for patriotic celebrations by all sections of society. Friedrich Wendeborn, a German visitor at the end of the 18th century, envied even the poorest Londoners for the liberty and independence they possessed. 'A foreigner will at first hardly be pleased with the manner of living in London', he wrote, 'but if he has sense enough to perceive and value that freedom in thinking and acting which is to be enjoyed in England, he will soon wish to conclude his days there'.

Map below The extent of Georgian London at its peak is contrasted to the size of the city today.

EXTENT OF LONDON 1820

LONDON 1990

St. Paul's

LONDON 1990

# GREAT ESTATES AND BUILDING DEVELOPMENT

During the 18th century London expanded over a larger area and at a faster rate than at any previous period. Buildings advanced unevenly in different directions from the centre and building booms alternated with periods of inactivity. Demand for houses was stimulated by rising commercial prosperity and by an increase in population from over 500,000 in 1700 to over 900,000 in 1801 and well over 1,000,000 in 1811. Movement away from the centre of the metropolis was precipitated by a thickening pall of smoke caused by a changeover in domestic fuel from wood to Newcastle coal, by a proliferation of epidemics (no longer plague, but of consumption, dysentery, smallpox, typhus and dropsy) and by high incidences of alcoholism, violence and other social disorders. Opportunities to meet the demand for new accommodation were seized by owners of great estates. The Crown and the church were less active than City livery companies and charitable foundations; and all these public bodies were much less active than private landowners in promoting building development.

A few great estates led the development of the West End as a fashionable residential district. Landowners and their agents designed the layout of streets and squares and drew the boundaries of building plots. Speculative builders were invited to submit plans and elevations of their proposed buildings and, having gained approval for these plans, were granted building leases to carry out the work. The builder sold a leasehold interest in the house he built to an occupier. The occupier was given security of tenure for a long lease of up to 99 years, at the end of which possession of the premises reverted to the ground landlord. The landlord retained a freehold interest in the soil, controlled the use of the land and buildings erected on it and charged a ground rent to the occupier.

While the rich moved west from Soho along Piccadilly and Oxford Street, the poor crowded into districts forming a belt around the City of London: St Giles', Clerkenwell, Spitalfields, and eastward into Bethnal Green, Whitechapel and Wapping. Once the social reputations of the east and west were widely acknowledged the process was cumulative: where the poor moved in the rich moved out. Archenholtz, visiting England in about 1780, remarked: 'the East End, especially along the shores of the Thames consists of old houses; the streets there are narrow and ill-paved; inhabited by sailors and other workmen who are employed in the construction of ships and by a great part of the Jews. The contrast between this and the West End is astonishing.'

The outer edges of the built-up area were scarred with gravel workings, brick pits, smoking kilns and tileries, stinking piles of horse manure, ashes, night soil and indescribable dumps of garbage. The fringe had a 'floating' population of dustmen, carters, rag-pickers, bone-boilers, horse-dealers and washerwomen. It also provided accommodation for pig keepers, dairymen, market gardeners, tanners, candle-makers and it offered space for some rough sports including dog-fighting, bull-baiting, boxing and, on occasion, duelling. It was not an idyllic rural retreat.

The first 18th century building boom began after the Treaty of Utrecht in 1713. Mayfair, west to Hyde Park and north to Oxford Street, was laid out in spacious squares and neat terraces. North of Oxford Street, the Cavendish-Harley family began developing their estate before the boom fizzled out in the 1730s. A fresh burst of activity opened with the Peace of Paris in 1763 and lasted until 1793 when war with France again halted building. During this golden age of Georgian architecture, John and Robert Adam designed the Adelphi, and adorned new developments in Piccadilly, Berkeley Square, Cavendish Square, Portland Place and Fitzroy Square with their gracefully proportioned buildings. Sir William Chambers designed Somerset House and left his mark on Piccadilly, the Albany, Berners Street and Whitehall. Many other architects contributed to the elegance of developments on the Portman, Berners, Portland, Bedford, Southampton–Fitzroy and Foundling Hospital estates. When peace returned in 1815 building activity was slow to recover. By 1820, the Prince Regent had commissioned a grandiose scheme for the development of Regent's Park and the

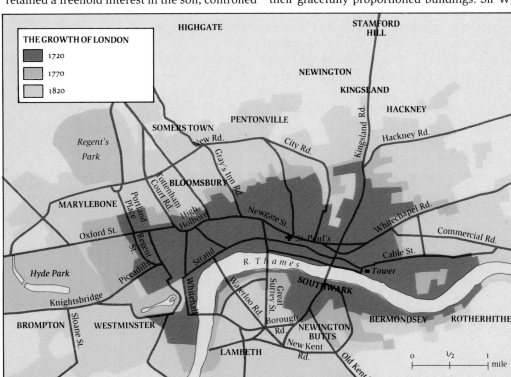

## MAJOR ESTATES IN CENTRAL LONDON

| | |
|---|---|
| 1. Angell | 50. Kensington Gore |
| 2. Audley | 51. Kilburn Priory |
| 3. Bartholomew's Hospital | 52. Ladbroke |
| 4. Battle Bridge | 53. Lambeth Wick |
| 5. Bedford, Duke of | 54. Lambs Farm |
| 6. Berkeley | 55. Leicester |
| 7. Berners | 56. Lloyd-Lisson |
| 8. Brett | 57. Maddox-Pollen |
| 9. Brewers' Company | 58. Maryon-Wilson |
| 10. Cadogan | 59. Mawby |
| 11. Calthorpe | 60. Mercers' Company |
| 12. Camden Charities | 61. Mildmay (Newington Gre- |
| 13. Camden, Earl of | 62. Minet |
| 14. Charterhouse | 63. Morden College |
| 15. Chelsea Hospital | 64. New River |
| 16. Choumert | 65. Norland |
| 17. Christ Church College, Oxford | 66. Norris |
| 18. Christie | 67. Northampton |
| 19. Church Commissioners | 68. Penton |
| (various estates) | 69. Phillimore |
| 20. Church Commissioners | 70. Pickering |
| (formerly Bishop of London) | 71. Portland-Soho |
| 21. Clothworkers' Company (Packington) | 72. Portland (Cavendish, Har- |
| 22. Conduit Mead | 73. Portman |
| 23. Corporation of London Bridge House | 74. Powell |
| 24. Craven | 75. Rugby School |
| 25. Crown | 76. St. John's College Cambri- |
| 26. Curzon | 77. St. Quintin |
| 27. Dartmouth, Lord | 78. St. Thomas's Hospital |
| 28. De Beauvoir | 79. Salisbury |
| 29. De Crespigny | 80. Sir John Cass Charity |
| 30. Duchy of Cornwall | 81. Skinner Company |
| 31. Edwardes (Lord Kensington) | 82. Slade |
| 32. Eton College | 83. Sloane-Stanley |
| 33. Eyre | 84. Smith's Charity |
| 34. Foundling Hospital | 85. Somers |
| 35. French School | 86. Southampton |
| 36. Gascoigne | 87. Stonefield (Richard Cloud |
| 37. Graham | 88. Sutton |
| 38. Grand Junction Canal Company | 89. Talbot |
| 39. Grosvenor, Duke of Westminster | 90. Thornhill |
| 40. Gunter | 91. Thurloe |
| 41. Hall | 92. Tredegar, Lord |
| 42. Harrison | 93. Trinity House |
| 43. Harrow School | 94. Tyssen-Amhurst |
| 44. Holland (Ilchester) | 95. Vallotten |
| 45. Hope | 96. Vaughn |
| 46. Hutchins | 97. Vauxhall, Manor of |
| 47. Inderwick | 98. Walcott |
| 48. Ironmongers | 99. Wenlock |
| 49. Jesus College, Oxford | 100. Wright |

THE GROWTH OF LONDON

1720
1770
1820

HIGHGATE
STAMFORD HILL
NEWINGTON
KINGSLAND
HACKNEY
PENTONVILLE
SOMERS TOWN
New Rd.
City Rd.
Kingsland Rd.
Hackney Rd.
Regent's Park
Gray's Inn Rd.
BLOOMSBURY
Tottenham Court Rd.
MARYLEBONE
Portland Place
High Holborn
Newgate St.
Whitechapel Rd.
Commercial Rd.
Oxford St.
Regent St.
St. Paul's
Cable St.
Strand
R. Thames
Tower
Hyde Park
Piccadilly
Whitehall
SOUTHWARK
Knightsbridge
Waterloo Rd.
Great Surrey St.
BERMONDSEY
ROTHERHITHE
BROMPTON
WESTMINSTER
Sloane St.
Borough Rd.
NEWINGTON BUTTS
New Kent Rd.
LAMBETH
Old Kent Rd.
Tothill Fields
WALWORTH

0     ½     1 mile

opening of a broad carriage-way to Carlton House and later to Trafalgar Square. At the same time, the Bedford estate was planning Tavistock Square and Gordon Square, the Grosvenor estate was laying out Belgrave Square and Eaton Square as part of a general design for Belgravia, the Bishop of London was embarking on the development of his lands at Paddington and dozens of small proprietors were calling in surveyors, architects and builders.

**The growth of London (map below left)** *Around Westminster the capital had begun to encroach upon Tothill Fields and Chelsea. To the south, Southwark spread over St. George's Fields into Newington. Long fingers of artisan housing and industrial premises stretched out to the north and west. But nowhere was private enterprise more vigorous than on the rural fringes: by the end of the 17th century the villages of St. Marylebone, Pentonville and Camden Town had been absorbed into the metropolis.*
**Grosvenor Square (centre left)** *This engraving of 1754 shows one of the earliest and grandest developments in Mayfair, the largest of its kind in London, covering six acres.*
**The development of Mayfair** *John Rocque's map (top right) of 1744 shows the regular pattern of streets in Mayfair beginning to take shape. Grosvenor Square is already built and the Chelsea Water Company's reservoir has been constructed in Hyde Park. South Mayfair remains in pasture around Shepherds Market. Richard Horwood's map of 1799 (centre right) shows the building of southern Mayfair completed by the development of Berkeley Square and Curzon Street.*
**Great Estates** *The map (below) shows the concentration of the largest estates in the West End. Some estates were owned and managed by public institutions such as the Church, City guilds, hospitals and universities. Others were owned by families, such as the Grosvenors, Portlands, Portmans and Curzons whose large tracts of land in the area left a legacy of orderly Georgian development.*

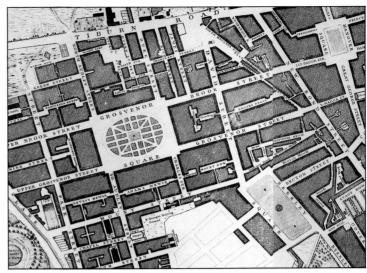

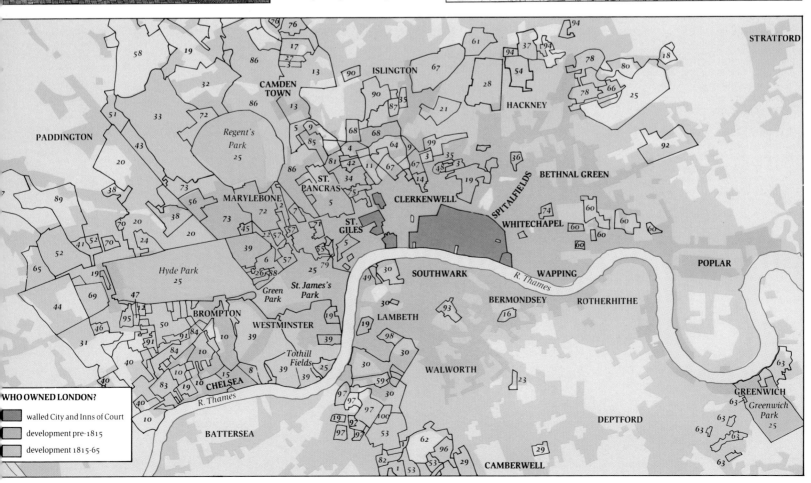

WHO OWNED LONDON?

■ walled City and Inns of Court
□ development pre-1815
□ development 1815-65

# PLANNING AND PUBLIC BUILDING

Private developers left London a substantial legacy of 18th-century buildings: noble yet comfortable mansions, orderly terraces of fine-looking commodious houses, elegant rows of shops, coffee houses, clubs, coaching inns, and solid commercial and industrial structures including shipyards and warehouses. A no less valuable legacy of public buildings comes from this period. When private house-building slackened, public bodies remained active. Government offices in Whitehall, Newgate Prison, docks, naval yards and barracks were all built or added to in the war years. At the same time, new bridges were thrown across the Thames and road improvement schemes were started, but not primarily for military purposes – London has no elaborate fortifications or military roads.

Public works replenished and consolidated the social infrastructure in the periods following building booms. Hence the provision of churches, almshouses, schools, museums and hospitals. The hospitals built in the 18th century reflect the rational humanitarian spirit of the era. Old medieval foundations were re-built and new hospitals were constructed – either through private generosity, as with Guy's and the Foundling Hospital, or through annual-subscription schemes as was the case with St. George's, the Middlesex and Westminster Hospitals, all of them built between 1720 and 1760.

Many churches designed to replace those destroyed in the Fire of London were built before 1713. Others designed by Hawksmoor, Archer, Flitcroft, Gibbs and Dance were commissioned by Parliament in 1711 and some of them were not completed until after 1730. A later phase of

*Georgian public buildings* The Adelphi (below), *John and Robert Adams, 1768. This river frontage has now been replaced by Savoy Place and Victoria Embankment Gardens.* Right (clockwise) Christ Church, Spitalfields. *This baroque design by Nicholas Hawksmoor was completed in 1727.* The Bank of England, Threadneedle St. *Designed by George Sampson and built 1732-36, it is now entirely encased in later building.* The Mansion House *Designed by George Dance the elder and built 1739-53. The portico remains unaltered.* The Imperial War Museum, Lambeth *Designed by J. Lewis in 1812 to rehouse old Bedlam, now Bethlehem Hospital for the insane. A dome was added in 1838.*

church building was initiated by the Church Building Act in 1818. One million pounds was spent furnishing new residential districts with Anglican churches. Dissenting congregations also built impressive places of worship during the 18th century.

The period between the Peace of Paris and the beginning of the French wars (1763-1793) was the golden age of Georgian architecture, dominated by two geniuses, William Chambers and Robert Adam. Virtually none of their work survives today – the two contrasting riverside developments of Somerset House (Chambers) and the Adelphi (Adam) were their most outstanding achievements. But it was in the London of George IV that a distinct urban vision is clearly evident. The King wanted to make London a truly magnificent capital, and city improvements and building initiatives, financed by the State, were undertaken on a large scale. John Nash's plans for Regent Street, with its dramatic vistas and the close attention paid to the siting of buildings, epitomises this era. It was also

**Regent's Park** *When Marylebone Park reverted to the Crown in 1811, it was suggested that the park be turned into a 'garden city' and that a new street should link Carlton House (the Regent's residence) and the park. In 1812 John Nash submitted his dramatic plans – a vision, never fully realised, of villas set in woodland, flanked by grandiose terraces. Regent Street (map right) cut through the West End, dividing the new squares and terraces of Mayfair and the untidy streets of Soho. The irregularities of the route allowed Nash to make a virtue out of necessity: the sweeping colonnades of the Quadrant to the north of Piccadilly Circus and – at a kink in the road between Oxford Circus and Portland Place – the vista of the church of All Soul's, Langham Place (below).*

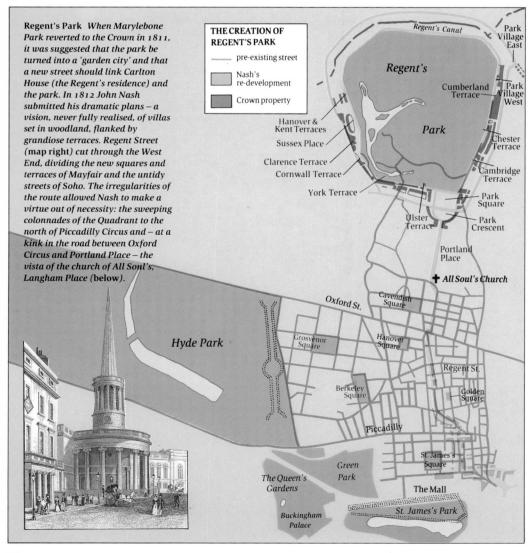

**THE CREATION OF REGENT'S PARK**

— pre-existing street

Nash's re-development

Crown property

**GEORGIAN ARCHITECTURE**

✝ place of worship    🏛 theatre

🏛 public building    🪑 club

🏥 hospital    🏬 shopping development

⌂ educational establishment    ▨ area of Georgian development

🏛 museum or gallery

1. Bank of England
2. Apothecaries' Hall (remodelled late 18thC)
3. Watermen's Hall (late 18thC)
4. Lancaster House (1820-33)
5. St. Mary-le-Strand (1714-17)
6. St. Anne, (1714-25)
7. St. Mary Woolnoth (1716-24)
8. St. Clement (Dane's) (tower) (1719-20)
9. St. Michael (1721)
10. St. Peter (1721-4)
11. St. Martin-in-the-Fields (1722-6)
12. Admiralty (1723-6)
13. St. Botolph (1725-9)
14. St. Bartholomew's Hospital (1730s onwards)
15. St. Giles-in-the-Fields (1731-4)
16. Paymaster General's Office (1732-3)
17. Treasury (1734-6)
18. St. George the Martyr (1734-6)
19. Mansion House (1739-53)
20. Foundling Hospital (1742-52)
21. Horse Guards (1750-8)
22. Dover House (1755)
23. All Hallows (1765-7)
24. Marlborough House (alterations 1771)
25. Adelphi (1772-4)
26. Boodles Club (1775)
27. Somerset House (1776-86)
28. Wesley's Chapel (1777-8)
29. Brooks's Club (1778)
30. Middlesex Sessions House (1779-82)
31. St. Luke's Hospital (1782-4)
32. St. Paul (rebuilt 1795-8)
33. Stationer's Hall (1800)
34. St. Anne (1802-6)
35. Royal Mint (completed 1807-9)
36. Drury Lane Theatre (1810)
37. Custom House (1813-17)
38. Royal Hospital (ancillary buildings, 1814-19)
39. Burlington Arcade (1815-19)
40. Royal Opera Arcade (1816-18)
41. St. Pancras (1818-22)
42. Haymarket Theatre (1820)
43. British Museum (1823-7)
44. Royal College of Physicians (1824-7)
45. Presbyterian Church (1824-7)
46. Buckingham Palace (1824-30)
47. St. Mark (1825-8)
48. Carlton Club (1826-7)
49. United Services Club (1827)
50. University College (1827)
51. Covent Garden Market (1828-30)
52. Athenaeum Club (1829-30)
53. St-Dunstan-in-the-West (1829-33)
54. Goldsmiths' Hall (1829-35)
55. Fishmongers' Hall (1831-3)
56. Charing Cross Hospital (1831-4)
57. National Gallery (1834-8)

during this period that work was begun on two major national institutions: Smirke's British Museum (originating in George IV's gift of his father's library to the nation) and Wilkins' National Gallery.

The return of peace and prosperity was marked by a resurgence of private building as well as the construction of theatres, banks, insurance offices and clubs. These

*The map (below) shows the major churches and public buildings of the Georgian period, and indicates (in brown tone) the principal areas of Georgian residential expansion.*

buildings still leave their imprint on London: the clubs of St James's, their grandiose architecture owing much to the pioneering style of Smirke's United Services Club (1816-1817); the first designed shopping streets, such as Woburn Walk, St Pancras (1822) and covered arcades, such as Burlington Arcade (1815-1819); the facade of Nash's Theatre Royal, Haymarket (1820-21).

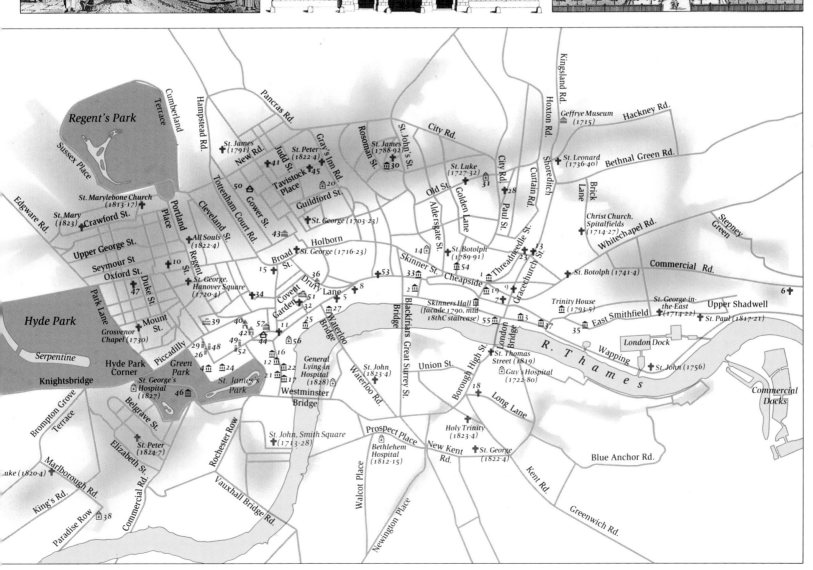

# FEEDING LONDON

At the beginning of the 18th century, the country within five or ten miles of London was entirely tributary to the metropolitan market. It supplied fruit, vegetables, meat and milk to the urban population as well as providing grazing land and hay for livestock. With changes in diet throughout the ensuing century, per capita consumption of fresh food increased, and London's agricultural hinterland had to meet that demand. The surface of land in orchards, nurseries and market gardens increased, extending westwards along the Thames as far as Brentford and northwards up the Lea to Homerton.

Not only did urban dairy herds and numbers of pigs increase but numbers of town horses grew rapidly. More and more were employed in ploughing as horses took the place of oxen. Ever greater numbers were used for riding, drawing coaches, carts, wagons and for towing barges on navigable waterways. Vast quantities of hay and oats were shipped and carted into London and vast quantities of manure were hauled out. Agriculture was directed at least as much towards feeding domestic animals as humans.

In 1800, the innermost edge of the built-up area was scarred with gravel workings, clay pits, brick kilns and mountains of metropolitan rubbish. At night, The Rev. Henry Hunter depicted it as forming 'a ring of fire and pungent smoke' around the City. Beyond the pits and tips lay the pastures where London's horses and cattle were put out to graze and butchers fattened their stock. On the Taplow Terrace west of the River Lea, strips of loam soil were intensively cultivated in orchards and market gardens. Further out lay an extensive area of meadows that supplied London with hay. A tract of arable farming persisted on the lighter soils of west Middlesex. A surprisingly large amount of land remained agriculturally unproductive. It was estimated in 1775 that 200,000 acres of waste land lay within 30 miles of the capital. Hounslow Heath and Finchley Common, very close to the built-up area, were described in 1793 as 'fitted only for Cherokees and savages' while Epping Forest was notorious for sheltering robbers. Firewood, gravel and sparse grazing for commoners' cattle were the meagre resources of these wild tracts.

At the beginning of the 18th century London was already the central market place for British agriculture. The prices of the principal grain crops were fixed at Mark Lane by the Tower. Cattle and sheep bred in the uplands of Wales and Scotland were driven to the east Midlands and East Anglia and from there as fatstock they made their last journey to Smithfield Market. Three dozen other markets dealt in different commodities: fruit and vegetables at Covent Garden, hides and leather at Bermondsey, and so on, and as the built-up area spread, new market places such as the Fleet, Oxford and Shepherds Markets, were established.

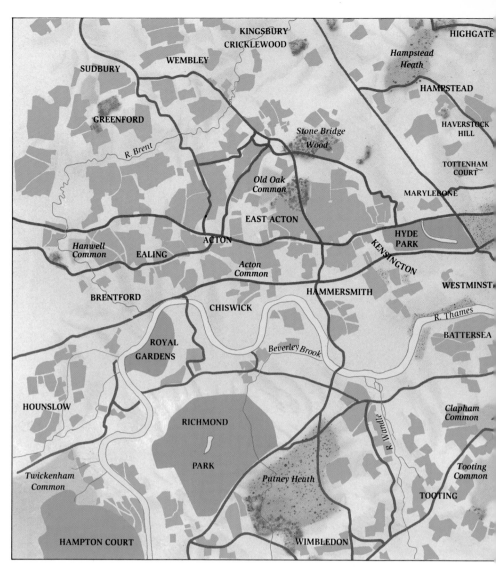

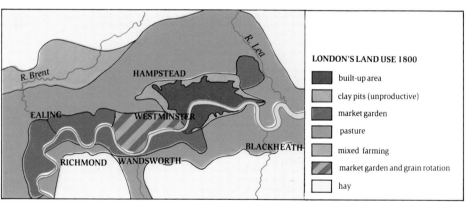

**LONDON'S LAND USE 1800**

- built-up area
- clay pits (unproductive)
- market garden
- pasture
- mixed farming
- market garden and grain rotation
- hay

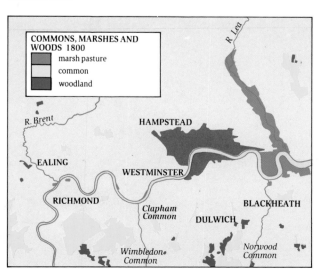

**COMMONS, MARSHES AND WOODS 1800**
- marsh pasture
- common
- woodland

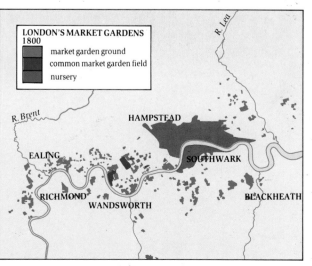

**LONDON'S MARKET GARDENS 1800**
- market garden ground
- common market garden field
- nursery

*Land use, 1746-1800  The map (top) is based on John Rocque's map of London and its environs (1746) and shows that the countryside beyond the pastoral fringe had a mixture of arable and agriculturally unproductive land. In 1800, Thomas Milne's survey (maps above, left and centre) indicate that land use was much more regularly zoned than it had ever been, the zoning being produced by market forces, not by state regulation. They also show the use of each field or parcel of land around London. A large area is unproductive marsh, wood or heath. The loams of the Thames terraces are intensively cultivated as nurseries and market gardens.*

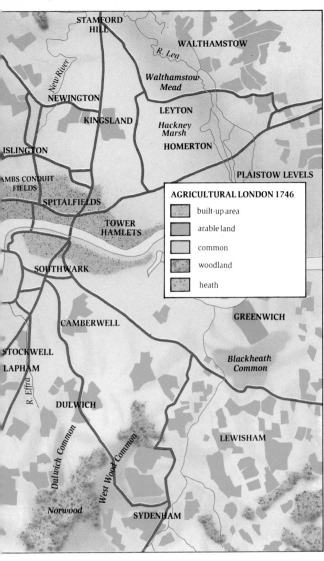

**AGRICULTURAL LONDON 1746**

- built-up area
- arable land
- common
- woodland
- heath

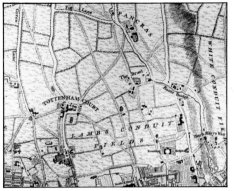

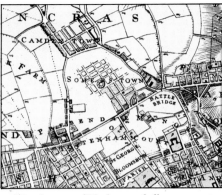

**The loss of arable land around 18th century London** is clearly evident when Rocque's map of 1746 (above left) is compared to Milne's survey of 1800 (above right). The brick and gravel pits have gone and Somers Town and Camden Town have been built.

**The 18th-century markets of London** (map below) Many markets were created during the Georgian period to serve the needs of the new building developments in the western suburbs. Other markets were Medieval legacies. As an eye-witness observed, 'Through these filthy lanes and alleys no one can pass without being butted with the dripping end of a quarter of beef, or smeared with a greasy carcase of a newly slain sheep.' The Monday market, Smithfield, shown (below) in 1811.

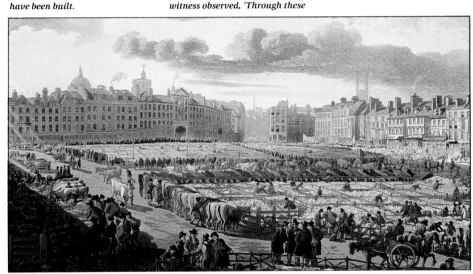

**18TH CENTURY FOOD MARKETS**

* 18th century creations
† exact date unknown

→ main droving routes into London

1. Southampton (general) 1662
2. Carnaby (general) 1690
3. St. James's (general) 1680
*4. Marylebone Fields (general) 1732
†5. Great Conduit Fields (general)
6. Great Brookfield (cattle) 1686
*7. Mortimer (general) 1768
8. Spital Square (fruit, vegetables) 1682
*9. Whitechapel (cattle, hay) 1708
10. Newgate (corn, meat) 1666
11. Honey Lane (meat, general) c.1670
†12. Holborn Bar (general)
13. Covent Garden (fruit, vegetables) 1670
14. Leadenhall (poultry, game, fruit) medieval
†15. Butchers Close (meat)
16. Fish Street Hill (fish) medieval
*17. St. George's (general) 1789
18. Smithfield (cattle) medieval
19. Billingsgate (fish, corn) medieval
†20. Whitecross Street (general)
21. Clare (meat, fish) 1657
22. Hungerford (meat, fish, vegetables) 1680
23. Berwick (general) c.1680
24. Strutton Ground (general) c.1680
25. Newport (general) 1686
†26. St. John Street (general)
27. Queenhithe (corn) 1547
†28. Bermondsey (general)
†29. Lower Marsh (general)
†30. Borough (fruit, vegetables)
*31. Fleet (fruit, vegetables) c.1740
*32. Shepherd (meat, fish, vegetables) 1735
*33. Oxford (meat, fish, vegetables) 1721
34. Haymarket (hay) 1657
35. The Stocks (meat, fish) medieval
†36. Bear Quay (corn)
†37. Islington (cattle)
38. Brooke (meat) 1692

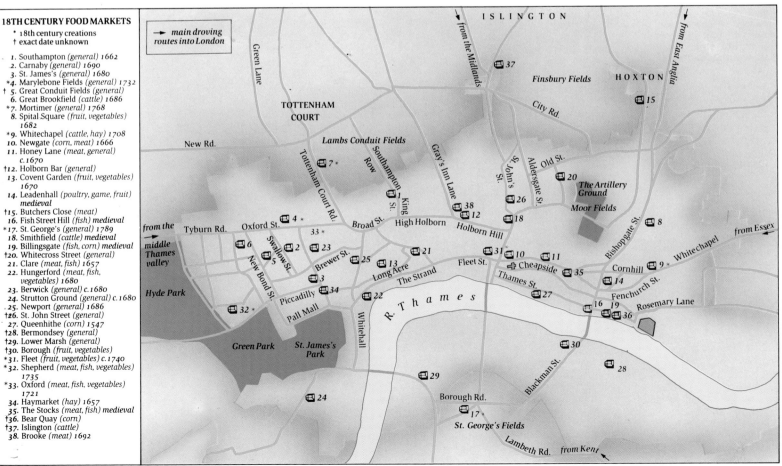

# ROADS AND BRIDGES

As London expanded it depended more and more on road transport to supply the growing metropolis with food, fodder and fuel, to carry people from home to work and to link the provinces with the capital. During the 18th century the volume of traffic on the roads into London increased prodigiously. A new and rapidly growing body of road-users consisted of those making daily journeys to work from the outskirts of London and later from places further afield. In 1725, Daniel Defoe remarked upon the large number of businessmen holding jobs in the City, at the Treasury or at Court, who lived in Epsom, where 'they look as if they had left all their London thoughts behind them'. A century later, William Cobbett observed that 'great parcels of stock jobbers ....skip backward and forward on the coaches, and actually carry on stock jobbing in Change Alley, though they reside at Brighton. There are not less than twenty coaches that leave the Wen every day for this place.'

Roads subjected to increasing wear and tear were less and less able to bear the loads thrust upon them, and in wet winter weather some roads became almost impassable. By transferring the responsibility for road maintenance from parishes to turnpike trusts and granting trusts powers to collect tolls on different classes of road users, parliament hoped improvements would be carried out, especially on heavily used roads. The earliest turnpikes were set up on the Great North Road and by 1750 trusts were established along most of its length from London to the Scottish border. The road to Harwich was turnpiked at an early date and sections of roads to Birmingham, Bristol and Portsmouth were in the hands of turnpikes before mid-century. Remarkable reductions in journey times were achieved in the second half of the 18th century. In 1706 and still in 1754 a coach from London to York took four days. By 1774 the schedule had been reduced to two days. Similar reductions were achieved on journeys to Shrewsbury and other places. Techniques of building and surfacing roads were improved, and by the end of the century investment in turnpikes was booming. Between 1790 and 1835 the number of coach passengers travelling to and from London multiplied sixteen-fold. Although stretches of turnpike roads over the clays of Middlesex, Surrey and Essex

**The principal roads from London (map below)** *The direct roads supplied the capital with food and fuel, acting as the nerve fibres of the nation's communication system. Marble Arch Turnpike, shown in a watercolour by Thomas Rowlandson, 1750 (right). A horseman, coach and trap are shown speeding away from the toll-gate on the newly laid road surface. Horse-drawn carts and coaches had difficulty climbing the steep ascents to Hampstead, Highgate and Muswell Hill (map right). Many inns offered both travellers and horses rest and refreshment.*

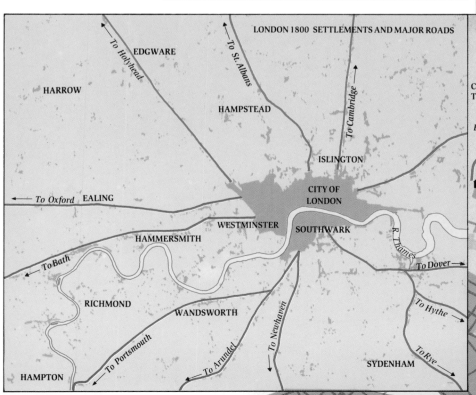

were still in no better condition than parish roads, some of the most serious defects had been remedied.

Within the built-up areas, problems caused by traffic congestion were growing worse rather than bettter. A little relief had been afforded by road-widening schemes and by laying down hard surfaces, but the greatest benefits were obtained from the building of new arterial roads. The most spectacular was the New Road, on the line of the present Marylebone, Euston and City Roads, built in 1756-61 to by-pass the built-up area between Watling Street, present Edgware Road, and Ermine Street, the present Kingsland Road. The building of Westminster Bridge in 1750 and the approach to St George's Circus provided a southern by-pass.

Until 1750 the Thames was a major barrier to road transport. There was only one bridge across the river, London Bridge, and that was encumbered with houses and shops. Upstream, the next bridge was at Putney. To cross the water or go up and down, people and goods were taken by boat. The building of six new bridges between 1750 and 1827 and the removal of buildings from London Bridge in 1759 greatly assisted movement and opened the south bank to development.

**Road improvements**  *In the early 18th century the main roads out of London were legacies from the Roman period (map top right). Medieval road builders had filled the spaces between Roman roads with an intricate network of narrow streets, lanes, alleys and courts. Every kind of traffic from droves of livestock and funeral processions to galloping courtiers exercised their rights of way and many streets also served as open sewers. An engraved view of Cornhill looking westwards (centre right), shows carriages and coaches jostling for space with draymen and wagoners. More was done to improve London's roads between 1750 and 1835 than had been done in the previous thousand years. On the north side of the metropolis, a by-pass was constructed in 1756-61 which was 120 feet wide (Marylebone, Euston and City Rd.). South of the Thames, road improvements – such as St. George's Circus, Westminster Bridge Rd. and Blackfriars Rd. – followed the building of new bridges. The first and most important was Westminster Bridge designed by the Swiss engineer Charles Labelye in 1750. It is illustrated by Canaletto in 1749 before the central arches were completed (below). In the post-Napoleonic war years, three new bridges – Vauxhall (1816), Waterloo (1817) and Southwark (1819) – were opened. Before these bridges were built, however, Londoners had to cross the Thames by boat. The King, Lord Mayor and wealthy citizens owned their own barges. Other Londoners boarded ferries at scores of stairs and landing stages (map below). The illustration of Westminster Bridge (below) shows a number of beached ferries and their passengers. The new bridge meant substantial losses in income for the Thames ferrymen, who protested bitterly, and were eventually awarded £25,000 in compensation.*

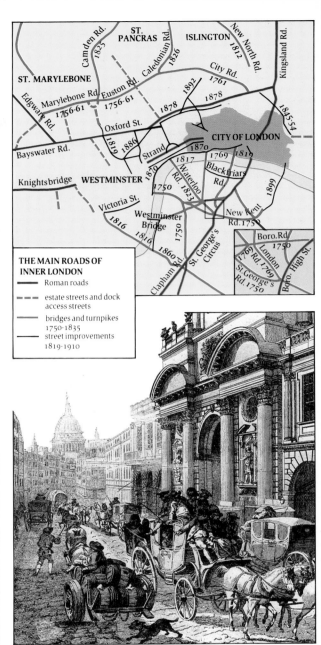

THE MAIN ROADS OF INNER LONDON
— Roman roads
--- estate streets and dock access streets
— bridges and turnpikes 1750-1835
— street improvements 1819-1910

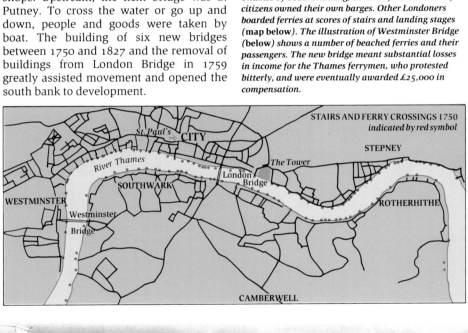

STAIRS AND FERRY CROSSINGS 1750
*indicated by red symbol*

# LONDON'S WATERWAYS

Throughout the 18th century London's maritime trade increased steadily, but the dominance of the port was challenged by an even more rapid expansion of trade at Liverpool, Bristol and other west coast ports. London retained a clear lead in the import of goods from Europe and the east: tea, coffee, pepper, spices, silks, precious metals, gemstones, porcelain, mahogany, teak and raw wool. Western ports were attracting more and more trans-Atlantic trade, importing raw cotton, tobacco, sugar, rum, furs, pine and taking increasing quantities of cocoa, rice and wine. Manufactured goods – cotton cloth from Lancashire, woollens from Yorkshire and Staffordshire pottery – were leaving the country by way of western ports.

The Thames continued to handle an enormous amount of coastal traffic. Portland stone, lime, a great variety of other building materials, shipbuilding timber as well as large quantities of staple foods reached London by water. By far the largest volume of coastal shipping was engaged in carrying sea coal from Newcastle and Sunderland: amounts carried tripled, to 1.4 million tons per annum, over the 18th century. The wherries returned laden with ballast, some of which was dug from pits at Charlton and some dredged from Dagenham Breach.

In 1700 about 435,000 tons of shipping were registered in London; by 1790 the volume had risen to 509,000 tons. In 1800, in addition to 1200 or more sea-going vessels, the waterway was crowded with 1200 coal barges, 500 timber barges, 800 lighters and over 1000 smaller craft handling freight. Ships waited days for favourable winds, high tides and berths at legal quays where customs officers could inspect cargoes. Delays added to the risks of damage and plundering. In 1801 West Indies merchants lost on average 2% of their revenue through theft on the waterway. Partly because of silting in the channel, large ships, drawing 6.7 tons of water could not sail beyond Blackwall.

To relieve crowding in the Pool of London between the Tower and London Bridge, it was decided to construct secure, deep water basins off the busy waterway. The London Docks downstream from the Tower were first opened in 1801. They were accompanied by the building of massive blocks of warehouses in Wapping. The cutting of the West India Docks across the neck of the Isle of Dogs was followed by the opening of Commercial Road in 1803 and the erection of ranges of well-guarded warehouses. Smaller docks for the East India trade were dug at Blackwall, accompanied by an extension of East India Dock Road. The Surrey Commercial Docks were connected to the river by the Grand Surrey Canal and traffic from the midlands was brought by the Grand Junction Canal to Paddington and round the northern fringes of London to the Western Docks at Limehouse.

Above the Pool of London the Thames was a major inland waterway, with a catchment area extending over much of southern and central England. Surrey, parts of Sussex and Hampshire were reached by the Mole and Wey navigations. Reading was connected by the Kennet-Avon Canal with Bath and Bristol and the navigable Thames was linked to Birmingham through the Oxford and Coventry Canals.

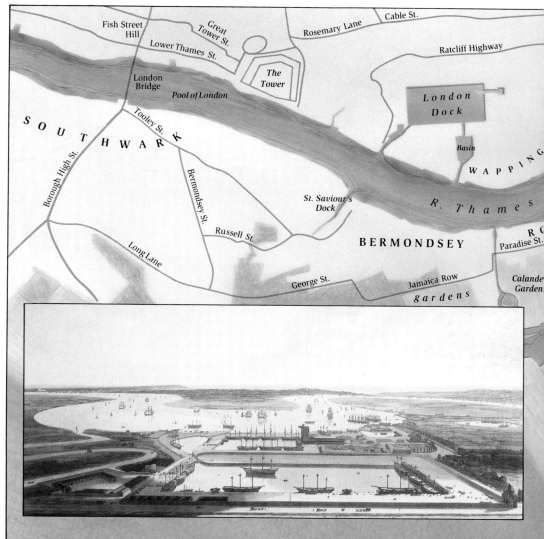

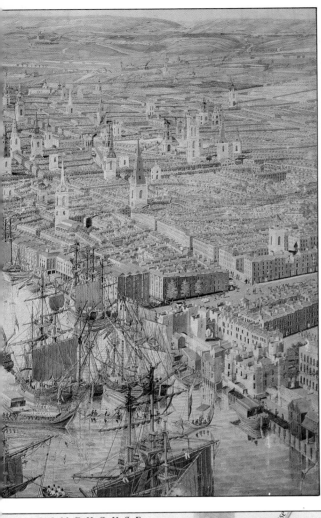

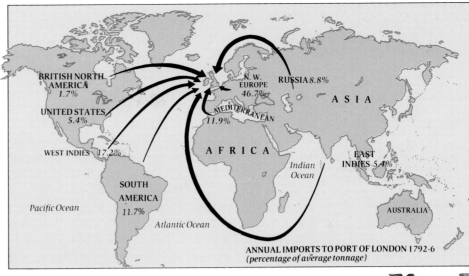

ANNUAL IMPORTS TO PORT OF LONDON 1792-6
(percentage of average tonnage)

**BRITISH NORTH AMERICA** *1.7%*
**UNITED STATES** *5.4%*
**WEST INDIES** *17.2%*
**SOUTH AMERICA** *11.7%*
**N. W. EUROPE** *46.7%*
**RUSSIA** *8.8%*
**MEDITERRANEAN** *11.9%*
**EAST INDIES** *5.4%*

**The Pool of London, c. 1820 (left)**
*The Rheinbeck Panorama depicts the Thames below London Bridge crowded with the masts of ships moored alongside wharves and warehouses. Above London Bridge lighters, barges and ferries carried passengers and freight upstream.*
**World trade 1792-96 (map above)**
*Arrows showing the comparative tonnage of goods imported to London indicate that increasing volumes of trade were with Britain's colonial territories. By far the largest growth in tonnage handled during the 18th century as the coastal trade in coal. The old Coal Exchange, (right) was on Lower Thames Street adjacent to St Dunstan's workhouse*

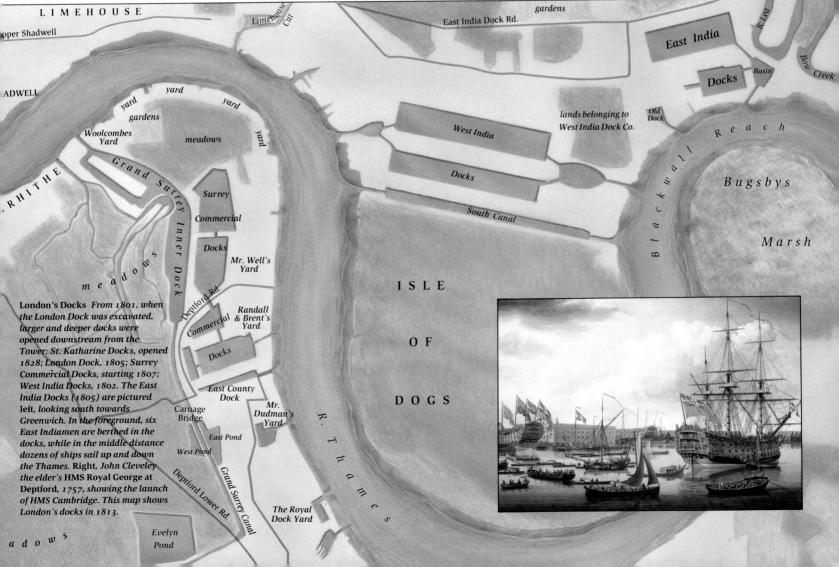

**London's Docks** *From 1801, when the London Dock was excavated, larger and deeper docks were opened downstream from the Tower: St. Katharine Docks, opened 1828; London Dock, 1805; Surrey Commercial Docks, starting 1807; West India Docks, 1802. The East India Docks (1805) are pictured left, looking south towards Greenwich. In the foreground, six East Indiamen are berthed in the docks, while in the middle distance dozens of ships sail up and down the Thames. Right, John Cleveley the elder's HMS Royal George at Deptford, 1757, showing the launch of HMS Cambridge. This map shows London's docks in 1813.*

# CHAPTER 7
# VICTORIAN LONDON

A hundred years ago smoke from Doulton's potteries polluted the atmosphere of Lambeth almost opposite the Houses of Parliament. The owners claimed the hydrochloric acid was harmless, despite trees in the neighbourhood being killed. In 2002 archaeologists excavated the remains of five kilns packed behind a pub and a row of tenements. Abundant evidence was found of the mundane stoneware bottles for ginger beer, lemonade and ink made on this site. Other potteries in Lambeth produced drain pipes, art ware and architectural ceramics, for which the name of Doulton is remembered.

Refer to pages 92-93 for a discussion of changes in the industrial structure of London.

THE 19TH CENTURY saw an unprecedented explosion in London's population: in 1801 the population of Greater London was just over one million, by 1911 it had increased to over seven million. The enormous physical expansion that accompanied this population growth meant that new forms of public transport became increasingly necessary: horse buses after 1829; railways in the 1830s; an underground railway system from the 1860s; trams in the 1870s; deep-level electric 'tube' trains in the 1890s. However, access to buses, trams and trains was linked to ability to pay, and this led to an increasing segregation of different classes. The better-off moved to suburbia first, while the poor remained in inner London within walking distance of work. The introduction of 'workmen's fares' in east London in the 1860s and more widely after 1883, and the electrification of tramways during the early 1900s, meant that the regularly employed could also move to new working-class suburbs, but casual labourers on building sites and in docks and markets still needed to live close to places where they might be able to find employment.

In Regency London, many of the poor still lived close to the rich, directly dependent on them for their employment. Gradually the class structure changed. New business practices and the expansion of administration called into being a 'lower middle class' of clerks and book-keepers, caricatured by George and Weedon Grossmith in the person of Mr Pooter, in *The Diary of a Nobody* (1892). Mechanisation in industry led to 'de-skilling', as artisans found themselves superseded by machines. This, in turn, led to the creation of a labour aristocracy of skilled workers, especially engineers, who built and maintained the new machines. These new classes provided an additional source of demand for manufactured goods. Instead of providing made-to-order goods for the elite, London's artisans increasingly concentrated on mass production of off-the-peg items for the newly affluent. The links between manufacturer and customer became impersonal and indirect. Factories replaced workshops and domestic industry; and the owners of businesses were less likely to know their employees by name.

In such a rapidly growing city, where for most people status was now earned rather than inherited, families sought to emphasise their position in society by retreating into one-class residential areas, ensuring that they had the best address that they could afford. In the novels of George Gissing, characters

Refer to pages 90-91 for a detailed discussion of the evolution of transport in Victorian London.

A visitor to the Wandle Valley in 1805 asserted that this was 'the hardest worked river for its size in the world'. That industrial activity has now disappeared from the suburban landscape of Merton but recent discoveries confirm that the valley once contained 90 watermills. In the 17th century the site produced textiles, including calico handkerchiefs using fine cotton imported from India. In 1881 William Morris set up workshops to print wallpaper there.

See pages 88-89 for a discussion of the evolution of London housing over the 19th century.

often lived not just in genuine districts of London, but in particular streets; to know their address was to know their status, their morals and their lifestyle. Having become part of London's class of *nouveaux riches*, the Frothinghams (in *The Whirlpool*, 1897) 'after obscure prosperity in a southern suburb ... fluttered to the northern heights' to a house in 'Fitzjohn Avenue', almost certainly Fitzjohn's Avenue, Hampstead. Later, after Bennet Frothingham's suicide, following the collapse of his 'Britannia Loan, Assurance, Investment, and Banking Co.', his widow and daughter moved to a flat in Swiss Cottage, supposedly a new and simple lifestyle: 'Just one servant, who can't make mistakes, because there's next to nothing to do. No wonder people are taking to flats.' Flats were frequently associated with an amoral modernism. They were at first called 'French Flats' to signify both their origin and the cosmopolitan, reputedly scandalous lifestyle of their inhabitants. In *The Whirlpool* Gissing situated the much travelled, dissolute and, significantly, childless Carnabys first in a house in Hamilton Terrace, St John's Wood, but later in Oxford and Cambridge Mansions, a real block of apartments, built in 1882, just four years before the setting of the novel, on the edge of Hyde Park. By contrast, the more conventional, established middle-class Harvey Rolfe moves, after his marriage, to a house in Pinner, outside the built-up area of London, but conveniently situated on the Metropolitan Railway, which had reached Pinner from Baker Street in 1885. Farther down the social hierarchy were suburbs like Crouch End, to which Sidney and Clara Kirkwood moved (in *The Nether World*, 1889) in an effort to escape the oppressive poverty of Clerkenwell. Crouch End in 1885 was 'still able to remind one that it was in the country a very short time ago. The streets have a smell of newness, of dampness; the bricks retain their complexion, the stucco has not rotted more than one expects in a year or two; poverty tries to hide itself with venetian blinds'.

Gissing was the literary counterpart to social researchers like Charles Booth, who worked in conjunction with School Board officers whose job was to ensure that all children of school age attended elementary schools, thereby acquiring an enormous fund of information about families in their area. Charles Booth calculated that more than 30% of Londoners were living below the poverty line in the 1890s. He reckoned that 'questions of employment', especially irregular earnings, accounted for 68% of cases of poverty, 'questions of circumstances', such as illness or large families, for 19%, and 'questions of habit' – drunkenness and thriftlessness – for only 13%. Yet it was the latter causes of poverty, focusing on the inadequacy of the individual, which attracted most attention among Booth's contemporaries. London was described as a 'modern Babylon', a decadent society sure to suffer ultimate destruction. The East End was variously described as an 'inferno', a 'city of dreadful night', 'outcast London', inhabited by 'people of the abyss', trapped in a 'nether world'. These perceptions could be sustained because, of course, most middle-class Londoners never went anywhere near the East End. Increasing residential segregation provided an environment in which ignorance and prejudice could flourish, reinforced by a press which seized every opportunity to spread panic among middle-class readers with tales of incest, crime, riot and the breakdown of social order. Not surprisingly, these rumours made the middle classes even less likely to settle in east London.

The housing problem of Victorian London was attributable to both the city's size and its industrial structure. To live within walking distance of work in, for instance, Covent Garden, Smithfield, London Docks or the major railway termini, was to live

*See pages 102-103 for a full discussion of Charles Booth's social research. An examination of the Victorian church on page 97 is also based on research by Charles Booth.*

*Left  A bird's eye view of the City from the west (1832-46). Although London was already beginning to spread, the massive expansion of the 19th century had not yet begun and countryside was still visible at the edges of the city. By 1900, successive building booms had transformed London into a scattered metropolis which continued to absorb, organically, the villages and local communities still visible on this panorama. This scattered city was tied together by the innovation and adaptation of new modes of transport; carriages, cabs, omnibuses, trams, railways. By 1900, railway-based tentacles of suburban growth were beginning to extend away from the city, precursors of an even greater dispersal that would come to dominate the 20th century.*

*The social researcher, Charles Booth, estimated that 30% of Londoners were living in poverty in 1890. Among his contemporaries William Booth, founder of the Salvation Army, blamed the habits of the poor as much as their economic circumstances. While he acknowledged the lack of sanitation and the inhumanity of sweated labour he stressed: 'Drunkenness and all manner of uncleanness, moral and physical, abound ... As in Africa streams intersect the forest in every direction, so the gin-shop stands at every corner with its River of the Water of Death flowing seventeen hours of the twenty-four for the destruction of the people'. Below  a typical Victorian slum street, Little Saffron Hill, in the 1890s.*

within an inner ring of pre-Victorian houses that had decayed into overpriced and overcrowded slums by the middle of the 19th century. Moreover, compared to smaller cities, London had proportionally more casual workers who needed to live close to places where they might find work. London was also the country's largest industrial city; in 1861, there were more manufacturing workers in London than the entire population of Manchester, but most worked for very small firms. Unlike industrialists in northern towns, few London employers were either sufficiently wealthy or felt it necessary for the success of their business to provide housing for their employees. Consequently, working-class Londoners depended for their accommodation on speculative builders and private landlords. Under the Cross Act (1875), the Metropolitan Board of Works could engage in slum clearance but was not permitted to undertake new housing construction. The cleared sites were sold to philanthropic or 'five per cent' agencies like the Peabody Trust and the East End Dwellings Company. Rebuilding *in situ*, however sanitary the new buildings, did not relieve problems of congestion so, from the 1880s, more reformers favoured a suburban solution, building cottage estates and garden suburbs, although these were only practicable when cheap fares on public transport became widely available. Suburban living might be healthier, but it had its drawbacks. Food was more expensive in suburban shops than inner-city markets, workers could not go home for lunch, there were few jobs for women. Although housing was better in quality, it was rarely any cheaper. For casual labourers a suburban base was impracticable.

In 1800 most Londoners lived in terraced houses. Middle-class Londoners often shared the use of a communal garden, situated in the centre of a square, as in Bloomsbury, Bayswater and Islington. Working-class Londoners were more likely to live facing an enclosed court, sharing more mundane facilities, like communal privies or water taps. Alternatively, they took rooms in old

*Refer to pages 100-101 for a discussion of slum conditions and philanthropic solutions to the housing problem.*

**Below** *The Charing Cross Hotel in the Strand. Designed by E. M. Barry and built in 1863-4, it was one of the first major buildings in London to be faced with artificial stone. Railway hotels were a 19th century phenomenon, attached to all the mainline railway termini. Charing Cross Hotel was built over Charing Cross station, which in turn was built on the site of the old Hungerford Market at the same time as the hotel. Charing Cross was the terminus of the South Eastern Railway.*

middle-class houses that were subdivided among several families. Nobody lived in purpose-built flats. By 1900, detached and semi-detached villas with their own private gardens typified middle-class suburbs; the better-off working classes lived in suburban terraced housing; in inner London an increasing proportion of both rich and poor lived in purpose-built flats – the latter in philanthropic dwellings and, after 1890, in blocks of council flats, the former in luxury apartments that first appeared near Victoria Street in the 1850s and around the Albert Hall in the 1870s.

London was also a city of migrants. Between 1841 and 1871, almost a million migrants came to London; many moving directly from East Anglia or the West Country to suburban Essex, Middlesex and Surrey. Whereas the majority of English migrants were skilled artisans or domestic servants, migrants from Ireland congregated in the poorest districts of inner London and in the worst jobs, as casual labourers or in tailoring or shoemaking sweatshops. By 1861 there were an estimated 178,000 Irish in London, nearly all Catholic, concentrated in Holborn, St Giles (which was nicknamed 'Little Dublin'), Whitechapel and Southwark. There was already a long established Jewish population in London, but London Jewry increased rapidly in the 1880s, as Jews fled from persecution in eastern Europe. By 1914, there were 140,000 Jews in London. They concentrated in the East End, working like the Irish before them in the sweated trades, but also establishing their own businesses, usually employing co-immigrants. Their presence provoked resentment and violence, especially at times of economic depression.

*Refer to pages 136-137 for a discussion of both Jewish and Irish immigration in the 19th century.*

For all the squalor of slum life, Victorian London was also the 'Heart of the Empire' and the financial capital of the world. New types of building for new business and administrative activities ranged from the office blocks of the City and Whitehall to the department stores of the West End. Mainline railway termini contained spectacular train sheds, such as W. H. Barlow's magnificent 240-feet single span in glass and iron at St Pancras, and Brunel's more cathedral-like pattern of aisles and transepts at Paddington. There were also exhibition buildings, museums, art galleries and concert halls. The Crystal Palace, designed for the 1851 Great Exhibition in Hyde Park, was intended to be temporary, but was subsequently re-erected in south London. The Victoria and Albert Museum opened in 1857, the National Portrait Gallery moved to its present site in 1895, and the Tate Gallery was erected on the site of Millbank Prison in 1897. The non-denominational University College was founded in 1826, while a rival, Anglican-inspired, King's College opened in 1831. More starkly utilitarian buildings included workhouses, prisons, hospitals and infirmaries.

*For the story of Harrods see page 149.*

*The Great Exhibition is discussed in full on pages 94-95.*

*For further details of hospitals, refer to page 96, and for a discussion of prisons refer to page 99.*

Both the layout and the geographical distribution of pubs, theatres and even churches reflected the Victorian compulsion to classify and segregate their patrons, audiences and congregations. Even in death, social geography was critical. Private cemetery companies divided their cemeteries into separate consecrated and unconsecrated areas for different denominations and graded the size and cost of grave plots. Pubs were divided up into separate compartments, or at least into lounge, saloon and public bar. Huge theatres like the Britannia, Hoxton, which had seats for 3,450 people, contained a variety of tiers with differential pricing. There were also music halls, predominantly suburban in location, although the most prestigious were in the West End, notably the Alhambra Palace in Leicester Square. As early as 1896 the Alhambra began to incorporate film scenes in its performances, including newsreels of events such as the Queen's Diamond Jubilee in 1897, and also short melodramas, initially filmed on an open-air set on the roof of the music hall. By the early 1900s a film industry had been created, with studios concentrated in upwind, fog-free suburbs like Ealing. London was entering the age of mass consumption, mass transit and mass media.

*Cemeteries are discussed on page 166.*

**Map below** *The extent of Victorian London at its peak is contrasted to the size of the city today.*

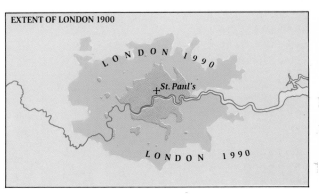

EXTENT OF LONDON 1900

LONDON 1990

+St. Paul's

LONDON 1990

# THE GROWTH OF 19TH-CENTURY LONDON

In the 1820s William Cobbett described London as 'The Great Wen', a cancer-like growth on the face of Britain, already embracing a population of one and a half million. By the end of Queen Victoria's reign, London's population included four and a half million inhabitants within the administrative limits of the County of London, but another two million in 'Greater London' beyond the jurisdiction of the newly-created London County Council. The map (*right*) plots this spectacular expansion.

Rates of housebuilding fluctuated much more than rates of population growth. In general, builders over-reacted to economic booms and slumps. In response to boom conditions they would build too many houses too late, so that, by the time the houses were ready for occupancy, demand was on the wane, leaving a glut of unsaleable properties. When prosperity returned, builders would react too slowly, and working-class families would be forced to take in lodgers to help pay increasing rents, or to 'double-up' with other families.

As in Georgian and Regency London, the great landed estates in the West End controlled development by specifying what kinds of buildings could be erected and how they were to be used, forbidding industrial and commercial uses, and sometimes employing gatekeepers to regulate access by non-residents. Some landowners introduced forms of land-use zoning: along the northern edge of Mayfair, between Grosvenor Square and Oxford Street, the Duke of Westminster promoted the construction of blocks of working-class 'model dwellings' as a kind of *cordon sanitaire* between the luxury houses in the heart of his estate and the commercial disorder of Oxford Street. The houses could also accommodate the army of artisans and tradesmen who relied upon the patronage of the rich.

It is interesting to compare the terraced houses, squares and crescents of Bayswater and Belgravia with the detached villas and individual private gardens on the Clapham Park Estate, developed by Thomas Cubitt in south London. Substantial terraces continued to be built in west London but many quickly became unfashionable; in North Paddington, for instance, large terraced houses were subdivided for occupancy by several working-class or lower middle-class families. There were always more middle-class houses built than there were families to occupy them. Hence the decline into seedy shabbiness of estates in Notting Hill and south of King's Cross, the latter brilliantly depicted in George Gissing's *The Nether World* (1889) and Arnold Bennett's *Riceyman Steps* (1923).

The new lower middle class of clerks, bookkeepers and schoolteachers mostly found homes in suburbs like Holloway and Camberwell, linked to the City by horse trams and suburban trains. These suburbs, in turn, were a cut above respectable working-class districts, which were located close to major industrial zones – around the Great Eastern Railway works in Stratford, for example, or following the line of the London and Greenwich Railway through Bermondsey and Deptford. London was not only developing into a 'monster city', but its population was becoming distributed into distinctive social areas by its status and ability to pay.

**LONDON'S POPULATION 1801-1911**

1801 — City / Rest of Greater London / County of London — TOTAL POPULATION 1,114,000

1861 — City / Rest of Greater London / County of London — TOTAL POPULATION 3,223,000

1911 — City / County of London / Rest of Greater London — TOTAL POPULATION 7,251,000

*The population of Greater London increased during the Victorian period, but the City and many inner districts lost residents: Finsbury, Marylebone, Westminster and Shoreditch all peaked in 1861; Islington, Southwark, Bermondsey and St. Pancras in 1896. The pie-charts (above) illustrate the disposition of London's inhabitants.*

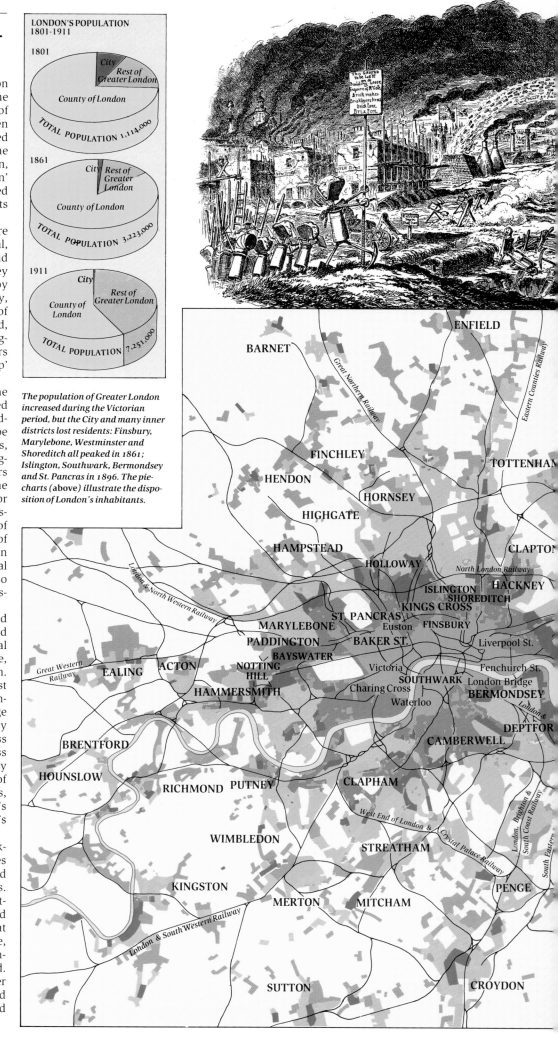

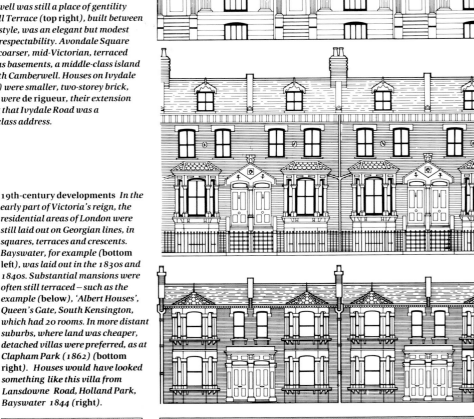

**The urban expansion** *As early as 1829 George Cruikshank dramatically caricatured the trauma of urban expansion in his cartoon of 'London Going Out of Town – The March of Bricks and Mortar' (left). Cruikshank lived in Amwell Street, close to Islington Fields, which were undergoing just such an invasion in the 1820s: farmland first became brickfields; streets were marked out by developers such as Thomas Cubitt; finally, a host of small speculative builders would acquire 'building leases'.*

*Until the 1840s Camberwell was still a place of gentility and even rusticity. Glengall Terrace (top right), built between 1843 and 1845 in Grecian style, was an elegant but modest expression of the suburb's respectability. Avondale Square (1875) (right) comprised coarser, mid-Victorian, terraced houses with attics as well as basements, a middle-class island in otherwise decaying North Camberwell. Houses on Ivydale Road (1900) (below right) were smaller, two-storey brick, slate-roofed; bay windows were de rigueur, their extension over both floors indicating that Ivydale Road was a respectable lower middle-class address.*

**19th-century developments** *In the early part of Victoria's reign, the residential areas of London were still laid out on Georgian lines, in squares, terraces and crescents. Bayswater, for example (bottom left), was laid out in the 1830s and 1840s. Substantial mansions were often still terraced – such as the example (below), 'Albert Houses', Queen's Gate, South Kensington, which had 20 rooms. In more distant suburbs, where land was cheaper, detached villas were preferred, as at Clapham Park (1862) (bottom right). Houses would have looked something like this villa from Lansdowne Road, Holland Park, Bayswater 1844 (right).*

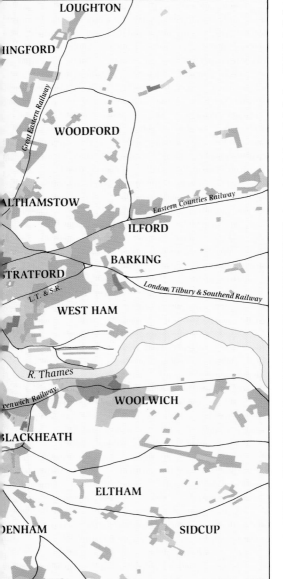

LONDON'S GROWTH 1800-1914

| | |
|---|---|
| ▨ 1800 | ▨ 1900 |
| ▨ 1845 | ▨ 1914 |
| ▨ 1860 | —— main railways, 1914 |
| ▨ 1880 | |

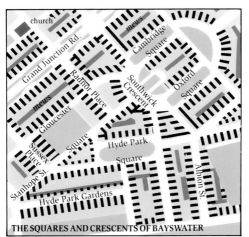

THE SQUARES AND CRESCENTS OF BAYSWATER

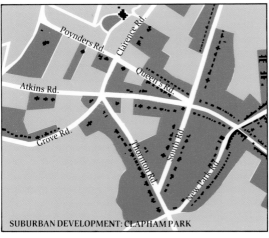

SUBURBAN DEVELOPMENT: CLAPHAM PARK

# THE TRANSPORT REVOLUTION

At the beginning of the 19th century, 'public transport' in London comprised short-stage coaches, hackney carriages, and ferry-boats, all affordable only by the better-off. So, when George Shillibeer introduced his 20-seater coaches in 1829, which operated along the New Road from Paddington to the City with fares as low as sixpence, he followed the Parisian practice of calling them 'omnibuses', for *all* the people. Even sixpence was beyond the means of most Londoners, and horse-buses remained a middle-class form of transport. Nevertheless, by 1850 there were more than 1300 buses on the streets of London; fierce competition between rival private operators, larger vehicles with rooftop seats, and tax cuts all allowed cheaper fares. Reduced profit margins led inevitably to rationalisation later in the 1850s, and most operators were taken over by the French-backed London General Omnibus Company. By 1875, the company could boast almost 50 million passengers per annum.

Many omnibus routes linked the City and West End to the earliest railway termini, sited on the edge of the built-up area, often some way short of the termini we know today. The London & Southampton Railway ended at Nine Elms (1838), extending to Waterloo ten years later; the first 'West End' terminus of the London & Brighton and South Eastern Railways was at Bricklayers Arms, off the Old Kent Road (1844). On these peripheral sites, land was relatively cheap and there were less likely to be delays negotiating the compulsory purchase of property that was already in profitable use. Even so, some demolition was usually necessary: the cutting of the path of the London & Birmingham Railway through Camden Town is dramatically described by Dickens in *Dombey and Son*.

The earliest passenger railway in London was the London & Greenwich (1836), running south-east from London Bridge on a four-mile viaduct. The company planned a 'promenade' alongside the viaduct, and hoped to utilise the arches for shops and houses, but in fact, urban railway viaducts everywhere brought blight, not prestige, to their surroundings. While the London & Greenwich was a commuter railway from the beginning, companies to the north and west of London regarded suburban trains as an awkward inconvenience, getting in the way of more lucrative mainline traffic. When the Great Western opened in 1838, the first station out of Paddington was West Drayton, thirteen miles away. Suburban traffic did become more important; but for the moment it remained primarily middle-class.

The Railway Mania of the 1840s generated so many competing schemes, all vying for access to the heart of the city, that a Royal Commission recommended in 1846 that no further railway lines should be built in central London. Where extensions were subsequently authorised, for example from London Bridge to Charing Cross (opened in 1864) and Cannon Street (1866), large-scale demolition proved necessary, displacing at least 76,000 of the poorest Londoners between 1855 and 1900, and intensifying overcrowding in the slum districts that survived. From the 1860s some companies were obliged by government to run cheap workmen's trains, to compensate for the displacements they had caused: this was the price paid by the Great Eastern Railway for its extension from Bishopsgate to Liverpool Street (1874). More generally, the Cheap Trains Act (1883) required all companies to offer workmen's fares on early morning and evening services, as directed by the Board of Trade. By October 1911, out of 390,000 passengers carried each weekday by twelve leading companies from stations 4-30 miles distant from central London, more than 105,000 travelled on workmen's tickets. There were also workmen's fares on new tube railways, such as the City & South London (1890), and on trams. Nevertheless there were still few working-class commuters on the Great Western or London

& North Western lines; the East End–West End dichotomy in London's social geography was re-emphasised and extended.

Railways left their mark in other ways. Mainline termini attracted grand hotels. Regular shopping trips to the West End became possible, stimulating the growth of department stores. Offices, shops and newly fashionable luxury flats lined Victoria Street, linking Victoria Station to Westminster. Farther out, tangles of junctions and marshalling yards isolated communities on 'the wrong side of the tracks'. Engine sheds and railway works became foci for suburban employment, for example in Stratford and Battersea.

Apart from three short-lived demonstration lines laid by an American promoter, George Francis Train, in 1861, the earliest horse tramways in London date from the 1870s. Horse trams were cheaper than buses, carried more passengers and operated earlier in the morning and later at night. They were the making of modest but respectable suburbs like Holloway and Camberwell. But the electrification of tramways in the early 1900s heralded a new era. The electric tramcar became the 'gondola of the people', used for weekend trips to parks, countryside and football matches, as well as for journeys to work. Neither horse-drawn nor electric trams were allowed in the City or West End; the only connection between north and south London systems was through the Kingsway Tunnel, opened in 1908.

*The railway era Two paintings depict the romance of the railway: John O'Connor's 'St Pancras Hotel and Station from Pentonville Road: Sunset' (1884) (above) and Camille Pissarro's 'Lordship Lane Station, Upper Norwood' (1871) (bottom). The clock-tower at King's Cross (1852) can be seen to the right of St Pancras Hotel, begun in 1867. Lordship Lane, on the Crystal Palace & South London Junction Railway, opened in 1865. A few substantial villas had already been built in the area (below left). By 1888 (below right) much more development had occurred to the north of the station and around the railway station at Forest Hill. The map (top right) shows the evolution of London's railways, and includes shallow underground lines (such as the Metropolitan and District), but omits the first deep tubes which date from the 1890s. Two graphs (right) show patterns of suburban passenger traffic in October 1911, by company and by distance travelled.*

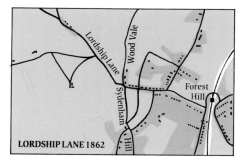

LORDSHIP LANE 1862

LORDSHIP LANE: 1888

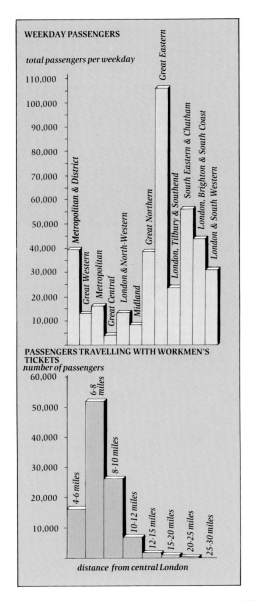

## WEEKDAY PASSENGERS

*total passengers per weekday*

110,000
100,000
90,000
80,000
70,000
60,000
50,000
40,000
30,000
20,000
10,000

Metropolitan & District
Great Western
Metropolitan
Great Central
London & North-Western
Midland
Great Northern
Great Eastern
London, Tilbury & Southend
South Eastern & Chatham
London, Brighton & South Coast
London & South Western

## PASSENGERS TRAVELLING WITH WORKMEN'S TICKETS
*number of passengers*

60,000
50,000
40,000
30,000
20,000
10,000

4-6 miles
6-8 miles
8-10 miles
10-12 miles
12-15 miles
15-20 miles
20-25 miles
25-30 miles

*distance from central London*

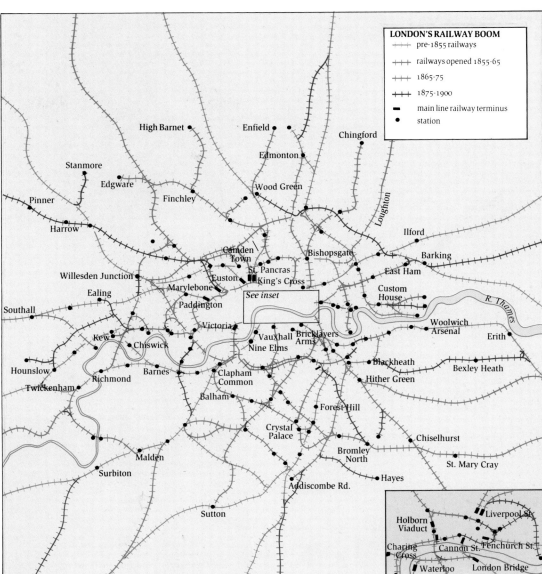

### LONDON'S RAILWAY BOOM

- pre-1855 railways
- railways opened 1855-65
- 1865-75
- 1875-1900
- main line railway terminus
- • station

High Barnet · Enfield · Chingford · Stanmore · Edmonton · Edgware · Finchley · Wood Green · Loughton · Pinner · Ilford · Harrow · Camden Town · Bishopsgate · Barking · Willesden Junction · St. Pancras · King's Cross · East Ham · Ealing · Marylebone · Custom House · Southall · Euston · Paddington · R. Thames · Victoria · Woolwich Arsenal · Kew · Chiswick · Vauxhall · Bricklayers Arms · Erith · Hounslow · Barnes · Nine Elms · Blackheath · Bexley Heath · Twickenham · Richmond · Clapham Common · Hither Green · Balham · Forest Hill · Malden · Crystal Palace · Chiselhurst · Surbiton · Bromley North · St. Mary Cray · Addiscombe Rd. · Hayes · Sutton

*See inset*

**Inset:** Holborn Viaduct · Liverpool St. · Charing Cross · Cannon St. · Fenchurch St. · Waterloo · London Bridge

**London's trams** *The map (right) shows the chronology of tramway construction prior to 1895. Services were run by private companies, of which the largest was the North Metropolitan, one of whose cars is shown outside the West Ham Union workhouse in 1890 (far right). The City remained the preserve of cabs and horse buses (bottom right); the bridge across Ludgate Hill carried the only mainline railway to cross central London.*

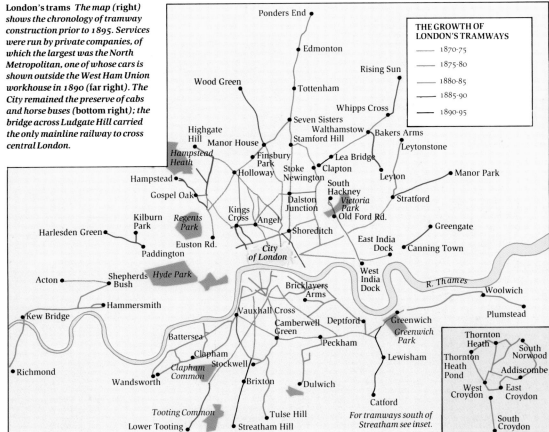

### THE GROWTH OF LONDON'S TRAMWAYS

- 1870-75
- 1875-80
- 1880-85
- 1885-90
- 1890-95

Ponders End · Edmonton · Rising Sun · Wood Green · Tottenham · Whipps Cross · Seven Sisters · Walthamstow · Bakers Arms · Highgate Hill · Stamford Hill · Leytonstone · Manor House · Finsbury Park · Lea Bridge · Hampstead Heath · Holloway · Stoke Newington · Clapton · Leyton · Hampstead · South Hackney · Manor Park · Gospel Oak · Dalston Junction · Victoria Park · Stratford · Kilburn Park · Regents Park · Kings Cross · Old Ford Rd. · Harlesden Green · Angel · Shoreditch · Greengate · Euston Rd. · East India Dock · Paddington · City of London · Canning Town · Acton · Shepherds Bush · Hyde Park · West India Dock · Kew Bridge · Hammersmith · R. Thames · Woolwich · Vauxhall Cross · Deptford · Plumstead · Richmond · Battersea · Camberwell Green · Greenwich · Clapham · Peckham · Greenwich Park · Wandsworth · Stockwell · Clapham Common · Brixton · Dulwich · Lewisham · Tooting Common · Tulse Hill · Catford · Lower Tooting · Streatham Hill

**Inset:** Thornton Heath · South Norwood · Thornton Heath Pond · Addiscombe · West Croydon · East Croydon · South Croydon

*For tramways south of Streatham see inset.*

# VICTORIAN INDUSTRY

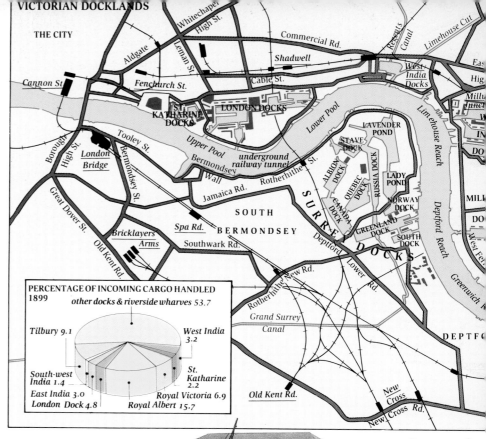

19th-century London was a city of small workshops. In 1851, 86 per cent of industrial employers in London had less than ten workers; and only 17 establishments employed more than 250 persons. During the century, some major London industries declined as a consequence of technological change and the extension of free trade. London's shipbuilding industry, for example, collapsed in the 1860s; timber hulls had been replaced by iron, and the more spacious sites on the Clyde and Tyneside provided the room to build and launch much larger vessels.

18th-century trades, such as clothing and shoe-making, had concentrated in small workshops, mostly in the West End, close to the homes of wealthy customers. During the 19th century, they were replaced by a mass-produced industry, making lower quality goods for purchase 'off the peg' by the new proletariat and lower-middle class. New forms of production were much larger in scale, but involved less skill and a more intricate division of labour: workers were now more often female, paid by the piece, employed either in sweat-shops or, as outworkers, in their own homes.

By the early 20th century, however, new and larger-scale industries in suburban London – Greenwich, Woolwich, West Ham, Enfield – were increasing in importance. In 1907 there was an average of 20 employees per factory or workshop in Greater London; but the figure in Woolwich was 69. The Edwardian era also saw the beginning of new electrical industries, vehicle manufacture (such as the Matchless motorcycle works, established in Plumstead in 1899), and an entertainment industry, prompting the location of film studios in relatively unpolluted areas of west London such as Ealing. Printing and photographic industries also moved to the pure air of western suburbs; Kodak located in Harrow as early as 1892.

The fortunes of Thameside industrial districts such as West Ham and Poplar were closely associated with the 19th-century expansion of the docks, intended to rid the river of growing congestion. By 1830, the docks dealt with most overseas trade, much of it with the British Empire, but riverside wharves still accommodated coastal traffic (from the British Isles), almost three-quarters of the total. Labour relations in the docks were often strained, reflecting a system of mainly casual labour which denied most dockers any guarantee of regular work, and culminating in a bitter Dock Strike in 1889. On average, 55 per cent of labourers seeking dock work were turned away. It is not surprising that dockers' wives and children were obliged to seek paid work themselves. Boys left school at the earliest opportunity to become newsvendors and errand boys, work which appeared well-paid in the short term, but which condemned them for life to the ranks of the uneducated and unskilled, thereby perpetuating a vicious circle of poverty.

**Victorian Docklands** *The map (top) and table (far right) show the evolution of London's docks. The Port of London Authority took control of the entire system in 1909. By the 1880s, between 50,000 and 100,000 men depended on the docks and riverside wharves for their employment. The graph (above right) shows the number of vessels engaged in foreign trade entering and leaving the Port of London. The average size of ships increased dramatically between 1861 and 1899. Net registered tonnage rose from 3.1 million tons in 1861 to 9.2 million in 1899 (imports), and from 1.6 million to 6.0 million tons (exports). The photograph (right) shows the busy waterfront between Yardley's Wharf and Braithwaite & Dean's Wharf (on the south bank, backing onto Rotherhithe Street), as it existed in 1937. The labour-intensive nature of cargo-handling in the docks in pre-container days is clearly evident (far right).*

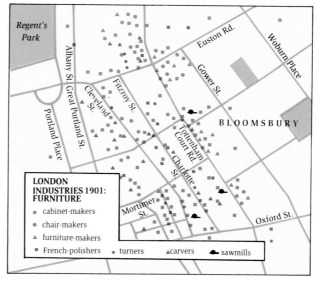

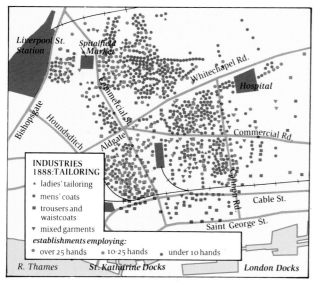

**London's Industry** *The map (far left) plots the vast number of tiny tailoring workshops in the East End, each with its own speciality. By the 1900s small workshops were giving way to much larger clothing factories, such as Schneider's in Whitechapel (above), which employed mainly young immigrants. Similar patterns and degrees of specialisation characterised other industries, such as furniture manufacturing around Tottenham Court Road (map left) and Curtain Road. The map (right) shows large factories in the County of London in 1898. West Ham, just outside the LCC area, had a wide range of industry (far right): from the Royal Docks, sugar refineries, chemical works and distilleries in the lower Lea Valley, to the Stratford railway works in the north.*

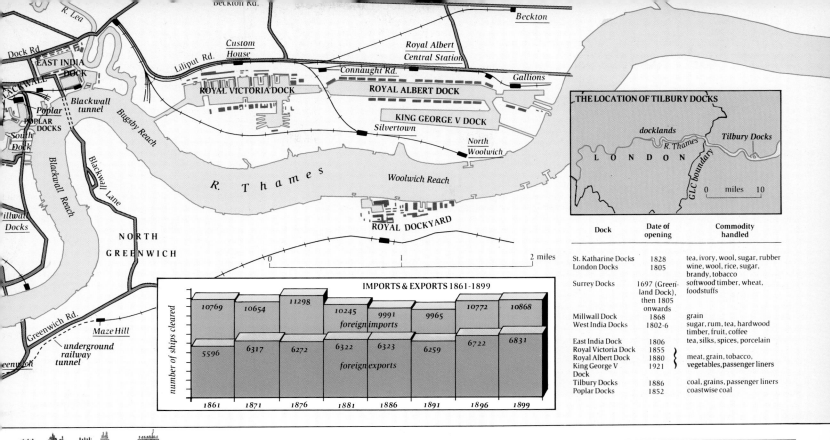

**THE LOCATION OF TILBURY DOCKS**

docklands

LONDON

R. Thames

Tilbury Docks

GLC boundary

0 miles 10

| Dock | Date of opening | Commodity handled |
|---|---|---|
| St. Katharine Docks | 1828 | tea, ivory, wool, sugar, rubber |
| London Docks | 1805 | wine, wool, rice, sugar, brandy, tobacco |
| Surrey Docks | 1697 (Greenland Dock), then 1805 onwards | softwood timber, wheat, foodstuffs |
| Millwall Dock | 1868 | grain |
| West India Docks | 1802-6 | sugar, rum, tea, hardwood timber, fruit, coffee |
| East India Dock | 1806 | tea, silks, spices, porcelain |
| Royal Victoria Dock | 1855 | meat, grain, tobacco, vegetables, passenger liners |
| Royal Albert Dock | 1880 | |
| King George V Dock | 1921 | |
| Tilbury Docks | 1886 | coal, grains, passenger liners |
| Poplar Docks | 1852 | coastwise coal |

**IMPORTS & EXPORTS 1861-1899**

number of ships cleared

foreign imports

| 1861 | 1871 | 1876 | 1881 | 1886 | 1891 | 1896 | 1899 |
|---|---|---|---|---|---|---|---|
| 10769 | 10654 | 11298 | 10245 | 9991 | 9965 | 10772 | 10868 |

foreign exports

| 5596 | 6317 | 6272 | 6322 | 6323 | 6259 | 6722 | 6831 |

# FACTORIES WITH OVER 100 WORKERS: 1898

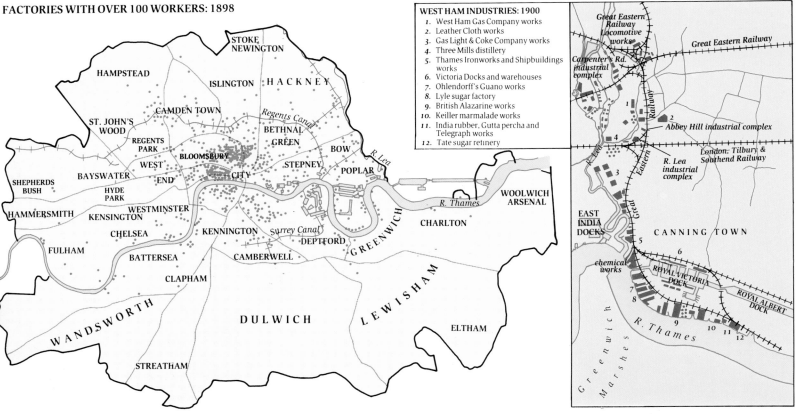

**WEST HAM INDUSTRIES: 1900**

1. West Ham Gas Company works
2. Leather Cloth works
3. Gas Light & Coke Company works
4. Three Mills distillery
5. Thames Ironworks and Shipbuildings works
6. Victoria Docks and warehouses
7. Ohlendorff's Guano works
8. Lyle sugar factory
9. British Alazarine works
10. Keiller marmalade works
11. India rubber, Gutta percha and Telegraph works
12. Tate sugar refinery

# HEART OF EMPIRE

The 19th century saw the transformation of the City of London from a bustling trading and mercantile centre to the commercial heart of the world's largest and wealthiest city and the financial centre of a vast Empire. The Napoleonic Wars had dealt a blow to rival European financial centres and increasingly London was seen as a safe haven – the merchant bankers of London became world financiers, investing vast sums in overseas development and industry.

This explosion in financial and business activity was accompanied by the extensive redevelopment of the City itself. The Bank of England had lost its monopoly on joint-stock banking in 1824, opening the way for the appearance of a large number of new joint-stock banks such as Barclays and the Midland. New headquarters were built for the new joint-stock banks and large insurance companies, especially in the area near

the Bank of England. The model of these buildings was the Italian palazzo, with public rooms on the ground floor, the board room on the first floor, other offices (some for letting) on the second floor, and a caretaker's flat in the attic. Although these buildings often had more space than their owners required, they promoted an impressive corporate image and allowed for future expansion. As the number of small firms

proliferated, and as banks and other major institutions began to occupy all the space in their own buildings, so speculatively-built office blocks became popular. In the 1860s, as schemes increased in size and therefore in capital requirements, limited companies took over from individual speculators. Many of these buildings were now occupied by several firms: in 1881 a City Corporation daytime census counted 1,320 lettings in only 26 buildings.

London directories recorded about 570 stock and share brokers in 1861, but over 5000 in 1901. 86 bankers were listed in 1861, 224 in 1901, of whom 85 were classified as 'foreign and colonial'. Insurance became big business: marine insurance revived from a slump after the Napoleonic Wars and the number of Lloyd's underwriters increased from 189 in 1849 to over 400 in 1870. London fire insurance companies established agencies and branch offices all over the world. By 1839 there were also 72 life assurance offices in London. In 1852, a deputation of working men asked the recently established Prudential Mutual

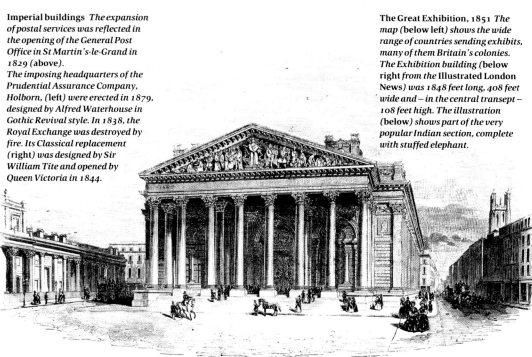

NEW ROYAL EXCHANGE.—(FROM THE ARCHITECT'S DRAWING.)

**Imperial buildings** *The expansion of postal services was reflected in the opening of the General Post Office in St Martin's-le-Grand in 1829 (above).*
*The imposing headquarters of the Prudential Assurance Company, Holborn, (left) were erected in 1879, designed by Alfred Waterhouse in Gothic Revival style. In 1838, the Royal Exchange was destroyed by fire. Its Classical replacement (right) was designed by Sir William Tite and opened by Queen Victoria in 1844.*

**The Great Exhibition, 1851** *The map (below left) shows the wide range of countries sending exhibits, many of them Britain's colonies. The Exhibition building (below right from the Illustrated London News) was 1848 feet long, 408 feet wide and – in the central transept – 108 feet high. The illustration (below) shows part of the very popular Indian section, complete with stuffed elephant.*

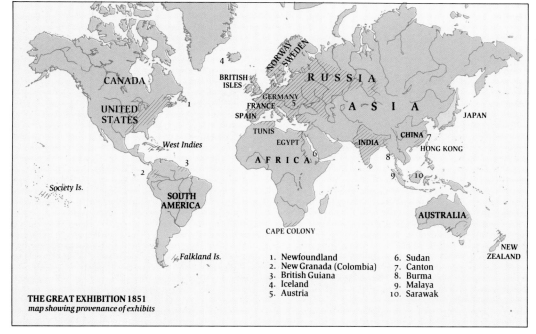

**THE GREAT EXHIBITION 1851**
*map showing provenance of exhibits*

1. Newfoundland
2. New Granada (Colombia)
3. British Guiana
4. Iceland
5. Austria
6. Sudan
7. Canton
8. Burma
9. Malaya
10. Sarawak

Assurance, Investment and Loan Association whether it would entertain assurances as small as £20, payable by weekly instalments. By 1875 the Prudential alone had more than 2 million 'industrial' assurance policies.

Britain's role in the world was also celebrated in 'The Great Exhibition of the Works of Industry of all Nations', staged in Joseph Paxton's 'Crystal Palace' in Hyde Park in 1851. Exhibits were requested from all over the world, including 'natural' wonders such as the Koh-i-Noor diamond, machinery, manufactures and crafts and fine arts. In all, over 100,000 exhibits were provided by 13,937 exhibitors: 7,381 from the United Kingdom and its Dependencies, 6,556 from the rest of the world. Exhibits from the former were grouped westward of the central transept, while those of other nations were placed together eastward. The position of each country's display was determined by its latitude, Mediterranean and tropical states nearer the transept than temperate nations. In all, about two million people visited the exhibition between 1st May, when it was formally opened by Queen Victoria, and 15th October, most paying several visits. In an effort to attract all social classes, entrance fees were varied: on two days when admission cost £1, only a few wealthy visitors came; on 80 days when the charge was a shilling, nearly 4.5 million tickets were sold. The British Museum was one of many attractions where tourist attendance increased. But there was disappointment that only 58,427 foreigners arrived in England between April and September 1851. Even then, it was reported, 'the proverbial expense of a London season must, in many instances, be a serious impediment against frequent visits'.

*Administering the Empire involved a major expansion of government offices in Whitehall (map below right). Less than 20 years after the Board of Trade offices were built in 1827, they were remodelled by Sir Charles Barry, incorporating existing buildings, such as Dorset House, behind a new facade. The whole block now constituted 'New Treasury Offices' (top right). More spectacular, especially when viewed from St. James's Park, were the New Government Offices designed by Sir George Gilbert Scott to house the Foreign, Colonial, India and Home Offices (top left), and erected south of Downing Street (1868-73). The march of Government southwards continued with the 'New Public Offices' (1899-1915); other new buildings included the War Office (1899-1906) and the Admiralty extension (1895).*

*North of Whitehall lay Trafalgar Square, completed in 1843 with the construction of Nelson's Column. In the popular imagination, Trafalgar Square truly was the 'heart of Empire'; the setting for mass meetings, demonstrations (sometimes violent), victory celebrations and New Year revels.*

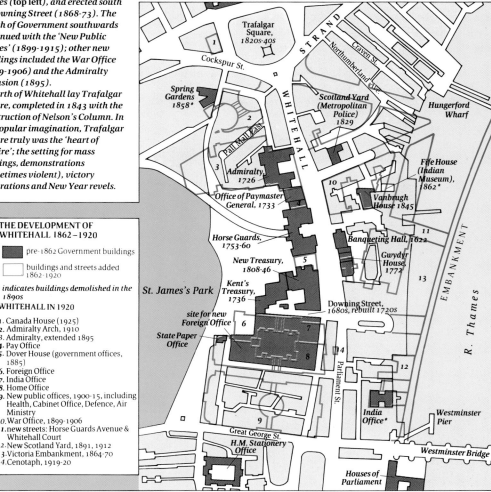

### THE DEVELOPMENT OF WHITEHALL 1862–1920

- ▇ pre-1862 Government buildings
- ☐ buildings and streets added 1862-1920

\* indicates buildings demolished in the 1890s

**WHITEHALL IN 1920**

1. Canada House (1925)
2. Admiralty Arch, 1910
3. Admiralty, extended 1895
4. Pay Office
5. Dover House (government offices, 1885)
6. Foreign Office
7. India Office
8. Home Office
9. New public offices, 1900-15, including Health, Cabinet Office, Defence, Air Ministry
10. War Office, 1899-1906
11. new streets: Horse Guards Avenue & Whitehall Court
12. New Scotland Yard, 1891, 1912
13. Victoria Embankment, 1864-70
14. Cenotaph, 1919-20

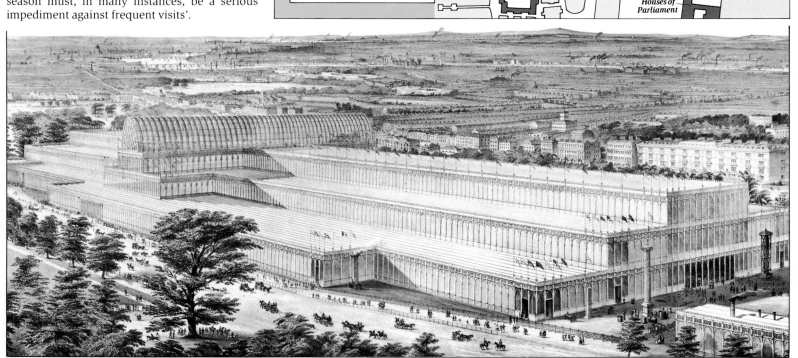

# VICTORIAN LONDON: HOSPITALS AND CHURCHES

## DISEASE AND HOSPITALS

Although by 1861, there were 80 hospitals in London, there was still little provision for the poor, apart from the sick wards of workhouses, until a public hospital system was established in 1867, funded out of Poor Law rates. The first Metropolitan Asylums Board hospital, opened in 1870, was only for paupers suffering from smallpox or scarlet fever,

**Victorian Hospitals** *The map (below) shows the main hospitals of central London in 1902. Many of London's specialist hospitals (see table, right) had opened since 1800. They included eye hospitals, orthopaedic hospitals, children's hospitals and several which catered only for women. But apart from isolation and mental hospitals, and a few Poor Law infirmaries, there were still very few hospitals in South London.*

**HOSPITALS NOT NAMED ON MAP (CENTRAL LONDON)**

1. Belgrave Hospital for Children (1866)
2. Royal Dental Hospital (1901)
3. British Lying-In Hospital (1749)
4. Cancer Hospital (1851)
5. Chelsea Hospital for Women (1871)
6. City Orthopaedic Hospital (1851)
7. Central London Throat & Ear Hospital (1875)
8. Evelina Hospital for Sick Children (1869)
9. French Hospital (1867)
10. General Lying-in Hospital (1765)
11. Hospital for Consumption & Diseases of the Chest (1841)
12. Central London Ophthalmic Hospital (1843)
13. Hospital for Diseases of the Throat (1863)
14. West End Hospital for Nervous Diseases (1878)
15. Hospital for Sick Children (1852)
16. Hospital for Women (1843)
17. Hospital for Women & Children (1866)
18. London Homeopathic Hospital (1849)
19. National Hospital for Diseases of the Heart (1857)
20. National Hospital for the Paralysed & Epileptic (1859)
21. National Orthopaedic Hospital (1836)
22. Queen Charlotte's Lying-in Hospital (1739)
23. Royal Hospital for Children & Women (1816)
24. Royal Orthopaedic Hospital (1838)
25. Royal South London Ophthalmic (1857)
26. Royal Westminster Ophthalmic (1816)
27. London Temperance Hospital (1873)
28. St. Peter's Hospital for Stone and other Urinary Diseases (1860)
29. Victoria Hospital for Children (1866)
30. Cheyne Hospital for Women (1874)
31. St. Saviour's Cancer Hospital (1875-7)
32. Italian Hospital (1884)
33. New Hospital for Women (Elizabeth Garrett Anderson) (1872)
34. Paddington Green Children's Hospital (1883)
35. Western Ophthalmic Hospital (1856)
36. Lock Hospital (for prostitutes) (1862)

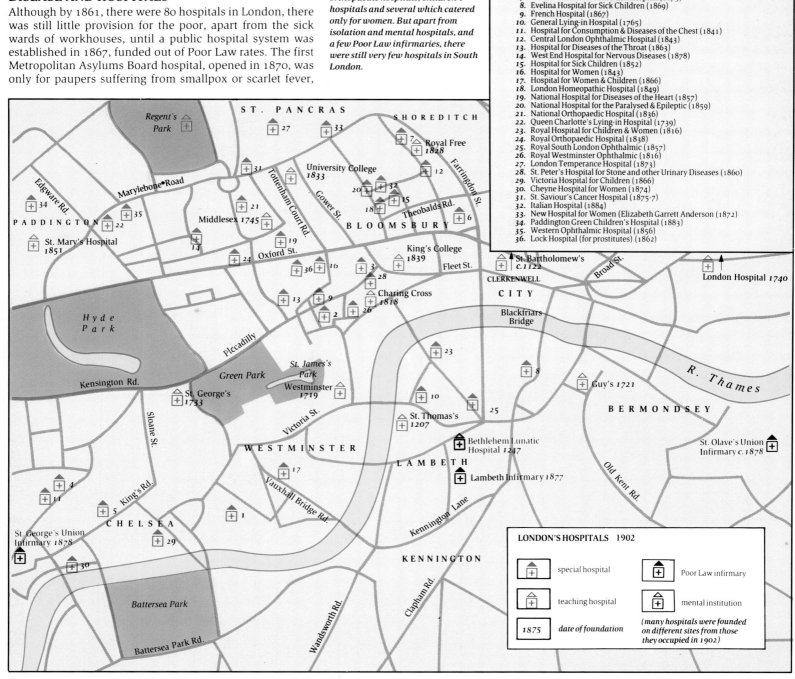

**LONDON'S HOSPITALS 1902**

- special hospital
- teaching hospital
- 1875 — date of foundation
- Poor Law infirmary
- mental institution

*(many hospitals were founded on different sites from those they occupied in 1902)*

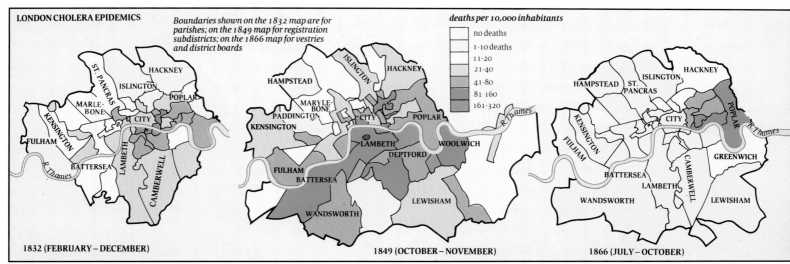

**LONDON CHOLERA EPIDEMICS** *Boundaries shown on the 1832 map are for parishes; on the 1849 map for registration subdistricts; on the 1866 map for vestries and district boards*

**deaths per 10,000 inhabitants**

- no deaths
- 1-10 deaths
- 11-20
- 21-40
- 41-80
- 81-160
- 161-320

**1832 (FEBRUARY – DECEMBER)**

**1849 (OCTOBER – NOVEMBER)**

**1866 (JULY – OCTOBER)**

but free admission was later extended to people who were not paupers, and to those suffering a wider range of illnesses. By 1877, five fever hospitals, on the edges of the built-up area, in Hampstead, Homerton, Stockwell, Fulham and Deptford provided 1,450 beds. By 1890 there were a further 26 Poor Law Infirmaries with a total of 13,203 beds.

London suffered major epidemics of cholera in 1832, 1848-49, 1853-54 and 1866. Thinking that the disease was spread by the inhalation of miasmas, invisible noxious gases emitted by excrement and rotting waste, sanitary reformers tried to prevent the spread of cholera by flushing sewers and watering streets to wash away the waste. In fact, cholera is primarily water-borne, and the first effect of this enthusiastic cleansing was to make the 1848-49 epidemic, with a death rate of 6.6 per 1,000 persons, even worse than that of 1832, where the death rate was 3.4 per 1,000. The distribution of deaths in successive cholera epidemics clearly reflects the comparative cleanliness of the water supply in different parts of London. In 1832, for example, cholera was worst in south London, where the Southwark Waterworks Company supplied appallingly polluted water pumped direct from the Thames, opposite a sewer outfall near London Bridge. In North London, water supplied by the New River Company was relatively pure, and death rates were correspondingly lower.

## VICTORIAN CHURCH-BUILDING

Despite massive church-building campaigns in the first half of the century, by 1851 the Church of England could provide sittings for only 17% of Londoners. Nonetheless, the lack of adequate buildings could not really be blamed for the finding that fewer than 25% of Londoners attended church on Census Sunday in 1851. Fifty years later the *Daily News* found that attendances still amounted to only 22% of the population. Allowing for 'twicers' who attended morning and evening services, it seemed that 19% of Londoners went to church, but the proportion varied from 40% in wealthy suburbs to less than 10% in parts of the East End. Anglicans were most numerous in areas of high social status, especially in west London, while non-conformists predominated in upper working-class and lower middle-class districts. There was also a regional factor; church-going was more common in north-east than in south-west London, reflecting the strength of nonconformity in East Anglia where many north-east Londoners had originated. Charles Booth's survey in the 1890s shows a proliferation of Baptist chapels south of the Thames, perhaps attributable to the charismatic impact of Charles Spurgeon, who became minister of a chapel in Southwark when aged only 19, and subsequently based his ministry at the Metropolitan Tabernacle, Elephant & Castle. In contrast, Catholicism was at its strongest in inner west London, where a poor Irish population combined with wealthier 'old Catholics' and with high Anglicans who had converted to Catholicism, following the example of the theologian, author and cardinal, John Henry Newman.

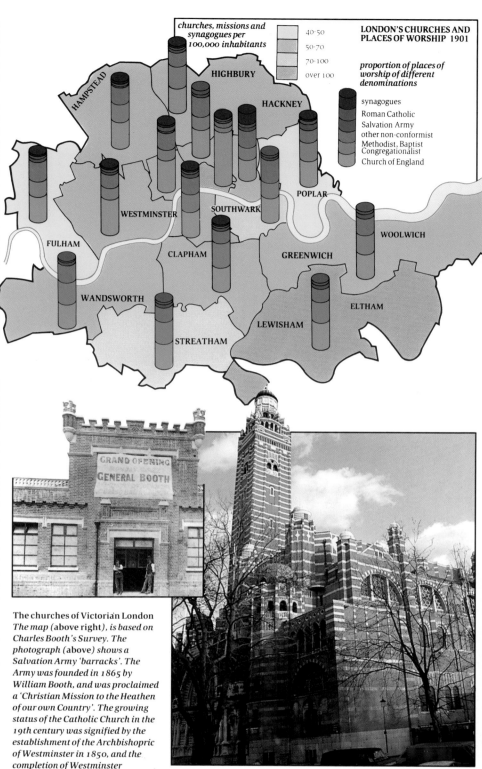

**The churches of Victorian London**
*The map (above right), is based on Charles Booth's Survey. The photograph (above) shows a Salvation Army 'barracks'. The Army was founded in 1865 by William Booth, and was proclaimed a 'Christian Mission to the Heathen of our own Country'. The growing status of the Catholic Church in the 19th century was signified by the establishment of the Archbishopric of Westminster in 1850, and the completion of Westminster Cathedral (above right) in 1903 on a site near Victoria Street.*

**Disease and health reform** *The maps (left) show the comparative mortality rates in three cholera epidemics. Distribution of deaths closely reflects contaminated water supplies. Drinking water frequently came untreated from the polluted River Thames, a common target in Punch. The cartoon (near left) of 1858, shows 'Father Thames Introducing His Offspring to the Fair City of London'. The offspring are labelled Diptheria, Scrofula and Cholera. John Snow's map of cholera deaths in Soho (right) shows the concentration of cases around a contaminated water-pump in Broad Street, vital evidence for his argument that cholera was water-borne.*

DIPTHERIA.   SCROFULA.   CHOLERA.

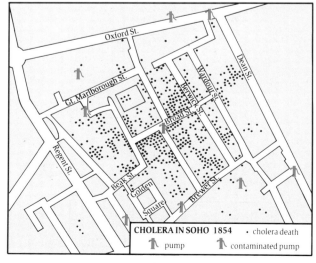

CHOLERA IN SOHO 1854   • cholera death
↟ pump    ↟ contaminated pump

# CRIME AND PUNISHMENT

London in the early 1800s was a violent and unsafe place to live. There was no London-wide police force until Robert Peel established the Metropolitan Police in 1829; and parish constables and night watchmen were no match for hordes of pickpockets, 'footpads' and garotters (equivalent to today's muggers). Districts with the most reported crimes included the City, Soho, Covent Garden and Wapping, where ragged mudlarks (who scavenged in the Thames mud) pilfered rope or coal from barges, while lightermen carried off bales of silk worth hundreds of pounds.

Yet, by the 1880s, London was considered 'the safest capital for life and property in the world'. In 1831, 378 persons per 100,000 had been taken into custody for crimes of violence; sixty years later the rate was 216 per 100,000. Improvement was not continuous; crime increased when real wages fell and the price of bread rose, and most petty larcenies occurred in winter, reflecting links between crime and poverty. But overall, the image created by dramatic outrages such as the Whitechapel Murders detracts from the reality that, for most people most of the time, London was getting safer.

Many Victorians believed that there was a hereditary 'criminal class', reproducing itself in London's 'rookeries', such as Saffron Hill (where Fagin lived in Oliver Twist). Thieves' lodging houses, 'dolly shops' (unlicensed pawn-brokers), whose proprietors acted as fences for stolen property, and 'nests of brothels' abounded in rookeries in Whitechapel, Shadwell and Spitalfields in the East End, and Drury Lane and Seven Dials in the West End. Reformers hoped that destruction of such rookeries would mean the end of criminal culture. In practice, slum clearance merely displaced criminal quarters to more suburban districts, such as Hoxton and Poplar, Vauxhall and Deptford, where the 'honest poor' might be led astray by their new, dishonest neighbours. With the ending of transportation to the colonies and a reduction in death sentences, more criminals were eventually released from prison and returned to the slums.

With the end of transportation more prisons had to be built. 'Convict prisons', for prisoners who previously would have been transported, included Millbank (1816-1903),

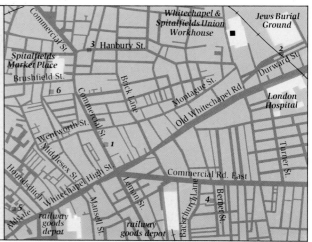

**THE WHITECHAPEL MURDERS 1888**

1. *Martha Turner – found at George Yard Buildings (now Gunthorpe St.) 7 August.*
2. *Mary Ann Nichols (also called Polly) – found at Bucks Row (now Durward St.) – 31 August.*
3. *Annie Chapman – found at the rear of 29 Hanbury St. – 8 September.*
4. *Elizabeth Stride – found at the rear of the International Working Men's Club, 40 Berner St. (now Henriques St.) – 30 September.*
5. *Catherine Eddowes – found at 30 (s-w corner) Mitre Square (off Mitre St.), just north of Aldgate – 30 September.*
6. *Mary Jane Kelly – found at 9 Miller's Court, Dorset St. (off Commercial St.) Spitalfields – 9 November.*

**The Whitechapel murders** *Six brutal murders of prostitutes in Whitechapel between August and November 1888 (map above) have been attributed to the mysterious 'Jack the Ripper', variously identified as a failed barrister, a minor aristocrat, an East End Jew (pure anti-semitism), or a doctor (because of his evident skill at dissection). Panic was whipped up by sensational reports in newspapers such as* Illustrated Police News *(left).*

**Legal London** *The City House of Correction, Holloway (above right), opened in 1882. The map (right) shows the complex array of London's courts and prisons in 1862, centred on the Inns of Court around Chancery Lane. There were over 1500 resident barristers, 3500 solicitors, and more than 5000 law clerks and court officers employed in London's legal district in 1851. The superior courts for civil law were brought under one roof with the opening of the Royal Courts of Justice (or Law Courts) in the Strand in 1882 (from the* Illustrated London News, *top). Designed by G. E. Street, the building contains over 1000 rooms.*

**Inns of Court:**

| | |
|---|---|
| 1. Lincoln's Inn | 8. Clement's Inn |
| 2. Temple | 9. New Inn |
| 3. Gray's Inn | 10. Lyon's Inn |
| 4. Furnival's Inn | 11. Symond's Inn |
| 5. Staple Inn | 12. Barnard's Inn |
| 6. Sergeant's Inn | 13. Thavies' Inn |
| 7. Clifford's Inn | |

**LONDON'S PENAL SYSTEM**

■ Inns of Court

⚖ Law courts

🏛 County courts

▲ Police courts

● prisons

**PENAL INSTITUTIONS NOT SHOWN**

*County Courts:*
    Lambeth
    Bow

*Police Courts:*
    Hammersmith
    Wandsworth
    Greenwich
    Woolwich

*Prisons:*
    Female Convict Prison, Brixton
    Hulks, Woolwich
    City House of Correction, Holloway
    Surrey House of Correction

Brixton (1819) and Pentonville (1842). When transportation to America ended, and before Australia became an alternative destination, prisoners were incarcerated in old warships called 'hulks', anchored in the Thames at Woolwich. Even in the 1850s two dilapidated hulks continued to accommodate convicts. There were also 'correctional prisons' for sentences of less than two years, for example at Wandsworth (1849) and Holloway (1852), and 'detentional prisons', such as Newgate and Clerkenwell, for prisoners awaiting trial following committal by a magistrate. Nearly 40,000 prisoners passed through these London prisons annually during the 1850s.

A variety of theories influenced prison layout. 'Classification' involved separating young from old, and novices from 'old lags'. The 'silent associated system' prevented prisoners from speaking to one another. Prisoners were placed in radiating wings, supervised by a centrally-positioned warder. Under the 'separate system' prisoners were prevented from mixing or talking by being confined to separate cells for long periods. All three ideas were evident at Holloway (*right*). There were six separate wings, each with its own exercise yard. Front left was for juvenile males, up to the age of 17; front right was for females; the rear, radiating wings were for adult males whose days were spent working a treadwheel, picking oakum (unravelling old rope), shoemaking, mat-making or tailoring.

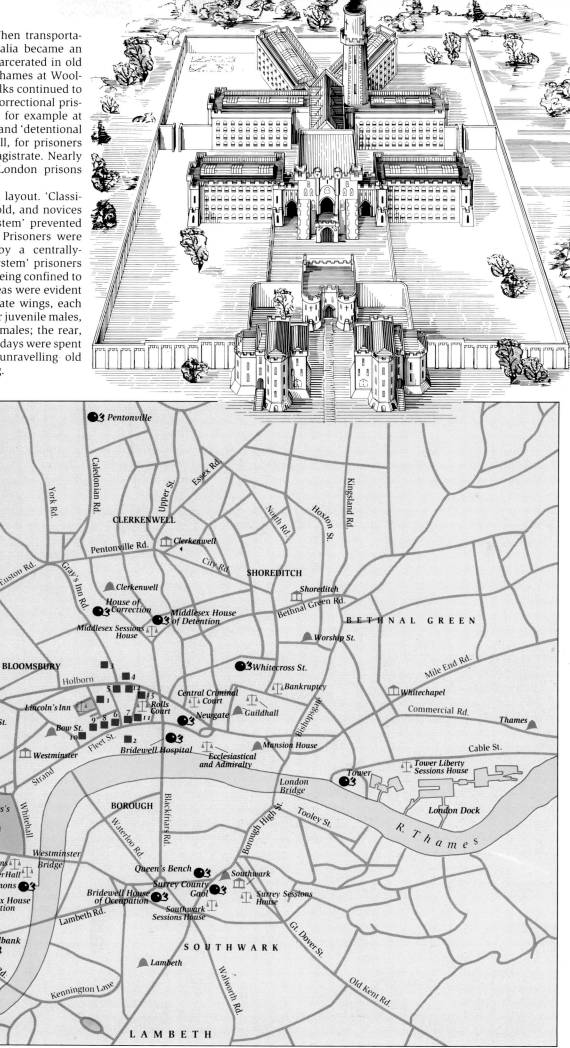

# VICTORIAN HOUSING IMPROVEMENTS

The first reaction of many well-to-do Victorians was to blame London's poor for the squalor and degradation in which they lived. But in the early 1840s a series of government inquiries prompted by Edwin Chadwick, a leading sanitary reformer, began a change in attitudes. Two pioneer agencies – the Metropolitan Association for Improving the Dwellings of the Industrious Classes and the Society for Improving the Condition of the Labouring Classes – started to erect 'model dwellings' for the poor. Their example was followed on a larger scale in the 1860s by the Peabody Trust, funded by the benevolence of George Peabody, a London-based American banker, and the Improved Industrial Dwellings Company, founded by Sydney Waterlow, a prominent stationer and printer, later Lord Mayor of London and a Liberal MP. The IIDCo. became the most important example of 'five per cent philanthropy', so called because dividends to shareholders were restricted to a modest five per cent. Another leading reformer, Octavia Hill, preferred to improve existing houses, which she acquired from slum landlords. She also employed 'lady visitors' who would offer advice on home economics at the same time as they collected the weekly rent. Along with many other philanthropists, she feared that cheap housing would discourage self-help and prove literally demoralising.

With the publication in 1883 of Andrew Mearns' tract, *The Bitter Cry of Outcast London*, which linked overcrowding to irreligion, immorality and incest among the labouring classes,

and the setting up of a Royal Commission on the Housing of the Working Classes (1884-85), several more model dwellings agencies were established. The East End Dwellings Company (1884) resolved to provide for the very poorest families, who had hitherto been neglected while the Four Per Cent Industrial Dwellings Company (1885), founded by Lord Rothschild, was mainly intended for poor Jewish families. Yet by 1900, seven of the largest trusts and companies still housed fewer than 80,000 people – at a time when London's population was increasing by more than this every year.

**Philanthropic schemes** *The Peabody Trust typically erected 'associated dwellings' (where tenants shared sculleries and toilets), as at Blackfriars Road (1871, above). Both the Trust and the Improved Industrial Dwellings Co. preferred sites near the West End (right), often on land provided by aristocratic landlords or the Metropolitan Board of Works. The Four Per Cent Industrial Dwellings Company did build in the East End, as at Rothschild Buildings (1887), pictured (left) in 1902; the graph shows the different class structure of the new residents.*

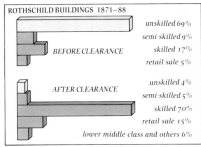

ROTHSCHILD BUILDINGS 1871–88

BEFORE CLEARANCE
unskilled 69%
semi-skilled 9%
skilled 17%
retail sale 5%

AFTER CLEARANCE
unskilled 4%
semi-skilled 5%
skilled 70%
retail sale 15%
lower middle class and others 6%

**Victorian slums** *The worst housing conditions were in shanty towns like 'The Potteries' in North Kensington (top right), inhabited by pigkeepers, brickmakers and day labourers, and in central London 'rookeries', where former middle-class houses were converted to tenements (above). Many more Londoners lived in drab terraced houses, like those in the shadow of railway viaducts near London Bridge, depicted by Gustav Doré in 1871 (top left).*

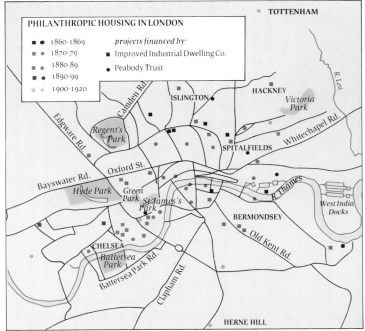

PHILANTHROPIC HOUSING IN LONDON

1860-1869
1870-79
1880-89
1890-99
1900-1920

*projects financed by:*
■ Improved Industrial Dwelling Co.
● Peabody Trust

TOTTENHAM
Camden Rd.
Edgware Rd.
ISLINGTON
HACKNEY
Victoria Park
R. Lea
Regent's Park
Whitechapel Rd.
SPITALFIELDS
Oxford St.
Bayswater Rd.
Hyde Park
Green Park
St James's Park
R. Thames
West India Docks
BERMONDSEY
CHELSEA
Battersea Park
Battersea Park Rd.
Old Kent Rd.
Clapham Rd.
HERNE HILL

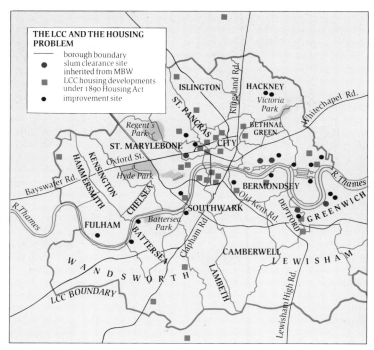

THE LCC AND THE HOUSING PROBLEM

— borough boundary
● slum clearance site inherited from MBW
■ LCC housing developments under 1890 Housing Act
● improvement site

BOUNDARY STREET ESTATE BEFORE RE-DEVELOPMENT (*below*)

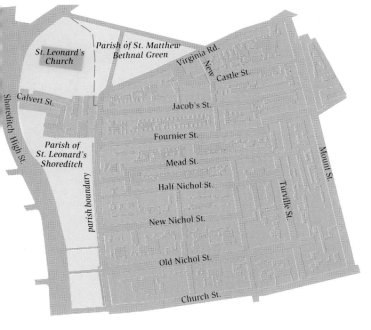

AFTER RE-DEVELOPMENT

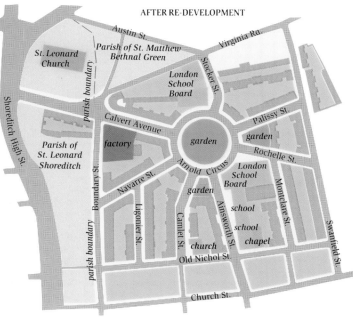

**Slum clearance** *The London County Council (LCC) inherited several slum clearance sites which its predecessor, the Metropolitan Board of Works (MBW), had hoped to sell to model dwellings companies. Under the 1890 Housing Act, the LCC obtained permission to rebuild cleared slums and to build on greenfield sites. The LCC was also obliged to provide housing where existing dwellings were demolished to make way for urban improvements, such as new streets and schools. The map (above left) shows the sites of LCC housing erected between 1890 and 1914. The most extensive slum clearance scheme in the 1890s was in Bethnal Green, where 'Old Nichol', a maze of narrow streets (left), similar in character to Little Britain, in Southwark (photograph right), was replaced by the Boundary Street Estate completed in 1900. This was distinguished by wide streets and impressive blocks of flats focused on a central garden (below left and right). The LCC then turned to a suburban solution, erecting 'cottage estates' at Totterdown in Tooting, south London (1903, photograph top right) and Old Oak in Acton (1912), just inside the county boundary, and at White Hart Lane (1904) and Norbury (1906), just 'out-county'.*

While many 'model dwellings' were erected on slum sites, the slum-dwellers who were the previous occupants, could not afford the rents demanded even for the plainest one- or two-room flats. New residents in Rothschild buildings (1887), for example, were predominantly skilled workers and their families. This experience was repeated when the London County Council began building council flats in the 1890s: in much of the East End and Docklands, their dwellings proved 'hard to let', primarily because they were too expensive for casually employed dockers and sweat-shop workers.

# THE SOCIAL FABRIC

Social surveys of London had been undertaken as early as the 1840s, laying bare the extent of poverty and overcrowding in slums such as St Giles. Investigative journalists, such as Henry Mayhew, reported on their interviews with the poor, while a few intrepid social explorers dressed as tramps and experienced at first-hand a night in the casual ward of a workhouse. But it was Charles Booth, a successful businessman, who produced the most detailed and comprehensive survey of the living conditions and culture of the London poor. His *Life and Labour of the People of London* ran to seventeen volumes, including series on 'Industry', 'Religious Influences' and 'Poverty'.

The population of London was divided into eight categories; classes A-D constituted 'the poor', on incomes of less than 21s. per week 'for a moderate family'; classes E and F were also 'working class', but better-paid and in regular employment; and classes G and H comprised the middle class and above. Booth was shocked to find that over 30 per cent of Londoners were living in poverty, and that a much larger proportion could expect to pass through periods of real poverty at some stage in their life. While he recognised a residuum of 'loafers and semi-criminals', he paid much more attention to the majority of the poor, whose poverty was no fault of their own. He identified the structural causes of poverty: seasonal and casual labour markets, which required a pool of excess, underemployed labour; a life cycle in which most working-class families would experience poverty during child-rearing and old age. Unsurprisingly, Booth was prominent in calling for old age pensions.

Booth produced two kinds of 'poverty map' of London. The first showed degrees of poverty in 1889-90 in 134 areas, each of about 30,000 inhabitants. In many districts around the City, from Clerkenwell through Hoxton, Whitechapel and Wapping, to Bermondsey and Southwark, more than 40 per cent of families were classed as poor. More surprising outliers of poverty included parts of Paddington, Notting Hill, Pimlico and Battersea. In a second map, Booth assigned each street to one of seven colours 'according to the general condition of the inhabitants', ranging from black and dark blue, corresponding to classes A and B, to red and yellow, streets inhabited by middle-class, servant-keeping families. This map clearly shows the very fine grain of poverty.

Booth saw beyond the details to generalise about the social geography of London. He noted the tendency for the colours on his maps to lighten with increasing distance from the river, and identified a pattern of concentric rings 'with the most uniform poverty at the centre'. He saw an obvious link between poverty and overcrowding; while one of his assistants (Llewellyn Smith, later a prominent social researcher in his own right) argued that London was breeding an unskilled, unhealthy and morally degenerate race: districts with most poverty were those with the largest proportion of their inhabitants born in the metropolis.

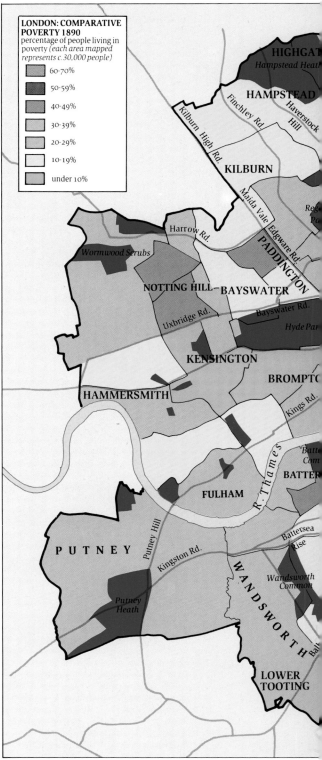

**LONDON: COMPARATIVE POVERTY 1890** percentage of people living in poverty *(each area mapped represents c.30,000 people)*

60-70%
50-59%
40-49%
30-39%
20-29%
10-19%
under 10%

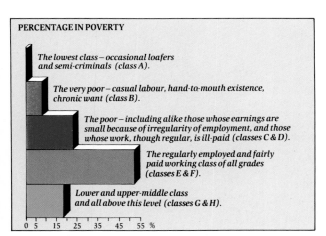

PERCENTAGE IN POVERTY

*The lowest class – occasional loafers and semi-criminals (class A).*

*The very poor – casual labour, hand-to-mouth existence, chronic want (class B).*

*The poor – including alike those whose earnings are small because of irregularity of employment, and those whose work, though regular, is ill-paid (classes C & D).*

*The regularly employed and fairly paid working class of all grades (classes E & F).*

*Lower and upper-middle class and all above this level (classes G & H).*

0   5    15   25   35   45   55 %

**Wealth and poverty** *The graph (left) shows Booth's definition of poverty classes and the percentage of families found in each class. The map (right) is based on Booth's 1889-90 map, showing the degree of poverty in 134 subdivisions of London. The facsimile (top right) from Booth's 'Descriptive Map of London Poverty 1889' shows wealth and poverty on a detailed street-by-street basis, clearly indicating the slums east of Woburn Place and south of King's Cross (dark blue), only a few hundred yards from exclusive Bloomsbury squares and terraces (red and yellow).*

**The 'habits of the people'** *Booth also produced detailed tabulations and maps of licensed premises. The map (near right) shows the distribution of licensed premises in the East End. Pubs with full licences were concentrated along main streets like Whitechapel Road. There were also numerous beerhouses on side streets, vying with grocers' shops for street-corner sites, and established in the wake of the Beershop Act of 1830, which allowed ratepayers easy access to licences (called 'on' licences) to brew and sell their own beer, but not spirits. After 1834, licences for off-sales (including spirits) were also granted, but there were few off-licences in the East End.*

*The geography of pubs throughout London in 1900 is summarised in a second map (far right) based on Booth's statistics. In the City there were large numbers of all kinds of licensed premises – one for every 44 residents (most served visitors and workers). In inner east London there was one pub for every 400 residents, but few off-licences – they proliferated in middle-class suburbia where drinking in pubs was less 'respectable' than drinking at home.*

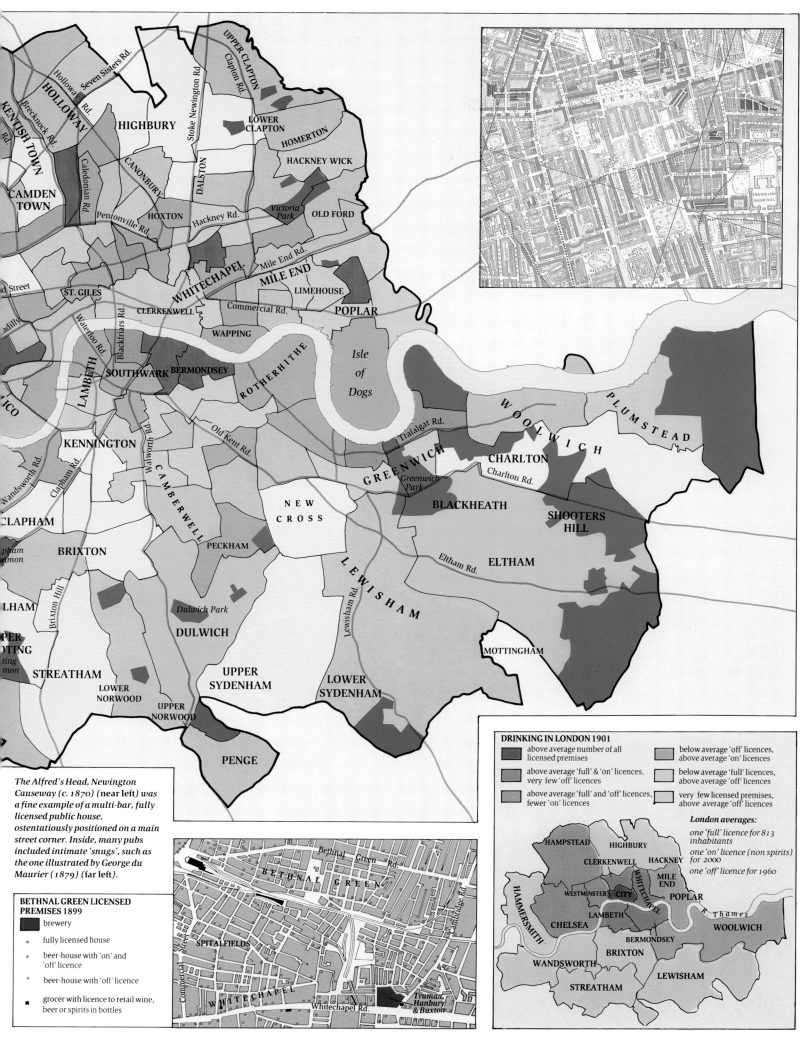

The Alfred's Head, Newington Causeway (c. 1870) (near left) was a fine example of a multi-bar, fully licensed public house, ostentatiously positioned on a main street corner. Inside, many pubs included intimate 'snugs', such as the one illustrated by George du Maurier (1879) (far left).

**BETHNAL GREEN LICENSED PREMISES 1899**

| | |
|---|---|
| ▮ | brewery |
| • | fully licensed house |
| ▪ | beer-house with 'on' and 'off' licence |
| ▲ | beer-house with 'off' licence |
| ■ | grocer with licence to retail wine, beer or spirits in bottles |

**DRINKING IN LONDON 1901**

- above average number of all licensed premises
- above average 'full' & 'on' licences, very few 'off' licences
- above average 'full' and 'off' licences, fewer 'on' licences
- below average 'off' licences, above average 'on' licences
- below average 'full' licences, above average 'off' licences
- very few licensed premises, above average 'off' licences

*London averages:*

one 'full' licence for 813 inhabitants

one 'on' licence (non spirits) for 2000

one 'off' licence for 1960

103

# METROPOLITAN IMPROVEMENTS

By the mid-19th century, London's fragmented urban infrastructure could not support its growing population. Outside the City of London, there was a patchwork of parish vestries, some relatively democratic and efficient, others inactive or corrupt. There were also special trusts for the provision of street lighting and maintenance of turnpike roads, and no fewer than eight sets of commissioners of sewers. Nobody took responsibility for London as a whole until, in 1855, the Metropolis Management Act established the Metropolitan Board of Works (MBW), which was empowered to levy a rate for improvements.

The most urgent problem for the MBW was sewage. Up until then, sewers had dealt only with surface water and discharged directly into the Thames, from which water companies were still extracting drinking water. Household waste went

**Local government** *The map (right) shows the vestries and district boards responsible for local government, 1855-99.*

**The reform of the sewers** *An engraving of the 1840s (below left) shows an open sewer running under the floor of a lodging house in Fish Lane, Holborn. The map (below) shows how the sewage system was improved by the MBW. By the mid-1860s, existing main-line sewers had been diverted into newly-built intercepting sewers. New storm relief sewers, carrying surface run-off, were constructed in the 1880s. To improve flow, pumping stations raised 'low-level sewers' (those closest to the Thames) to provide a gradient for the continuing flow downstream. Abbey Mills Pumping Station (bottom) was opened in 1868, powered by 8-feet Cornish beam engines. It was Gothic in style, with wrought-iron staircases and decorative cast-iron columns.*

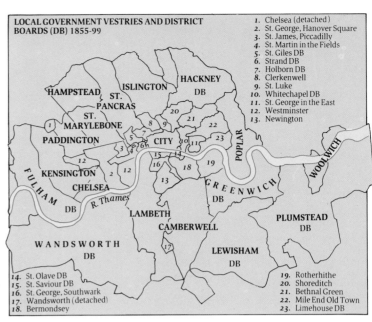

LOCAL GOVERNMENT VESTRIES AND DISTRICT BOARDS (DB) 1855-99

1. Chelsea (detached)
2. St. George, Hanover Square
3. St. James, Piccadilly
4. St. Martin in the Fields
5. St. Giles DB
6. Strand DB
7. Holborn DB
8. Clerkenwell
9. St. Luke
10. Whitechapel DB
11. St. George in the East
12. Westminster
13. Newington
14. St. Olave DB
15. St. Saviour DB
16. St. George, Southwark
17. Wandsworth (detached)
18. Bermondsey
19. Rotherhithe
20. Shoreditch
21. Bethnal Green
22. Mile End Old Town
23. Limehouse DB

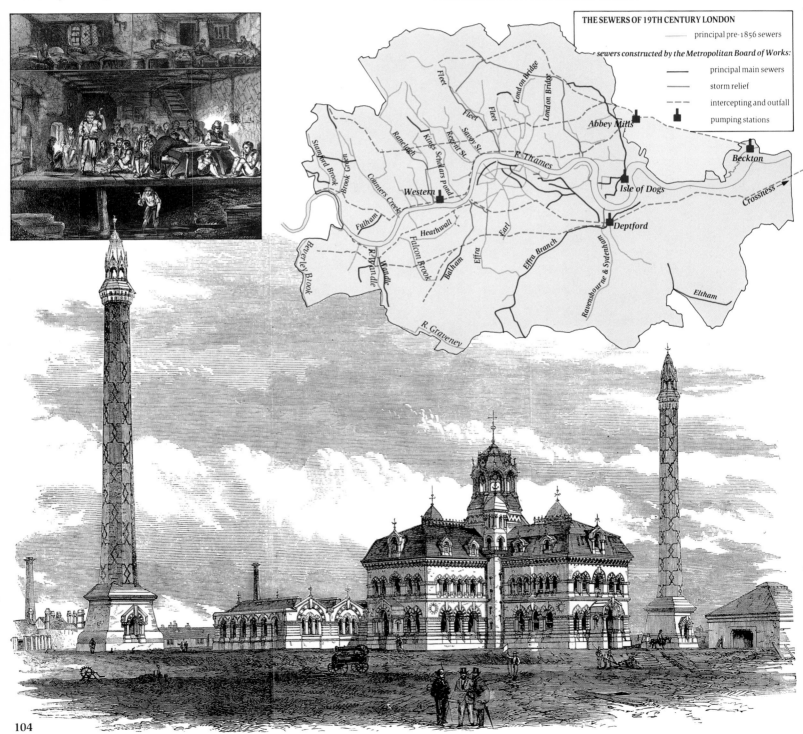

THE SEWERS OF 19TH CENTURY LONDON

— principal pre-1856 sewers

sewers constructed by the Metropolitan Board of Works:

— principal main sewers
— storm relief
--- intercepting and outfall
■ pumping stations

into cesspits, which leaked their contents into adjacent wells, thereby ensuring that water supplies were polluted. Successive cholera epidemics highlighted the severity of the problem, which was finally brought home to parliament by the 'Great Stink' of 1858, when the stench from the Thames became overpowering. Under its chief engineer, Sir Joseph Bazalgette, the MBW constructed 82 miles of 'intercepting sewers'; smaller, pre-existing sewers draining into the Thames were intercepted, so that their effluent could be discharged much farther downstream, at Beckton and Crossness, where outfall sewage works were completed in 1864 and 1865. The MBW also embarked on an ambitious programme of road-building and improvement, combining traffic engineering with slum clearance.

Despite these improvements, the MBW was still regarded as undemocratic and corrupt. The demands of Liberal and East End politicians for a directly-elected, London-wide council, able to transfer resources from rich West End areas to poorer East End districts, led to the creation of the London County Council (LCC) in 1888. In 1899, to counter the power of the LCC, the vestries and District Boards were replaced by 28 new metropolitan borough councils. This new administrative structure lasted until the 1960s, yet, even in the 1880s, the built-up area of London extended beyond LCC boundaries.

*Street improvements Holborn Viaduct (under construction near right, and complete far right, below) was built between 1863 and 1869, designed to ease traffic flows between the City and West End, avoiding the steep hills into and out of the Fleet Valley. The only visible section is the cast-iron bridge across Farringdon Street, but the whole viaduct is a quarter of a mile in length, hidden between offices and warehouses. Even more impressive was the Victoria Embankment, completed in 1870. A new river wall was built up to 500 feet out into the Thames, providing 37 acres of new land. A cross-section through the Embankment beneath Charing Cross station (far right, above) shows an underground conduit carrying water and gas mains and telegraph cables; beneath that was the low-level intercepting sewer; the Metropolitan District Railway occupied a tunnel under the newly laid-out Embankment Gardens.*

## THE THAMES TUNNEL 1843

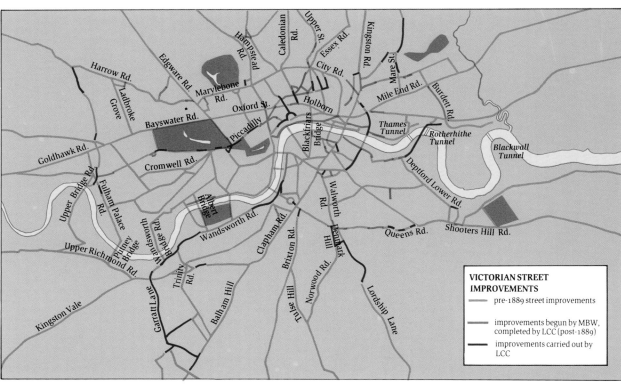

R. Thames

Thames Tunnel

staircase from surface

*Street improvements by the MBW (map right) culminated in the construction of Shaftesbury Avenue (1877-86) and Charing Cross Road (1887), and the enlargement of Piccadilly Circus around the statue of Eros. Further improvements were undertaken by the LCC, including the clearance of 28 acres to create Kingsway and Aldwych, opened in 1905, and the building of road tunnels under the Thames, at Blackwall (1897) and Rotherhithe (1908).*

*The first Thames Tunnel (cross-section above right, entrance above), between Wapping and Rotherhithe, was a private initiative, promoted by the engineer, Marc Brunel. It was started in 1825 but not completed until 1843. Within 15 weeks of its opening, one million pedestrians had paid 1d each to walk through, but once the novelty wore off, it became the haunt of thieves and prostitutes. The tunnel had cost over £600,000, but in 1865 it was sold to the East London Railway Company for only £200,000 and converted into a railway tunnel.*

### VICTORIAN STREET IMPROVEMENTS
— pre-1889 street improvements
— improvements begun by MBW, completed by LCC (post-1889)
— improvements carried out by LCC

# VICTORIAN COMMERCE

The 19th century saw dramatic changes in the geography and character of London's shops. From the beginning of Victoria's reign there was a movement westwards, along the lines of Holborn, Oxford Street, Fleet Street and the Strand, following the continuing shift of the better-off into West End estates. Later in the century a 'new West End' developed in Knightsbridge, Kensington and Bayswater. Major suburban shopping centres, for example in Clapham, Brixton and Holloway, also acquired their own department stores and, by 1914, chain stores such as Marks & Spencer. In many suburbs single-storey, flat-roofed extensions were built to accommodate shops on what had previously been the front gardens of private terraced houses. By the end of the century new, purpose-built department stores were replacing such makeshift extensions.

There were also changes to London's markets. In 1855, the live cattle market moved from Smithfield to Copenhagen Fields, north of King's Cross. A new meat market opened at Smithfield in 1866, and the insanitary Newgate Shambles was closed. Many central London markets were displaced by the construction of new streets and railways, while others, such as Covent Garden, Spitalfields, Billingsgate and Leadenhall, were rebuilt. These, and other new markets with direct rail access to the rest of the country – at King's Cross, Somers Town and Stratford – increasingly restricted their activities to the wholesale trade. Most markets were owned by the City Corporation, railway companies or local authorities, but a few philanthropic ventures were promoted, including Angela Burdett-Coutts' Columbia Market in Bethnal Green, a spectacular failure from the day it opened in 1869. Street markets were increasingly subject to regulation under public health and nuisance laws, and regarded as sources of public disorder, especially as they did most of their business late on Friday and Saturday nights, and on Sundays. Yet the number of street traders increased, as underemployed casual labourers, in a last attempt to avoid the workhouse, tried to earn a living as streetsellers.

The growth of a new class of shop and office workers, aspiring to middle-class standards, and the building of thousands of modest but comfortable suburban homes that needed furnishing and decorating, increased the demand for consumer goods. As public transport improved, West End stores attracted customers from all over London. William Whiteley commenced business in Westbourne Grove in 1863, the same year as the Metropolitan Railway was opened to nearby Paddington. Selfridge's, opened in

1909, was located immediately above the 'Twopenny Tube', opened in 1900 (now part of the Central Line). Some multiple retailers, such as W. H. Smith, were directly associated with public transport, with their chain of station bookstalls; others, such as J. J. Sainsbury, used improved road and rail transport to distribute standardised, mass-produced goods. J. J. Sainsbury started out with a dairy in Drury Lane in 1869, followed by branches in working-class market streets, such as Chapel Market in Islington. In the 1880s, the firm expanded into more distant middle-class suburbs such as Croydon and Lewisham. By 1914, there were 115 branches of Sainsbury.

Most department stores began as drapers' shops, only gradually increasing the range of goods they sold. By the 1840s there was a cluster of stores on Tottenham Court Road (Shoolbred's, Maples, Heal's), reflecting the concentration of furniture manufacturers in adjacent streets. On Oxford Street, Peter Robinson, linen draper, expanded from one shop in 1833 to take over five adjacent shops by 1860. But the most spectacular 19th-century department store was Whiteley's, described in 1887 as 'an immense symposium of the arts and industries of the nation and of the world'. By 1906, it boasted 159 separate departments, including services such as refreshment rooms, estate and ticket agencies, laundry and dry cleaners. The new department stores

*London's Victorian Markets The distribution of wholesale and retail markets in central London, including the numbers of costermongers at each market, as recorded by the journalist, Henry Mayhew, in 1849 (map below left). The Hay Market moved in 1830 to Cumberland Market, east of Regent's Park. Robert Bevan's painting (below) depicts hay carts at Cumberland Market in 1915. West End stores The map (above right) shows the distribution of London's department stores in 1910, and indicates whether they were purpose-built, or originated as bazaars. By 1850, there were at least ten bazaars in central London, usually arcaded structures where individuals could rent stalls, mostly selling items of female dress, and luxury goods such as jewellery and toys.*

**LONDON'S MARKETS 1849**

street market in 1849    wholesale market (named on map below)

*street markets
(number of costermongers given in brackets)*

1. New Cut, Lambeth (300)
2. Lambeth Walk (104)
3. Walworth Road (22)
4.* Camberwell (15)
5. Newington (45)
6. Kent St., Borough (38)
7. Bermondsey (107)
8. Union St., Borough (29)
9. Great Suffolk St. (46)
10. Blackfriars Rd. (58)
11. Brill & Chapel St. (300)
12. Camden Town (50)
13. Hampstead/Tottenham Court Rds. (333)
14. St. George's Market, Oxford St. (177)
15. Marylebone (37)
16. Edgware Rd. (78)
17. Crawford St. (145)
18. Knightsbridge (46)
19. Pimlico (32)
20. Tothill St. (119)
21. Drury Lane (22)
22. Clare St. (139)
23. Exmouth St. (142)
24. Leather Lane (150)
25. St. John's St. (47)
26. Old St. (46)
27. Whitecross St. (150)
28. Islington (79)
29. City Road (49)
30. Shoreditch (100)
31. Bethnal Green (100)
32. Whitechapel (258)
33. Mile End (105)
34. Commercial Rd. (114)
35. Limehouse (88)
36. Ratcliffe Highway (122)
37. Rosemary Lane (119)
38. Columbia

* not shown on map
† wholesale markets opened 1850-1893
*wholesale markets not shown on map*
† Stratford (fruit, veg.)
† Brentford (fruit, veg.)

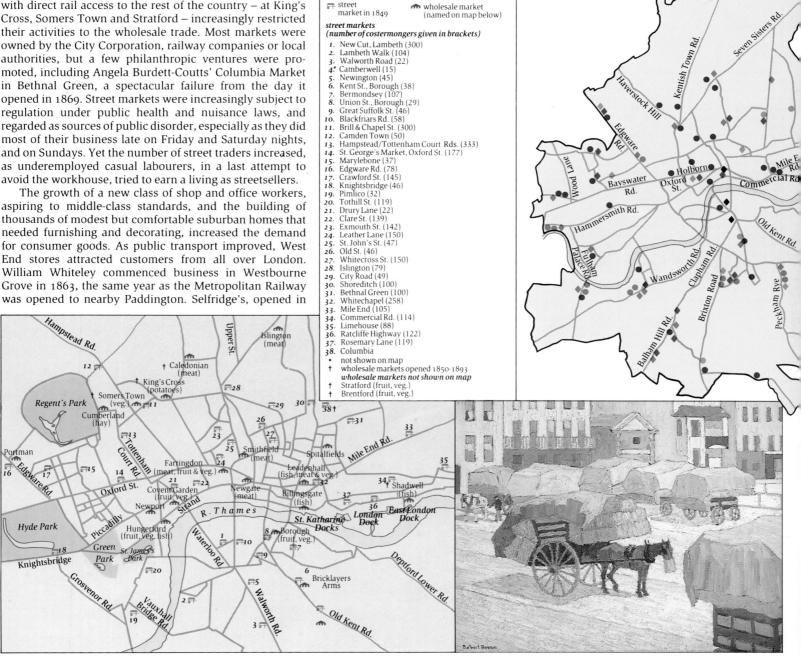

advertised fixed prices, required payment in cash, and encouraged the general public to enter with no obligation to buy. Up until the 1870s they had remained collections of existing small shops knocked together and extended piecemeal. The first purpose-built department store was the Bon Marché in Brixton, opened in 1877, named in imitation of the Parisian store. As West End land values increased, so store-owners preferred to build upwards: multi-storey premises extended from bargain basements to roof gardens. By the 1890s lifts were common, and in 1898 Harrods installed the first moving staircase. An earlier technological innovation had been plate glass, allowing much more impressive window displays, while from the 1880s electric lighting was introduced, increasing the attractions of night-time shopping. To raise capital for these changes, stores ceased to be private family businesses and became limited companies.

The most impressive brand-new department store was built in 1909 by Harry G. Selfridge, who had previously worked in the Chicago store of Marshall Field. Selfridge's was almost a town in its own right; by 1914, 950 men and 2,550 women were employed in its 160 departments. With restaurants, hairdressers, writing, reading and rest rooms, Selfridge's was the equivalent of a gentleman's club for women. Indeed, Selfridge's proclaimed itself as being 'dedicated to the service of women'.

**Selfridge's** *An advertisement (above) proclaims the opening of London's grandest purpose-built department store in 1909. The cross-section (right) shows the layout of Selfridge's, from the mail order department in the basement to the elegant tea-rooms on the top floor.*

**SELFRIDGE'S** *London's New & Wonderful Shopping Centre Dedicated to Woman's Service – devoted to the Children's Needs – the Main Best Buying Place with best assorted Stocks at London's Lowest Prices* **NOW OPEN TO THE WORLD** OXFORD STREET LONDON W

**LONDON'S DEPARTMENT STORES 1850–1910**

■ bazaar established pre-1850
○ shop established pre-1850
● shop developed 1850-80
■ department store established after 1880 *(named)*

**SHOPPING IN THE SUBURBS 1898-1930**

◆ Marks & Spencer
● Woolworth

*store founded:*

◆ pre-1904
◆ 1904-11
◆ ● 1912-16
◆ ● 1917-24
● ● 1925-30

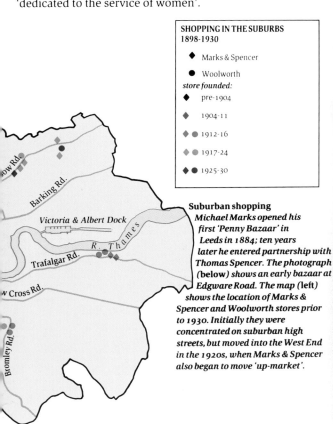

**Suburban shopping**
*Michael Marks opened his first 'Penny Bazaar' in Leeds in 1884; ten years later he entered partnership with Thomas Spencer. The photograph (below) shows an early bazaar at Edgware Road. The map (left) shows the location of Marks & Spencer and Woolworth stores prior to 1930. Initially they were concentrated on suburban high streets, but moved into the West End in the 1920s, when Marks & Spencer also began to move 'up-market'.*

MARKS & SPENCER LTD.
ORIGINATORS OF PENNY BAZAARS.
PENNY ADMISSION BAZAAR
ADMISSION FREE

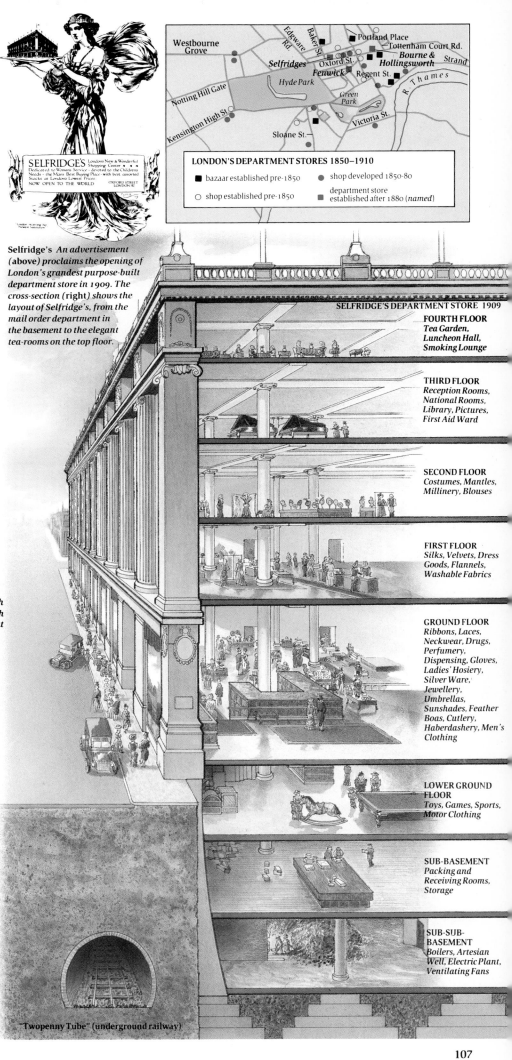

**SELFRIDGE'S DEPARTMENT STORE 1909**

**FOURTH FLOOR**
*Tea Garden, Luncheon Hall, Smoking Lounge*

**THIRD FLOOR**
*Reception Rooms, National Rooms, Library, Pictures, First Aid Ward*

**SECOND FLOOR**
*Costumes, Mantles, Millinery, Blouses*

**FIRST FLOOR**
*Silks, Velvets, Dress Goods, Flannels, Washable Fabrics*

**GROUND FLOOR**
*Ribbons, Laces, Neckwear, Drugs, Perfumery, Dispensing, Gloves, Ladies' Hosiery, Silver Ware, Jewellery, Umbrellas, Sunshades, Feather Boas, Cutlery, Haberdashery, Men's Clothing*

**LOWER GROUND FLOOR**
*Toys, Games, Sports, Motor Clothing*

**SUB-BASEMENT**
*Packing and Receiving Rooms, Storage*

**SUB-SUB-BASEMENT**
*Boilers, Artesian Well, Electric Plant, Ventilating Fans*

"Twopenny Tube" (underground railway)

THE FIRST HALF of the 20th century saw a more radical transformation of London's appearance and physical extent, and of its inhabitants' lifestyles, than any comparable period of history. Passing through an era of spectacular urban expansion in the 1930s, by 1950 London had begun a marked population decline. Dominated at the beginning by Victorian values and social inequalities, by the middle of the century welfare-state idealism offered the prospect of a new beginning. These transformations were partly brought about by continuing dissatisfaction with the city's legacy of social division and physical decay. National life at the time was dominated by these problems, and the political means of resolving them, but the status and size of London focused the issues with special intensity.

London retained its historic status in international affairs through the administration of the Empire and its share of British seaborne trade. Throughout the period it also dominated national, political, administrative, economic and cultural life. In some ways, for example through the growth of manufacturing and office activities and the developing role of central government, the city's role within Britain was even greater by the end of the period than at the beginning. Its most pressing problems in the early years, however, were associated with the Victorian legacy of industry and overcrowded housing. In the wake of the First World War there was a severe housing shortage. Initially, the official response was to placate post-war expectations of 'homes fit for heroes' by subsidising publicly-built, rented ('council') housing. The London County Council (LCC) became by far the largest public sector developer, both within London and on land acquired elsewhere in south-east England. This surge of building nevertheless petered out in the early 1920s, and subsequent rates of council house building fluctuated with the economic and political conditions of the period.

*For an examination of the post-war housing boom, refer to pages 114-115.*

These pioneering schemes set higher standards, both for amenities and space, than ever before for London working-class housing. The 'Garden City' ideas of Ebenezer Howard, writing in the 1890s, were already being put into practice at Hampstead Garden Suburb, Letchworth and, later, at Welwyn Garden City. These were privately-sponsored examples of what could be done to improve living conditions. They influenced standards of council housing in the 1920s, as well as the programme of new town building which was begun later, in the 1940s. Although supported by Liberal views on state intervention to alleviate the plight of the poor, the move from *laissez faire* solutions towards public intervention was also promoted by the growth at local, and later national levels, of the Labour Party. Within a few years the same models were adapted by private companies, building for middle-class owner-occupiers, to create an even more radical transformation of London's housing. This explosion of house-building would be on a scale that could scarcely have been imagined before the First World War, and which the public sector could never match.

In the early years of the century, plans were already being prepared to improve road and public transport in London. At this time many people worked relatively near to their homes within the city, but longer distance commuting was growing, using surface railways and the few privately-built underground lines. Even before motor lorries, and to a lesser extent private cars, began to multiply in the 1920s, congestion on the streets was a major issue. The First World War itself radically affected transport in London.

*Below* The years after the Great War saw a spectacular growth and consolidation of the London Underground system. Under the aegis of Frank Pick, the commercial manager of the Underground Group, this expansion was marked by a series of promotional posters, their unique style owing much to the special typeface called 'Underground', which had been designed during the Great War and was used throughout the system. Posters, such as 'Brightest London' (Horace Taylor, 1924), were not simply design classics. The Underground was well-used at peak travel times, but it also made commercial sense to encourage Londoners to use the Underground for day excursions, shopping trips and evenings in the West End.

**BRIGHTEST LONDON**
IS BEST REACHED BY
U̲N̲D̲E̲R̲G̲R̲O̲U̲N̲D̲

*The expansion of public transport is mapped on page 113.*

Many of the munition factories were located around the edge of the city, on sites which were often to become major factory estates in the 1920s and 30s. Movement therefore became less tightly confined to the area of the Victorian city. As people and jobs migrated outwards, so did the diversity of transport; electric railways, the expanding underground, trams and trolley buses, omnibuses and bicycles were each employed in an increasing variety of combinations to get around the city. This 'mobility revolution', based on public transport, owed little to private car ownership.

As well as these transport developments, other forms of new technology wrought significant changes in London's life. These included the spread of electrical power and the telephone, and the introduction of new industrial products and methods of mass manufacture. Large private companies, which could support the growing scale of manufacturing and marketing, became increasingly important. These various opportunities came together most spectacularly in the expansion of the inter-war suburbs, which served a growing demand from small, lower middle-class families who could afford to buy houses for the first time, instead of renting them in the older parts of the city. Stable, if often modest incomes, derived from the growing numbers of office and skilled manual jobs, enabled many to obtain mortgages with affordable deposits and repayment rates. Entirely new domestic lifestyles could also be evolved, based on the latest household gadgetry, including gas and electric cookers, vacuum cleaners, refrigerators and the increasingly available 'wireless'. The design of houses, furniture, domestic appliances and vehicles came under the influence of mass production techniques and modernist ideals.

*The rise of 'Metroland' is examined on page 114, and the impact of the mass movement out of the inner city during the 1930s is mapped in detail on page 112.*

*Above  The Odeon, Leicester Square, with black granite facade, shortly after it opened in 1937. Perhaps the most far-reaching development in this period was the expansion of the 'media': mass-circulation newspapers, radio broadcasting, and cinema. American culture – styles of dress, music, dancing and, above all, films – permeated British life between the wars, and had an extraordinary impact on a society which only twenty years before had been largely Victorian in cultural values and attitudes.*

*A full discussion of London's industry in the first half of the 20th century can be found on pages 116-117.*

The attractions of the suburbs were not just confined to private citizens. Manufacturing companies, until then concentrated by the availability of transportation links and labour into the crowded areas of inner and east London, were also able to move out. This was encouraged by improved communications, and by road transport for both freight and workers. Expansive industrial estates, mainly of single-storey factories, dotted the suburbs along the new trunk roads and on other readily available vacant land. These estates not only attracted traditional industries, they also became the sites for many new firms, sometimes American-owned, serving the London consumer boom. Typical products included domestic electrical goods, radios, new types of building materials, furniture, processed foods and pharmaceuticals. Whole new industries also developed around the production of aeroplanes, motor vehicles, machine tools and production control apparatus. To some extent the economic depression of the early 1930s favoured the production and building industries of London by keeping down labour, materials and land costs. The city, with its prosperous suburban-dweller, was also the main national focus of demand.

All of these innovations inevitably changed ways of life, especially for women. Although the war had expanded the range of acceptable jobs for single women, few middle-class wives worked; their task was to run the new home in which machines had replaced the servants of the Victorian era. Communities were less 'communal' than in the old city areas, and problems arose, especially for women, in adjusting to the solitary suburban life. This was especially true for working-class women moving to the LCC's 'out county' estates, which were situated outside London. A new type of 'commuter settlement' began to dominate London life, based upon the ideal of separate, semi-detached family homes, with large gardens on extensive estates. Of course, some of the areas of earlier development in inner London continued to support large, older and often still prosperous populations, including upper-class families with servants. With time, however, their residents moved to the owner-occupied life of the outer suburbs, and many 'respectable' areas declined physically and socially, as poorer people moved in to rent part of the large subdivided properties.

Wembley Stadium symbolises much about London at this time. First used for the Cup Final of 1923, it was the centrepiece of the 1924-25 British Empire Exhibition, designed to assert the continuing significance of Britain's imperial power. In all, 27 million people attended the Exhibition over the two years. Like the stadium itself, with its 120,000 capacity, the Exhibition thus heralded the era of mass entertainment. Over the next 15 years a wave of characteristic 'Metroland' suburbia surrounded the site and engulfed much of the rest of Middlesex. After the Exhibition, Wembley became a major focus for suburban industrial development in the 1930s. It was not unique in this; Park Royal, less

than two miles to the south, had been the site of the Royal Agricultural Society showground, abandoned in 1905, and pressed into service for war purposes. By the Second World War it had become the largest industrial area in London.

Between the World Wars, two major problems associated with the 'liberation' of people from the pressures of overcrowded urban life emerged as time progressed. The first was the increasing separation, on a large scale, of areas where the 'haves' and 'have-nots' lived. The latter remained concentrated in the deprived industrial slums around the city centre and in the East End. Secondly, the rapid physical encroachment of the city into the surrounding countryside, often through tentacles of 'ribbon development', attracted increasing concern. By the late 1930s these two consequences of post-war development had created a rare consensus across a broad spectrum of opinion over the need to control the sprawl of London. Two ideals, one for social unity which would be brought about by improving health and social conditions of the poorer people, and the other for the conservation of the countryside, were engaged to support the first efforts to define 'green belts' which would contain the growth of London.

Social conditions in many of the old parts of London remained desperately poor. Punitive Poor Law regulations remained the principal way of relieving poverty until the late 1920s, when national public assistance was first introduced. The alleviation of poverty attempted by the London County Council and the boroughs had created political and social upheavals in the 1920s. In spite of council slum clearance and campaigns to improve child health, education and recreation, many of London's poor were still trapped in slum housing close to the factories and docks of inner London. The poor quality and insecurity of such employment meant that incomes were low, with the ever-present threat of lay-offs, or redundancies. The depression of the early 1930s, although less acute and shorter-lived in London than elsewhere in Britain, created special hardships in the heavy industrial and sweatshop areas of the East End. These overcrowded areas were particularly difficult and expensive to redevelop. A good deal of the worst housing was finally demolished by German bombing during the Second World War, thus establishing conditions in which massive urban renewal schemes, including demolition of the remaining slums, were undertaken after 1950.

*Bethnal Green, an area of inner-city deprivation between the wars, is mapped and discussed in detail on page 115.*

The movement to halt the suburban sprawl of London, which originated in the late 19th century, gathered pace during the 1930s. After 1935, local authorities in rural areas began to purchase open land around London to preserve it from private development. Initially this was undertaken with the financial backing of the LCC, but later the rural authorities increasingly undertook land purchasing schemes on their own initiative. The motives for this expenditure were mixed; the LCC wished to preserve accessible open spaces for Londoners, while the rural councils wanted to stop established communities being swallowed up by London's growth. Others pointed with alarm to the reduction of farmland, and its effects on national food production. These various interests came together after the Second World War, when it was seen that huge resources would be needed to purchase all the land needed around London. Local authorities were empowered to refuse planning permission for non-conforming developments in the statutory green belt. With the New Towns Act of 1946, this move established the regional framework for planning London's post-war development.

*Map below The extent of London on the eve of the Second World War is contrasted to the size of the city today.*

Of the many radical changes affecting London during this period, it was the Second World War and its devastating physical impact on the city that was the most important culminating event. It is remarkable that, even in the darkest days of the war, plans were already being laid, not only for reconstruction, but also for government policy in the city. Post-war priorities were not merely to repair the damage of the Blitz, but also to tackle the long-term problems of housing, transportation and social conditions.

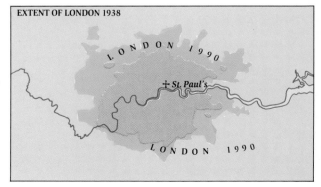

EXTENT OF LONDON 1938

LONDON 1990

+ St. Paul's

LONDON 1990

# SUBURBANISATION AND SPRAWL

The suburban development of London had been progressing for at least 300 years before the beginning of the 20th century. Nevertheless, suburbs are most commonly associated in the public mind with the vast unplanned housing developments of the 20s and 30s and the rise of 'semi-detached' London. This suburban expansion was the result of both high birth rates and increased levels of migration into the capital. However, while Greater London's population grew from 7.5 million in 1921 to 8.7 in 1939, the numbers living in the inner city fell by almost 450,000 as people moved out to the suburbs.

It was the rising numbers of middle class administrative and clerical workers in commercial life and the civil service who enjoyed the new lifestyle, living in the suburbs and commuting to work. But by far the most dynamic changes in lifestyle between the wars were being created by American-style consumerism. A growing range of goods was available for mass sale; cookers, fridges, furniture, radios, processed foods – all the accoutrements of home decoration, gardening and increased leisure time. These commercial changes created employment for a growing number of managers, clerks, production and maintenance workers, drivers, design and sales staff.

**Commuting to work** *increased between the wars, as people left the city for the outer London suburbs* (**maps below**). *The new Carreras cigarette factory at Mornington Crescent* (**below**), *employed 2,600 workers and the map* (**above**) *shows where they lived and how far they had to travel to work.*

Far-sighted plans to accommodate the growth of goods and freight traffic were reflected in the construction of new trunk roads around and out of London, including Western Avenue and the North Circular Road. Improved road networks also meant that industry could move out of the crowded inner city. Estates of factories grew up around the periphery of London, taking advantage of the new road transport, both for freight and workers.

As people and jobs migrated outwards, more varied

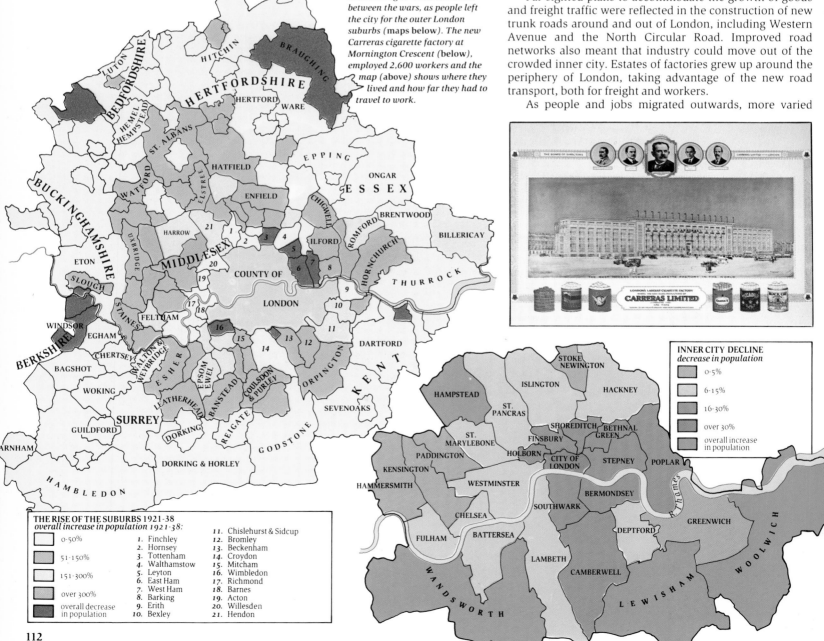

**THE CARRERAS FACTORY: JOURNEY TO WORK 1936**
— London area postal boundary
— postal district boundary
Starting point of journey
up to 100 workers
over 100 workers

**THE RISE OF THE SUBURBS 1921-38**
*overall increase in population 1921-38:*
- 0-50%
- 51-150%
- 151-300%
- over 300%
- overall decrease in population

1. Finchley
2. Hornsey
3. Tottenham
4. Walthamstow
5. Leyton
6. East Ham
7. West Ham
8. Barking
9. Erith
10. Bexley
11. Chislehurst & Sidcup
12. Bromley
13. Beckenham
14. Croydon
15. Mitcham
16. Wimbledon
17. Richmond
18. Barnes
19. Acton
20. Willesden
21. Hendon

**INNER CITY DECLINE**
*decrease in population*
- 0-5%
- 6-15%
- 16-30%
- over 30%
- overall increase in population

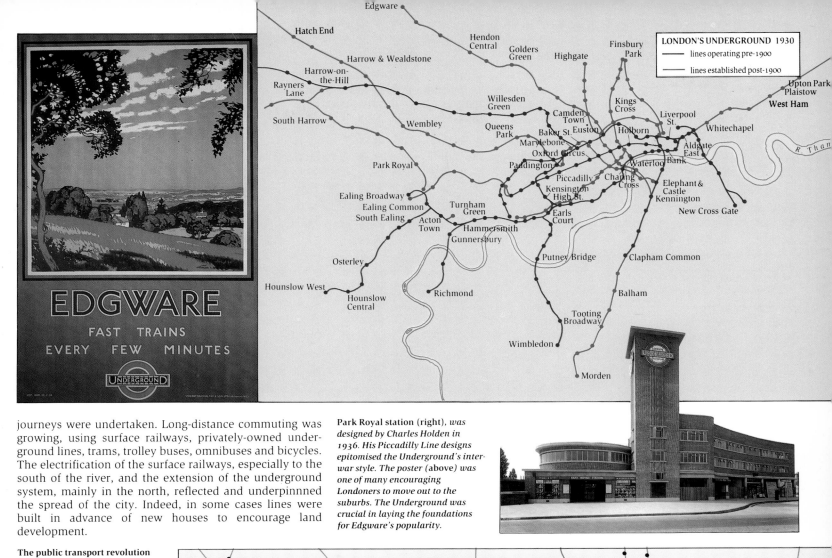

journeys were undertaken. Long-distance commuting was growing, using surface railways, privately-owned underground lines, trams, trolley buses, omnibuses and bicycles. The electrification of the surface railways, especially to the south of the river, and the extension of the underground system, mainly in the north, reflected and underpinnned the spread of the city. Indeed, in some cases lines were built in advance of new houses to encourage land development.

Park Royal station (right), *was designed by Charles Holden in 1936. His Piccadilly Line designs epitomised the Underground's inter-war style. The poster (above) was one of many encouraging Londoners to move out to the suburbs. The Underground was crucial in laying the foundations for Edgware's popularity.*

**The public transport revolution**
*This period was the Golden Age of public transport in London. Its rapid growth was already under way at the beginning of the century, as numerous companies introduced electric and petrol-driven services to displace the steam trains and horse trams of the last century. The expansion and electrification of both underground (map above) and surface railways (map right) were to continue for the next 40 years. The increasing scope of the system was dictated by a few dominant private companies, especially the Underground Group, the Metropolitan Railway and Southern Railways.*

*The London County Council and some boroughs had also become involved in the electrification of tramways before the Great War. London Transport was established in 1933, finally ending the freewheeling chaos of London's public transport development, with the underground system, buses and trams all placed under the co-ordinating control of a single public corporation.*

LONDON'S RAILWAYS 1930
*stations closed post-1930 are named in italics*

main railway lines pre-1900

pre-1900 lines electrified 1900-1930

steam lines built 1900-1930

electric lines built 1900-1930

0    2
miles

# THE SUBURBAN DREAM

The lives of Londoners in the first fifty years of this century were dominated by two world wars and the Depression of the 1930s. One of the immediate effects of the First World War was the loss of able-bodied men and consequently the employment for the first time of women in many factory, transport and clerical jobs. These war-time upheavals, and the new social attitudes that went with them, radically altered the life prospects of many ordinary Londoners, sweeping aside Victorian and Edwardian formality, raising aspirations and offering fundamental and lasting changes in lifestyle.

Unlike the rest of the country, London appeared to benefit from the Depression. It was not dependent on heavy industry, but instead had developed the new manufacturing technologies of the time, and so attracted cheap labour from other parts of the country. At the same time, employment in offices – both government and commercial – was expanding. The result of London's resilience in the depressed job market of the post-war years was a huge housing and consumer boom. The economic and social trauma of the post-war years made home-ownership a stable and attractive prospect to the rapidly-growing middle classes, and from the early 1920s private building contractors began to buy cheap land on the outskirts of the city for building purposes – this was the birth of 'semi-detached' London. Throughout the 20s and 30s this ring of suburban development expanded, and new houses were to spring up especially quickly in areas which were served by new railway and Underground extensions – a trend which was enthusiastically endorsed by London Underground advertising campaigns which celebrated the lure of 'Metroland'. Houses were also built along new arterial roads and by-passes. The more expensive up-market houses were concentrated in the north and north-west of London in areas such as Finchley, Hendon and Barnet, and around the southern fringes, at Coulsdon, Purley and Epsom. Architecturally eclectic, the favoured styles included 'mock Tudor', a reflection of aspirations towards an idealised rural past. Cheaper, more down-market 'semis' sprung up all round London, and – with small down-payments and low mortgage repayments – were well within the reach of many Londoners. Although mass-produced to a few basic designs, styles were subtly varied to give individuality, including mock-Tudor and Gothic details, with variations in porches, bay windows and tiling.

Surrounding the private, family-centred world of semi-detached London, the most dynamic changes in lifestyle between the wars were being created by commercial pressures towards American-style mass consumerism, and its promotion through both advertising and the media. A growing range of goods was being manufactured using new production techniques for mass sale: cookers, washing machines, fridges, furniture, electrical heaters, radios, processed food, lighting accessories, bathroom fittings, popular newspapers, magazines and books – all the accoutrements of home ownership and improvement, gardening and increased leisure time.

At the same time, new styles of mass retailing were opening up, initially in the West End, which could be reached quickly and easily by improved

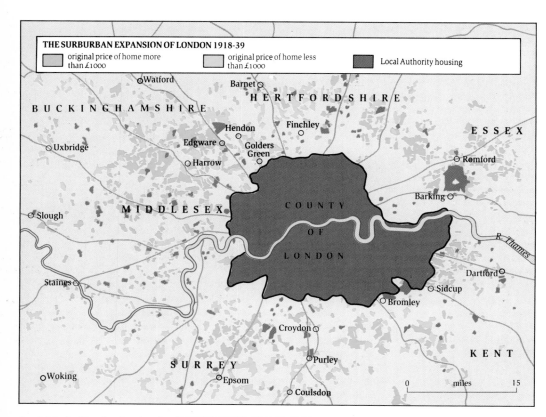

**THE SURUBURBAN EXPANSION OF LONDON 1918-39**

original price of home more than £1000

original price of home less than £1000

Local Authority housing

Watford · Barnet · HERTFORDSHIRE · BUCKINGHAMSHIRE · Hendon · Finchley · ESSEX · Uxbridge · Edgware · Golders Green · Romford · Harrow · MIDDLESEX · Barking · R. Thames · Slough · COUNTY OF LONDON · Staines · Dartford · Sidcup · Bromley · Croydon · KENT · SURREY · Purley · Woking · Epsom · Coulsdon

0 miles 15

**Semi-detached London** *In spite of the suburbs' reputation for dull uniformity, there were considerable variations in house size, style and cost (map above). The majority of semi-detached houses sold at less than £1,000 (photograph right), and encircled London (map above). Larger, often detached houses were typical of areas away from the growing industrial zones (below right). The map (right) shows a suburban estate at Finchley, with its gardens, shops, tennis court, woodland fringe and 'rustic' street names. The LCC's council estates, built after the First World War, set high standards (below).*

Cissbury Ring North · Lullington Garth · Chanctonbury Garth · Cissbury Ring South · tennis court · Woodside Park · Walmington Fold · shops · Dollis Brook

**WOODSIDE PARK GARDEN SUBURB FINCHLEY c.1935**

public transport, and then in the expanding suburban centres. The siting of chain stores, such as Woolworths, became the best indicator of the status of local shopping centres. New means of mass communication, such as the popular press and the 'wireless', which had spread to most homes by 1939, also created a common basis of information. But it was the cinema which was to have the greatest impact on the lives of ordinary Londoners. Picture palaces, lavishly decorated and hugely popular, were sited away from the traditional theatrical heartland of the West End, their locations mirroring the new prominence of suburbia. By 1929, there were 266 cinemas in the LCC area alone.

Nevertheless, inherited inequalities between rich and poor, especially in incomes and housing, remained etched on the map of the city. Many of the slums of the 1930s showed little improvement from the beginning of the century. Initially, the LCC and inner city boroughs had embarked on an ambitious policy, building large quantities of high-quality council houses and estates on the semi-rural fringes of London. Typical houses had three or more bedrooms, running water, inside toilets and bathrooms, electricity and spacious gardens. However, the Depression and the economic difficulties it caused meant that these standards were not always maintained, and public and political concern was slow to be translated

into effective large-scale action. The Second World War devastated large parts of London, including many of the areas of worst social deprivation. Whereas the effort of building between the wars had resulted in almost a million suburban, largely private dwellings, the drive after the War was towards rebuilding the inner areas, or alternatively offering people a new life outside London altogether, in the first new towns, established after 1947. In both cases, public intervention, under the new 'Welfare State', was essential – the Victorian combination of market forces and philanthropy deployed to solve social inequality was finally superseded by concerted State action.

**Inner City deprivation** *Poverty dominated many areas of inner and east London throughout the interwar period. This area of Bethnal Green* (right) *shows the close intermingling of poor housing with industry (in an area dominated by small furniture and sweatshop clothing firms), warehousing, public buildings, and shops in the early '30s. Employment was uncertain in these areas, often casual and in trades with marked seasonal and cyclical fluctuations. Housing lacked most basic amenities, including electricity and water supply; toilet, bathing and cooking facilities had to be shared. Many houses, built over 100 years ago, were now overcrowded, damp and dilapidated (photograph below right). In spite of these deprivations, such areas enjoyed an intense, street-based communal life, often missed by those who moved to new LCC estates (bottom).*

**Selling the suburbs** *London Underground was instrumental in promoting the suburbs – often new Underground lines preceded development. The booklet (left), Metroland (1928-9), was one of a series put out by the Metropolitan Railway to encourage travel to the suburbs. It contained advertisements from estate agents and building contractors. The line from Golders Green to Edgware was extended 1923-4, and London Underground posters (below left, by William Kermode 1924), promoted the suburban dream – 'that I might be Master of a small House and a Large Garden'.*

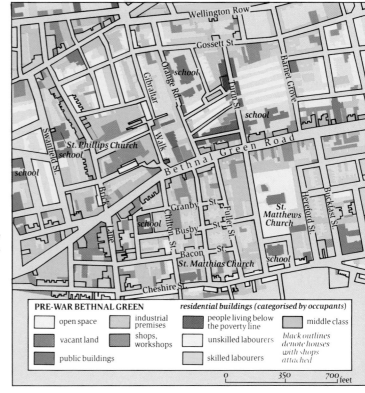

# INDUSTRIAL LONDON

The industrial inheritance of London in 1900 was twofold: the port and the Victorian manufacturing belt. The latter was a densely packed arc of small-scale specialist industries in the inner suburbs to the north, east and south of central London, frequently the successors of long-established crafts which originated in the medieval city. With some small exceptions, these specialised areas were still clearly identifiable fifty years later. They survived by specialising in labour-intensive, skilled production, such as tailored clothing or furniture in the East End and precision engineering in Clerkenwell and Tottenham Court Road, and depended

on a skilled, local labour supply. Many larger firms, however, had already moved out to areas such as Hackney, Camden Town, or even farther afield, where modern production methods could be more easily applied. The migration of London's skilled labour force to the suburbs also continued, especially during the immediate aftermath of the Second World War.

The other old-established industrial zone in London was associated with the port. The diverse shipping activities connected with the port itself were augmented by heavy industries based on large sites, such as marine engineering and repairs, construction materials, timber, food processing, and gas and electricity production. Many of these industries were extensions of port activities, servicing shipping or processing imported materials, which were then

**The Victorian Legacy** *The inheritance of Victorian manufacturing was spread throughout the London County Council area in 1947 (map below), often intermingled with residential areas, and it was the aim of the planning authorities to improve the living environment by disentangling this intermixture. However, the old-established industrial quarters (map below left) – from the tailoring districts of the East End to furniture-making in Shoreditch – had always depended on skilled workers living nearby. Heavier industries were found farther east (map below right), near the port and along the River Lea and the canals. These industries supported shipping, through engineering and repair yards, and processed imported raw materials, such as timber, food and chemicals. In time, however, many industries moved out to London's suburbs, where skilled workers increasingly preferred to live. The wartime bombing of central London and the devastation it caused to the city's traditional industrial heartland, accelerated this trend.*

LONDON'S INDUSTRY 1947
- open space
- 500 workers per dot
- location of industry

THE INDUSTRIAL QUARTERS OF NORTH-EAST LONDON 1948
- concentration of industry
- industrial quarter
- other areas with industrial specialisations

INDUSTRIES USING WATER TRANSPORT 1948
- timber merchants and sawmills
- food product manufacturers
- constructional engineers and metal industries
- ship and barge repairs
- chemical industries
- other manufacturers
- gas and electricity

transported by rail to other parts of the British Isles, or re-exported abroad. Whilst they provided some diversity for the economy of the East End, they attracted only low wages, and were particularly susceptible to the depression conditions of the 1930s.

The main change after 1918 was the development of factories outside these old-established areas, especially in the new suburban industrial estates which were located around the outer periphery of the city and accessible to the new trunk road networks. These estates provided an ideal environment for spacious factories, which used electric power and automated processes, and were therefore less dependent on the old craft skills. One such industrial zone in the north-east of London spread along the Lea valley from the port area as far north as Enfield. Inner-city firms, such as clothing and furniture-makers, moved out here, and were joined by newer factories specialising in activities such as electrical engineering.

The same pattern was repeated on an even larger scale in west London, as the spread of suburban housing accelerated. The largest area was in and around Park Royal, built on the site of a failed agricultural show and First World War munitions factory. Although a few large companies moved in later, most firms here were small, occupying ready-made factories. Wembley Stadium (*page 143*), the site of the British Empire Exhibition in 1924, also subsequently offered extensive areas for industrial development. Among other areas that became prominent were Hayes, Southall and Acton, and locations along the new arterial roads and the North Circular, such as Colindale and Cricklewood. The main industries that grew up at this time were general and electrical engineering, vehicle manufacture and food processing. By 1933, the Lea valley industrial zone employed almost 38,000 people, and west Middlesex 75,000.

**Inter-war industrial expansion**
*Many factories were built along London's new arterial roads between the wars, exploiting the new potential of road transport, which freed industry from the old ties of rail and water transport. One of the new industrial areas was the Great West Road, opened in 1925. Many now-familiar factories moved into new premises: Smith's crisps (poster below); Curry's cycles and radios (below); Gillette razors (bottom). These spacious, showcase factories depended on the spread of the electricity supply, from new river-based power stations, such as at Battersea (right).*

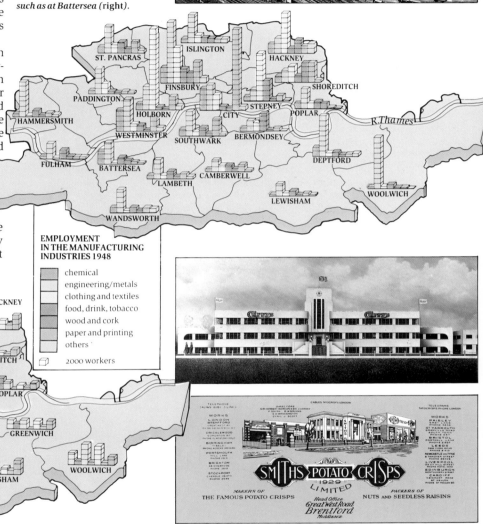

**EMPLOYMENT IN THE MANUFACTURING INDUSTRIES 1948**

- chemical
- engineering/metals
- clothing and textiles
- food, drink, tobacco
- wood and cork
- paper and printing
- others
- ◻ 2000 workers

**EMPLOYMENT IN THE NON-MANUFACTURING INDUSTRIES 1948**

- building
- transport & commercial
- distribution
- insurance, banking, finance
- administration
- professional
- miscellaneous
- ◻ 2000 workers

**Distribution of industry, 1948**
*Different districts within the city came to specialise in distinct manufacturing trades (map top right), often because of local concentrations of skilled workers, as well as long-established traditions – for example printing in Fleet Street and the City. London was, however, a predominantly service-based city (map above), and by the late '40s its financial, administrative and professional functions had come to dominate the City and the West End.*

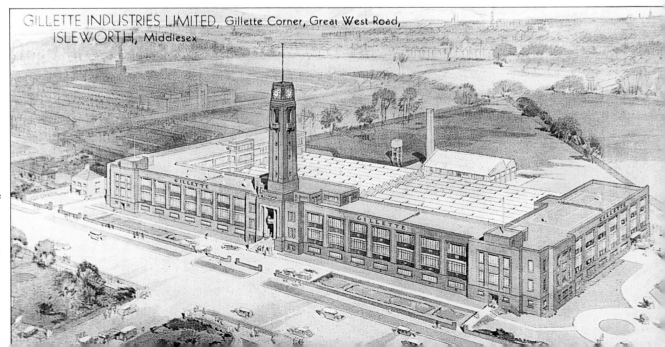

# LONDON AT WAR

The outbreak of war in 1914 coincided with the early development of military aviation. German strategists argued that bombing their city would undermine morale so much that Londoners would force their government to sue for peace, and in July 1915 the Kaiser finally gave approval to attacks on the enemy capital. From then until May 1918 London became a limited field of conflict; German attacks were few and far between and were relatively ineffective. At first they were confined to Zeppelin raids; airships dropped 196 tons of bombs on London and the surrounding counties. In 1917 the German air force developed a long-range bomber, the Gotha IV, capable of reaching London. From June 1917 a series of raids was carried out in fine weather; these attacks killed 835 Londoners and injured 1,437. London turned into an armed camp: an outer circle of airfields provided fighter protection; an inner circle of searchlights and anti-aircraft guns covered the capital itself.

The experience of the first war prepared London for the next. In the later 1930s the government developed plans for the air defence of London: air raid shelters were built; civil defence training and advice were established; the evacuation of the city was planned in great detail. The first bombs were not dropped until September 1940, which was the start of the Blitz, a sustained six-month bombardment of London which produced 71 major raids during which 18,000 tons of high explosive bombs were dropped and 20,000 Londoners killed. At first, German aircraft attacked military and port facilities, but in alleged retaliation for British attacks on German cities the bombing became more indiscriminate. Londoners were forced to spend sleepless nights in air raid shelters and Underground stations. The bombing cut gas, water and electricity supplies, and brought transport chaos after heavy raids. Yet the Blitz failed to destroy London's economy or to undermine London's morale. When Londoners were asked by Mass Observation what made them most depressed in the winter of 1940-1, they rated weather above air-raids. Over half of Londoners polled were against vengeance attacks on Germany.

In May 1941, the bombing abruptly came to an end with the great raid of May 10th. Over the next three years

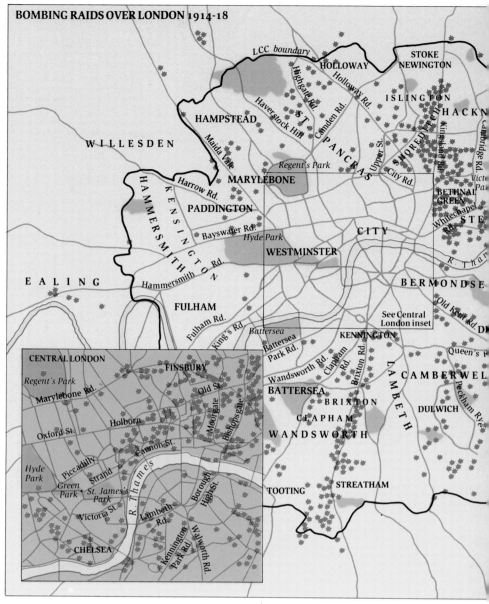

BOMBING RAIDS OVER LONDON 1914-18

CENTRAL LONDON

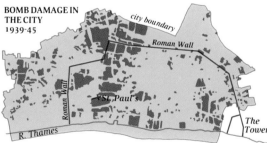

BOMB DAMAGE IN THE CITY 1939-45

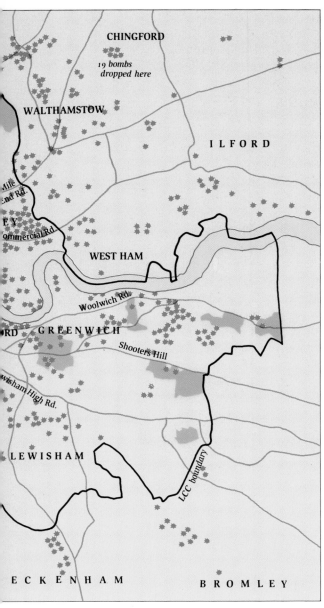

**Aerial bombardment** *On the morning of 13 June, 1917, fourteen German bombers launched the first aircraft attack on London. They dropped four tons of bombs, most of them falling within a mile of Liverpool Street Station. From then until May 1918, a series of raids brought destruction to many parts of the capital (map left). Barrage balloons, anti-aircraft artillery and searchlights were mobilised to combat the raiders. The same system was used during the Blitz, when German air forces attacked London repeatedly between September 1940 and May 1941. The most famous raid took place on 29 December, 1940 when large parts of the city were destroyed (map below).*

London's defences were strengthened and it became a major centre of wartime production, despite its proximity to German air bases. The long lull made the renewed assault in the summer of 1944 harder to take. The Allies were mounting ever-heavier attacks on German cities. Hitler demanded retaliation and launched the new wonder-weapons, the V1 flying-bomb and the V2 rocket, against London. The first bombs landed in June 1944 and continued almost to the end of the war. The damage they did was slight compared with the Blitz, but the attacks were indiscriminate and loss of life was high. The V-weapons killed 9,200 and injured 22,000 others. In total, 29,890 Londoners were killed by enemy action in the capital, and 50,507 were injured. Large areas of central London were reduced to rubble. It was this destruction which helped to accelerate the trend towards centralised town-planning, as well as hastening the re-location of London's population, from city to suburbs, which had begun in the 1930s.

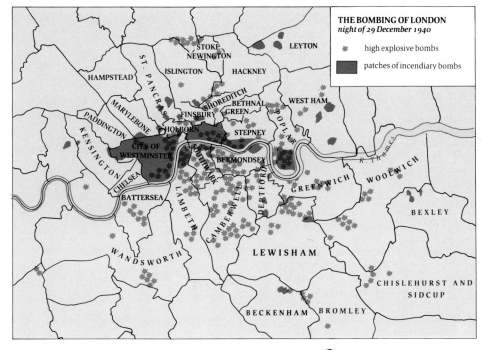

**THE BOMBING OF LONDON**
*night of 29 December 1940*

high explosive bombs

patches of incendiary bombs

**London at war** *When the Second World War broke out, London was prepared for extensive bombing. In September 1939, 690,000 children were evacuated from London to safer provincial areas and London's main stations were thronged with diminutive travellers (photograph far left). By the time of the Blitz many had returned to the city. Two maps (centre left and below right) give a stark picture of the damage sustained by Greater London and, in particular, the City during the Second World War. An artist's drawing of the City (left), made from a low-flying hot air balloon, gives a vivid impression of the destruction. An exhortation to 'Dig for Victory' is emblazoned across the Royal Exchange, ironically surrounded by vast craters (left), while bowler-hatted office workers pick their way across flattened streets in Moorgate in 1941 (above left). London Underground posters celebrated the City's survival – Walter Bradberry's 'The Proud City' (above right) shows the Chelsea power station lit up by searchlights. Although the worst of the Blitz was over by May 1941, German attacks returned again in 1944, with Hitler's 'Vengeance' weapons, the V1 flying bomb and V2 rocket (map far right).*

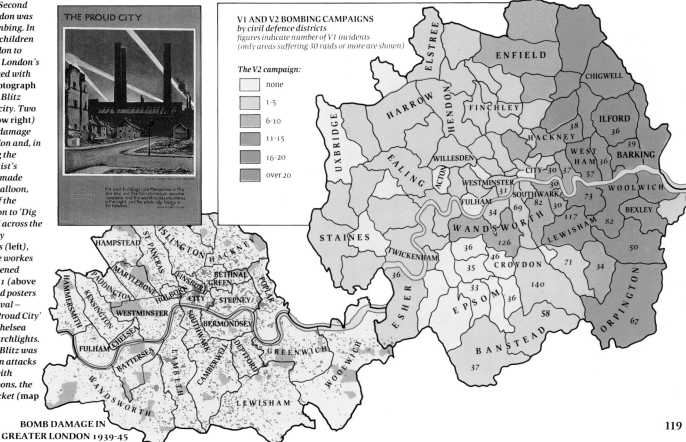

THE PROUD CITY

*'...the poor buildings lose themselves in the dim sky and the tall chimneys become campanili and the warehouses are palaces in the night, and the whole city hangs in the heavens.'*

**V1 AND V2 BOMBING CAMPAIGNS**
*by civil defence districts*
*figures indicate number of V1 incidents*
*(only areas suffering 30 raids or more are shown)*

**The V2 campaign:**

1-5

6-10

11-15

16-20

over 20

**BOMB DAMAGE IN GREATER LONDON 1939-45**

119

# CHAPTER 9
# POST-WAR LONDON

*The brave new world of post-war Britain was proclaimed at the Festival of Britain on London's South Bank, previously a place of wharves and industry. King George VI performed the inauguration ceremony on 3 May 1951. There was a sense of holiday in the air and the crowds came in droves. People were fascinated by the bold architecture of the buildings, the detail of exhibits, attractions of cafés, and views over the Thames that took them out of their everyday world of rationing and deprivation – at least for a few hours. At the end of September, the Festival closed; nearly 8.5 million people had visited the South Bank, and over 8 million had gone to the Pleasure Gardens at Battersea. Almost all the Festival buildings, including the massive Dome of Discovery, were temporary and were soon demolished. The Royal Festival Hall, with almost 3,000 seats, remains at the heart of the cultural focus of the South Bank.*

**Below** *In popular mythology, post-war London's success reached its peak with the emergence of the pop music and fashion cultures of the 'swinging sixties'. During this period, London became the focus of world attention as a leading 'style capital', and nowhere epitomised this new-found status as a trend-setting city more vividly than Carnaby Street, with its fashionable boutiques and lively street culture.*

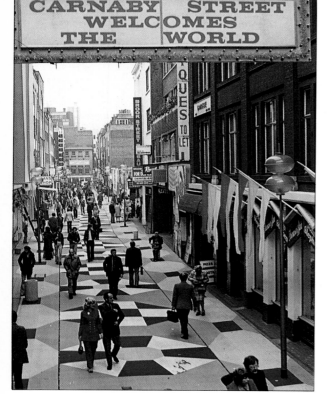

LONDON HAS CHANGED radically since the Second World War. During the first 20 years of the period, the city's status as the hub of the British Empire progressively diminished, followed within 15 years by the final decline of the old Port of London. In the 1980s, however, the expansion of global financial markets enabled the City to renew and sustain its leading world position. Other areas of the city were also transformed by changes in the international situation; as declining seaborne trade undermined the economy of east London, so the rise of mass air transport focused expansion in the west around Heathrow, and in the south around Gatwick. Perhaps the most startling consequence of this expansion was the growth of London as a major centre of international tourism, a development certainly not anticipated by planners at the end of the war.

London's manufacturing industries and the port – the traditional employers of the working-class – continued to thrive until the mid-1960s, but then began to close down or move out of the city with increasing speed. Unemployment rose, and the quality of the remaining types of employment declined. Jobs tended to be less secure, poorly paid and often associated with the tourist trade, consumer services or construction work. The public sector, always a vital part of the London economy, took up some of the slack in the 1970s, but this was followed by a reduction of employment in national and local government, the health service and public transport.

Changes in city life, however, reflect not only economic and social realities, but also involve attitudes to the image of the city and the buoyancy of its culture. In popular mythology, post-war London's success reached its first peak with the emergence of the pop music and fashion cultures of the 'swinging sixties'. The coming-of-age of the post-war baby-boom, the development of the modern 'media' industries – led by film, television, radio and advertising – all combined to focus world attention on London in the late 1960s. Two decades later, with the burgeoning of business and financial services, the 1980s equivalent of the 1960s was the 'yuppy' generation. Although based more upon commercial opportunism than artistic flair, this offered a similarly dominant, and ephemeral, image of London, reflected in many aspects of life from property development to fashion.

London also enjoyed a post-war artistic revival. During the 1960s and 70s it became an international centre of music, drama and the visual arts. This achievement had been stimulated by public and private sector investment in orchestras, theatre and opera companies and in such developments as the South Bank and Barbican Arts Centres. It also depended on expanding opportunities in higher education and rising middle-class cultural aspirations. The artistic dynamism of the capital was further enhanced by the growing number of immigrants from Ireland, Europe and the Commonwealth. They, in turn, generated new, and exotic, sources of music, fashion and lifestyle.

Another key change in post-war London was a greater awareness of the need to preserve the city's dwindling cultural and architectural heritage. In the view of many, such sentiments emerged much too late; the 20th-century transformation of London's appearance had been radical, piecemeal and generally of mediocre quality. As investment in manufacturing industries was withdrawn, successive booms in private property development satisfied an apparently insatiable demand for modern office accommodation. The West End and the City were transformed by periods of virulent land speculation and soaring land prices. This pattern has been frequently repeated in London's history;

*A discussion of London's history of immigration can be found on pages 136-137.*

*A discussion of the unrealised plans to redevelop Piccadilly Circus in the 1960s, and the contrasting plans to redevelop, and at the same time conserve, Spitalfields in the 1990s can be found on page 129.*

the needs of private capital have always taken precedence over regulation or planning. Ironically, less than 25 years on, some of the 1960s developments were being demolished under the influence of the 'heritage' movement, to be replaced by buildings which revived historical styles.

By the 1970s London's 'inner city' problems were multiplying. To the problems of unemployment were added ethnic conflicts, public sector under-funding, unsuccessful education reforms, overstrained welfare and health services, and increasingly inadequate housing provisions. Although most of the houses built in London immediately after the war were intended for council renting, there were long waiting lists which increased as rates of building diminished after the 1960s. Much of the post-war housing built by public authorities was criticised for its alienating design, poor construction and inadequate maintenance. For people moving into the city, whether from northern England, Ireland, Barbados or Bangladesh, neither private ownership nor council renting was readily available. The provision of privately rented accommodation – best suited to the shifting population of the city – declined, and what remained rose in price. The early 1960s were marked by the scandal of 'Rachmanism' whereby unscrupulous developers forced out tenants who were paying low, controlled rents, and redeveloped the properties either to sell them or charge higher rents. The optimistic attitude of the 1950s to house building and urban redevelopment was therefore the prelude to a long-term intensification of London's housing problems. In its most extreme form, this was demonstrated by the growth of the homeless population during the 1980s.

Nowhere were the difficulties of reconciling conflicting interests in post-war London more evident than in formulating a cohesive transport policy.

*The gentrification of London's Georgian and Victorian housing is discussed on page 127.*

**Above** *The 1980s saw a period when London's business and financial services burgeoned. London's industrial legacy had been supplanted in the post-war years by the rise of the service sector. By the 1980s, London was exploiting its status as a leading world financial centre, and the square mile of the City was being transformed by a speculative building boom. This view of the Stock Exchange at night clearly demonstrates the mixture of old and new which now characterises the architecture of the City, with the measured classicism of the Mansion House (centre) and the Bank of England (left) contrasted against the looming height of the NatWest Tower in the distance.*

121

Right *London's status as an international capital in the postwar years was reinforced by the opening of a new London airport, at Heathrow, in 1946. Development proceeded there over the ensuing forty years, the most recent addition being Terminal Four (opened in 1986). In 1977, the Piccadilly Line was extended to Heathrow, improving transport links with the capital. Heathrow is one of the world's busiest airports; Terminal Four can handle up to 4,000 passengers an hour. A fifth terminal will add further capacity at Heathrow, and important expansion is planned at Stansted. Noise pollution and urbanisation of rural land are major environmental threats that should not be underestimated. Radical commentators have even called for the closure of Heathrow and its replacement by a vast new international airport on the Cliffe marshes along the Thames estuary of northern Kent.*

*A map of the Greater London Development Plan can be found on page 128.*

Far-sighted plans for road improvement had been laid down in the 1930s, but they were soon overwhelmed by the scale of traffic growth in the 1960s. The Greater London Development Plan of 1967 proposed a 'motorway box' around the centre of London, orbital motorways in the suburbs, and routes to connect the city centre to the national motorway system. Some argued that the building of motorways in cities simply encouraged the greater use of vehicles, swamping other aspects of city life wherever they decanted traffic into local areas. The most telling opposition, however, came from localities directly threatened by motorway building, and the strength of opposition to the GLDP scheme led to its eventual abandonment. Transport policy has long been the

subject of heated political debate. Questions have been asked about appropriate levels of subsidy required to maintain British Rail and London Transport services, road-building schemes, the introduction of bus lanes, the possibility of taxing road users, and the high proportion of cars in rush-hour queues that were company-subsidised. The rise of tourism and the revival of commuting into central London in the 1980s added to the problems. Meanwhile, it was universally agreed that the quality of public transport continued to decline, dragging the quality of the environment of inner London down with it. In 1986 the completion of the M25 orbital motorway around London vividly demonstrated the problems of preserving the city in an age of escalating road transport. It connected many areas around London for the first time, but generated as much as six times the traffic anticipated, and quickly became a byword for congestion and motorists' frustration.

In 1945 the dominant administrative and political authority in London was the London County Council. This elected authority governed inner London, but its powers to represent the whole of London became increasingly limited by the expansion of the city beyond the LCC boundaries. In spite of opposition, the Greater London Council was instituted in 1965, covering 610 square miles and including most of the built-up area of the city. The whole of Middlesex and parts of the other surrounding counties were added to the former LCC area. A new two-tier metropolitan government was established, with 32 London Boroughs and the City of London. The GLC was given a significant range of powers which included strategic planning, the administration of the LCC's housing and parks, main sewers, drainage and flood prevention, main roads and traffic planning, the fire and ambulance services, and refuse disposal. The old LCC educational service was separately preserved as the Inner London Education Authority, while the outer boroughs administered their own education.

The GLC was able to draw on the rating resources of outer London to help inner London; as the wealth gap between these two areas increased however, political resistance from outer London to this redistribution of finances grew. The GLC's administrations were often out of step with central government, which frequently led to political conflict. One trend which in part reflected this situation was the erosion of the GLC's powers, sometimes as part of wider administrative reforms. In 1974, for example, the establishment of Regional Water and Health Authorities removed the GLC's drainage and flood prevention functions, and the ambulance service. The GLC's housing, both within the city and in the overspill communities outside it, was transferred in 1980-82 to local boroughs. The Council's supervisory control of the London Transport Executive granted in 1970, was removed once more in 1984. By the 1980s, the net effect had been to diminish the GLC's role in London to activities such as transport studies, arts and recreation, and grants to voluntary bodies.

The GLC was finally abolished in 1986 and for the first time for 97 years, there was no unified representative government for the city, a situation unique among major world cities. In 1990, the Inner London Education Authority, the last remnant of the old LCC, was also abolished.

In the post-war decades, the major contrast in development was between the declining east of the city, and the prosperous, 'overheating' west. This was, if anything, encouraged by planned investment in new towns, motorways, Heathrow Airport, research and development, and military establishments. Only by the mid-1980s did the completion of the M25, the final designation of the third London airport at Stansted, the imminent completion of the Channel Tunnel, and the prospect of major investment in eastern Docklands and lower Thamesside, seem to shift the emphasis eastwards. Nevertheless, the huge established pressures for development west of the capital remained the single most powerful force shaping the geography of the London region as the last decade of the 20th century approached.

*The construction of the M25, the increase in traffic congestion and the rising pressures on public transport within London are all discussed on pages 126-127. Construction of additional lanes along some stretches of the M25 is an attempt to ease traffic flows on this severely over-crowded motorway.*

**Map below** *London as it is today.*

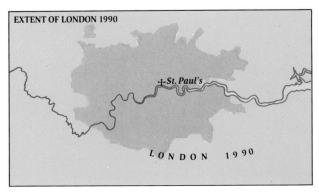

EXTENT OF LONDON 1990

+ St. Paul's

LONDON 1990

# THE POST-WAR CITY

In the twenty-year period after the Second World War the reconstruction of London was often localised and piecemeal. As economic recovery occurred the initiative for rebuilding in both the City and the West End was taken largely by landowners and commercial developers. Public agencies, however, channelled their efforts into neighbourhoods that had suffered serious war-

*The Lansbury Estate in Poplar was built as the Festival of Britain's Exhibition of Living Architecture. This pioneering neighbourhood scheme (left) was intended to act as a blueprint for the redevelopment of the deprived areas of the East End. Unfortunately, its intimate scale, low-rise design and generous provision of open space, was not widely adopted because of the pressure for mass-production building techniques which grew in subsequent years.*

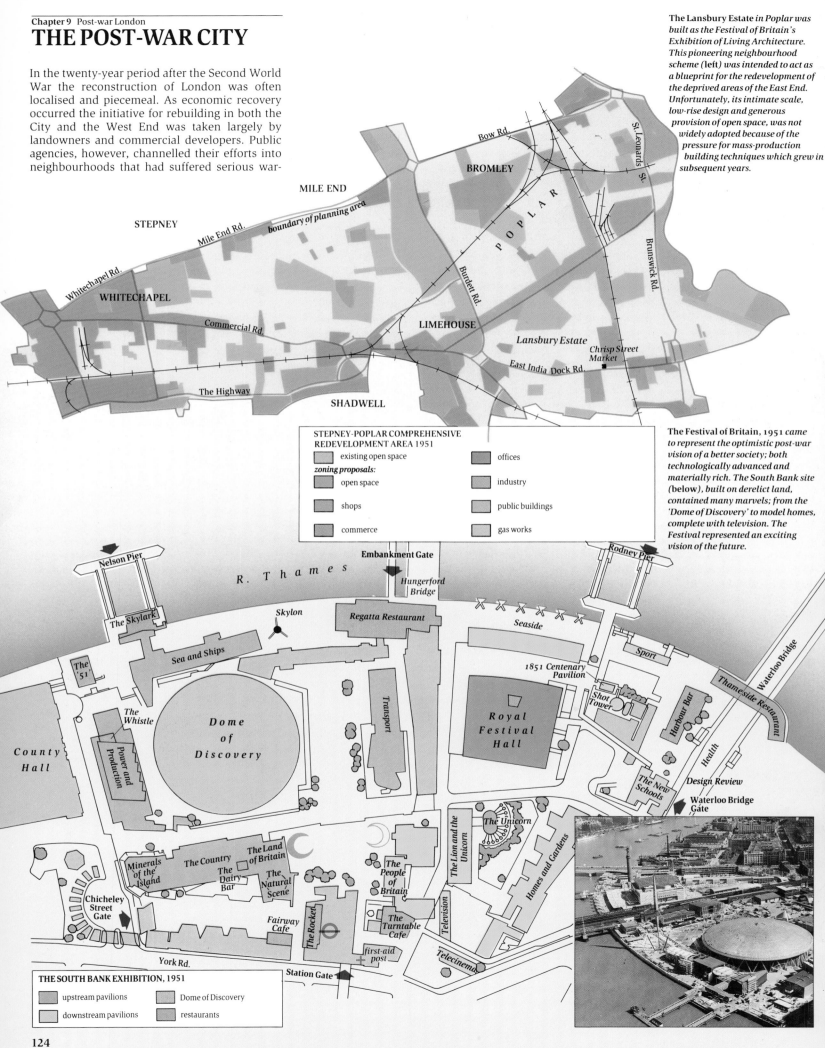

STEPNEY
Mile End Rd.
MILE END
*boundary of planning area*
Whitechapel Rd.
WHITECHAPEL
Commercial Rd.
The Highway
SHADWELL
Bow Rd.
BROMLEY
P O P L A R
St. Leonards St.
Burdett Rd.
Brunswick Rd.
LIMEHOUSE
Lansbury Estate
Chrisp Street Market
East India Dock Rd.

**STEPNEY-POPLAR COMPREHENSIVE REDEVELOPMENT AREA 1951**

- existing open space
- *zoning proposals:*
- open space
- shops
- commerce
- offices
- industry
- public buildings
- gas works

*The Festival of Britain, 1951 came to represent the optimistic post-war vision of a better society; both technologically advanced and materially rich. The South Bank site (below), built on derelict land, contained many marvels; from the 'Dome of Discovery' to model homes, complete with television. The Festival represented an exciting vision of the future.*

Nelson Pier
The Skylark
R. Thames
Embankment Gate
Hungerford Bridge
Rodney Pier
Waterloo Bridge
Skylon
Regatta Restaurant
Seaside
Thameside Restaurant
The '51'
Sea and Ships
Sport
1851 Centenary Pavilion
Shot Tower
Harbour Bar
The Whistle
Dome of Discovery
Transport
Royal Festival Hall
Health
County Hall
Power and Production
The New Schools
Design Review
Waterloo Bridge Gate
Minerals of the Island
The Country
The Land of Britain
The Dairy Bar
The Natural Scene
The Lion and the Unicorn
The Unicorn
Homes and Gardens
Chicheley Street Gate
The People of Britain
Fairway Cafe
The Rocket
The Turntable Cafe
Television
*first-aid post*
York Rd.
Station Gate
Telecinema

**THE SOUTH BANK EXHIBITION, 1951**

- upstream pavilions
- downstream pavilions
- Dome of Discovery
- restaurants

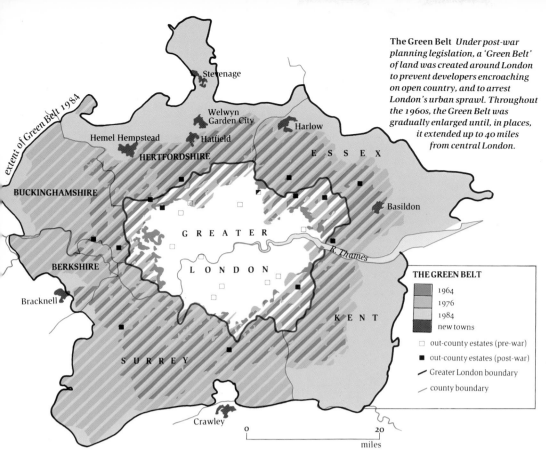

extent of Green Belt 1984

**The Green Belt** *Under post-war planning legislation, a 'Green Belt' of land was created around London to prevent developers encroaching on open country, and to arrest London's urban sprawl. Throughout the 1960s, the Green Belt was gradually enlarged until, in places, it extended up to 40 miles from central London.*

**THE GREEN BELT**

- 1964
- 1976
- 1984
- new towns
- ☐ out-county estates (pre-war)
- ■ out-county estates (post-war)
- Greater London boundary
- county boundary

Perhaps the real embodiment of the Festival spirit can be found in the new towns ideology. Although sometimes attached to small existing settlements, they were intended to create a totally new living environment. They were to be medium-sized communities (around 60,000, although most are now well above this), with a preponderance of council housing for poor families from London, set in rural surroundings. They would have enough employment in new industries, often relocated from London, to prevent the need for commuting back to the city. Housing areas were grouped into neighbourhoods of 10-12,000 people, with local shopping and schools clearly segregated from the industrial areas. Green belts – areas of farmland and open country protected by law from urban infringement – were instituted in 1946. The new towns thus presented a planned outlet for the growth of London's population, protecting the countryside of the south-east from indiscriminate sprawl.

The planned approach to London's many long-standing problems, adopted after the Second World War, can claim several successes. The Green Belt has been regularly extended and remains one of the most secure features of British planning policy. In their early years the new towns did suffer teething problems – many residents from crowded, intimate inner-city areas found the planned vision of a better future antiseptic, and suffered greatly from the towns' lack of community. However, over the years many new towns have matured into pleasant, well-established settlements and have been among the major growth centres of the 1980s.

The idealism of the Festival of Britain could not, however, anticipate the 'baby boom' of the 1960s, and the resulting pressures placed on space in the London region. Nor did it foresee the effects of growing affluence on people's housing expectations, or the huge impact of general car-ownership, with its resultant effects on transportation in the city. Furthermore, post-war optimism did not anticipate the collapse of London's manufacturing and port economy some twenty years later. The new towns have been able to adapt to, and even benefit from, these changes. The redevelopment of the East End in the 1950s and '60s appeared to eradicate the legacy of poverty, but many high-rise estates built then developed serious problems in the following years. Characterised by high levels of crime and socio-economic deprivation, they form a major challenge for the future planning of London.

time devastation and into major redevelopment schemes, designed to solve the problems of London's poor housing, social amenities and infrastructure. The 1947 Town and Country Planning Act legislated for the comprehensive redevelopment of the slum areas of the old Victorian city. The largest schemes were in the East End, where the old patterns of roads, services, housing and land-use were almost completely replaced over a twenty-five year period on the basis of a master plan drawn up in the 1940s.

Another approach to redevelopment involved moving people out of the city altogether, initially to the eight 'first generation' new towns, established in 1947-8: Basildon, Bracknell, Crawley, Harlow, Hatfield, Hemel Hempstead, Stevenage and Welwyn Garden City. The two strategies were linked, since the rebuilt inner city areas could house barely half the population that was living there before. The new centres, along with established towns where expansion had been planned, such as Thetford in Norfolk or Swindon

in Wiltshire, were intended to receive 'overspill' from the reconstruction of London.

The idealism of the time was perhaps best symbolised by the South Bank Exhibition, the centrepiece of the 1951 nationwide Festival of Britain. One hundred years after the Great Exhibition in Hyde Park, this was intended to 'demonstrate the contributions to civilisation made by British advances in 'Science, Technology and Industrial Design' against a background representing the living and working world. Built on derelict land on the south bank of the river, the most striking features were the 'Dome of Discovery', containing exhibits on modern exploration, and the cigar-shaped 'Skylon', balanced on wires high above the spectators. After wartime and post-war deprivations, exhibits on 'The Land' of Britain, and 'The People', presented the morale-boosting prospect of a planned, technologically-based Welfare State. The Festival's permanent legacy to London was a section of river wall bounding the site, and the Festival Hall.

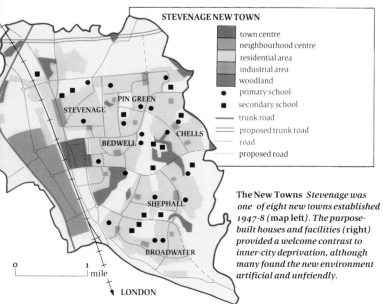

**STEVENAGE NEW TOWN**

- town centre
- neighbourhood centre
- residential area
- industrial area
- woodland
- • primary school
- ■ secondary school
- trunk road
- proposed trunk road
- road
- proposed road

**The New Towns** *Stevenage was one of eight new towns established 1947-8 (map left). The purpose-built houses and facilities (right) provided a welcome contrast to inner-city deprivation, although many found the new environment artificial and unfriendly.*

# LIVING AND WORKING IN LONDON

After the Second World War, the population of inner London, especially of skilled workers, was in decline. Londoners were moving out to the suburbs, satellite settlements and the new towns which were a major component of post-war planning. In the 1960s, inner London was also affected by the collapse of manufacturing. Many national firms closed their London factories, while small firms in the traditional textiles, clothing, furniture and metal-working quarters were going out of business, unable to compete with firms outside the city which were better placed to introduce new technology and compete internationally. Suburbs and new towns offered far better living conditions for the skilled workforce than deprived inner-city areas had done.

A further blow came with the equally rapid collapse of the port, caused by increased competition from continental and smaller east coast ports which used new container-handling and 'roll-on roll-off' ferry technologies. Hampered by poor labour relations and management, London's docks were progressively closed between 1969 and 1981, with the loss of about 25,000 jobs. A workforce of only 2-3,000 was left at the Tilbury and other downstream docks. Firms dependent on the port closed, adding to the general decline of inner city manufacturing.

Meanwhile, London's service role was being reasserted. London was becoming increasingly dependent on financial business in the 1970s and 80s, competing with New York and Tokyo. Most of the new jobs were filled by white collar workers from the suburbs and outside London, leading in turn to an increase in commuting during the 1980s as more people travelled into the city for work. This added to the strains on transportation that the decentralisation of manufacturing should have relieved.

Although offices were encouraged to move out of central London in the 1960s and 70s, this had only a marginal impact on the overall pattern of commuting, especially as demand for office space grew. Massive new schemes for road improvement had also been proposed to relieve some of the strain on public transport, but met with fierce opposition from local and environmental groups during the 1980s. The capital's commuting hinterland now extended to the south coast and into East Anglia, the Midlands and the West Country. In 1939, 8,600,000 people lived within Greater London; the total has now fallen to 6,500,000 as many Londoners have moved to new homes beyond the Green Belt.

Despite this movement away from the city, London's most pressing problem is still a substantial shortfall in satisfactory housing – 32,000 families in London are now recognised as homeless. Local Authorities are confronted with generations of London housing in a serious state of disrepair: solidly-built Victorian houses, inter-war semis and shoddily-built 1960s apartment blocks are all in need of massive investment.

London's residents are highly varied in wealth, age and household size and composition. In 1900, 90 per cent of Londoners rented their

**Developing the Green Belt** *Many Londoners have opted to move away from the problems of inner-city dilapidation into the surrounding countryside. The illustration (top right) shows a proposed shopping centre at Colnbrook, one mile west of Heathrow airport. Its neo-classical style is very different from the architecture of other new shopping centres and may make the project more acceptable to the substantial lobby who oppose the building of homes and other facilities within the Green Belt.*

*The whole of the M25 orbital motorway cuts through Green Belt land and sites close to motorway junctions offer prime locations for new development of all kinds (map below).*

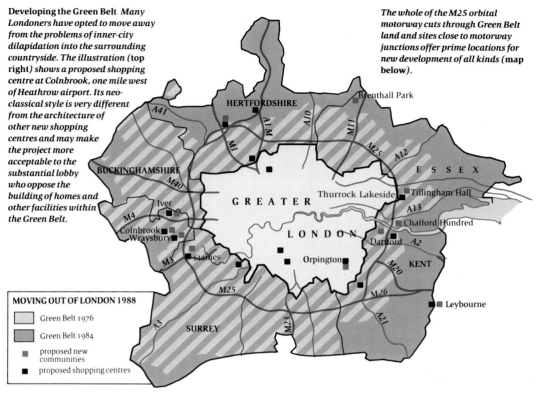

**MOVING OUT OF LONDON 1988**

- Green Belt 1976
- Green Belt 1984
- proposed new communities
- proposed shopping centres

**Gentrification** *The map (right) shows areas in Islington where significant influxes of professional and managerial residents occurred in the 1960s. The photographs (far right) show the run-down state of Canonbury housing before this trend (above), and the refurbished houses (below). The map (centre right) shows other districts gentrified in the 1960s. Renovation has occurred more widely in recent years.*

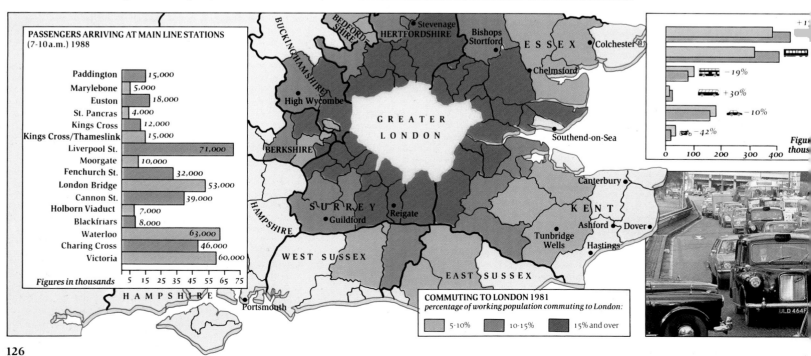

**PASSENGERS ARRIVING AT MAIN LINE STATIONS** (7-10 a.m.) 1988

| Station | Figures in thousands |
|---|---|
| Paddington | 15,000 |
| Marylebone | 5,000 |
| Euston | 18,000 |
| St. Pancras | 4,000 |
| Kings Cross | 12,000 |
| Kings Cross/Thameslink | 15,000 |
| Liverpool St. | 71,000 |
| Moorgate | 10,000 |
| Fenchurch St. | 32,000 |
| London Bridge | 53,000 |
| Cannon St. | 39,000 |
| Holborn Viaduct | 7,000 |
| Blackfriars | 8,000 |
| Waterloo | 63,000 |
| Charing Cross | 46,000 |
| Victoria | 60,000 |

*Figures in thousands*

−19%
+30%
−10%
−42%

Figu
thous

**COMMUTING TO LONDON 1981**
*percentage of working population commuting to London:*

- 5-10%
- 10-15%
- 15% and over

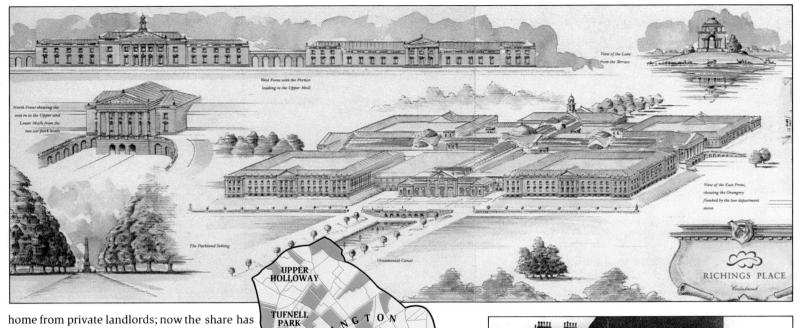

*View of the Lake from the Terrace*

*West Front with the Portico leading to the Upper Mall*

*North Front showing the way in to the Upper and Lower Malls from the two car park levels*

*View of the East Front, showing the Orangery flanked by the two department stores*

*The Parkland Setting*

*Ornamental Canal*

RICHINGS PLACE
*Colnbrook*

home from private landlords; now the share has dropped to below one-fifth. Just over half of London's homes are now owned by their occupants; the remaining 30 per cent are rented from local authorities or housing associations. The number of new homes built in Greater London declined sharply from 32,000 in 1972 to 8,000 in 1980. Until the building recession of the later 1980s, the figure ran at approximately 10,000 each year. Private rehabilitation of housing stock is widespread, especially in accessible inner suburbs with attractive but often run-down housing dating from Victorian and Edwardian times. Such areas have been discovered by managerial and professional households in recent years and a process of 'gentrification' has taken place – not only the houses themselves, but entire neighbourhoods are transformed by influxes of relatively affluent newcomers, who replace working-class residents. House prices subsequently rise, home-owners replace tenants, and local shops and restaurants cater for a wealthier clientele. In the 1990s London housing is a mosaic of great complexity with respect to age, appearance, comfort and quality. Like New York and Paris, some of the best accommodation in this cosmopolitan city is owned by members of London's large, diverse foreign community.

UPPER HOLLOWAY

TUFNELL PARK

ISLINGTON

Holloway Rd.

HIGHBURY

CANONBURY

LOWER HOLLOWAY

Canonbury Rd.

BARNSBURY

PENTONVILLE

ANGEL

0    1/4
miles

**LONDON GENTRIFICATION 1961–1971**

CAMDEN

ISLINGTON

HACKNEY

WESTMINSTER

TOWER HAMLETS

CITY

KENSINGTON & CHELSEA

HAMMERSMITH

WANDSWORTH

LAMBETH

SOUTHWARK

GREENWICH

LEWISHAM

**LONDON GENTRIFICATION 1961–1971**

'gentrified' areas 1961

1971

**COMMUTING TO CENTRAL LONDON**
(7·10 a.m.)

1983
1987

British Rail
Underground
Bus
commuter coach
private car
motor/pedal cycle

**A city of commuters**
*London commuters use a wide range of transport (table left). During the 1980s the number of commuters travelling by train, Underground or coach increased, while journeys by bus, private car or cycle declined. The map (far left) shows how London's commuting area has grown since mid-century. In 1951 it hugged the continuously built-up area; by 1981 it extended far into surrounding counties, and long-distance commuters travelled from East Anglia, the Midlands and the West Country. The table (inset) shows that Liverpool St. Station (serving East Anglia and Essex) receives the largest number of commuters, followed by Waterloo and Victoria. Roads, notably the M25, have been built to take some of the strain (map right), but under-investment in transport generally has made road congestion (left) and railway over-crowding (above left) an all too frequent occurrence.*

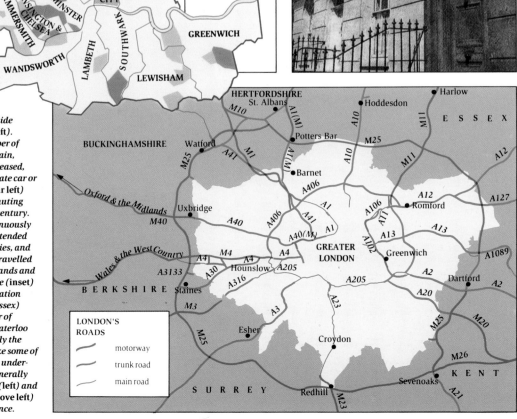

HERTFORDSHIRE
St. Albans
Harlow
Hoddesdon
M10
A1(M)
A10
M11
ESSEX
BUCKINGHAMSHIRE
Watford
Potters Bar
M25
A41
M1
M1(M)
A10
M11
A12
M25
Barnet
A406
A1
A12
Oxford & the Midlands
Uxbridge
A40
M40
A406
A41
A1
A106
A11
Romford
A127
A40(M)
A1
A13
A13
Wales & the West Country
A4
M4
A4
A4
GREATER LONDON
A102
Greenwich
A1089
A3133
A30
Hounslow
A205
A2
Dartford
A316
Staines
A205
A20
A2
BERKSHIRE
M3
A3
A23
M25
M20
Esher
Croydon
M26
KENT
SURREY
Redhill
M23
Sevenoaks
A21

**LONDON'S ROADS**

motorway
trunk road
main road

# PLANS FOR LONDON

During the Second World War it was widely accepted that public authorities would have to take the initiative in post-war reconstruction. The devastation wrought by the war gave London a unique opportunity to tackle the city's long-standing social, housing and environmental problems. The planning pioneer, Sir Patrick Abercrombie, advocated that development should be co-ordinated across the whole city and, as early as 1944, he anticipated reconstruction up to 30 miles from the centre in his 'Greater London Plan'. After 1947, when local authorities and a new Ministry of Town and Country Planning were given powers to control the change of land use, Abercrombie's vision became the basis of London's planning for the next thirty years. These years proved to be a period when market forces increasingly encouraged the decentralisation not only of people, but also of an increasing number of economic and social activities.

The late 1960s were the high-point for urban planners. As a result of his innovative proposals for the Green Belt and the building of the new towns, Abercrombie's influence was still strong, but these schemes were becoming increasingly inadequate to serve fast-developing needs. Population and employment in the London region were growing more rapidly than expected. Affluence created extra housing demands, while ever-increasing car ownership – the number of private cars quadrupled in the London area between 1945 and 1960 – necessitated a massive investment in road building schemes. There were constant pressures to make Green Belt land available for housing, but powerful lobbies still argued for countryside conservation.

A succession of plans was presented to reconcile these regional conflicts. In 1964 the Ministry of Housing and Local Government produced the 'South-East Study'. On top of existing 'overspill' policies for Londoners, it predicted that a further 3.5 million people would need houses by 1981. About one third of these were to be in new growth centres outside London. As in each of the subsequent plans, the Green Belt was to be sustained, or even strengthened. The 1964 Labour Government established Planning Councils for each region, and tightened controls on industrial and office

*Planning Greater London In 1965 London gained a new planning body which replaced the London County Council. Like the LCC at its inception, the Greater London Council (GLC) effectively encompassed the whole city, combining the administration of 32 metropolitan boroughs as well as the City of London. One of its tasks was to produce a strategic plan for the capital to act as a framework within which the boroughs could carry out more detailed development planning. This was the Greater London Development Plan (GLDP). The 'Strategy for the South East' had already emerged in 1967 (map below), placing London's development in its wider regional context. The GLDP sought to integrate policies for transportation, housing, land use, retail and commercial activity, historical conservation and recreation and open space.*

*The Plan was widely criticised. By far the most contentious issue was the imposition of a comprehensive motorway network. But with London's employment contracting rapidly and inner city housing problems escalating, the realism of many of the GLC's planning ambitions was also questioned. Political changes ensured that road proposals were never adopted. A modified plan was eventually approved in 1976 (map right), but even this had only limited relevance in the rapidly changing circumstances of the late 1970s and '80s. Throughout the 1980s there was no coherent regional planning policy for London; development was often held up or radically altered by a conservationist lobby dedicated to ensuring that it was modified to enhance the existing buildings and landscape.*

growth in the South-East. 'A Strategy for the South-East' followed in 1967. This proposed promoting major new city regions as counter-magnets to London, linking them to the metropolis by transportation 'corridors'. In the event, only Northampton and Milton Keynes were eventually developed.

In 1970 local authorities co-operated to produce the 'Strategic Plan for the South East'. This acknowledged the uncertainties which had bedevilled earlier plans, and proposed a flexible approach based on five major and seven smaller growth areas. The anticipated population boom predicted in the 1960s had proved to be greatly exaggerated; by the mid-1970s new towns and regional growth centres could only expand at the expense of London itself. A review of the Plan was published in 1976 but, with the decline in economic prospects, regional planning in the South East was effectively abolished in 1979. Throughout the 1980s, regional strategy was seldom considered by the Government, unless under pressure from local authorities and private developers requiring guidance for their activities.

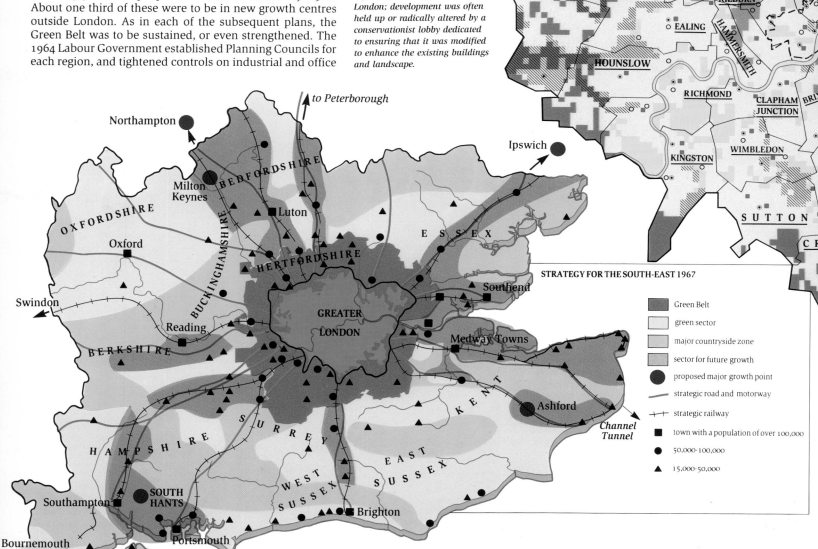

**GREATER LONDON DEVELOPMENT PLAN 1976**

- Green Belt
- metropolitan open land
- housing problem area
- area of opportunity
- ILFORD strategic centre
- ○ action area
- ■ preferred office location
- ■ preferred industrial location
- ● transport interchange
- --- central London
- — borough boundary

ENFIEL / HARROW / WOOD G / WEMBLEY / HOLLOW / UXBRIDGE / KILBURN / EALING / HAMMERSMITH / HOUNSLOW / RICHMOND / CLAPHAM JUNCTION / BRIXTO / KINGSTON / WIMBLEDON / SUTTON / CRO

**STRATEGY FOR THE SOUTH-EAST 1967**

- Green Belt
- green sector
- major countryside zone
- sector for future growth
- ● proposed major growth point
- — strategic road and motorway
- +++ strategic railway
- ■ town with a population of over 100,000
- ● 50,000–100,000
- ▲ 15,000–50,000

to Peterborough
Northampton / Milton Keynes / BEDFORDSHIRE / Luton / OXFORDSHIRE / Oxford / BUCKINGHAMSHIRE / HERTFORDSHIRE / ESSEX / Ipswich / Swindon / Reading / BERKSHIRE / GREATER LONDON / Southend / Medway Towns / HAMPSHIRE / SURREY / KENT / Ashford / Channel Tunnel / WEST SUSSEX / EAST SUSSEX / SOUTH HANTS / Southampton / Portsmouth / Brighton / Bournemouth

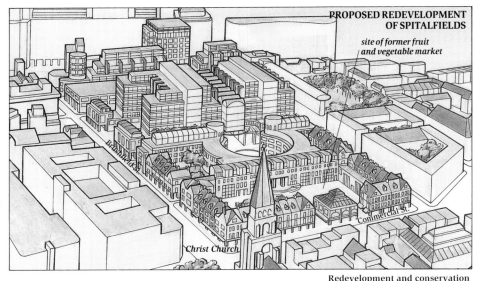

**PROPOSED REDEVELOPMENT OF SPITALFIELDS**

*site of former fruit and vegetable market*

Christ Church

Commercial St.

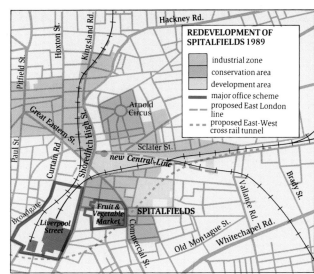

**REDEVELOPMENT OF SPITALFIELDS 1989**

- industrial zone
- conservation area
- development area
- ▬ major office scheme
- ▬ ▬ proposed East London line
- ∙∙∙∙ proposed East-West cross rail tunnel

Hackney Rd.

Hoxton St.

Pitfield St.

Kingsland Rd.

Great Eastern St.

Paul St.

Curtain Rd.

Shoreditch High St.

Arnold Circus

Sclater St.

*new Central Line*

Broadgate

Liverpool Street

Fruit & Vegetable Market

**SPITALFIELDS**

Vallance Rd.

Brady St.

Commercial St.

Old Montague St.

Whitechapel Rd.

**Redevelopment and conservation**
*The pace of commercial property development in London during the 1960s was one part of the argument for regional and London-wide strategic planning. Developers began acquiring multiple blocks of land and proposing ever-larger schemes. These exploited the economics of high-rise building technology, transforming the appearance of the city in ways which, it was argued, were not for the better. Planning scrutiny modified some of this impact and campaigns, sometimes successful, were waged to save the city's heritage. The illustration (above) shows the proposed (1989) redevelopment of Spitalfields to replace the market with offices. The map (top right) shows much investment and redevelopment occurred around Great Eastern Street in the 1990s, with loft apartments, wine bars and clubs.*

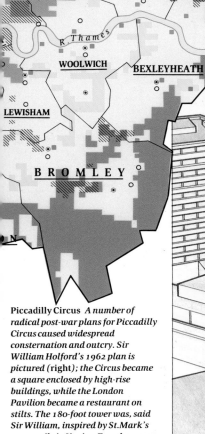

WALTHAMSTOW

ILFORD

ROMFORD

ISLAND

STRATFORD

BARKING

R. Thames

WOOLWICH

BEXLEYHEATH

LEWISHAM

**BROMLEY**

Haymarket Tower

London Pavilion

Piazza

Eros

Regent St.

**Piccadilly Circus** *A number of radical post-war plans for Piccadilly Circus caused widespread consternation and outcry. Sir William Holford's 1962 plan is pictured (right); the Circus became a square enclosed by high-rise buildings, while the London Pavilion became a restaurant on stilts. The 180-foot tower was, said Sir William, inspired by St. Mark's campanile in Venice. Eros, however, still graced the central piazza. In the late 1970s, after decades of controversial plans for Piccadilly Circus, it was decided that it should be left virtually intact (above right), and so it has remained.*

# CHAPTER 10
# LONDON THEMES

FOR VIRTUALLY A thousand years the might of London has been inextricably bound up with its role as the nation's capital, seat of its rulers and home of its Parliament, administration and courts of law. Coupled to that vital power base, London flourished as a centre of commerce and manufacture, with a port that served not only the trade routes of western Europe but of the British Empire and the entire world. London's role as the nation's capital has shaped large parts of the city centre. The Tower of London encapsulates William the Conqueror's royal residence and stronghold, defending the city from water-borne invasion along the Thames Estuary. Royal palaces grace the river banks from Greenwich in the east to Hampton Court in the west, and royal parks provide expanses of public open space in many parts of the metropolis. But it is the palaces and parks, streets and statues of Westminster which most powerfully evoke the presence of 'royal London'. Following the initiative of the Saxon kings, who established a monastery and residence on Thorney Island upstream of *Londinium*, successive monarchs fashioned and refashioned Royal Westminster, making it the official setting for the most solemn occasions of national life, such as coronations, royal weddings and state funerals. The City of London, on the other hand, displays a different kind of grandeur; its dense network of streets, the cathedral of St. Paul's, its historic churches and great buildings all reflect the dynamism generated by trade and international finance. During the working week the City is vibrant and busy, but at night and during weekends it is virtually deserted. The City never used to be like this. For almost all of its history it housed merchants and bankers, craftsmen and apprentices, reaching a peak population of more than 200,000 in the early 18th century. But as the suburbs grew, the old City became a specialised 'central business district' of offices and banks and its residential population declined. Railway building in the second half of the 19th century eradicated numerous workshops and homes, as did the bombing raids and fires of World War II. The City's population dwindled to 4,000 in 1971 but climbed again to 5,300 as apartments were built in the fire-bombed warehouse district of the Barbican.

Just as the City and Westminster acquired increasingly specialised functions during the past two centuries, so did other sections of the expanding capital. Downstream from the City, especially on the north bank, enclosed docks of ever increasing dimensions were dug from the soft alluvium of the Thames floodplain in the late 18th and throughout the 19th centuries. The new enclosed docks captured a large share of Thames trade, but cargo ships continued to be loaded and unloaded at wharves and jetties along the river. Many docks spawned a range of industries, processing goods as diverse as edible oils, timber, chemicals and metals. Each complex of docks was fringed by housing for its employees. Docklands formed a distinctive but oddly isolated part of London, well connected to the rest of the world but with very few public transport links to the heart of the city. During the 1960s and 1970s the docks closed, and many traditional industries died. Imaginative redevelopment schemes have transformed the upstream docks and the Isle of Dogs, but the Royal Docks downstream present a major challenge not only for the 1990s but for the 21st century.

Victorian London witnessed the powerful emergence of a second 'central business district', with a different set of businesses and offices from those in the City. High quality shops had long served the fasionable clientele of Mayfair, and towards the end of the 19th century were joined by new department stores. The West End was London's 'theatreland' and between the wars the most prestigious cinemas were opened there. Unlike the City, where life was geared almost exclusively to the pursuit of commerce, the West End was home to a wide range of cultural activities which included the great museums and galleries as well as many colleges of the University.

Beyond the City, Westminster, the West End and Docklands there developed the largest and in some ways the most diverse component of London – its suburbia. Despised by many Londoners but home to most, the suburbs grew in complexity over the past two centuries. Successive innova-

For a full discussion of the evolution of Westminster and Whitehall, see pages 154-155.

For an examination of the evolution of London's docks see pages 82-83 and 92-93, and for a review of present-day Docklands, see pages 158-159.

On the south bank of the Thames, archaeologists have recently discovered the remains of a large ten-sided building in Bear Gardens, only 100 m from the site of the new Globe Theatre. The remains may be those of the Hope Theatre, built in 1613–14 to replace the Globe that had been destroyed by fire one year earlier. It is possible that the building was used for animal baiting as well as staging plays. The Hope was closed in 1642, when the Civil War started, and was demolished by the middle of the next decade.

See reconstruction of Tower of London and discussion of London's royal parks and palaces, pages 138-139.

The present-day City is examined in detail on pages 152-153.

See discussion of Selfridge's (page 107) and an examination of the evolution of West End shopping districts and the growth of Harrod's on page 149. London's 'theatreland' is examined on page 147.

tions in private and public transport enabled the tide of bricks and mortar to wash further into the London Basin, incorporating villages, hamlets and market towns and engulfing commons, heaths and parks. The term 'urban sprawl' does not do justice to the dramatic rise of Greater London. Every omnibus route, railway line or tramway had to be planned. Each portion of land had to be purchased or leased and provided with an appropriate selection of housing, shops and local facilities. The net result is an intricate fabric of old and new. Historic parish churches, Georgian and Victorian houses fringe ancient village greens. Main roads twist and turn in obedience to long-lost field patterns. Shop fronts stand along building lines defined by tram lines that have long since disappeared, or push forward where suburban front gardens have been built over to provide more retail space.

*London's urban sprawl and the gradual absorption of villages into the city boundaries are mapped on pages 156-157.*

*Sources of stone and brickearth are mapped on pages 132-133.*

The growth of London from a population of 15,000 in the reign of William the Conqueror to 8,193,000 in 1951 required massive supplies of building material. In early times most dwellings in London were made of local materials, such as timber and thatch. Only ceremonial buildings or monuments of great importance merited costly imports of stone or the manufacture of bricks and tiles. The Great Fire of 1666 brought this tradition to an end. The new London became a tidy, brick-built town whose houses were roofed with tiles or slates to withstand fire. Brick continued to be the most widespread medium of construction until it was overtaken by concrete in the present century. The opening of railways enabled bricks to be hauled from the great clayfields of the East Midlands, and London no longer had to rely on local brickfields. Prestigious buildings still demand materials from other parts of Britain or from distant corners of the globe.

The growing city needed to be equipped with much more than housing and business premises. The bulk of historic London had developed north of the Thames and only modest expansion occurred on the south bank. Old London Bridge had been rebuilt several times, but many more bridges were needed if London was to become a less 'lop-sided' capital. New bridges were built in the middle of the 18th century and these permitted a burst of suburban growth south of the river. During the subsequent two and a half centuries many more bridges have been added and the old ones replaced; two more will be completed soon. Bridges are far more than functional links in the communication system since they also provide a fascinating complement to the sweep of London's river.

*For a reconstruction of old London Bridge, see pages 162-163.*

Beneath the city streets there exists another London, vital but little known. The brightly coloured Tube map is familiar to Londoners and visitors alike, but few have a clear idea of where the tunnels run. Even less is known about the 'lost rivers', intercepting sewers and local drains which carry waste and prevent flooding. With so many people concentrated in such a small area the pollution of London's environment has been notorious since medieval times. Remarkable progress in waste disposal and water supply was achieved between 1850 and 1950 but not until recent years was the Thames cleaned up and London's air purged of its smoke and dust. Unfortunately, substances emanating from vehicle emissions now pollute London's air and degrade its environment, posing yet another challenge for scientists and legislators.

*Sewers are plotted on pages 160-161.*

*The pollution of London's environment is mapped on pages 134-135, while the underground city is examined on pages 160-161.*

*Vehicle-clogged London contains eight of the ten most polluted streets in the UK, with Park Lane having the highest concentrations of nitrogen dioxide. Other major concentrations of traffic pollution include: the North Circular Road at Brent Cross and Neasden; Grosvenor Place, Victoria; Hyde Park Corner; the Great West Road; Westway; the Hammersmith Flyover.*

Throughout history monarchs, architects and planners devised schemes for 'improving' London with new thoroughfares, triumphal buildings, docks, cemeteries and a host of other projects. Some of their visions became reality but other ideas remained in draft, forming the London that never was. Even now, bold plans are being announced to revitalise several parts of the capital. Their massive cost, social implications and innovative styles make them highly controversial. Time alone will tell whether they will contribute to the London of the future or will join so many yellowing pages of architectural dreams and lost opportunities.

*Unrealised visions of London are illustrated on pages 168-169, while contemporary visions of a future London are examined on pages 170-171.*

London's present condition can only be fully understood by appreciating its long and complex history. All the issues mentioned above are explored in the final pages of this Atlas. The present chapter illustrates a selection of themes that characterised London in the past and still continue to do so, while the final chapter concentrates on places within the capital.

# THE FABRIC OF LONDON'S BUILDINGS

Good building stone is absent from the London area. For much of the city's history, therefore, many ordinary buildings were made from timber and roofed with thatch. Brick fashioned from local clay was used for more solid buildings; only churches and great civic buildings were constructed from stone, which had to be brought into the city from other regions. Disastrous fires were a frequent occurrence, and after the Great Fire (*page* 68) legislation stipulated that brick and stone, tiles and slates should be used in new

buildings. The story of London's building stone reflects, primarily, the evolution over the centuries of transport which enabled materials to be brought from ever greater distances. A similar background characterises the history of the use of brick – when local clays became exhausted, increasingly distant clay deposits had to be used.

Rather than try to trace the history of stone use throughout the whole City of London, it is easier to concentrate on the buildings in one particular area such as Trafalgar Square. The oldest is the church of St. Martin in the Fields which was designed by James Gibbs in 1726, when he encased an older structure of Kentish Ragstone and Reigate Stone, brought by boat from the Medway Valley or North Downs, in a

classical exterior of Portland Stone. Portland is the best English building stone, and had already been used extensively by Sir Christopher Wren for rebuilding the City after 1666. This pure white limestone is quarried exclusively on Portland Island off the south coast of Dorset, whence it was shipped to London. For the National Gallery (1835), William Wilkins also chose to use Portland Stone. There, however, loss of the original smooth surface of the limestone through the effects of wind and rain has caused fossil shell fragments to stand out. This demonstrates that the limestone was once a sea-bed sediment, rich in broken debris of oysters.

The National Westminster Bank in the south-west corner of the square was designed in 1871

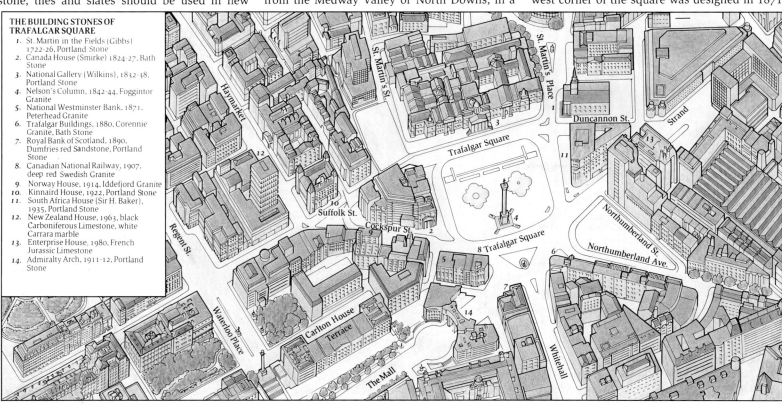

**THE BUILDING STONES OF TRAFALGAR SQUARE**

1.  St. Martin in the Fields (Gibbs) 1722-26, Portland Stone
2.  Canada House (Smirke) 1824-27, Bath Stone
3.  National Gallery (Wilkins), 1832-38, Portland Stone
4.  Nelson's Column, 1842-44, Foggintor Granite
5.  National Westminster Bank, 1871, Peterhead Granite
6.  Trafalgar Buildings, 1880, Corennie Granite, Bath Stone
7.  Royal Bank of Scotland, 1890, Dumfries red Sandstone, Portland Stone
8.  Canadian National Railway, 1907, deep red Swedish Granite
9.  Norway House, 1914, Iddefjord Granite
10. Kinnaird House, 1922, Portland Stone
11. South Africa House (Sir H. Baker), 1935, Portland Stone
12. New Zealand House, 1963, black Carboniferous Limestone, white Carrara marble
13. Enterprise House, 1980, French Jurassic Limestone
14. Admiralty Arch, 1911-12, Portland Stone

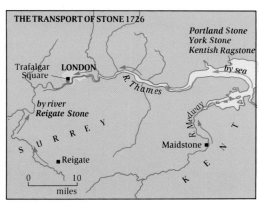

**THE TRANSPORT OF STONE 1726**

Portland Stone
York Stone
Kentish Ragstone

*by sea*

Trafalgar Square **LONDON**

*by river* Reigate Stone

R. Thames

R. Medway

**SURREY**

**KENT**

Reigate

Maidstone

0 — 10 miles

**The transport of stone** *The three small maps (left and below) show the routes that were used to bring various stones to Trafalgar Square: in the early 18th century, before a variety of transport was available; in the 1780s, when the building of canals meant that more distant sources of stone could be used; and in the mid-19th century, when the railway carried stone from far more distant sources to London. Nelson's Column, for example, erected in 1842, was built of several different granites from as far afield as Cornwall and Scotland.*

**The building stone of Trafalgar Square** *The map (above) shows the location of selected buildings around Trafalgar Square, and the varied stones in which they are built. The modern block of New Zealand House (left), built of Carboniferous Limestone, contrasts with the National Westminster Bank (1877, right), built of Portland Stone, with Peterhead Granite columns. The fine facade of the National Gallery (1835, below) is constructed of Portland Stone, favoured by Sir Christopher Wren.*

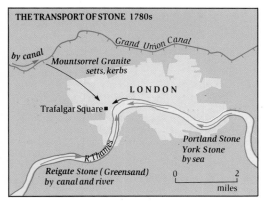

**THE TRANSPORT OF STONE 1780s**

*by canal*

Grand Union Canal

Mountsorrel Granite setts, kerbs

**LONDON**

Trafalgar Square

R. Thames

Portland Stone
York Stone
*by sea*

Reigate Stone (Greensand) *by canal and river*

0 — 2 miles

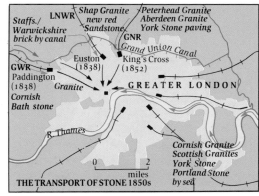

Staffs./ Warwickshire brick by canal

**LNWR**

Shap Granite
new red Sandstone

Peterhead Granite
Aberdeen Granite
York Stone paving

**GNR**

Grand Union Canal

**GWR**

Euston (1838)
King's Cross (1852)

Paddington (1838)

Cornish Bath stone

Granite

**GREATER LONDON**

R. Thames

Cornish Granite
Scottish Granites
York Stone
Portland Stone
*by sea*

0 — 2 miles

**THE TRANSPORT OF STONE 1850s**

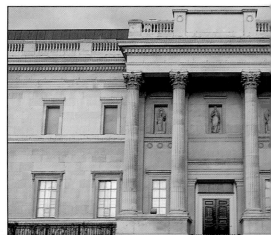

by F.W. Porter, the architect of branches of the original National Provincial Bank. White Portland Stone walling is set off by distinctive pink columns of polished Peterhead Granite from coastal Aberdeenshire. The steep-pitched roofing carries green Lake District Slate from quarries in the Borrowdale Volcanic Series, which is an ancient accumulation of volcanic ash. The Edwardian building, bearing the initials 'C.N.' (Canadian National Railway), is built of deep red Swedish Granite and has interiors of Italian Marble. In the background, rises New Zealand House (1963), a tower mainly of steel and glass. The basal stalk to the building, however, is faced with dense black natural stone. Rare fossils (white against the black surface) prove that this Carboniferous Limestone is from either Tournai in Belgium or from southern Ireland. It is evident from this limited survey that the range of stone being used in this prestigious London square became much greater and more exotic as new and more effective modes of transport – roads, canals, railways, shipping – became available.

Brick had been used for buildings in London since Roman times but after the Great Fire it entered into renewed favour. Sir Christopher Wren claimed: '... the earth around London, rightly managed, will yield as good brick as were the Roman bricks ... and will endure, in our air, beyond any stone our island affords'. Throughout the 17th and 18th centuries, brickearth and London Clay were used to produce 'stock bricks' which varied in colour from bright yellow to deep earthy purple, and were used as good facing bricks. They contrasted with cheaper 'place bricks' which were not intended to be left exposed to the elements. Some stock bricks were carried up the Thames from Kent but most were made in the immediate environs of London.

Natural brickearth contains lime and can yield a yellow or whitish brick, unlike other clays whose iron oxide gives rise to red bricks unless lime or chalk is added. By the early 19th century, local supplies of pure brickearth were almost expended. Builders relied increasingly on a mix of chalk, London Clay and a little brickearth.

As well as suburban brickfields, which extended ever-further into the countryside, more distant sources of clay were used in Kent, Essex and the Upper Thames Valley. The bricks they yielded were carried to London along the Thames or along the new canal system. The opening of the Grand Union Canal through Middlesex in 1794 was soon followed by a proliferation of brickfields along its banks. In the 1830s and 1840s, brickmaking by hand started to be replaced by machinery which meant that it was possible to use the harder clays of the Midlands. The building of the Great Northern Railway in 1852 enabled the clays of Bedfordshire (some 35

**Building in Brick** *Gray's Inn (1676, right) was built using 'stock bricks', a mixture of brickearth and London Clay, ranging in colour from dark red to the deep purple of Bedford Square (below right). The Victorian houses (1880s, below) were built of brick made up of a mixture of chalk, clay and a little brickearth, a practice known as 'soiling'.*

miles north of the capital) to be used in steam-powered mechanised brickworks. In 1881, a grey-brown clay deposit, very suitable for brickmaking, was discovered below the brownish top layer of the Oxford Clay at Fletton near Peterborough. This became the new focus of mechanised brickworks. Even more were opened in the 1890s alongside railway lines in Bedfordshire and Buckinghamshire. Despite the great reliance in recent decades on concrete, brick is still popular with many of London's architects and builders at the end of the 20th century.

**London Brick** *The maps (right) show sources of Brickearth and other clays that were used for making London's bricks from medieval times to the 18th century. In 1811, Henry Hunter described London as being surrounded by 'a ring of fire' from brick kilns. For him '... the face of the land is deformed by the multitude of claypits from which is being dug the brickearth fused in the kilns which smoke all around London'. By the early 19th century, bricks were being produced at slightly greater distances in areas that are now covered by suburbia. These outer-London brickfields were often small and temporary operations – worked-out brickpits were used as pasture or were filled with urban rubbish and then sold for building land. Building the railways enabled distant clay deposits near Bedford and Peterborough (far right) to be used to provide the rapidly growing city with essential supplies of bricks.*

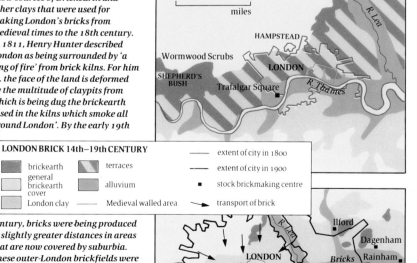

**LONDON BRICK 14th–19th CENTURY**

| | | |
|---|---|---|
| ▨ brickearth | ▨ terraces | —— extent of city in 1800 |
| ▨ general brickearth cover | ▨ alluvium | —— extent of city in 1900 |
| ▨ London clay | — Medieval walled area | ■ stock brickmaking centre |
| | | ↘ transport of brick |

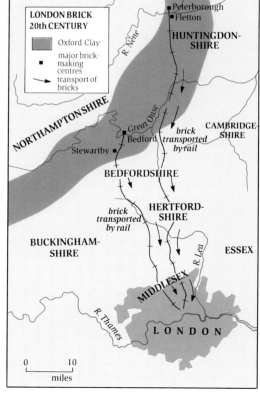

**LONDON BRICK 20th CENTURY**

▨ Oxford Clay
■ major brick-making centres
↘ transport of bricks

133

# LONDON AND POLLUTION

The demographic growth and economic success of London was at the cost of profound damage to the environment. Concern for high concentrations of smoke can be traced back to the 13th century when a commission was established to investigate the problem and recommended that burning of sea coal be prohibited. This was not implemented and in the 17th and 18th centuries there was growing awareness of the adverse effects of smoke on the health of the citizens of London. King James I complained about the soiling of St. Paul's Cathedral in 1620; John Evelyn in 'Fumifugium' (1661) noted decreased visibility; in 1784 the naturalist Gilbert White recorded dark plumes rising from London.

In late Victorian times the word 'smog' was coined to describe the combination of smoke and fog evoked so graphically in the novels of Dickens. The Smoke Abatement Act (1853-56) and the Sanitation Act (1866) had attempted to curb smoke emissions but there was little improvement in conditions until the Clean Air Acts of 1956 and 1968. There were also important changes in energy sources. Industry and commerce switched largely from coal to oil and gas; the railways were powered by electricity rather than steam; domestic central heating using oil, gas and electricity replaced open coal fires. Finally, slum clearance and urban renewal

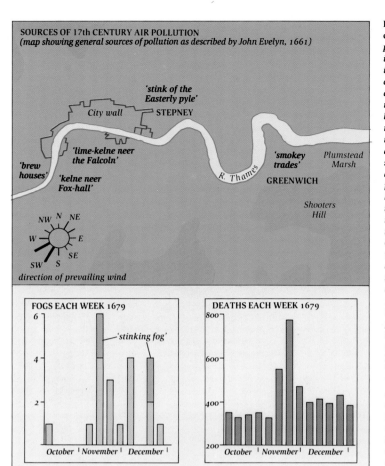

SOURCES OF 17th CENTURY AIR POLLUTION
(map showing general sources of pollution as described by John Evelyn, 1661)

'stink of the Easterly pyle'
STEPNEY
City wall
'lime-kelne neer the Falcoln'
'brew houses'
'kelne neer Fox-hall'
R. Thames
'smokey trades'
Plumstead Marsh
GREENWICH
Shooters Hill

direction of prevailing wind

FOGS EACH WEEK 1679
'stinking fog'
October | November | December

DEATHS EACH WEEK 1679
October | November | December

London's air pollution, 17th-19th centuries *The sources of air pollution described by John Evelyn in 'Fumifugium' (1661) are shown in the map (left). The city was covered with a 'hellish and dismal cloud of sea-coal' emanating from the premises of brewers, dyers, lime burners, salt boilers and soap makers. Pollution from industries to the west of the city was blown across London by the prevailing south-westerly winds. Smoke damaged plants, buildings, clothes, furnishings and paintings, and human health (graphs left) was impaired. Evelyn advocated the removal of noxious industries 5 or 6 miles east of the city to the Greenwich peninsula, where winds would sweep pollution far downstream. The map (below left) shows the amount of sulphate deposited in rain around London in 1869-70. Highest levels of pollution were found in densely-populated poorer residential districts fringing the City and in the East End, with concentrations extending east of London and into the lower Lea Valley. Some of the atmosphere of Victorian smog is captured in H. Medleycott's painting, 'The Pool of London', c.1880 (bottom). A Punch cartoon of 1905, (below left) illustrated the difficulty of finding one's way round streets where atmospheric conditions led to negligible visibility.*

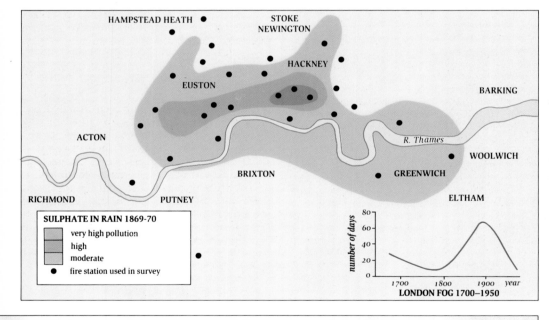

HAMPSTEAD HEATH
STOKE NEWINGTON
HACKNEY
EUSTON
BARKING
ACTON
R. Thames
WOOLWICH
BRIXTON
GREENWICH
RICHMOND
PUTNEY
ELTHAM

SULPHATE IN RAIN 1869-70
very high pollution
high
moderate
• fire station used in survey

number of days
1700  1800  1900  year
LONDON FOG 1700–1950

A QUALIFIED GUIDE.—*Befogged Pedestrian.* "Could you direct me to the river, please?" *Hatless and Dripping Stranger.* "Straight ahead. I've just come from it."

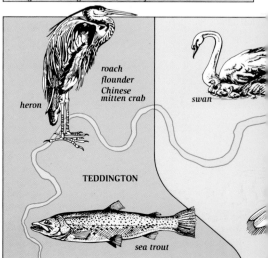

roach
flounder
Chinese mitten crab
heron
swan
TEDDINGTON
sea trout

## SMOKE: AVERAGE CONCENTRATION 1957

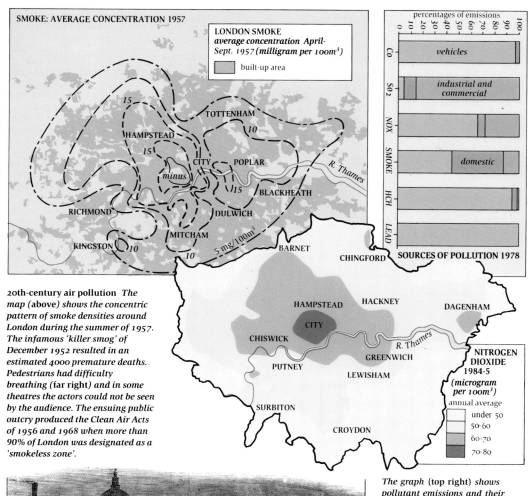

**LONDON SMOKE**
*average concentration April-Sept. 1957 (milligram per 100m³)*

built-up area

TOTTENHAM
HAMPSTEAD
CITY    POPLAR
minus
BLACKHEATH
RICHMOND
DULWICH
MITCHAM
KINGSTON
BARNET
*R. Thames*
5 mg/100m³

percentages of emissions

**SOURCES OF POLLUTION 1978**

vehicles — Co
industrial and commercial — SO₂
— NOX
domestic — SMOKE
— HCH
— LEAD

**20th-century air pollution** *The map (above) shows the concentric pattern of smoke densities around London during the summer of 1957. The infamous 'killer smog' of December 1952 resulted in an estimated 4000 premature deaths. Pedestrians had difficulty breathing (far right) and in some theatres the actors could not be seen by the audience. The ensuing public outcry produced the Clean Air Acts of 1956 and 1968 when more than 90% of London was designated as a 'smokeless zone'.*

CHINGFORD
HAMPSTEAD    HACKNEY    DAGENHAM
CITY
CHISWICK    *R. Thames*
GREENWICH
PUTNEY    LEWISHAM
SURBITON
CROYDON

**NITROGEN DIOXIDE 1984-5**
*(microgram per 100m³)*
annual average
under 50
50-60
60-70
70-80

*The graph (top right) shows pollutant emissions and their sources in London in 1978. The map (above) shows the pattern of concentration of nitrogen dioxide, an atmospheric gas derived mainly from vehicle exhausts, which contributes to problems experienced by asthma sufferers.*
**Cleaning the Thames** *The cartoon (left) appeared in Punch on 10th July 1858, graphically expressing widespread disquiet about the pollution of the Thames in the mid-1850s. The Thames has undergone an extensive clean-up over the past 30 years. The map (below) shows some of the birds and fish that have since returned to various sections of the Thames: after a century's absence the brown shrimp has returned; numbers of salmon, heron, swan and pochard have risen and shelduck now over-winter in their hundreds in Barking Creek.*

did away with thousands of sources of pollution as densely-packed houses were replaced by centrally-heated flats and spacious suburbs.

London has resolved the problem of smoke pollution but is now faced with a less visible but potentially more dangerous mix of pollutants resulting from vehicular emissions. Carbon monoxide is now the most common air pollutant in London. Vehicles also emit hydrocarbons and the action of sunlight on this mix of emissions can produce toxic secondary pollutants (for example, ozone, aldehydes and various aerosols) known as 'photochemical' smog. Nitrogen dioxide contributes to this smog and acid rain.

The Thames and its tributaries were also fouled by the growth of the city and its industries. Conditions became so bad, and the stench from the polluted river so great, that in 1858 Members of Parliament resolved to strengthen the powers of the newly created Metropolitan Board of Works (*page 104*). By 1865 80 miles of intercepting sewers had been installed, carrying still untreated sewage to outfalls on the Thames, well downstream of the built-up area. During the 20th century many more sewers were constructed and treatment works opened, but the condition of the Thames continued to decline, reaching its worst point in the 1950s. Since then there has been major investment in sophisticated treatment processes. A good indication of recent improvements in water quality is in the fish life in the Thames. In 1957 only eels could survive in London's river. Seventeen years later no fewer than 82 species of fish were living in the London stretches of the Thames, including the first salmon since 1833.

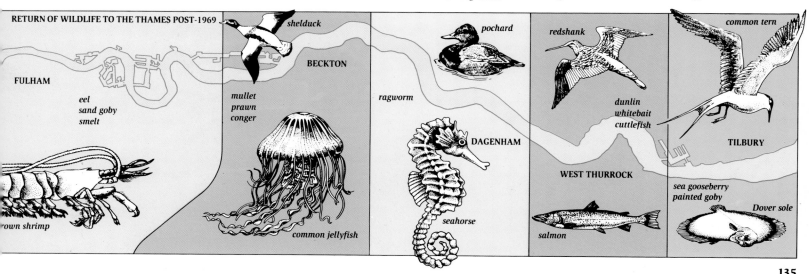

**RETURN OF WILDLIFE TO THE THAMES POST-1969**

shelduck
BECKTON
pochard
redshank
common tern
FULHAM
eel
sand goby
smelt
mullet
prawn
conger
ragworm
dunlin
whitebait
cuttlefish
TILBURY
DAGENHAM
WEST THURROCK
brown shrimp
common jellyfish
seahorse
sea gooseberry
painted goby
Dover sole
salmon

# LONDON AND IMMIGRATION

London has played a dominant role in Britain's long history of immigration, serving as a major port of entry, a place of economic opportunity and a hoped-for refuge from persecution. In medieval times, some foreigners lived in separate neighbourhoods, notably Jewish traders (who had come to England with the Normans but were expelled to the Continent in 1290) and Hanseatic merchants from northern Germany, who occupied the Steelyard alongside the Thames until they too were expelled in 1598. By contrast, Flemings, Dutch, French and Walloons were assimilated far more easily into the indigenous population. In the 1650s, Cromwell allowed persecuted Jews to return to England and Sephardic Jews settled in Whitechapel. They were followed by members of Ashkenazi Jewish communities from central Europe who brought their trades and skills to districts beyond the eastern limits of the City, where they could operate without interference from the guilds and City companies. Huguenots (Protestants) fled from France when religious toleration was ended by the Revocation of the Edict of Nantes in 1685. They moved to two main districts, setting up silk-working establishments in Spitalfields and opening craft workshops in Soho, which became a 'little France'.

Many immigrants came to London because their native countries formed part of the rapidly-expanding British Empire. By the late 18th century small numbers of Chinese had settled near the docks, having arrived on East India Company

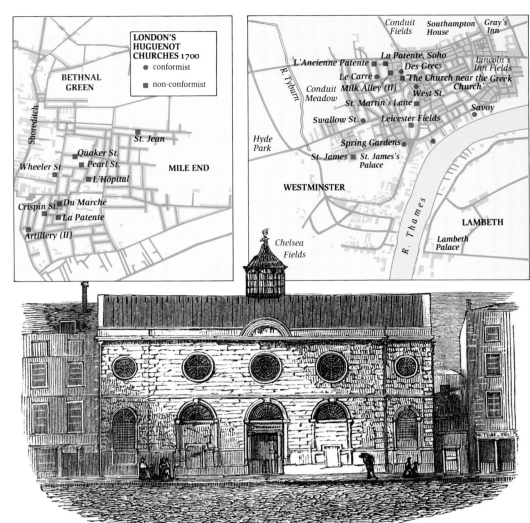

ships. Indians, many of whom were brought to London as servants of colonial families, also began to arrive in London at this time. Similarly, returning traders, plantation owners, army officers and government officials brought Afro-Caribbean migrants to London as slave-servants prior to the abolition of slavery in Britain in 1807, and in the British Empire in 1834.

Immigration in the 19th century was due to a number of new factors. The Great Irish Famine of the 1840s unleashed a new flood of immigrants, and by 1851 over 100,000 Irish were living in the capital, making up one in twenty of all Londoners. The rookeries of St. Giles, Whitechapel and Southwark contained particularly large numbers, many of whom lived in appalling poverty. Many worked in the docks, or in the workshops and factories of the East End, where sweated labour

**London and the Huguenots** *The two maps (above) show the distribution of Huguenot churches in Spitalfields and the West End in the early 18th century. A Huguenot church at Threadneedle Street (1669) is depicted (above) from the* **London Illustrated News.**

**Jewish London** *The map (left) shows the Jewish East End in 1900. Some streets had more than 90% Jewish inhabitants. The map (below left) shows Jewish dispersal from the East End. As they grew more prosperous during the 19th century, the Jewish population began to move to suburban areas, especially to the north and north-west. The photograph (below) shows Jewish immigrants arriving at London Docks in the late 1930s.*

**THE JEWISH EAST END 1900**
*Jews as proportion of total population:*

| less than 5% | 5-24% | 25-49% | 50-74% | 75-94% | 95-100% |
|---|---|---|---|---|---|

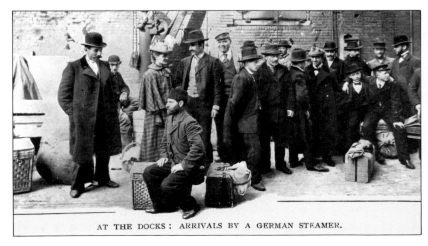

AT THE DOCKS : ARRIVALS BY A GERMAN STEAMER.

was firmly entrenched.

In 1881, the assassination of Tsar Alexander II gave rise to anti-semitic pogroms in Russia and Poland. Vast numbers of Jews fled westward, hoping to move to North America. Many settled instead in the East End and other parts of London, where they played a major role in the clothing and tailoring trades and in many branches of commerce and finance. 30,000 Germans lived in London before the First World War – the German businesses and restaurants in Charlotte Street earned it the nickname 'Charlottenstrasse'. When war broke out, many returned to the fatherland, while remaining Germans of military age were interned (a fate which also befell the German population at the outbreak of the Second World War). Numerous German families in London adopted English-sounding surnames.

The receptive role of the East End has continued in recent years with many thousands of migrants from the West Indies and the Indian subcontinent settling there in the 1950s and 1960s. Other recent migrant groups have contributed to the complex mosaic of modern London; the West End has its Chinatown, while Greek and Turkish Cypriots settled in North London in sizeable numbers during the 1960s and 1970s. The capital's ethnic and racial diversity contributes a richness and vitality to its restaurants, entertainment, religion, music, cultural and commercial life. Nevertheless, every major immigrant group has faced hostility and discrimination on arrival in London. Jewish and Irish migrants experienced persistent religious intolerance, while Asians have faced a barrage of racist taunts and physical violence. Racial harassment is widespread, but at its most severe in deprived East End boroughs such as Tower Hamlets.

**Irish London** *The map (above right) shows the distribution of Irish-born residents in London in 1851 – very soon after the Great Potato Famine, which had driven large numbers of Irish people to seek a better life elsewhere. High concentrations of Irish residents can be seen in areas such as St Giles and Whitechapel. Here 'rookeries' (overcrowded tenements) provided meagre accommodation for the new arrivals.*

**Commonwealth immigration** *The post-war economic boom created an enormous demand for labour, and from the early 1950s Commonwealth immigrants began to flood into the city seeking work. This immigration was to have a profound impact on the social geography of the capital (maps right). Once 'pioneer' immigrants had become established in certain areas, friends and families arriving later tended to cluster together, forming clearly demarcated communities, such as Jamaican Brixton and Punjabi Southall. The photos show: the Whitechapel Mosque; the recently completed Hindu temple at Neasden; new arrivals to London in the 1950s; the Fournier Street Mosque (formerly a Huguenot church and a Jewish synagogue).*

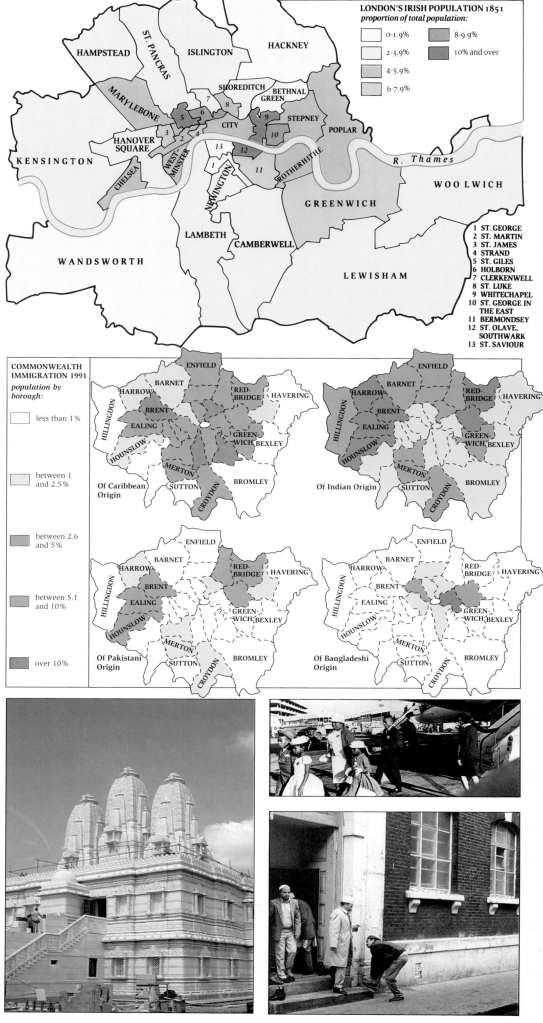

LONDON'S IRISH POPULATION 1851
*proportion of total population:*

0-1.9%  8-9.9%
2-3.9%  10% and over
4-5.9%
6-7.9%

1  ST. GEORGE
2  ST. MARTIN
3  ST. JAMES
4  STRAND
5  ST. GILES
6  HOLBORN
7  CLERKENWELL
8  ST. LUKE
9  WHITECHAPEL
10 ST. GEORGE IN THE EAST
11 BERMONDSEY
12 ST. OLAVE, SOUTHWARK
13 ST. SAVIOUR

COMMONWEALTH IMMIGRATION 1991
*population by borough:*

less than 1%

between 1 and 2.5%

between 2.6 and 5%

between 5.1 and 10%

over 10%

Of Caribbean Origin

Of Indian Origin

Of Pakistani Origin

Of Bangladeshi Origin

# ROYAL LONDON

For most people 'Royal London' conjures up thoughts of palaces, parks and pageantry. It is, of course, much more than that. The unique structure of London owes its origin to the decision of the Saxon king, Edward the Confessor, to locate his main residence upstream of the ancient city, selecting the site where the church of St. Peter – soon to be known as Westminster Abbey – was being built (*page 42*). Edward died before his projects were complete but his choice of Westminster was accepted by many later sovereigns. Courtiers and servants settled nearby, ensuring that Westminster and its environs would be endowed with palaces, parks and the highest functions of government and adminstration in the land. For two centuries following 1650 the Crown and members of the nobility developed their estates on the western side of London, gracing them with splendid streets, fine houses and elegant squares (*page 75*). For virtually a thousand years successive kings and queens have lived in London, often favouring Westminster but sometimes preferring palaces located some distance from the heart of London. Many were built adjacent to the Thames which provided a beautiful setting and guaranteed the most rapid and efficient means of transport during many centuries when road conditions were poor.

These royal homes vary in size and sophistication, from the austere stone of the Tower of London, through the fine Tudor brickwork of St. James's and Hampton Court, to the elegant splendour of Buckingham Palace. Several originated as mansions built for courtiers, passing into royal hands by purchase, gift or seizure at a later stage. All have undergone extensive remodelling and enlargement as fashions changed and standards of space and comfort were transformed. Much the same is true of the royal parks and the private gardens which surround the capital's royal houses. Many began as ancient hunting grounds or were acquired as Church lands or were confiscated by Henry VIII in the 1540s. The imagination of landscape designers, combined with the craft of generations of gardeners, has endowed London with a unique legacy of 5,700 acres of lawns, trees and lakes which act as a haven for many species of birds.

Eleven miles south-west of Westminster – but much further along the meandering Thames – Hampton Court epitomises all that is best about Royal London. Its pure air, woodlands and proximity to the river made it the favourite country home for successive generations of English monarchs. Work on the palace, which was designed to be the grandest in Europe, was started in 1514 by Cardinal Wolsey, Lord Chancellor to Henry VIII. Fifteen years later Wolsey presented it to his King in a futile attempt to remain in favour. Henry greatly loved the palace and had it enlarged. At the request of Charles II and William and Mary its gardens were redesigned, with three broad avenues leading away from the palace and the Long Water extending for three quarters of a mile through the deer park almost to the Thames. Sir Christopher Wren rebuilt the eastern section of the palace in neo-classical style but its brick-built western part remains largely unchanged.

**Buckingham Palace** *has been the London home of the monarchy since Victoria became Queen in 1837. It originated in 1703 as a brick mansion for the Duke of Buckingham, (depicted left in an aquatint of 1819 by W. Westall) and was purchased by George III in 1762. In 1825 George IV engaged John Nash to make substantial alterations and over the next 12 years a new palace of Bath Stone was constructed around the old house. The east wing was built in 1847 and was heightened and faced in Portland Stone in 1912-13 to harmonise with the Victoria Memorial (1910). The present building has some 600 rooms (photograph below); the royal apartments are in the north wing. When the monarch is in residence the royal standard flies over the building and the Changing of the Guard takes place in the forecourt at 11.30 each morning.*

**London's royal parks** *Royal palaces and parks grace central London and some of its suburbs (map right). Manicured lawns at Green Park (53 acres) and flowerbeds in St. James (93 acres) contrast with plantations and greensward in Richmond Park (2,358 acres). This originated as a hunting preserve enclosed by Charles I in 1637 and is still a home for deer. Greenwich Park was enclosed in 1433. Leases on farmland at Marylebone Fields reverted to the Crown in 1811 and John Nash and the Prince Regent created Regent's Park (472 acres) (page 76). A water feature to commemorate the life of Diana, Princess of Wales, is being constructed near the Serpentine in Hyde Park. The area is on the site of a Roman settlement and has not been investigated archaeologically since 18th century landscaping.*

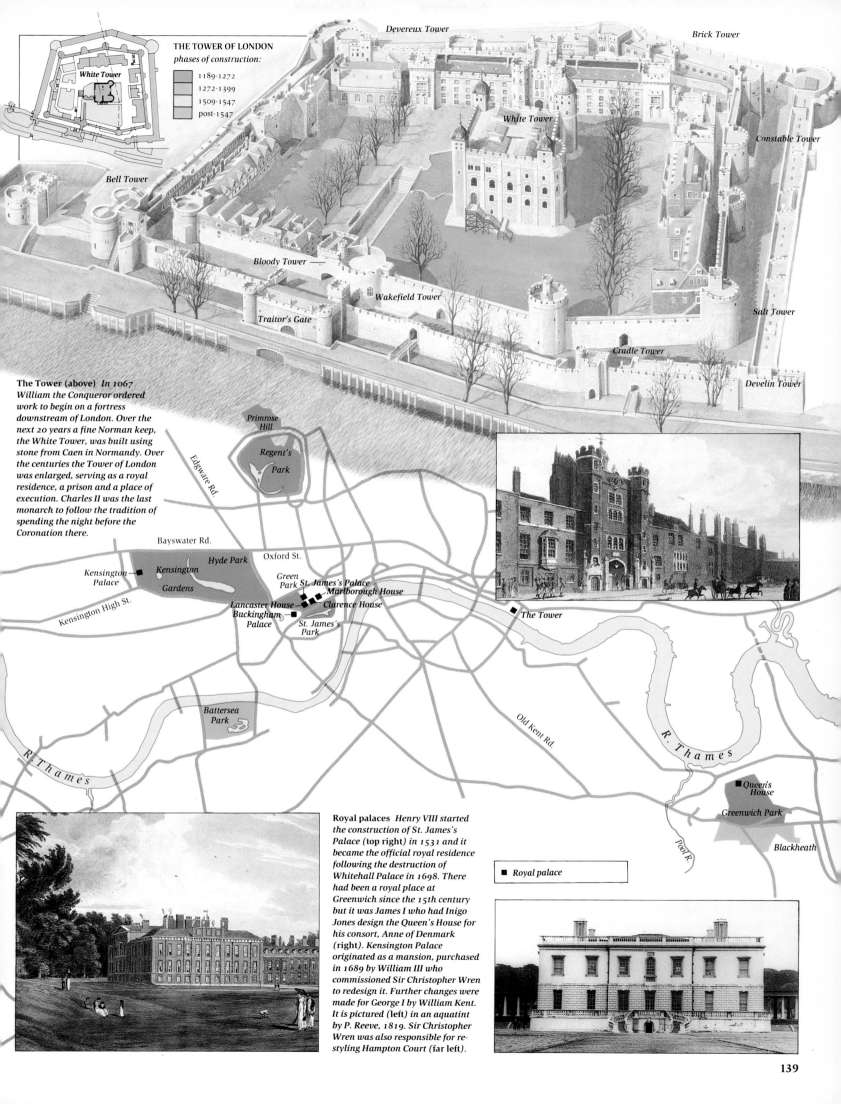

THE TOWER OF LONDON
*phases of construction:*

1189-1272
1272-1399
1509-1547
post-1547

*White Tower*

Devereux Tower

Brick Tower

White Tower

Constable Tower

Bell Tower

Bloody Tower

Wakefield Tower

Salt Tower

Traitor's Gate

Cradle Tower

Develin Tower

**The Tower (above)** *In 1067 William the Conqueror ordered work to begin on a fortress downstream of London. Over the next 20 years a fine Norman keep, the White Tower, was built using stone from Caen in Normandy. Over the centuries the Tower of London was enlarged, serving as a royal residence, a prison and a place of execution. Charles II was the last monarch to follow the tradition of spending the night before the Coronation there.*

Primrose Hill

Regent's Park

Edgware Rd.

Bayswater Rd.

Oxford St.

Kensington Palace

Kensington Gardens

Hyde Park

Green Park

St. James's Palace

Marlborough House

Lancaster House

Clarence House

Buckingham Palace

St. James's Park

Kensington High St.

The Tower

Battersea Park

Old Kent Rd.

R. Thames

R. Thames

Queen's House

Greenwich Park

Pool R.

Blackheath

■ Royal palace

**Royal palaces** *Henry VIII started the construction of St. James's Palace (top right) in 1531 and it became the official royal residence following the destruction of Whitehall Palace in 1698. There had been a royal place at Greenwich since the 15th century but it was James I who had Inigo Jones design the Queen's House for his consort, Anne of Denmark (right). Kensington Palace originated as a mansion, purchased in 1689 by William III who commissioned Sir Christopher Wren to redesign it. Further changes were made for George I by William Kent. It is pictured (left) in an aquatint by P. Reeve, 1819. Sir Christopher Wren was also responsible for re-styling Hampton Court (far left).*

# GREEN LONDON

Londoners enjoy a great wealth of public open spaces, ranging from historic royal parks, ancient commonlands and the grounds of great mansions, to municipal parks created in Victorian times or in the present century. Many of London's squares are blessed with public gardens and numerous urban churchyards have been converted into green havens. Greater London has no fewer than 1,700 public open spaces greater than one acre in size, covering in all 67 square miles. Many are much smaller: even the densely built-up City of London has 400 green spaces.

Much of the land now occupied by the great royal parks was acquired from the Church in the 1540s after the Dissolution of the Monasteries. Tudor monarchs kept these areas on the outskirts of London for hunting and other private pleasures, but under the Stuarts and the Prince Regent they were laid out as parks and opened for public enjoyment – central London's largest green space, Hyde Park, originally one of Henry VIII's deer parks, was opened to the public in the early 17th century. The large flocks of deer still in evidence at Richmond Park reveal its antecedents as a royal hunting ground. As the capital grew, so did the need for parks in other districts. Despite various campaigns, it was not until 1842 that funds were granted from the Crown for London's first real public park to be created. This was Victoria Park in Hackney, soon to be followed by Battersea Park (1858) and, later in the century, by Finsbury and Southwark Parks (both opened in 1867). These parks were laid out replete with sweeping drives, ornamental lakes, bandstands and pavilions. Many of them were densely planted – reflecting the Victorian passion for horticulture and botany – places of education and instruction as well as pleasure.

Many areas of commonland around London had been enclosed for building or farming during the 18th and 19th centuries, but those that remained were protected under the Metropolitan Commons Act (1866). In this way, Hampstead Heath and Wimbledon Common were secured for public access. The Corporation of the City of London was also empowered to acquire and conserve land up to 25 miles away from the city for public recreation and enjoyment; Epping Forest (1878) and Highgate Woods (1885) are notable examples.

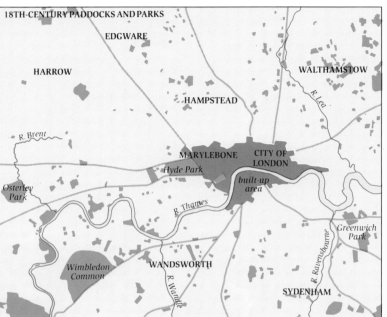

18TH-CENTURY PADDOCKS AND PARKS

London's parks *The fields at Marylebone (pictured by Chatelin, left) provided opportunities for Londoners to enjoy country air. In 1800 Thomas Milne mapped and recorded numerous stretches of private parkland (map left).*

*By the early 16th century, the royal park of St James was surrounded by bricks and mortar. Henry VIII had the area drained and formal gardens were laid out for James I. The park was redesigned after the fashion of Le Nôtre. It is pictured (below) in an engraving of 1794 by Canaleti Delin. In the 1820s the park was improved by John Nash.*

*Battersea Park formed one of the splendours of Victorian urban improvement. Until the mid 16th century this low-lying land had been flooded by the Thames, but parts were later farmed, as John Rocque showed in 1745 (bottom left). Following legislation in 1846 an embankment was built and the ground raised by earth excavated from the Victoria Dock. Reynold's map of 1883 (bottom right) show's the Park's plantations, avenues and lake which proved fashionable for skating. (The 'Ladies' Mile', 1867. is depicted centre.) The poster (top right), designed by Edward Bawden in 1936, was one of many encouraging Londoners to visit their city's parks.*

*With the help of the Heritage Lottery Fund, the Victorian design and fabric of the Park, together with features from the 1951 Festival Gardens, have been restored and enhanced.*

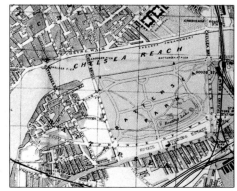

Many landscaped parks on private estates were converted into municipal parks and thereby saved from the suburban tide. Even now new parks are being laid out, such as the ambitious Burgess Park along the line of the old Surrey Canal in Southwark. However, public open spaces as shown on map (*below*) can only form part of the picture of green London, since the city also boasts hundreds of thousands of private gardens which yield flowers, fruit and vegetables.

As well as Greater London's impressive legacy of public open spaces and private gardens, there are also numerous sports-fields, reservoirs, sewage works, railway embankments and areas of derelict land. All of these areas support wildlife and most are valuable land for nature conservation. Abandoned wharves in Docklands, for example, have been colonised by plants and animals and now form important wildlife habitats in parts of the city that otherwise lack open spaces. Over 100 sites which contain especially varied or rare plants and animals have been identified, and three dozen of these have been designated as Sites of Special Scientific Interest. There are also five Local Nature Reserves.

The city centre, not surprisingly, is poor in wildlife compared with outer locations, but as a result of increased development and aggressive mechanised farming techniques in the countryside, birds of prey, grass snakes and foxes are being driven into the suburbs, attracted by the plentiful supplies of food. Aquatic habitats are important for many birds, with reservoirs, gravel pits and ornamental lakes supporting large populations of resident and migratory birds. Good examples are found in the Colne and Lea valleys, the royal parks and alongside the Thames in west London (*page 135*). Habitat management affects the number of plants and animals found in various parts of the capital. Sports pitches and some amenity grasslands are managed intensively and do not support much wildlife.

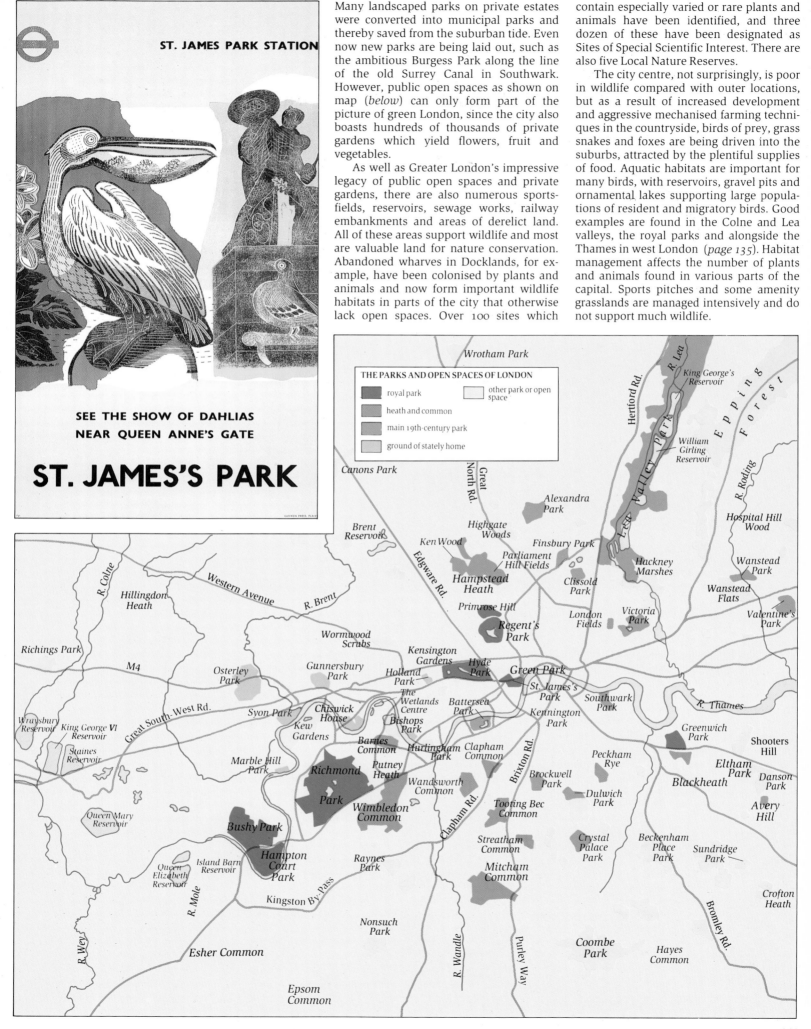

ST. JAMES PARK STATION

SEE THE SHOW OF DAHLIAS
NEAR QUEEN ANNE'S GATE

# ST. JAMES'S PARK

**THE PARKS AND OPEN SPACES OF LONDON**

- royal park
- heath and common
- main 19th-century park
- ground of stately home
- other park or open space

# LONDON AT LEISURE

Medieval Londoners enjoyed varied entertainment: ball games; wrestling; shooting with bow and arrow; swimming; and skating on bone skates on the Thames in cold winters. Mystery plays, pageants and fairs provided more organised entertainment. Cock-fighting and bull- and bear-baiting were certainly known in Tudor times and may have been introduced in the 13th century. They flourished beyond the city limits, especially on the south bank. Animal fighting was not made illegal until 1835.

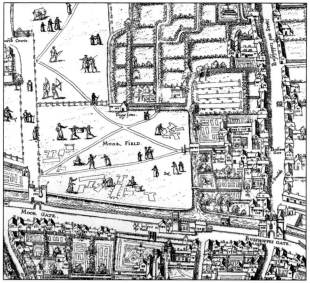

*Archery in Moorfields is depicted on the 'Copperplate Map' of 1559 (left), the oldest surviving map of London. Archery was encouraged by law – it supplied trained bowmen in times of war.*

*Frost fairs and pleasure gardens During exceptionally harsh winters the Thames froze over and frost fairs were held on the ice, with booths, dancing and ox-roasting. Freezing no longer occurred after 1831, when old London Bridge was demolished and river flow accelerated. A frost fair of 1683-4 is depicted in a painting by Hondius (above left). Alongside the Thames, Vauxhall Gardens in Lambeth formed one of the best known pleasure gardens to fringe London in the 18th and 19th centuries (map below). For over a hundred years, until the gardens closed in 1859, Vauxhall supplied music, suppers and entertainment. The Grand Walk at Vauxhall is shown (centre left) in an engraving by Wade and Muller, 1759.*

London's Elizabethan theatres *(page 146)* were sited east of the City and in Southwark, which was notorious for its brothels. Ordinary Londoners, not admitted to the Royal Parks until the 17th century, enjoyed visiting the pleasure grounds fringing the built-up areas. Spring Gardens, on the eastern edge of St James's Park, was an early example, but by 1630 scandalous activities were reported along its shady paths. Puritan zeal curtailed

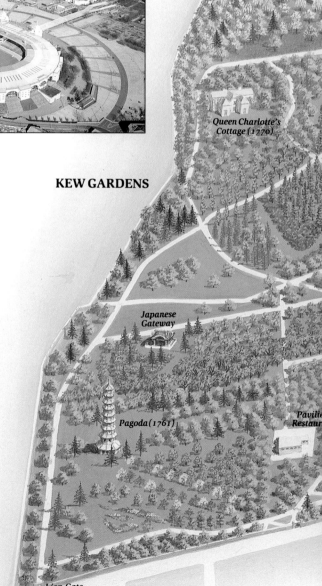

**KEW GARDENS**

*Queen Charlotte's Cottage (1770)*

*Japanese Gateway*

*Pagoda (1761)*

*Pavilion Restaurant*

*Lion Gate*

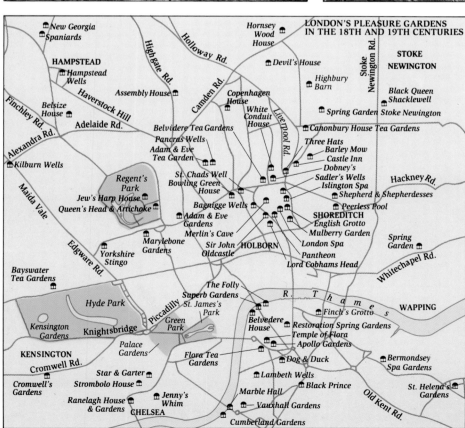

**LONDON'S PLEASURE GARDENS IN THE 18TH AND 19TH CENTURIES**

New Georgia
Spaniards
Hornsey Wood House
Devil's House
STOKE NEWINGTON
HAMPSTEAD
Hampstead Wells
Highbury Barn
Assembly House
Copenhagen House
Black Queen Shacklewell
Belsize House
White Conduit House
Spring Garden Stoke Newington
Kilburn Wells
Belvidere Tea Gardens
Canonbury House Tea Gardens
Pancras Wells
Three Hats
Adam & Eve Tea Garden
Barley Mow
Castle Inn
Regent's Park
St. Chads Well
Dobney's
Sadler's Wells
Jew's Harp House
Bowling Green House
Islington Spa
Hackney Rd.
Queen's Head & Artichoke
Bagnigge Wells
Shepherd & Shepherdesses
Peerless Pool
Adam & Eve Gardens
SHOREDITCH
Marylebone Gardens
Merlin's Cave
English Grotto
Mulberry Garden
Yorkshire Stingo
Sir John Oldcastle HOLBORN
London Spa
Spring Garden
Bayswater Tea Gardens
Pantheon
Lord Cobhams Head
Whitechapel Rd.
The Folly
Superb Gardens
Hyde Park
St. James's Park
WAPPING
Kensington Gardens
Green Park
Belvedere House
Finch's Grotto
Knightsbridge
Palace Gardens
Restoration Spring Gardens
Temple of Flora
Apollo Gardens
KENSINGTON
Flora Tea Gardens
Dog & Duck
Bermondsey Spa Gardens
Cromwell Rd.
Star & Garter
Cromwell's Gardens
Strombolo House
Lambeth Wells
St. Helena's Gardens
Ranelagh House & Gardens
Jenny's Whim
Marble Hall
Black Prince
CHELSEA
Vauxhall Gardens
Cumberland Gardens

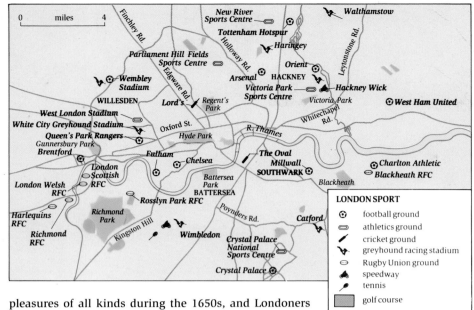

Sporting London *The city boasts a large number of sports facilities (map above). One of London's most famous sports venues was Wembley Stadium (below left). A new stadium is now being built on this site (see page 172).*

springs, such as Sadler's Wells and Hampstead Wells, became fashionable spas.

During Victorian times Londoners were provided with a great range of leisure facilities, ranging from parks and sports clubs to theatres and music halls. Regent's Park Zoo was opened in 1847, while Joseph Paxton's Crystal Palace was rebuilt at Sydenham after the Great Exhibition of 1851 *(page 95)*, where it offered an exotic setting for all kinds of entertainment until its destruction by fire in 1936. Many of the sporting teams that are supported today by dedicated fans were created or formalised during the 19th century. Rugby clubs were founded at Twickenham and Richmond in the 1860s and several of London's leading Football Association teams date from the 1880s. The All England Lawn Tennis Club was created in 1882, evolving from an earlier croquet association. Cricket was being played in Tudor London, but its rules were not formalised until 1744. Henley was the first site of the Oxford and Cambridge Boat Race (1829), but it was moved to its present Putney to Mortlake course in 1845. Perhaps London's most popular 20th-century sporting event is the London Marathon, run between Blackheath and Westminster Bridge in late April.

London hosts major events throughout the year. Thousands of visitors flock to Soho for the Chinese New Year and to the Notting Hill Street Carnival in late August. The Chelsea Flower Show displays the latest ideas in floriculture and garden design each May and, in November, following a tradition dating back to 1215, the Lord Mayor drives through the City of London in a gilded coach.

pleasures of all kinds during the 1650s, and Londoners rejoiced when the monarchy was restored in 1660. The 18th century was the era of pleasure gardens; Chelsea's Ranelagh Gardens, for instance, opened in 1742 and were graced with an ornamental lake, a Chinese pavilion and a great rococo rotunda. In more modest style, Londoners were attracted to inns and springs within easy access of their homes, and some of London's natural

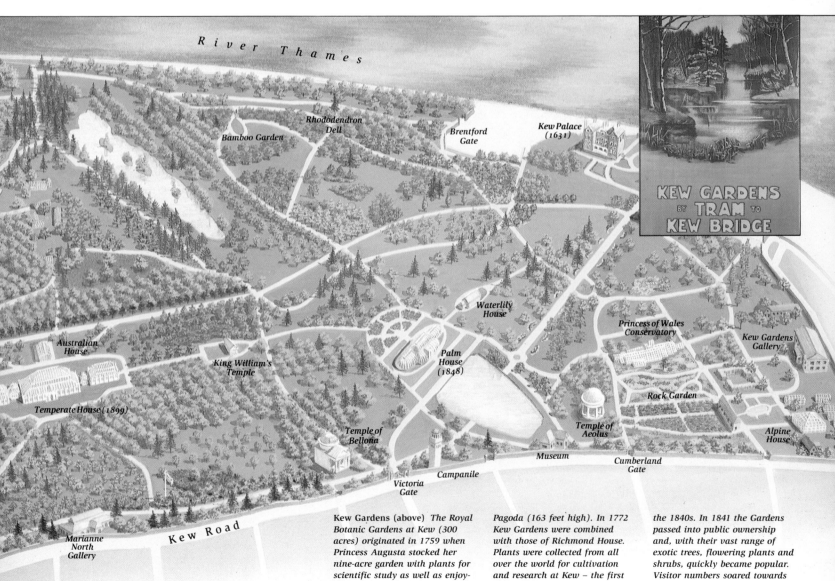

Kew Gardens (above) *The Royal Botanic Gardens at Kew (300 acres) originated in 1759 when Princess Augusta stocked her nine-acre garden with plants for scientific study as well as enjoyment. The surrounding parkland was subsequently adorned with classical temples and the Great Pagoda (163 feet high). In 1772 Kew Gardens were combined with those of Richmond House. Plants were collected from all over the world for cultivation and research at Kew – the first glasshouse to be built for this purpose was the Palm House, designed by Decimus Burton in the 1840s. In 1841 the Gardens passed into public ownership and, with their vast range of exotic trees, flowering plants and shrubs, quickly became popular. Visitor numbers soared towards the end of the 19th century, when public transport made Kew more accessible to Londoners.*

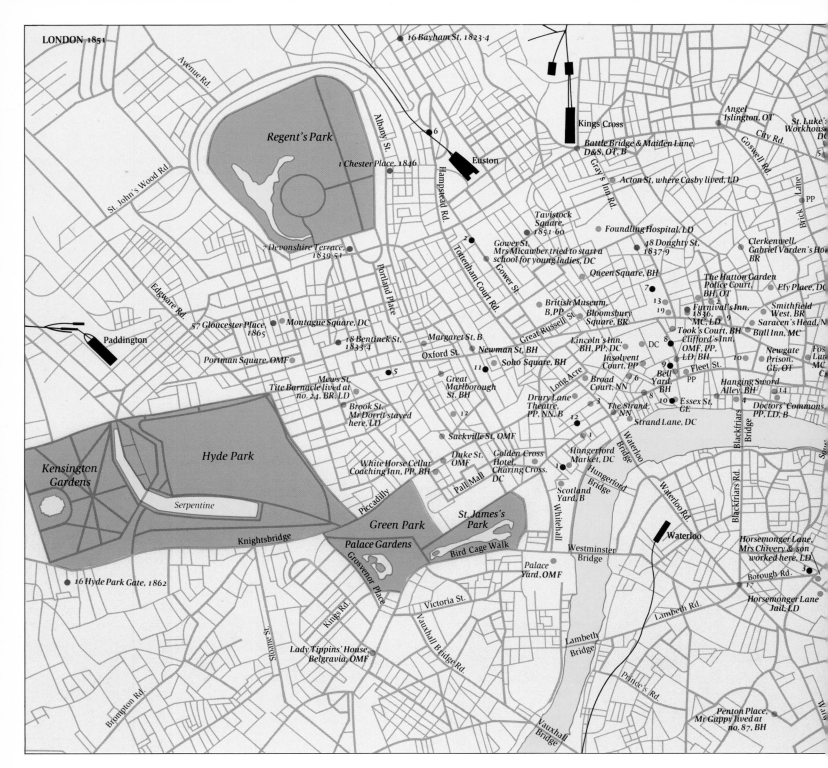

*Map labels:*

16 Bayham St, 1823-4

Regent's Park

Kings Cross

Angel Islington, OT
St. Luke's Workhouse
City Rd.
Goswell Rd.

Albany St.

6

1 Chester Place, 1846

Euston

Battle Bridge & Maiden Lane, D&S, OT, B
Gray's Inn Rd.
Acton St, where Casby lived, LD

Brick Lane

PP

Hampstead Rd.

St. John's Wood Rd.

Tavistock Square, 1851-60
Foundling Hospital, LD
48 Donghty St, 1837-9
Clerkenwell, Gabriel Varden's Ho, BR

7 Devonshire Terrace, 1839-51

2

Gower St, Mrs Micawber tried to start a school for young ladies, DC
Gower St.

Queen Square, BH

The Hatton Garden Police Court, BH, OT
Ely Place, DC

Edgware Rd.

Portland Place

Tottenham Court Rd.

British Museum, B, PP
Bloomsbury Square, BR

7

13
19

Furnival's Inn, 1836, MC, LD
Smithfield West, BR
Saracen's Head, MC
Bull Inn, MC

57 Gloucester Place, 1865
Montague Square, DC

Great Russell St.

Lincoln's Inn, BH, PP, DC

DC

8

Took's Court, BH
Clifford's Inn, OMF, PP, LD, BH

Newgate Prison, GE, OT
Fleet Lane, MC

Paddington

18 Bentinck St, 1833-4
Margaret St, B
Oxford St.
Newman St, BH

9

Bell Yard, BH

10

Fleet St.

PP

Hanging Sword Alley, BH

14

Portman Square, OMF

Insolvent Court, PP

6

Soho Square, BH

5

11

Great Marlborough St, BH

Long Acre

Broad Court, NN

8

10

Essex St, GE

4

Doctors' Commons, PP, LD, B

Mews St, Tite Barnacle lived at no.24, BR, LD

12

Drury Lane Theatre, PP, NN, B

3

The Strand, NN

Strand Lane, DC

Brook St, Mr Dorrit stayed here, LD

12

1

Hyde Park

Sackville St, OMF

Duke St, OMF

Golden Cross Hotel, Charing Cross, DC

Hungerford Market, DC

Hungerford Bridge

Waterloo Bridge

Blackfriars Bridge

Blackfriars Rd.

Kensington Gardens

White Horse Cellar Coaching Inn, PP, BH

Pall Mall

Scotland Yard, B

1

Serpentine

Green Park

St. James's Park

Whitehall

Waterloo Rd.

Waterloo

Horsemonger Lane, Mrs Chivery & son worked here, LD

Knightsbridge

Palace Gardens

Bird Cage Walk

Westminster Bridge

Borough Rd.

3

Piccadilly

Grosvenor Place

Palace Yard, OMF

16 Hyde Park Gate, 1862

Horsemonger Lane Jail, LD

Victoria St.

Lambeth Rd.

Kings Rd.

Vauxhall Bridge Rd.

Lambeth Bridge

Brompton Rd.

Sloane St.

Lady Tippins' House, Belgravia, OMF

Prince's Rd.

Penton Place, Mr Guppy lived at no. 87, BH

Vauxhall Bridge

## Chapter 10 London Themes
# THE LONDON OF CHARLES DICKENS

Throughout its history London has inspired works of literary genius but none can be compared with the powerfully evocative writings of Charles Dickens (1812–1870). Born in Portsea, Dickens came from Chatham to London when he was ten to join his family in their new home in Camden Town. It was not to be an easy or settled existence in the metropolis; just two days after his twelfth birthday the talented and ambitious boy was sent to pack boot-blacking in Warren's warehouse near Hungerford Stairs, reached after a 3-mile walk from Camden Town. A few days after the job started his father, John Dickens, was imprisoned as an insolvent debtor in Marshalsea Prison, Southwark. In the fashion

of the time (evocatively described in *Little Dorrit*) his wife and children moved into the Marshalsea with him, and young Dickens was forced to find new lodgings close to the prison. Although his father was released after a few months and Charles was able to attend school again, the squalor, smell and despair of Marshalsea remained imprinted in his mind. From an early age he was exposed to the hardship he was to portray so powerfully in his novels.

Dickens left school in 1827 and obtained work as a solicitor's clerk. Two years later he became a legal reporter and then moved to parliamentary reporting. His initial writings on London life were brought together as *Sketches by Boz* (1836). In later life, he felt compelled to constantly revive his sense of place by walking the streets and alleys of the capital, and visiting its markets, public houses, workhouses, police courts and prisons. Throughout his works of

'imaginative vision' Dickens embraced the essential contradictions of 19th-century London, but always dwelt on the harsher side. Next to the wealth he set appalling poverty, for his characters' hope was frequently tinged with despair. Splendid public buildings contrasted with terrifying slums, all shrouded in the fog which seemed to emanate from a million coal fires, factory chimneys and steamboats on the river.

The 'Great Oven', the 'Great Wen', the 'Fever Pitch' and 'Babylon' were the images of London that Dickens evoked as the capital grew from a densely-packed, filthy town of some 1,400,000 souls when he first arrived to a sprawling city of 3,000,000 inhabitants, complete with railways, underground lines and a constellation of suburbs, when he died. The grinding and widespread poverty of Dickens' adolescent vision was to remain a stark reality for many Londoners well beyond the time of his death.

London locations
mentioned

Titles are abbreviated
as follows:

| | |
|---|---|
| B | Sketches by Boz |
| BH | Bleak House |
| BR | Barnaby Rudge |
| DC | David Copperfield |
| D&S | Dombey & Son |
| GE | Great Expectations |
| LD | Little Dorrit |
| MC | Martin Chuzzlewit |
| NN | Nicholas Nickleby |
| OT | Oliver Twist |
| OCS | Old Curiosity Shop |
| OMF | Our Mutual Friend |
| OT | Oliver Twist |
| PP | Pickwick Papers |

*A selection of places and events (numbered on map):*

1. Adelphi Terrace and Hotel. Favourite watering hole of Mr Pickwick and Mr Wardle – PP
2. Bleeding Heart Yard. Home to the Plornish family and Daniel Doyce's factory – LD
3. Bow Street Police Court. The Artful Dodger – OT – and Barnaby Rudge were taken to Bow Street Police Station.
4. Bridewell Workhouse, House of Correction – where Miss Miggs was chosen to be Female Turnkey for the County Bridewell – BR
5. City Rd. Windsor Terrace. Where Mr Micawber lived – DC
6. Clare Market, site of the Old Curiosity Shop and gin shops – B
7. Custom House. Peepy worked here – BH; also the late Mr Bardell – PP. Pip left his boat at a wharf near the Custom House – GE
8. Johnson's Beef House where David Copperfield ordered a small plate of beef.
9. Field Lane, Saffron Hill. Fagin's Den – OT
10. Fleet Prison. Where Mr Pickwick was imprisoned – PP
11. Garraway's, the famous city coffee house. Mr Flintwich was a customer here – LD. Also Nadgett, the enquiry agent – MC
12. Golden Square. David Copperfield and Martha found Little Emily here – DC
13. Gray's Inn. David Copperfield stayed in the Gray's Inn Coffee House when visiting Traddles – DC
14. Horn Coffee House, 29 Knightrider St. Where Mr Pickwick sent for a few bottles of wine while in Fleet Prison, to celebrate Mr Winkle's visit – PP
15. Jacob's Island (Folly Ditch). Home of Bill Sikes and where he was hanged whilst trying to make his escape – OT
16. Leadenhall Market. In the Green Dragon Sam wrote the famous 'Walentine' – PP; the offices of Dombey and Son were here.
17. Obelisk, generally called the 'obstacle'. David Copperfield had his trunk and half guinea stolen and had to start his journey to Dover on foot – DC
18. St. Mary Axe. This is the location of the pretty roof garden where Lizzie and Jenny Wren used to sit and talk above the premises of Pubsey & Co. – OMF
19. Gray's Inn, South Square. Mr Phunky had chambers here – PP. Traddles lived at no. 2 Holborn Court, nearby.

DICKENS' LIFE

● places where Dickens lived
(dates shown on map)

● a selection of events in Dickens'
life:

1. Craven St. Site of Hungerford Market where Dickens worked as a boy in Warren's Blacking House at Old Hungerford Stairs.
2. Gower St. North. Dickens' mother opened a school here attempting to delay payment of debts.
3. The King's Bench Debtors' prison where John Dickens was imprisoned for debt in 1824.
4. The New Marshalsea Debtors' Prison to which Dickens' father was then moved. To save money, his wife and younger children moved in with him.
5. Tenterden St. The Royal Academy of Music. Dickens' sister Fanny was a boarder here.
6. Wellington House Academy (corner of Granby St. and Hampstead Rd.). Dickens was sent here for two years after his father's release from prison.
7. Gray's Inn, Holborn. Dickens, aged 15, came to work here at the law firm of Ellis & Blackmore.
8. Chancery Lane where Dickens then worked for the Solicitor Charles Molloy.
9. Bell Yard, Carter Lane. Dickens rented an office here while a reporter in Doctors' Commons.
10. Essex St. Dickens attended the Unitarian Chapel here in 1842.
11. Dean St. Fanny Kelly's Theatre (now gone) owned and run by a retired actress; Dickens acted here in 1845.
12. Maiden Lane. Rules Restaurant was one of Dickens' favourite eating places.

**Images of Dickens' London** *The Marshalsea Prison* (above right, *c.1895*) *must have held grim associations for Dickens, since his father was incarcerated there for debt in 1823-4. Dickens was taken out of school and worked at a blacking factory at Hungerford Stairs, near Charing Cross* (below left, *1823*). *He was to write powerfully about child exploitation in his novels. The criminal underworld was also an enduring obsession; at the beginning of* **Great Expectations**, *the hero, Pip, is surprised in a graveyard by Magwitch, who has escaped from the hulks* (see below right, *a prison ship at Deptford*), *where convicts awaiting transportation were held. Little of Dickens' London survives; the George Inn at Southwark* (right, *photographed in 1890*) *is an exception. Mentioned in* **Little Dorrit**, *it is the only surviving galleried inn in London.*

# THEATRICAL LONDON

In medieval London players were restricted to performing in galleried innyards, bull-baiting arenas and the houses of the nobility. The City authorities feared that plays could corrupt morals and kept a close watch on entertainments. In 1574 a law was passed forbidding the construction of playhouses inside the City walls, and so London's first purpose-built theatres were located outside the City. They were constructed to retain many of the qualities of the old galleried inns. In 1642 the Puritans closed down all London's theatres. Dramatic life revived just before the Restoration, but the old unroofed playhouses did not reopen.

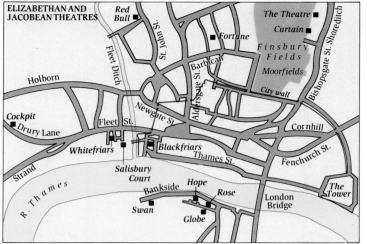

**Shakespeare's London** *The map (left) shows that Elizabethan and Jacobean playhouses were sited on the South Bank, which had housed entertainments since medieval times, in Shoreditch and off Fleet Street. Recent archaeological work has uncovered many details about the design of London's theatres in Shakespeare's day. The Curtain, London's first purpose-built theatre, was constructed in 1577, followed by the Rose on the South Bank in 1587. The Globe was built partly from materials salvaged from the Curtain, which had been demolished after objections from the Puritans.*

**The Globe** *The illustration (far right) shows an engraving by Wenceslas Hollar of the second Globe Theatre on Bankside. This was rebuilt in 1613 on the foundations of the original Globe Theatre, which had been constructed between 1598 and 1599.*

**Shakespeare's workplace** *The first Globe Theatre, in which Shakespeare performed, was destroyed by fire when a spark from a stage canon, used in a performance of* Henry VIII, *set light to the thatched roof.*

**The new Globe Theatre** *In 1993 construction of a new Globe Theatre began approximately 200 yards from the site of the original one. Like the first playhouse, known as Shakespeare's 'wooden O', the most recent version is polygonal and contains tiers of seating around an open yard for standing spectators. The roof is made of thatch and is open at the top, allowing natural daylight to illumine the action on stage. The photographs (above, left and right) show the new Globe as it appears from the outside, from the inside and under construction against the background of London's cityscape.*

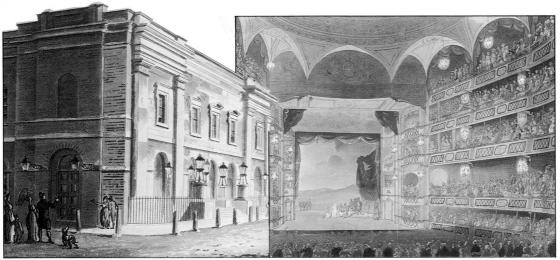

ALHAMBRA
Theatre of Varieties

LEICESTER SQUARE, LONDON.

Royal patents for presenting spoken drama were granted to two companies by Charles II. Demand for theatre could not be satisfied by the patent houses in Drury Lane and Covent Garden alone, so 'minor' theatres operated outside the law until the monopoly was abolished in 1843. By 1850 London had two dozen theatres, clustered in Covent Garden, Drury Lane and the Strand.

Music-halls offered more robust and popular fare. Originally garish, brightly-lit halls often connected with pubs, they had become veritable palaces of entertainment by the end of the 19th century. Their heyday was not to last: London's first cinematograph show was given in 1895, and soon many theatres and music-halls were showing moving pictures. Nevertheless, the late 20th century has not been devoid of new theatres in London – two notable examples are the National Theatre and the Barbican in the City.

*London's Theatreland The Theatre Royal, Drury Lane (above left, 1812), was opened in 1663. It became the home of David Garrick, one of England's great Shakespearean actors, seen performing in an aquatint (above centre) dated 1808. The corniced facade of the Alhambra music hall at Leicester Square can be seen, (above right), while the painting (right, 1861), shows an early music-hall interior (the Pavilion). The map (below left) shows the location of music halls in Victorian London. Many of London's theatres are now closed, and the map (below right) shows London's lost theatres. Today's theatreland is largely concentrated in the West End (map, bottom left), although the National Theatre (bottom right) is part of a major arts complex on the South Bank.*

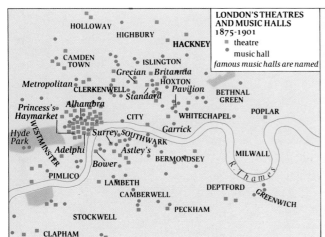

LONDON'S THEATRES AND MUSIC HALLS 1875-1901
- ■ theatre
- ● music hall
*famous music halls are named*

LONDON'S LOST THEATRES

1   Alhambra (1858-1936)
2   Daly's (1893-1937)
3   Empire (1883-1927)
4   Gaiety (1868-1903)
5   Globe (1868-1902)
6   Royal Connaught (1873-1886)
7   Holborn Theatre Royal (1866-1880)
8   Imperial (1876-1907)
9   Kingsway (1882-1941)
10  Little (1910-1940)
11  Olympic (1806-1899)
12  Opera Comique (1870-1899)
13  Princess's (1840-1902)
14  Royal Strand (1832-1905)
15  Royalty (1840-1938)
16  St. George's Hall (1867-1941)
17  St. James's (1835-1957)
18  Shaftesbury (1888-1941)
19  Terry's (1887-1910)
20  Toole's (1869-1895)
21  Scala (1905-1968)
22  Lyceum (1834-1939)
23  London Pavilion (1918-1934)
24  London Hippodrome (1900-1982)
25  Gate (1925-1940)
26  Queen's (1867-1879)
27  Carlton (1927-1930)

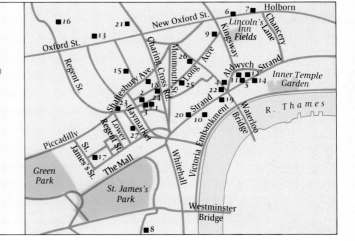

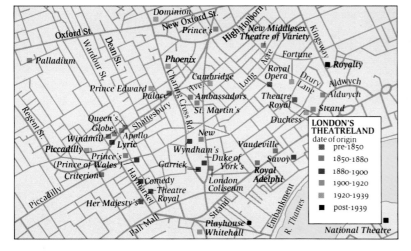

LONDON'S THEATRELAND
date of origin
- ■ pre-1850
- ■ 1850-1880
- ■ 1880-1900
- ■ 1900-1920
- ■ 1920-1939
- ■ post-1939

# SHOPPING AND MARKETS

## MARKETS

Great cities live by trade, and London is no exception. As the city grew and modes of transport improved, so it was supplied with goods from ever greater distances. In 1720, Daniel Defoe remarked that '... this whole kingdom, as well as the people, the land and even the sea in every part of it, are employed to supply London with provisions, fuel and timber'. As sailing ships gave way to steam, railways opened up hitherto unimaginable distances. The British Empire had reached its zenith and London's trade embraced the whole globe. Trade did not just mean goods; bonds, stocks and shares also played a role in the vast array of London's marketing.

The great Roman forum stood at the heart of *Londinium*, an emporium for goods brought by land and sea. Trade

*The history of London's markets stretches back to Roman times. Indeed, many of the names of medieval markets (top left) are still familiar to a 20th-century Londoner – Cheapside, Smithfield, Leadenhall. Commodities, too, have been immortalised in street names such as Poultry, Milk Street and Honey Lane. The distribution of markets in Stuart London (centre left) reflects the spread of the city outside the medieval walls: Covent Garden, opened in 1670 but relocated to Battersea in 1973, was the first of many markets which were founded specifically to serve the residents of the new suburbs.*

*Markets in the 20th century London's markets today (bottom) present a rich and varied array. Many of the medieval markets have been relocated further out, with Billingsgate moving to the Isle of Dogs and Spitalfields to Temple Mills, Stratford. However, the old-established market of Leadenhall still survives in the City. London's street markets capture a district's character in all its immediacy; markets such as Petticoat Lane and Brick Lane (to the east of the City) are both located in areas with a rich ethnic history – their Jewish and, more recently, Asian legacy.*

*The map shows the detailed range of specialities which characterise the street markets; flowers, antiques, furniture, second-hand clothes, tools, specialised foods, are all represented. Many residents of Greater London are within range of a street market (be it only a few fruit and vegetable stalls or a substantial street market selling a whole range of goods). Their vitality and variety are characteristics of the city.*

*Right The Sunday street market at Petticoat Lane. A thriving old clothes market since the beginning of the 17th century, it is still a busy general market today.*

declined when the Saxons overwhelmed the city, but by the 7th century London was re-established and open markets were developed in Cheapside. As in other medieval cities, specialised traders clustered in distinctive quarters to defend their interests, and these local trades (bread, honey, milk, poultry) are all immortalised in the surrounding street names. Market activities were closely regulated – trading was permitted only in established marketplaces and during specified hours; few goods could be hawked openly in the streets. In time, more distant markets flourished at Spitalfields and in Southwark.

In 1666, the Great Fire dealt a mortal blow to some of the city's oldest markets, some of which were rebuilt as covered markets under royal charter (e.g. Leadenhall, Newgate, Billingsgate, the Stocks). At the same time, the fashion for suburban development was paralleled by the creation of new markets. Covent Garden (1670), built on the Earl of Bedford's land was the first to be authorised; it was to be emulated by scores of other landowners during the next 200 years. The City's monopoly over all markets within a radius of six and two-third miles was widely challenged; many new markets developed unofficially.

With the advent of the railways, a number of wholesale food markets were opened near the main termini. The old sheds of Covent Garden had been replaced by an elegant market hall in 1830, Billingsgate and Leadenhall were rebuilt in the City, and handling of live cattle was transferred from Smithfield to the Caledonian cattle market in Islington (1855). It was closed during the Second World War. Over the past hundred years many of London's markets have been closed and others relocated (e.g. Billingsgate and Spitalfields) but eighty still survive in inner London and there are more in the suburbs and in surrounding towns.

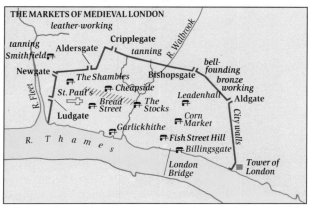

**THE MARKETS OF MEDIEVAL LONDON**

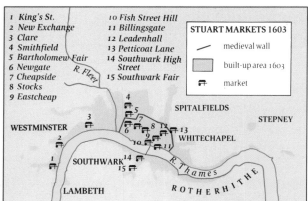

| | |
|---|---|
| 1 King's St. | 10 Fish Street Hill |
| 2 New Exchange | 11 Billingsgate |
| 3 Clare | 12 Leadenhall |
| 4 Smithfield | 13 Petticoat Lane |
| 5 Bartholomew Fair | 14 Southwark High Street |
| 6 Newgate | 15 Southwark Fair |
| 7 Cheapside | |
| 8 Stocks | |
| 9 Eastcheap | |

**STUART MARKETS 1603**

— medieval wall

▢ built-up area 1603

▤ market

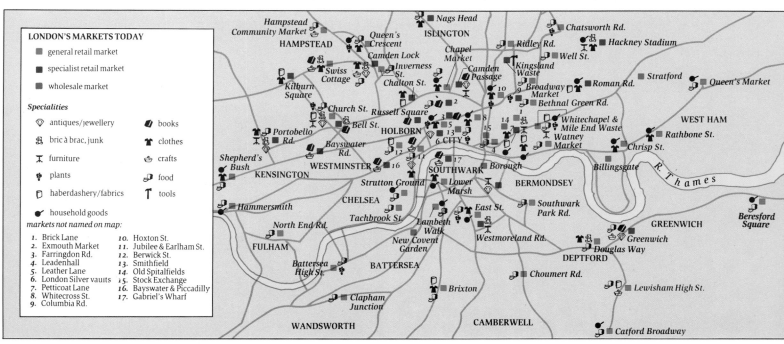

**LONDON'S MARKETS TODAY**

■ general retail market

■ specialist retail market

■ wholesale market

**Specialities**

♦ antiques/jewellery
🐗 bric à brac, junk
⊥ furniture
🌱 plants
◘ haberdashery/fabrics
🕯 household goods

📖 books
👕 clothes
🎨 crafts
🍴 food
⊤ tools

markets not named on map:

| | |
|---|---|
| 1. Brick Lane | 10. Hoxton St. |
| 2. Exmouth Market | 11. Jubilee & Earlham St. |
| 3. Farringdon Rd. | 12. Berwick St. |
| 4. Leadenhall | 13. Smithfield |
| 5. Leather Lane | 14. Old Spitalfields |
| 6. London Silver vaults | 15. Stock Exchange |
| 7. Petticoat Lane | 16. Bayswater & Piccadilly |
| 8. Whitecross St. | 17. Gabriel's Wharf |
| 9. Columbia Rd. | |

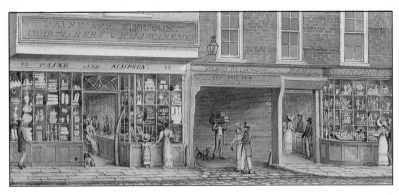

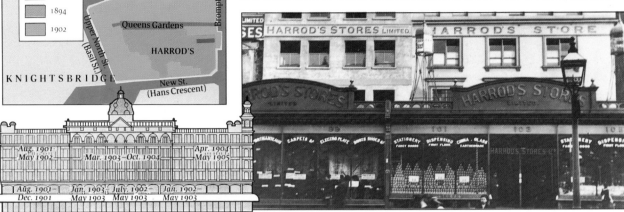

London's shopping history *From medieval times London was richly endowed with specialist shops. This view of the shopping street of Cornhill (early 18th century, above far right) clearly shows the elaborate overhanging signs, with which each individual shop advertised their wares. They were judged to be dangerous to passing pedestrians and were finally removed in 1762. 18th-century Londoners could be justly proud of their shops, with their enticing displays (above). A German visitor to London in 1786, Sophie v. la Roche, visited Oxford Street and remarked '... behind great glass windows absolutely everything one can think of is neatly, attractively displayed, and in such abundance of choice as to make one greedy...'.*

*Harrod's started life as a small grocer's shop in the Brompton Road, opened by H.C. Harrod, a tea retailer in 1853 (photograph far right 1891). Gradually, he acquired the surrounding terraces (map above right), until he had built up an 'island site', and the massive expansion of Harrod's store then began (diagram right). Harrod's now covers a 20-acre site.*

*19th-century Tobacco Dock is now a shopping village (illustration below), its vaults and upper levels converted into shops and boutiques. However, it ran into severe financial difficulties in 1990 as the dynamism of the Docklands revival declined.*

### SHOPPING

London's earliest shops surrounded marketplaces in the walled city and were adjacent to unloading points along the Thames. That pattern held good for many centuries, but as London spread westward after 1650 so new clusters of shops developed to serve rich households living around the elegant squares and streets which were springing up all over the West End. Many of these shops were also dedicated to serving the Royal Court, and the King's move to St. James's Palace at the end of the 17th century (after Whitehall Palace had been destroyed by fire) was to have a profound effect on the surrounding neighbourhoods. Many royal warrant-holders set up business in the streets of St. James, proclaiming that they sold goods 'By appointment from' His or Her Majesty – many have retained both their warrants and

premises to this day. Over 800 royal warrant-holders are concentrated in the elite shopping districts of St. James and Mayfair. Many of the shops in this district have a long history; William Fortnum (a footman in the household of Queen Anne) and Hugh Mason set up a grocer's shop in 1707. Fortnum secured orders from the royal household and the business consequently thrived; to this day Fortnum and Mason's occupies the same site. A few yards along Piccadilly is Hatchard's bookshop, which opened in 1797, while Burlington Arcade was built in 1819 to provide an exclusive shopping parade, subject to strict regulations.

During the 19th century, the shopping districts of the West End began to radiate outwards, along Regent Street, Oxford Street and Tottenham Court Road. This was the century which saw the advent of department stores. Originally an American concept, these vast trading emporia, boasted (in the words of William Whiteley) 'We can supply anything from a pin to an elephant'. By the end of the century, department stores of ever-increasing size were to be found in the residential areas of Kensington, Brompton and Chelsea. While shops in the West End flourished, many in the City closed as its residential population fell from 128,000 (1801) to 27,000 (1901).

In the 1920s and 30s, the growth of American mass-consumerism, supported by advertising and the mass media, created an even greater demand. This was the era when shops such as Woolworth and Marks & Spencer began to colonise London's suburbs (*page 107*). Their presence in a district is an accurate index of a suburb's status as a regional shopping centre.

As the 20th century has progressed, fashions in shopping have changed. Some of the large department stores, founded during the optimistic and expansionist days of the British Empire, have fallen on hard times and been forced to close. Others, such as Whiteley's in Queensway, have been born again as shopping complexes, playing host to many separate retail outlets. Purpose-built shopping centres, with cinemas, restaurants and car parks, characterise the outer suburbs, while in the inner city a wide range of unlikely buildings (such as abandoned and neglected warehouses in Docklands) have been put to similar use.

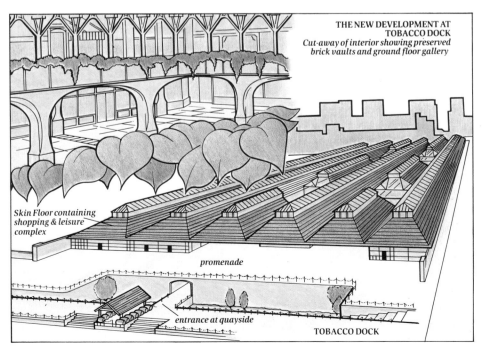

**THE NEW DEVELOPMENT AT TOBACCO DOCK**
*Cut-away of interior showing preserved brick vaults and ground floor gallery*

*Skin Floor containing shopping & leisure complex*

*promenade*

*entrance at quayside*

TOBACCO DOCK

# CHAPTER 11
# PLACES IN LONDON

*The Jubilee Line Extension from Westminster, through the archaeologically sensitive south bank of the Thames to Docklands, and on to Stratford was Europe's largest civil engineering operation in the late 1990s. Many important discoveries were made and reported in The Big Dig: archaeology and the Jubilee Line Extension (1998).*

## PALAEOECOLOGY

*Analysis of sediments and pollen remains, especially from Southwark and Canada Water, has allowed the environment and vegetation of early times to be investigated. The enormous span from the Mesolithic (10,000–5,000 BC) to the Iron Age (700 BC–AD 43) saw the change from hunting and gathering to a settled farming economy when cereals were cultivated, animals grazed and villages built. Woodland (oak, elm, ash, hazel) was found on higher ground, with boggier land near the Thames supporting alder and reed mace. A decline in tree species and an increase in evidence of herbaceous plants suggest clearing for settlement and farming the Bronze Age (c. 2000 BC). Evidence from medieval times is less useful than for earlier periods, since pollen from imported herbs later planted complicates the record.*

## EARLY PERIODS

*Neolithic arrowheads (5000–2000 BC) and fragments of polished axe suggest prehistoric occupation at Westminster, where Late Bronze Age or Iron Age pottery (c. 7000 BC) was also found. Analysis of fluvial deposits shows that woodland cover was removed in the Bronze Age (2000-700 BC) for cultivation and settlement. Iron Age (700 BC–43 AD) settlements and burials were found on gravel islands at Stratford.*

## ROMAN PERIOD

*Fragments of Roman tiles, floors and burials confirm that the Romans occupied Thorney Island at Westminster. Remains of clay-and-timber and masonry buildings were found along a rutted stone road to London Bridge. Many Roman jars (amphorae) for wine, figs and olives from the Mediterranean were discovered at Southwark, together with evidence of early Roman buildings. These remains were sealed by a layer of fire debris indicating a major fire on the south bank (AD 60-70), arguably coinciding with Boudica's revolt. Roman Southwark may have housed 3,000 residents in the late 2nd century, with evidence of smithies, granaries, bakeries, and butchers' shops being found.*

THIS ATLAS is both a visual celebration of two thousand years of London's history and an inventory of economic and architectural achievement, which has been punctuated by phases of disaster and destruction, as well as the poverty and deprivation which are the darker but inescapable sides of metropolitan life. The city is the sum total of its many neighbourhoods – some prestigious, others ordinary – which face the future with varying degrees of accumulated strength and potential. This final chapter focuses on a sample of these places. As the dual cores of old London, the City and Westminster stand proud in modern London and are obvious choices for our selection. So too is Docklands, which was so important to London's economy in the past and on which so much faith for London's future is pinned. 'Village London' evokes the historic settlements around which so many suburbs developed and much of the character of Greater London has been built. London's many bridges are of great visual and functional interest in their own right and remind us of how significant the Thames is in dividing Londoners' perceptions of their home town. Living 'north of the river' is very different from living 'south of the river', and few Londoners are equally familiar with both sides of the capital. London's universities and museums evoke the worldwide cultural importance of the city; its monuments and great cemeteries not only honour the dead, but also recall London's role as national capital and historic focus of a colonial empire. Perhaps less obvious is our choice of the hidden world beneath the surface of London and the many grand designs that were never realised to transform the capital. They contribute to the 'London that never was'. Equally surprising may be our selection of schemes that may fashion London's appearance and activities as it enters the third millennium.

As the 20th century drew to a close, London had lost most of its industry and now survives by providing services and managing international finance. If London, and the towns and villages in its commuting orbit, are to flourish in the years ahead, the city must respond to two challenges, one from within, the other from beyond. If it fails to do so then the future of the metropolitan region may be sombre. London's buildings and infrastructure are wearing badly. Much housing that had outlived its useful life was destroyed during the Second World War, and even more was erased in slum clearance schemes, but London still has a complex legacy of Victorian and Edwardian dwellings, inter-war suburban houses and post-war flats in need of expensive restoration or replacement. The surfaces of London's roads are pitted by repeated excavation and inadequate repair as old utilities are replaced and new ones, such as fibre-optics cables, are laid. Over 600,000 new holes are dug in London's streets each year. Many sewers were installed a century or more ago; frequent burst water mains reveal that many pipes need replacement. London's roads have to cope with lorries of ever increasing weight and dimension and are jammed with over 2 million cars each year. Average car speeds have fallen in recent years. The Underground system is often stifling, overcrowded, dirty and very expensive. London's buses are little better as they crawl through what seems to be an unceasing rush hour that lasts from morning to night. Political geography is changing fast and London's vitality and financial supremacy cannot be taken for granted in the 'new Europe' that is emerging as a result of the Single European Market, the unification of Germany, the dramatic changes in Eastern Europe, the enlargement of the European Union, and the future entry of states in Eastern Europe. Paris, Frankfurt and other European cities are planning to maximise their chances of capturing growing shares of business activity. Their success could be to the detriment of London unless effective action is taken to manage the city comprehensively, and meet the European challenge head on.

Paris provides the best example of a city that has been planned, managed and modernised over the past 35 years. No other city is promoting its future with such verve and commitment. If London is to compete with Paris and other European cities, it must be repaired, restored and reinvigorated. Its strengths and weaknesses must be evaluated and an integrated plan must be

## MEDIEVAL

*Many medieval buildings have been identified at New Palace Yard, Westminster, including parts of 'water gates' along the Thames. Drainage ditches with timber edging at Westminster have been radiocarbon dated to 950–1100. A 12th-century quay serving Westminster Palace has been excavated. At Southwark, the town house of the Prior of Lewes (Sussex) has been identified. Remains of the medieval abbey of Stratford Langthorne (founded 1135) have been excavated in the lower valley of the Lea. The history of this abbey, one of the richest houses of the Cistercian order, has been illuminated by excavating the monastic precinct, chapels, cloister, infirmary, drains and monks' graveyard (with almost 700 skeletons).*

## LATER PERIODS

*A large 17th-century cemetery was found on unconsecrated ground at Southwark. This was the Single Woman's Burial Ground for female paupers and prostitutes of Bankside. The 17th-century stone well of old St. Thomas' Hospital was uncovered near London Bridge, with the stable yards of taverns. A 17th-century Chinese cannon was found at Stratford, perhaps having been seized as booty, brought as ship's ballast, or perhaps intended for melting down. Much evidence of Stratford's varied industrial activities (printing of calico and silk, dyeing, carpentry) in the 18th and 19th centuries has been discovered.*

*As the new millennium arrived, Ford ceased making cars at Dagenham, epitomising both the profound deindustrialisation and the impact of globalisation that have affected the capital over the past quarter century.*

After a long period of neglect, land along London's canal is being redeveloped for housing, ranging from expensive apartments to affordable homes. Already projects are underway on the Grosvenor Basin (Victoria), Paddington Basin, and at other sites along the Grand Union Canal. Future schemes will involve the Limehouse Canal and canal-side locations in the Lower Lea Valley.

Installing the Channel Tunnel Rail Link through Kent has been accompanied by many archaeological digs along the route. Discoveries include: Bronze Age barrows, and Anglo-Saxon cemetery, and a 14th century castle at sites near the mouth of the Tunnel; an early medieval moated enclosure near Ashford; Mesolithic flint tools, a Roman villa and a Neolithic long house at sites near Maidstone; and a Roman cemetery and an Anglo-Saxon cemetery at two locations west of Rochester.

Proposals have been launched to transform abandoned land around the Wembley arena site into a complex of homes, restaurants, hotels, designer outlets and other activities around the new stadium. Such revitalisation will be an important factor in London's attempts to host the 2012 Olympic Games.

implemented, not just for the metropolis, but for the whole London region. Termination of the GLC (and Britain's other metropolitan authorities) in 1986 removed a politically controversial organisation, but also robbed the city of a London-wide framework for taking stock of problems. The City of London, plus 32 borough authorities with sharply different socio-economic and environmental characteristics and markedly divergent political sympathies, did not pull together in the way necessary for London as a whole to flourish in the future.

The metropolitan development that occurred in recent years has been disjointed. Much faith has been pinned on redeveloping Docklands, not only as a mechanism for dealing with a major problem area, but also as the means of attracting corporate finance to the metropolis and answering an anticipated explosion in demand for office facilities. The area is served by a light railway that has been extended to Bank and to the Royal Docks. New highways link Docklands to other parts of the region, and the Jubilee Line extension offers a great improvement. The task of regenerating vast areas around the Royal Docks downstream is being faced in the new millennium.

Other schemes are underway elsewhere in Greater London and more have been proposed: a fast rail link from Paddington to Heathrow has improved access to the airport; a CrossRail line tunnelled from beyond Liverpool Street to Paddington has been proposed to provide a fast east-west service with interchange facilities on several north-south Tube lines; rail services using the Channel Tunnel terminate at special facilities at Waterloo. The main terminal will, however, be at St Pancras, which will be served by a high-speed rail link through Kent. This will trim journeys to Paris and Brussels from three to two and a half hours. Unlike the North Circular Road, which is an identifiable highway being upgraded, the South Circular remains a bizarre string of suburban streets. Schemes for improving it and for installing motorways through congested suburbs have been shelved because of rising costs and widespread local opposition. The London Ring Main tunnel has been constructed to carry 285 million gallons of water at any one time from intake points to the south-west of London for distribution to many locations in the region. Some 120 feet beneath the surface, the 50-mile tunnel is deeper than most Tube lines and longer than the Channel Tunnel. There are proposals to increase its length early in this new century.

In 1993 the government launched a scheme to regenerate the East Thames Corridor, also known as the Thames Gateway. With a legacy of industrial decline and job losses, this area extends into south Essex and as far as the Isle of Sheppey in Kent. Its areas of derelict land offer great potential for accommodating new economic activities. Stations on the Channel Tunnel Rail Link will provide direct access to the European mainland; the Jubilee Line extension provides services to central London. However, the negative image of East London must be transformed if the area is to succeed in attracting the necessary volumes of investment for regeneration. After many delays and escalating costs, the major phases of the new British Library were finished, enabling many scattered holdings to be consolidated. The fate of redundant railway land at King's Cross and other sites remains controversial. The banks of the Thames on the Isle of Dogs have been invaded by an extravaganza of post-modern construction. Office developments have enveloped Charing Cross station, Cannon Street and several other sites. Schemes for redeveloping the South Bank and land opposite the Tower of London will bring more important changes to London's riverside in the years ahead. The former Bankside Power Station now houses the Tate Modern, but the future of the crumbling Battersea Power Station remains to be resolved. There is undoubted potential for redeveloping other areas in imaginative ways to enhance the sullied beauty of London's river.

In recent years many continental cities have been planned on a metropolitan scale and their economies are now forging ahead. This European experience suggested that London may be in peril without a grand design and an administrative mechanism to help implement it. The controversial plan announced by London's elected mayor in 2002 may offer some assistance in the drive toward urban renaissance.

Numerous projects in the area of the Thames Gateway offer great potential for economic growth and job creation, but only at considerable environmental costs. Conservationists wish to convert the vast and desolate expanse of Rainham Marshes (surrounded by scrapyards, electricity pylons, railways and a mammoth rubbish tip) into an enormous nature reserve to provide a haven for wild birds, rare insects and plants, and threatened animals. Now, the Royal Society for the Protection of Birds owns most of the marshes, having bought 900 acres from the Ministry of defence in 2000. Proposals for a new international airport for London, to be sited on the Cliffe Marshes across the Thames estuary, have given rise to major protests among environmentalists.

In November 2002 it was announced that half of an 80-year old extension to Spitalfields Market is to be demolished to make way for a vast office block. Opponents argued that the scheme represents a further encroachment by the financial quarter of the City into the historic but relatively impoverished neighbourhoods of the East End. They claimed that almost all local residents want the market site retained for community use. Conservation bodies, including English Heritage, have accepted that the 750,000 sq ft development, comprising four 'glazed fingers' up to 13 storeys high, should not overwhelm adjacent historic buildings. Tower Hamlets Borough Council have approved the project after thirteen years of controversy.

Cultural attractions on London's South Bank include (from east to west):
Design Museum
Bramah Museum of Tea and Coffee
Tower Bridge (and its exhibition)
HMS Belfast; Hay's Galleria
Britain at War Experience; London Dungeon
Southwark Cathedral
Golden Hinde replica ship
Clink Prison and Museum
Vinopolis
Globe Theatre
Tate Modern and Millennium Bridge
Bankside Gallery
Oxo Tower
Royal National Theatre, National Film Theatre, Hayward Gallery, Royal Festival Hall
Imax Cinema
London Aquarium

# THE CITY

The City of London is both the oldest and in some ways the most modern part of the capital. Narrow streets, dating from medieval times and re-established after the Great Fire, contrast with broad, straight thoroughfares created in Victorian times or as part of the great rebuilding programme after the Second World War. Historic churches and St Paul's cathedral still occupy their ancient sites, but underwent reconstruction in the 17th century and again in the 20th century. The Victorians transformed the Georgian City, with its small buildings and narrow streets, embarking on an ambitious scheme of road-widening and construction. Vast buildings, constructed in monumental style to house the banks, insurance companies and trading firms which managed the wealth of Victorian Britain and her Empire, are now being torn down and replaced by a new generation of office blocks designed to meet the requirements of computerised business transactions. New construction is drastically changing the face of the historic City – even offices built in the 1950s and 1960s are being demolished and replaced by striking buildings of post-modern design.

As offices and warehouses replaced homes in the City during the 19th century, so its residential population plummeted from 128,000 in 1851 to 9,000 in 1939 and a mere 4,000 in 1971. Since then, the figure has risen to 7,200 (2001) as a result of new blocks of flats being included in the Barbican development and construction of new apartments. In sharp contrast, over 300,000 people now commute into work in the 'Square Mile' each weekday.

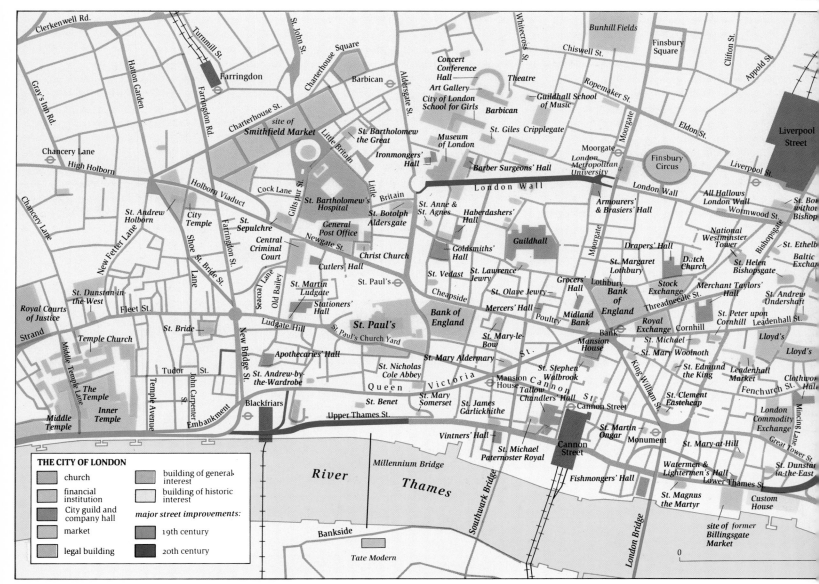

**THE CITY OF LONDON**

- church
- financial institution
- City guild and company hall
- market
- legal building
- building of general interest
- building of historic interest

*major street improvements:*
- 19th century
- 20th century

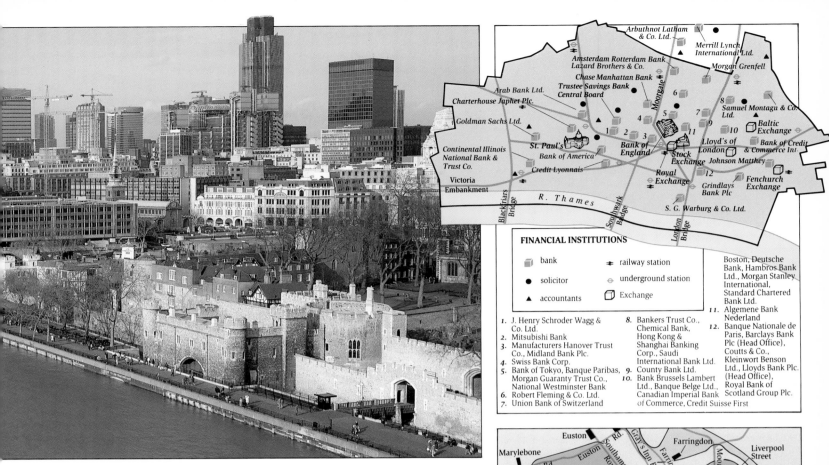

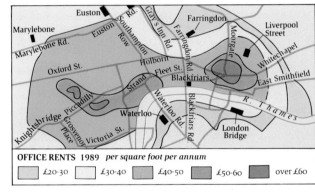

## FINANCIAL INSTITUTIONS

| | |
|---|---|
| 🏛 bank | 🚊 railway station |
| ● solicitor | ⊖ underground station |
| ▲ accountants | ⬒ Exchange |

1. J. Henry Schroder Wagg & Co. Ltd.
2. Mitsubishi Bank
3. Manufacturers Hanover Trust Co., Midland Bank Plc.
4. Swiss Bank Corp.
5. Bank of Tokyo, Banque Paribas, Morgan Guaranty Trust Co., National Westminster Bank
6. Robert Fleming & Co. Ltd.
7. Union Bank of Switzerland
8. Bankers Trust Co., Chemical Bank, Hong Kong & Shanghai Banking Corp., Saudi International Bank Ltd.
9. County Bank Ltd.
10. Bank Brussels Lambert Ltd., Banque Belge Ltd., Canadian Imperial Bank of Commerce, Credit Suisse First Boston, Deutsche Bank, Hambros Bank Ltd., Morgan Stanley International, Standard Chartered Bank Ltd.
11. Algemene Bank Nederland
12. Banque Nationale de Paris, Barclays Bank Plc (Head Office), Coutts & Co., Kleinwort Benson Ltd., Lloyds Bank Plc. (Head Office), Royal Bank of Scotland Group Plc.

The modern City *The map (below left) shows today's City, whilst the photo (above) shows the buildings of many centuries. Clearly visible as a cluster of skyscrapers is the 'Square Mile', and the map (top right) identifies its leading financial institutions. The map (right) shows the pattern of office rents, which peak around the Bank of England. Rents have declined over the 1990s.*

Fleet Street *Close to the lawyers of The Temple and the clerics of St. Paul's, Fleet Street was the home of London's publishing trade for many centuries, and national newspapers were published there between 1702 and 1989 (map below). From that point, corporate mergers, new technology and working practices meant that editorial offices and, frequently, printing works began to relocate – in Docklands (map below right).*

**OFFICE RENTS 1989** *per square foot per annum*

| £20-30 | £30-40 | £40-50 | £50-60 | over £60 |
|---|---|---|---|---|

## MAIN NEWSPAPER SITES IN AND AROUND FLEET STREET PRE-1987

1. W H Smith (from 1920)
2. Newspaper House (Westminster Press)
3. Fleetway House (Amalgamated Press)
4. Northcliffe House (Associated Newspapers)
5. Temple House (Horace Marshall and Sons) National Press Agency Carmelite House
6. New Carmelite House
7. St. Bride Foundation Institute
8. Printing House Square
9. Bracken House
10. Sheffield Daily Telegraph
11. Liverpool Daily Post
12. Glasgow Herald
13. The Scotsman
14. Punch
15. Daily Chronicle & Lloyd's Weekly News
16. Birmingham Daily Post
17. Reuters & Press Association

**NEWSPAPER MOVES SINCE 1987**

● editorial ▲ printing

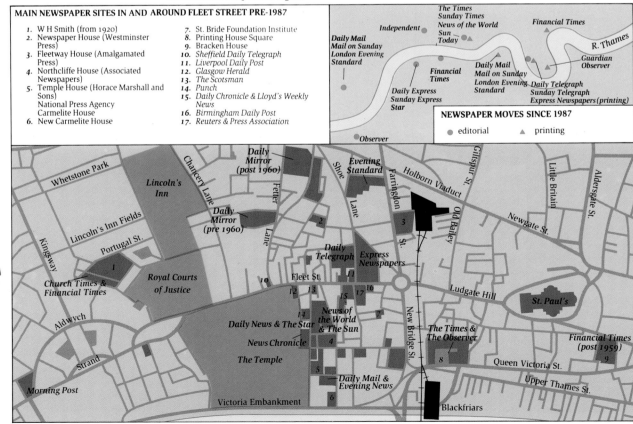

# WESTMINSTER AND WHITEHALL

Almost a thousand years ago, the Saxon king Edward the Confessor chose to build an abbey and a royal palace on Thorney Island, and ever since, Westminster has been quite different in character from the commercial City. Westminster Abbey with its monastery was dedicated in December 1065, within days of Edward's death. William the Conqueror was crowned there in 1066 and almost all monarchs have followed that precedent. Henry III added a Lady Chapel (1220) and in 1245 rebuilt the abbey, inspired by the Gothic cathedrals at Amiens and Reims. Work was finished in 1269 and thereafter the abbey served as the burial place of kings up to the reign of George III. Rebuilding continued during the 14th and 15th centuries, with the magnificent Henry VII Chapel being completed in 1519. In 1540, following the dissolution of the monasteries, the Abbey's property and treasure were confiscated and the Benedictine monks expelled, but its fabric survived. Sir Christopher Wren and Nicholas Hawksmoor added two 225-feet towers that were completed in 1745 and substantial renovation was carried out in the 19th century.

William the Conqueror had Edward the Confessor's palace completely reconstructed, while his son, William Rufus, added Westminster Hall, the largest Norman hall in Europe. The building was remodelled in the late 14th century and has survived almost intact. Its splendid hammer-beam roof means that supporting piers are not required. Early parliaments met in the Abbey's Chapter House until 1529 when Henry VIII moved to Whitehall Palace. It was not until the 17th century that Parliament assembled in

Westminster Hall. Almost all of the old palace of Westminster was destroyed by fire in 1834, only the Jewel Tower and Westminster Hall survive. Charles Barry and Augustus Pugin won a competition to design the new parliament house, and combined a simple ground plan with an intricate Gothic design. The building that resulted is 940 feet long, has over 1,000 apartments and covers more than eight acres. On the south side the Victoria Tower rises to 336 feet but it is the smaller Clock Tower (316 feet), housing the clock and bell named Big Ben, that has made Westminster world-famous.

The third component of Westminster is Whitehall, which was once the site of a great palace. In the early 16th century, Cardinal Wolsey acquired York House and remodelled it in magnificent Tudor style. Henry VIII seized it in 1529, renaming it the Palace of Whitehall. Apartments in this, the largest palace in Europe, were reserved for visiting kings from Scotland prior to union in 1603. The name Great Scotland Yard evokes that function. Further embellishments were undertaken for the Stuart kings, including the classical Banqueting Hall (1619-22) designed by Inigo Jones. William III disliked

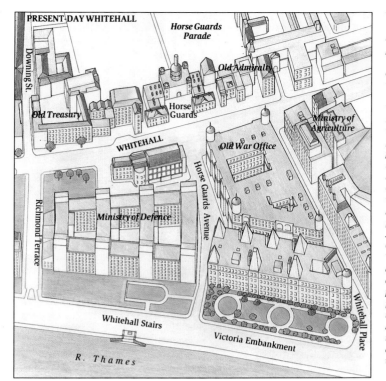

PRESENT-DAY WHITEHALL

The changing face of Whitehall  *Whitehall's ministries and official buildings span the period from the 17th century to the 1980s (map left). A reconstruction of the Palace of Whitehall as it would have appeared c.1695 (below) shows a marked contrast. The Banqueting Hall is all that remains of the vast Palace which was destroyed by fire in 1698. Just a few years earlier it was a maze of passages and yards traversed by two public highways running between Westminster and Charing Cross and down to the Thames. As well as the royal apartments, the Palace contained over 2,000 rooms for courtiers. To the west lay St. James's Park, redesigned for Charles II in the manner of Versailles, with shady avenues and an ornamental lake. 'Pelemele', a cross between croquet and golf, was played along the tree-lined walk in front of St. James's Palace and gave its name to Pall Mall and the Mall. Many plans were conceived to replace Whitehall Palace in an appropriately grand manner, but were never implemented.*

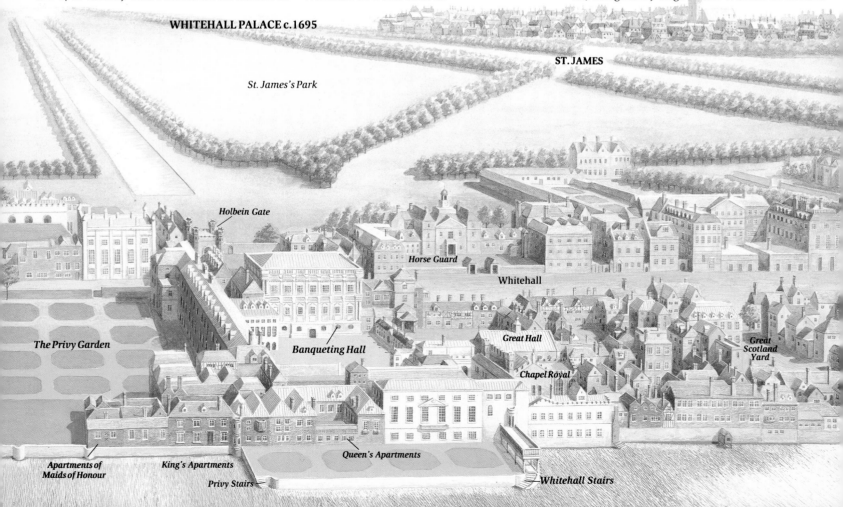

WHITEHALL PALACE c.1695

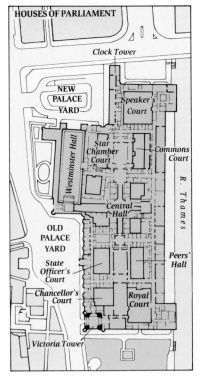

Clock Tower
NEW PALACE YARD
Speaker's Court
Star Chamber Court
Commons Court
Westminster Hall
Central Hall
R. Thames
OLD PALACE YARD
State Officer's Court
Peers' Hall
Chancellor's Court
Royal Court
Victoria Tower

*Sala Regalis cum Curia Westmonastery, vulgo. Westminster hall.*

Whitehall, preferring St. James's Palace and the clean air of Hampton Court, which was better for his asthma. In 1698 most of Whitehall Palace burned down; only the Banqueting Hall survived. The present appearance of Whitehall is the product of several centuries of building. Downing Street dates from the later 17th century and the Horse Guards from Georgian times. The Home Office, Foreign and Commonwealth Offices and the Treasury are Victorian (*page 95*). The massive Ministry of Defence was completed in 1959 and the Department of Health building as recently as the later 1980s.

*The palace of Westminster was turned over to the State in 1529. From 1547, Parliament met in St. Stephen's Chapel and subsequently Westminster Hall. The Palace is shown in an engraving of the 1640s by Hollar (above). Virtually all the palace was burnt down in 1834, a fact proclaimed in a contemporary poster (right). The present Gothic revival building (plan top) was designed by Sir Charles Barry and Augustus Pugin (1837-60), and is depicted (below) in a painting by John Anderson, 1872.*

DREADFUL FIRE!

**VILLAGE LONDON**
*area built up by:*

- 1813
- 1872
- 1897
- 1934
- present day
- parks and open spaces
- ○ village name in 1800

The urban sprawl *The map (above) shows the spread of London over the past two centuries. In 1800, the city was ringed with villages and hamlets set amidst meadows and market gardens. The vast majority of these villages were subsequently engulfed in suburbia. However, the remnants of old villages may still be traced in the form of street patterns, historic parish churches and houses, and fragments of village greens. The names of scores of London's villages survive on the name plates of railway and Underground stations.*

*Many of London's former villages retain elements of their identity, with annual fetes and carnivals. The most famous modern carnival is held in Notting Hill over the last weekend of August, drawing up to 2 million revellers from London and much further afield to celebrate its Caribbean identity.*

0  miles  4

Chapter 11 Places in London

# LONDON'S VILLAGES

London is richly endowed with neighbourhoods which, despite their absorption into the growing metropolis, have still retained their village character. The history of these villages varies greatly. Some, such as Shoreditch and Stepney, originated as agricultural settlements very close to the edge of the City, and soon became incorporated into the urban fabric. Others were at a greater distance from the City and remained free-standing settlements amidst the fields of Middlesex, Surrey, Kent or Essex until well into the 18th century and beyond. They were ultimately converted into suburbs by a number of factors:

turnpike roads brought Hampstead and Highgate into the parameters of 18th-century London, while 19th-century railway developments accounted for the absorption of Balham and Enfield. In the 20th century, Underground lines meant that even far-flung centres such as Edgware and Morden became part of Greater London. In addition, London has its share of planned 'villages' such as Hampstead Garden Suburb, which followed the opening of the Golders Green Underground station in 1907, and Bedford Park, which was described by John Betjeman as 'the most significant suburb built in the last century, probably in the western world'.

Tudor and Stuart monarchs had sought to contain the spread of London through legislation; James I feared that 'soon London will be all

England'. His attempts and those of successive administrations failed. The population of Middlesex, that most suburban of Home Counties, rose from a mere 70,900 living in hamlets, villages and market towns in 1801, to 792,000 in 1901 and an astonishing 950,000 just four years later. Not until the Green Belt legislation of 1938 and 1947 was London's suburban spread brought to a notable and controversial halt.

Villages such as Harefield are still distinctly recognisable as such, and not too much imagination is needed to identify the village structure of Blackheath, Clapham, Hampstead or Highgate. Traces, often more obscure, of London's historic villages abound elsewhere; beneath the fabric of present-day suburbia the structure of many of London's villages still survives.

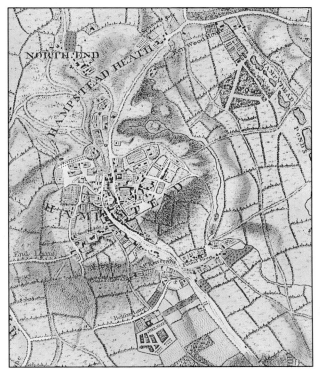

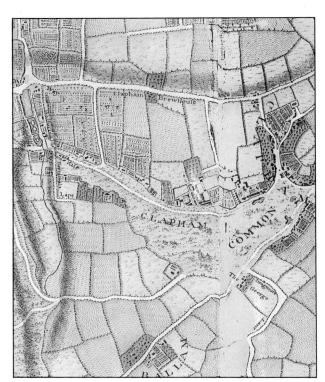

**From villages to suburbs** *The cartographer, John Rocque (1745), depicted Hampstead (above left) and Clapham (above right) when they were still largely rural, long before they were engulfed by bricks and mortar (maps centre). Constable's painting, 'Sir Richard Steele's cottage, Hampstead' c.1821 (above) shows a still rustic village street. The view of Holy Trinity Church, Clapham, 1845 (above right) is still much the same today.*

**Bedford Park** *This garden surburb (right) was laid out by Norman Shaw and other architects who designed the spacious, distinctive houses in the vernacular style of the 'Arts and Crafts' movement of the late 19th century. They were provided with their own church, inn, shops and tennis courts. The painting (below) depicts Tower House (right) and Queen Anne's Grove (1882), designed by Norman Shaw.*

**BEDFORD PARK
A GARDEN SUBURB 1896**

road forming part of
original plan

listed building 1991

0        yards        220

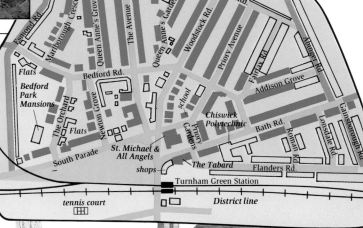

# DOCKLANDS

Before the 1980s the vast complex of dock basins stretching for five miles downstream from the Tower of London formed unknown territory for most Londoners. The individual docks and warehouses were surrounded by high walls for protection against theft. Only dockers and seamen entered this enclosed world on which so much of the wealth of London and Britain had once depended. By the late 1960s the small upstream docks were closed, overtaken by fierce competition from European ports, poor labour relations and a lack of space for modern ships and cargo-handling techniques. After a decade of great uncertainty, the large Royal Docks were closed in 1981, and the basins at Tilbury – 26 miles downstream – were all that remained of the Port of London. As the docks closed, so their associated industries collapsed. No fewer than 18,000 dock-related jobs were lost between 1966 and 1981, when local unemployment stood at 24 per cent.

In 1969 a project was launched to revitalise St Katharine Dock (25 acres in size), situated just beyond the Tower of London, by establishing a large hotel, a marina, a variety of housing and the World Trade Centre. In 1976 the Docklands Joint Committee, comprising representatives of local councils, presented the London Docklands Strategic Plan. It came at a most unpropitious time, at the height of a world economic crisis. The Plan sought to modernise the Docklands through more local authority housing and new industrial jobs. But private investment was sluggish, transport facilities outdated and large areas of derelict land remained. In 1981 the London Docklands Development Corporation (LDDC) was set up, and a year later an Enterprise Zone was created on the Isle of Dogs, enabling developers to enjoy rate and tax benefits.

The LDDC launched a vast regeneration programme, using public expenditure on new roads, sewers and public transport to attract market-led investment. A light railway was built – initially to link Docklands to Tower Hill. This now extends from Bank in the City to Beckton in the Royal Docks, and work has begun on extending the railway south of the river to Lewisham. In 1987 London City Airport was opened for business flights to

*Canary Wharf (bottom right) Early in 1988 the Canadian developers, Olympia and York, started work on the vast Canary Wharf scheme at the West India Docks. A 50-storey office tower, at One Canada Square, soaring to 800 ft and with 1.2 million sq. ft of office space, commands magnificent views of the dock basins and the Thames. The planners' dreams were challenged by the changing financial climate, fluctuating demand for office space and the terrorist bomb attack in 1996. Confidence has since returned and two vast new office towers have been constructed: the 1.1 million sq. ft HSBC building and the 1.2 million sq. ft Citigroup building.*

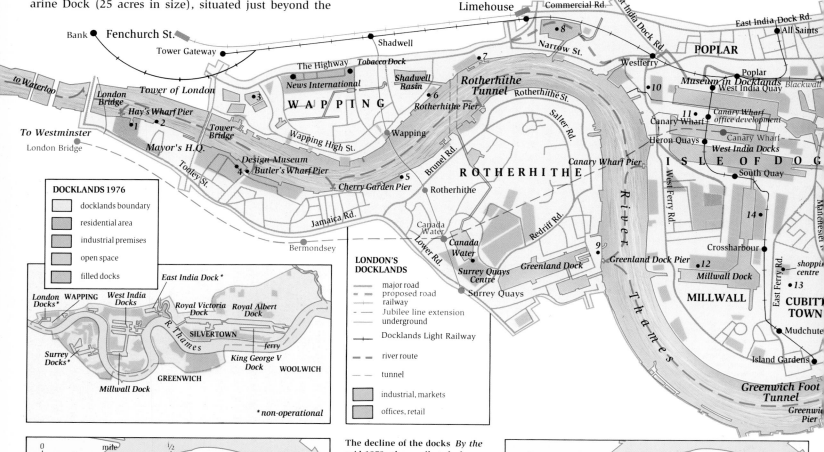

**DOCKLANDS 1976**

- docklands boundary
- residential area
- industrial premises
- open space
- filled docks

**LONDON'S DOCKLANDS**

- major road
- proposed road
- railway
- Jubilee line extension
- underground
- Docklands Light Railway
- river route
- tunnel
- industrial, markets
- offices, retail

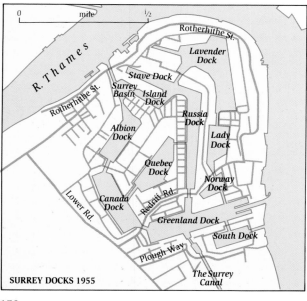

**SURREY DOCKS 1955**

The decline of the docks By the mid-1970s the smallest docks were no longer operational and the larger ones faced an uncertain future (map above left). Housing clustered outside their security walls, with industry still occupying important stretches of riverside. The Surrey Commercial Docks (map left) had flourished in the 19th century, importing timber from Scandinavia, grain and, later, dairy products. The docks were closed to traffic in 1970. Many basins were filled in and work started on landscaping and new roads. During the 1980s almost 5,000 dwellings were completed (map right), and many more have been built since. New industries moved in, including the Daily Mail's printing works. New open spaces on this site include a seven-acre ecological park.

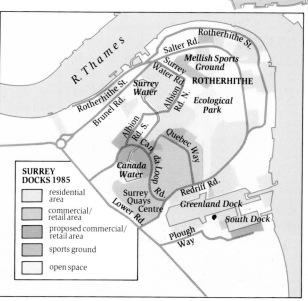

**SURREY DOCKS 1985**

- residential area
- commercial/ retail area
- proposed commercial/ retail area
- sports ground
- open space

Europe. By 1996 £1,744 billion of state money had attracted a further £6,277 billion of private investment. New offices, housing, shopping centres and recreation facilities were constructed and land values soared. Incoming professionals and executives purchased new homes at prices beyond the reach of most East Enders. Many new jobs in Docklands involved transferring firms from elsewhere in London, bringing skilled workers with them, and the LDDC has been criticised for promoting outsiders' interests rather than concentrating on locals' needs for jobs and homes. The future of Docklands remains poised delicately on the assumption that London will continue to grow as the world's leading financial centre, creating more jobs, requiring more office space and attracting more international investment.

*Transformation of Docklands (below) The small upstream docks were among the first to be closed in the late 1960s. Now, following projects at St Katharine Dock and Wapping, their transformation is complete. South of the river the Surrey Docks peninsula has experienced substantial regeneration. Work continues on the Isle of Dogs, where three towers on Canary Wharf soar above West India Docks, and new offices and homes are trans-*

*forming the Millwall Dock. East of the River Lea, vast stretches of land and water in the Royal Docks are now being regenerated. London City Airport, new housing and shopping facilities at Beckton, plus a new campus for the University of East London contribute to the revival of this area, which is now served by the Docklands Light*

*Railway. The challenge of area regeneration will continue to be met in the 21st century. In 2001, two vast office blocks were completed next to One Canada Square.*

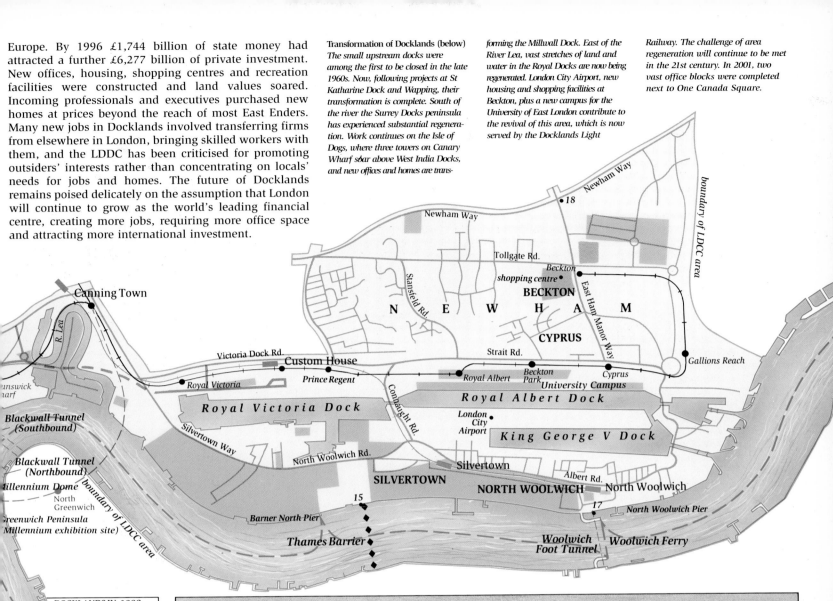

# UNDERGROUND LONDON

Every Tube passenger hurtling between stations knows that there is a London under London. Nevertheless, a comprehensive map of the tunnels, pipes and cables beneath the capital has never been drawn up, so developers have to scrutinise many individual documents to avoid damage. Some of these hidden underground features date back centuries; many were installed after 1850. New rail tunnels, water mains and fibre-optic cables are being positioned now and more are planned.

Throughout the centuries, many tributaries of the Thames have been covered over and integrated into London's sewer system. The Walbrook, in the heart of the ancient city, was covered in the late 15th century. The same fate awaited the Fleet, whose polluted lower course was covered in 1760. Soon its upper stretches were also culverted and in 1855 were converted into a sewer. The culverted Westbourne passes through an aqueduct visible above Sloane Square Underground Station.

Streams and specially-dug ditches were London's earliest sewers, but could not cope with ever-increasing quantities of effluent. Cesspools harboured disease, while flushing lavatories, which started to be used in 1810, added to the pollution of the Thames. Urban cesspools were banned in 1848 and still greater amounts of waste were directed into the river. The Thames became so badly polluted that in 1858 MPs resolved to strengthen the powers of the newly-created Metropolitan Board of Works. By 1865, 70 miles of intercepting sewers had been installed to carry effluent to two major outfalls downstream of London. A network of drains serving every street and ultimately every building was installed as the built-up area expanded. London's sewer authorities are now faced with the expensive challenge of repairing and replacing the Victorian brickwork. As sewers crumble and collapse, foul water can stagnate, providing breeding grounds for armies of rats.

Work on railways under London began in 1860, when a 'cut and cover' tunnel was started beneath New Road from Paddington towards Moorgate. Trains started to run in 1863, linking the northern rail termini with the City. Other 'cut and cover' sections were dug to complete a misshapen 'Circle' in 1884. Smoke-consuming engines, where smoke was diverted into a tank behind the engine by means of an exhaust and released when trains emerged overground, operated until electrification in 1905. The remainder of the Underground system was made up by deep 'tube' tunnels, excavated by special machines. Separate companies constructed individual lines and operated electric trains. First came what is now part of the City branch of the Northern Line (1890), followed by the middle stretch of the Central Line (1900). The Waterloo and City Line ('the Drain') had been opened in 1898. Additional tube tunnels were excavated in the 1930s, playing a crucial role in London's suburban expansion. Yet more tunnels were dug for the Victoria Line (opened 1968) and the original Jubilee Line (completed 1979). The Jubilee Line extension from the West End to Docklands and Stratford was completed in 1999. The Underground now runs over 100 miles of tunnels, though the total Underground network is considerably longer, since much runs on the surface.

Underground railways are not only used by the travelling public. For over 60 years the Post Office has operated its own underground electric railway to speed mail between sorting offices and main railway stations. During the Second World War, a three-mile section of the Central Line (Leytonstone to Gants Hill) served as an underground factory for aircraft components. Art treasures were stored in the Aldwych spur of the Piccadilly Line, and Down Street Station (closed in 1932) became a bunker for the War Cabinet. Platforms, shafts and even staircases in 79 tube stations provided makeshift night shelters for

This cross-section (above) shows the station at Piccadilly Circus after it was extensively rebuilt in 1923. The complex network of tunnels, platforms, cables and – a recent innovation – escalators, was an engineering triumph.

The map (right) shows an underground view of the city. London's first underground railway, the Metropolitan (between Paddington and Farringdon) opened in 1863. Early lines are just beneath street level; later ones were excavated much deeper. The latest addition is the Jubilee Line extension through Waterloo and London Bridge to Docklands. Some underground stations have since closed down, becoming 'ghost stations'. Main sewers and underground rivers form other important features of subterranean London.

Some churches in London have crypts or vaults, many of which are architecturally fine. The one pictured (below near right) is St Mary Magdalene in Paddington, dating from 1895.

Many of London's sewers are excellent examples of Victorian engineering, such as the one pictured (below centre right). They are now over 100 years old and need constant maintenance and, in some instances, replacement.

The Post Office operates its own railway system beneath central London. Its fully automatic, driverless trains run between main sorting offices and railway terminals. The photograph (far right) shows mail being loaded.

The construction of the first tunnel under the river – the Thames Tunnel – was greeted with some scepticism (cartoon, far right). Engineered by Marc Brunel, it took 18 years (1825-43) and cost £614,000 to complete. It never lived up to its promise as a pedestrian tunnel and was sold to the East London Railway Company.

The map (right) is the first edition of the Diagram of the London Underground drawn by Henry Beck and issued in January 1933. It shows the structure of the lines, but not their precise location or the relative distances between stations.

ordinary Londoners. In the early 1940s, eight deep tunnels were excavated beneath existing tube tracks, especially along the Northern Line. General Eisenhower used the Goodge Street tunnel as the HQ of America's wartime operations in Europe. In 1948 the deep tunnels at Clapham South provided temporary accommodation for 236 Jamaican immigrants who had sailed to Britain on *The Windrush*. Brixton was the nearest labour exchange and many settled nearby.

Subterranean London has also played a critical role in the city's defence. During the 1930s three subterranean civil defence 'citadels' were installed in north London and 'the Hole in the Ground' was excavated under the Treasury in Westminster to provide secure space for top politicians and

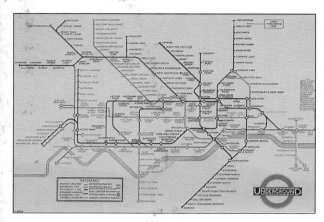

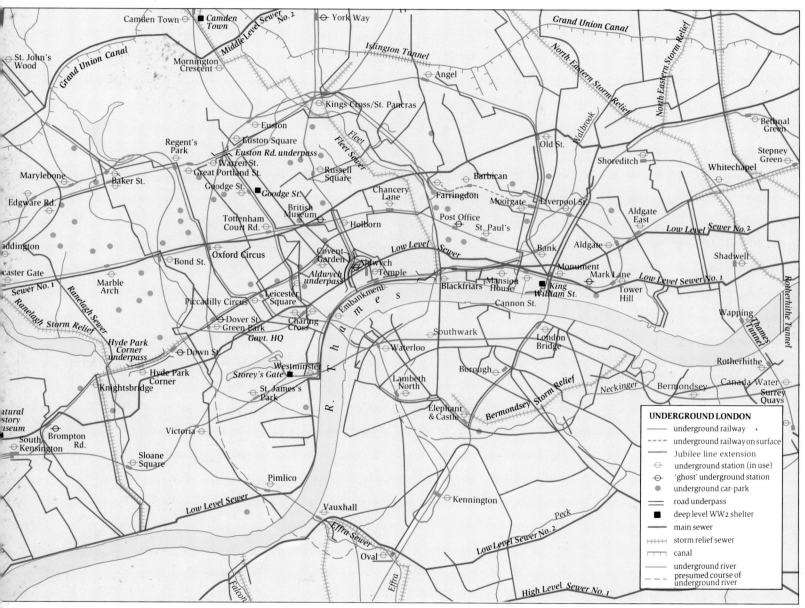

UNDERGROUND LONDON

- underground railway
- underground railway on surface
- Jubilee line extension
- ⊖ underground station (in use)
- ⊖ 'ghost' underground station
- ● underground car-park
- road underpass
- ■ deep level WW2 shelter
- main sewer
- storm relief sewer
- canal
- underground river
- presumed course of underground river

civil servants. It is possible to visit the Cabinet War Rooms, which accommodated Churchill and his Chiefs of Staff. Four subterranean fortresses were built more recently beneath central London to house vital government activities in event of nuclear war. The northern section of Kingsway Tram Tunnel has been equipped as an emergency control centre should London be faced with a major disaster.

The London 'Water Ring Main' has been excavated lower than the Underground and functions as a 50-mile aqueduct from Ashford-Sunbury in the south-west to Coppermills in the north-east. Located 120 feet below ground, it is designed to supply half the capital's water and plans are afoot for substantial extension early in the 21st century.

# LONDON'S BRIDGES

Over two dozen bridges span the Thames in London, but only Tower Bridge lies downstream of the point selected by the Romans for siting their bridge almost 2,000 years ago. The original, wooden London bridge needed constant repair against the force of the tide and storms. In 1176 work started on a stone bridge which was completed in 1209, with a wooden drawbridge which could be raised on the north side to defend the City, and twenty arches. The bridge was surmounted by tightly-packed shops and houses – 198 of them by the mid-14th century. In places, the bridge thoroughfare was barely more than 9 feet wide. Not surprisingly, traffic congestion posed a serious problem and water-men were kept busy rowing travellers across the river.

For nearly 700 years London Bridge re-mained the only Thames crossing, but in 1729 a wooden bridge was constructed at Putney far to the west. In 1736 an Act of Parliament autho-rised a bridge to be built at Westminster, in the face of fierce opposition from boatmen and the Archbishop of Canterbury, who owned the only ferry large enough to convey horses and carts. Westminster Bridge was opened in 1750 and was followed by another stone bridge at Blackfriars in 1769. Both played a vital role in enabling urban development to extend on to the south bank of the Thames. Between 1758 and 1762, the houses were removed from London Bridge and the two central arches replaced by a single

span to ease navigation. Four more bridges were built during the 18th century, two of wood (Kew, 1758-9 and Battersea, 1771-2) and two of stone (Richmond, 1774-7 and a second bridge at Kew, 1783-9). The first iron bridge came early in the 19th century (Vauxhall, 1811-16) and was soon followed by Waterloo (1811-17) and Southwark (1815-19), both designed by John Rennie, whose final task was to design a replacement for London Bridge.

The new century saw not only new styles of bridge but also new motives for construction.

Suspension bridges were built for speculative purposes at Hammersmith (1825-7), to encour-age building on the south bank, and in central London, where the old Hungerford Bridge (1841-5) was designed to attract trade to Hungerford market. It survived for less than 20 years and the market site was redeveloped for Charing Cross Station. The first railway bridge was the Grosve-nor (1858-66), which brought the Brighton line to Victoria. Legislation was passed in 1877 which enabled the Metropolitan Board of Works to buy all of London's privately-constructed

*London's Bridges  Old London Bridge was rebuilt in 1831, designed by John Rennie. It is pictured (left) in the late 19th century, congested with people and traffic. Westminster Bridge (top right, painted c. 1750) was opened in 1750, designed by Charles Labelye. A new technique was used, with caissons (large wooden boxes) being floated to where the piers were to be built, sunk and pumped dry to enable construction to take place inside them. Tower Bridge (1894) was designed to be in architectural harmony with the Tower of London. It is pictured (above right) under construction (c. 1889), and (far right) complete, with bascules raised (c. 1895) enabling tall ships to pass underneath. The Albert Bridge (right), 1873, designed by Roland Mason Ordish is one of several suspension bridges spanning the Thames.*

*London Bridge (reconstructed, below, as it might have appeared in the 16th century) was completed in 1209. The most extraordinary of the bridge buildings was the highly decorated Nonsuch House, brought in pre-fabricated sections from Holland and built in 1577. In stark contrast, traitors' heads rotted on pikes at the gateway to the Bridge.*

*Kew Bridge 1759 (1903)*

*Kew Railway Bridge  1869*

*Chiswick Bridge  1933*

*Barnes Railway Bridge 1849 (1891-5)*

*Hammersmith Bridge 1827 (1887)*

*Richmond Lock Bridge  1894*

*Twickenham Bridge  1933*

*Richmond Railway Bridge 1848 (1908)*

*Richmond Bridge 1777 (1939)*

*Putney Bridge 1729 (1886)*

*Putney Railway Bridge 1889*

*Teddington Lock Bridge (1888-9)*

bridges and abolish payment of tolls for their use. Previously only London and Westminster bridges had been toll-free. The pinnacle of achievement came with the construction of Tower Bridge (1885-94) which opened to enable tall shipping to reach the Pool of London. The story of London's bridges in the 20th century has been one of widening, rebuilding and replacement. John Rennie's London Bridge met a strange fate when it was replaced by the present bridge between 1968 and 1972 – it was sold for rebuilding at Lake Havasu City, Arizona.

Blackfriars Bridge 1769 (1869)

Alexandra Railway Bridge 1866 (widened 1890s)

Waterloo Bridge 1817 (1942-4)

Millennium Bridge 2000

Tower Bridge 1894

Hungerford (Railway) Bridge 1845 (1864)

Southwark Bridge 1819 (1921)

London Bridge late 1st century AD (1973)

Westminster Bridge 1750 (1862)

new pedestrian bridges (2001)

Lambeth Bridge 1862 (1932)

Grosvenor Railway Bridge 1858-66 (1963-7)

Chelsea Bridge 1858 (1937)

Vauxhall Bridge 1816 (1906)

Albert Bridge 1873

Battersea Bridge 1772 (1890)

**THE BRIDGES OF LONDON**

⟩⟨ bridge

+++ railway bridge

Battersea Railway Bridge 1863

where original bridge has been replaced, date of present bridge is shown in brackets

**Blackfriars Bridge** was designed by Robert Mylne, who completed the bridge in 1769. The picture (right) is taken from a stereoscopic card (1860).

Wandsworth Bridge 1873 (1940)

Nonsuch House

**LONDON BRIDGE**

# UNIVERSITIES AND MUSEUMS

London is one of the museum capitals of the world, with over 300 museums and galleries in the metropolitan area, visited 20 million times a year. They range in scale from national collections, such as the British Museum, to small specialist museums.

The British Museum was founded in 1753 and comprised three privately-owned public collections, bought by public lottery for £300,000 and kept in Montagu House, Bloomsbury. Other collections were incorporated over the ensuing half-century – Egyptian antiquities were acquired in the wake of the Napoleonic Wars and the still-contentious Elgin marbles soon afterwards. When, in 1823, George IV's library was added to the Collection, it became imperative to build new premises. A new building was designed by Sir Robert Smirke, and begun in 1823. Nevertheless, new acquisitions meant that space was still at a premium. This situation was alleviated when the Natural History collection was moved to South Kensington in 1881, housed in a building designed by Alfred Waterhouse. Some of the large profits made by the Great Exhibition of 1851 had been used to buy land in South Kensington, on which the Victoria and Albert, the Science and Natural History Museums were later built. Bloomsbury and South Kensington thus became the original focus of London's most famous collections. More recently, important local history collections in the suburbs have been opened to the public and new thematic museums have been created to celebrate design, the history of

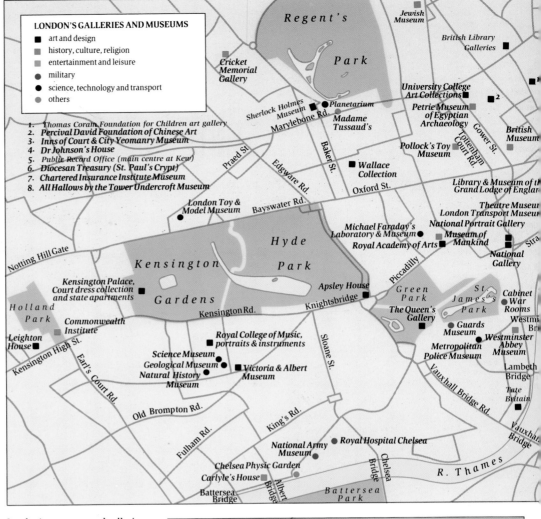

**LONDON'S GALLERIES AND MUSEUMS**
- ■ art and design
- ■ history, culture, religion
- ■ entertainment and leisure
- ● military
- ● science, technology and transport
- ● others

1. *Thomas Coram Foundation for Children art gallery*
2. *Percival David Foundation of Chinese Art*
3. *Inns of Court & City Yeomanry Museum*
4. *Dr Johnson's House*
5. *Public Record Office (main centre at Kew)*
6. *Diocesan Treasury (St. Paul's Crypt)*
7. *Chartered Insurance Institute Museum*
8. *All Hallows by the Tower Undercroft Museum*

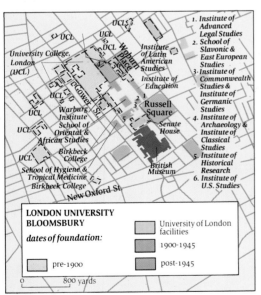

**LONDON UNIVERSITY BLOOMSBURY**

*dates of foundation:*
- ☐ pre-1900
- ☐ University of London facilities
- ☐ 1900-1945
- ☐ post-1945

0    800 yards

1. Institute of Advanced Legal Studies
2. School of Slavonic & East European Studies
3. Institute of Commonwealth Studies & Institute of Germanic Studies
4. Institute of Archaeology & Institute of Classical Studies
5. Institute of Historical Research
6. Institute of U.S. Studies

**London's museums and galleries**
*The map (above) shows the wide range of galleries and museums within the capital.*

**The academic quarter** *in Bloomsbury (left) has the British Museum on its southern fringe and the University of London's Senate House (1936) soaring at its centre. The view, below, from the* **Illustrated London News** *(1933), shows 'A great temple of learning to arise in Bloomsbury', designed by the architect Charles Holden but never completed. The classical facade of the main building of University College was built 1827-29, following the design of William Wilkins, architect of the National Gallery. A macabre sight of University College is the clothed skeleton of philosopher Jeremy Bentham, one of its founding fathers, displayed in the main building.*

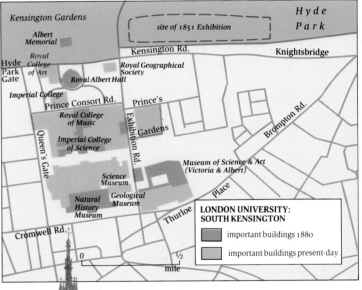

**LONDON UNIVERSITY: SOUTH KENSINGTON**
- ☐ important buildings 1880
- ☐ important buildings present-day

0    ½    mile

**South Kensington** *The museums and colleges of South Kensington were built on property acquired after the Great Exhibition of 1851 (map above). Museums devoted to Natural History, Science, Geology, and Science and Art (the Victoria and Albert) are found in the southern section. At the centre is Imperial College, famed for science and technology; to the north the Albert Hall (1870) and elaborate Albert Memorial, 1876 (engraving, left) in honour of Queen Victoria's consort. The whole complex is clearly visible in the aerial photograph (right).*

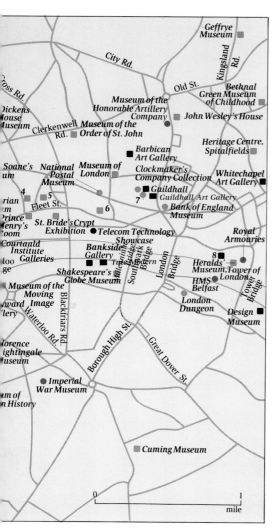

Map labels (Bloomsbury/City museum map):
Geffrye Museum · City Rd. · Kingsland Rd. · Old St. · Bethnal Green Museum of Childhood · Cross Rd. · Dickens House · Museum of the Honorable Artillery Company · John Wesley's House · Clerkenwell Rd. · Museum of the Order of St. John · Heritage Centre, Spitalfields · Barbican Art Gallery · Whitechapel Art Gallery · Soane's um · National Postal Museum · Museum of London · Clockmaker's Company Collection · 4 · 5 · rian m · Fleet St. · Prince Henry's Room · 6 · 7 · Guildhall · Guildhall Art Gallery · Bank of England Museum · St. Bride's Crypt Exhibition · Telecom Technology Showcase · Royal Armouries · Courtauld Institute Galleries · loo ge · Bankside Gallery · 8 · Heralds' Museum, Tower of London · Shakespeare's Globe Museum · London Bridge · HMS Belfast · Museum of the Moving Image · ward lery · London Dungeon · Design Museum · Waterloo Rd. · Blackfriars Rd. · Borough High St. · lorence ightingale Museum · Great Dover St. · Imperial War Museum · am of n History · Cuming Museum

0 · 1 · mile

**London's Museums** *The poster (left), designed by Edward Wadsworth in 1936, advertises the Imperial War Museum (1846), housed in the former Bethlehem Royal Hospital (Bedlam). Lord Leighton's house in Holland Park (1866), is now a museum. Its exotic Arab Hall (right, 1877-9), is based on drawings of Moorish Spain, its walls covered in tiles from Cairo, Damascus and Rhodes. The classical southern facade of the British Museum is depicted in a painting by Dudley Heath (below), 1890. Keats House (below right) Hampstead, was built 1815-16, Keats lived there 1818-21, and wrote Ode to a Nightingale there. Restored 1974-5, it is now a museum.*

London Transport, the moving image, theatre and, of course, London itself.

In the early 19th century, London contained the Inns of Court and historical medical schools but no actual university. In the 1820s, a group of politicians and scholars sought to establish a university which would charge moderate fees and be open to all, irrespective of race, creed or political belief. A site was purchased in Bloomsbury to house what is now University College (opened 1828). With the backing of the Archbishop of Canterbury, a rival university was opened at King's College in the Strand in 1831. In 1836 the University of London was set up as an examining and degree-conferring authority, a role it held until its reorganisation into a federal system of colleges in 1900. The University of London now has 50,000 undergraduates and 22,000 postgraduates. The capital also contains ten new universities. It also has the largest concentration of medical training in Britain.

**The University of London** *The organisation and geography of the federal University of London is highly complex (map below). A detailed map of the Bloomsbury focus of the University is shown (far left). Some colleges, such as Queen Mary and the London School of Economics, are tightly focused, but others occupy buildings in several parts of central and suburban London. Ten thousand students attend Brunel and City Universities, and a further 110,000 are enrolled at ten new universities (former polytechnics) in Greater London. Their premises are quite scattered, reflecting both the important expansion of higher education and the recent trend for institutional mergers.*

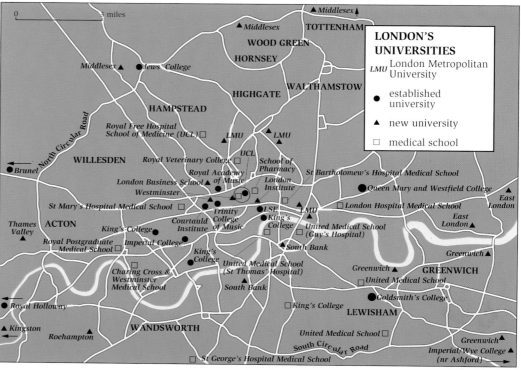

0 · 3 miles

**LONDON'S UNIVERSITIES**

*LMU* London Metropolitan University

● established university

▲ new university

□ medical school

Map labels: Middlesex · TOTTENHAM · WOOD GREEN · HORNSEY · WALTHAMSTOW · HIGHGATE · Jews' College · HAMPSTEAD · North Circular Road · Royal Free Hospital School of Medicine (UCL) · LMU · LMU · WILLESDEN · Royal Veterinary College · UCL · School of Pharmacy · St Bartholomew's Hospital Medical School · Brunel · Royal Academy of Music · London Institute · Queen Mary and Westfield College · East London · London Business School · Westminster · London Hospital Medical School · St Mary's Hospital Medical School · LSE · LMU · East London · Thames Valley · ACTON · King's College · Courtauld Institute · Trinity College of Music · King's College · United Medical School (Guy's Hospital) · Royal Postgraduate Medical School · Imperial College · King's College · Greenwich · GREENWICH · Charing Cross & Westminster Medical School · United Medical School (St Thomas' Hospital) · South Bank · United Medical School · Goldsmith's College · Royal Holloway · King's College · LEWISHAM · Kingston · Roehampton · WANDSWORTH · United Medical School · South Circular Road · Greenwich · St George's Hospital Medical School · Imperial/Wye College (nr Ashford)

# MONUMENTS AND CEMETERIES

## CEMETERIES

Over 100 cemeteries are to be found within a 9-mile radius of Charing Cross, varying in size from one to 182 acres. Together, they occupy 3,000 acres, the size of a small London borough. In the early 19th century over 50,000 burials were taking place in London each year. London's ancient churchyards were filled to bursting, and many burials took place in scandalous conditions. Campaigners sought to establish cemeteries out in the surrounding countryside, and in 1832 the cholera epidemic finally demonstrated that new cemeteries were essential. Legislation was passed that very year and within a decade commercial companies had established a ring of seven metropolitan cemeteries. Further laws in 1850 enabled more cemeteries to be created.

**LONDON'S CEMETERIES** (date of opening shown in brackets)

✠ general (Church of England and others)

✝ Roman Catholic

✡ Jewish

1. Abney Park (1840)
2. Acton (1895)
3. Alperton (1917)
4. Barkingside (1923)
5. Barnes Common (1854)
6. Battersea New (1891)
7. Battersea St. Mary's (1860)
8. Beckenham (1877)
9. Bexleyheath (1876)
10. Brockley (1858)
11. Bromley (1905)
12. Brompton (1840)
13. Bunhill Fields (1665)
14. Camberwell (1856)
15. Camberwell New (1927)
16. Charlton (1855)
17. Chingford (1884)
18. Chiswick Old (1888)
19. Chiswick New (1933)
20. City of London (1856)
21. Croydon (1876)
22. Crystal Palace (1880)
23. Ealing and Old Brentford (1861)
24. Eastcote Lane (1900)
25. East London (1872)
26. East Sheen (1903)
27. Edmonton (1884)
28. Edmonton & Southgate (1880)
29. Eltham (1935)
30. Fulham (1865)
31. Golders Green (1902)
32. The Great Northern (1861)
33. Greenwich (1856)
34. Grove Park (1935)
35. Gunnersbury (1936)
36. Hammersmith (1869)
37. Hammersmith New (1926)
38. Hampstead (1876)
39. Harrow (1887)
40. Hendon (1899)
41. Highgate (1839)
42. Isleworth (1879)
43. Alderney Road (1697)
44. Brady Street (1761)
45. East Ham (1919)
46. Fulham Road (1815)
47. Hoop Lane (1895)
48. Kingsbury Road (1840)
49. Lauriston Road (1788)
50. Montague Road (1884)
51. New Sephardi (1733)
52. Old Sephardi (1657)
53. Plashet Park (1896)
54. Rowan Road (1915)
55. West Ham (1857)
56. Willesden (1873)
57. Kensal Green (1832)
58. Kensington Hanwell (1855)
59. Kingston (1855)
60. Lambeth (1854)
61. Lee (1873)
62. Manor Park (1874)
63. Merton & Sutton (1947)
64. Mitcham, Church Road (1883)
65. Mitcham, London Road (1929)
66. Mortlake (1852)
67. North Sheen (1926)
68. South Metropolitan (1837)
69. Nunhead (1840)
70. Old Mortlake (1854)
71. Paddington, Mill Hill (1936)
72. Paddington, Willesden Lane (1855)
73. Pinner (1933)
74. Plaistow (1892)
75. Plumstead (1890)
76. Putney (1855)
77. Putney Vale (1891)
78. Queen's Road (1861)
79. Richmond (1853)
80. Roding Lane (1940)
81. Royal Hospital Chelsea (1692)
82. Royal Hospital Greenwich (1857)
83. St. Marylebone (1854)
84. St. Mary's (1858)
85. St. Pancras & Islington (1854)
86. St. Patrick's (1868)
87. St. Thomas's (1849)
88. Streatham (1892)
89. Streatham Park (1909)
90. Sutton (1889)
91. Teddington (1879)
92. Tottenham (1856)
93. Tottenham Park (1912)
94. Tower Hamlets (1841)
95. Twickenham (1868)
96. Walthamstow (1872)
97. Wandsworth (1878)
98. West Ham (1857)
99. Westminster (1854)
100. Willesden (1891)
101. Wimbledon (1896)
102. Woodgrange Park (1890)
103. Woolwich (1856)

*Highgate Cemetery* (map left), *is one of a ring of early Victorian cemeteries which encircle London. The cemetery was created out of the grounds of a 17th-century house. Its 17 acres were consecrated in 1839 and proved immediately popular. The house itself had long been demolished but beneath the surviving terrace 80-yard long catacombs were equipped with 840 recesses to receive coffins. A sunken 'Egyptian avenue', lined with burial vaults, was entered through a Pharaonic arch and flanked by obelisks. In 1845 a further 19 acres were purchased east of Swain's Lane. An hydraulic lift was installed in the Anglican chapel to enable coffins to be carried to a tunnel and thence under the roadway to the new burial ground. After 1945 graves became neglected and overgrown. In 1975 the Friends of Highgate Cemetery were established to promote its conservation and restoration, acquiring the freehold for £50 in 1981.*

*Right An ivy-clad angel adorns the tomb of V.W.J. Adamson in the west cemetery. Below A scene from the funeral of Tom Sayers, the last of the bare-knuckled prize fighters. 100,000 people attended his funeral in 1865 and his pet dog occupied the chief mourner's position, riding behind the hearse on a small phaeton. A sculpture of the dog lies in front of Sayers' grave in Highgate's west cemetery.*

Catacombs

Peter Robinson (1804-74), founder of the Oxford Circus department store

Charles Dickens (1812-70), memorial

Egyptian Avenue

Charles Cruft (1852-1938), founder of the dog show (1886)

John Galsworthy (1867-1933), memorial

Sir Edwin Landseer (1802-73), memorial

WEST CEMETERY

Michael Faraday (1791-1867), chemist

Rossetti family: Gabriele (1783-1854), poet and scholar; his son and daughter, both poets, and daughter-in-law

Edward Blore (1787-1879), the architect who completed Buckingham Palace

Chapel

William Foyle (1885-1963), founder London bookshop

George Eliot (1819-80), author

EAST CEMETERY

Karl Marx (1818-83)

Swain's Lane

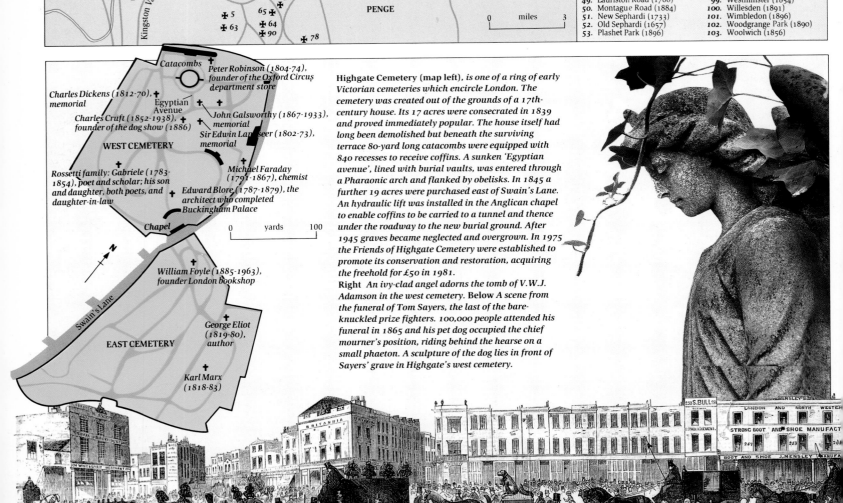

# MONUMENTS

Central London is rich in monuments of all kinds and every suburb has at least one memorial recalling the sacrifices of war. Every British ruler since Elizabeth I (with the exception of Edward VIII) is on view in central London, together with politicians, soldiers, admirals, explorers, writers, social reformers and many others – no fewer than 370 statues are found on the outside of the Houses of Parliament alone. The most elaborate monument to an individual is surely the Albert Memorial, composed of granite, sandstone, limestone, slate, marble and mosaics and unveiled in 1876 after more than a decade of work. By contrast, plain Portland Stone is used in two of London's best-known monuments. In the City a 202-feet-high Doric column, the Monument, was designed by Sir Christopher Wren to commemorate the Great Fire. In Whitehall Sir Edward Lutyen's massive Cenotaph, constructed in 1920, honours all the nation's dead.

*The oversize bronze statue of Sir Winston Churchill (1874-1965) half faces the House of Commons, (left). In Piccadilly Circus the aluminium statue of Eros (below) honours the philanthropy of the Seventh Earl of Shaftesbury (1801-85).*

*A stone replica of a howitzer surmounts the Royal Artillery Memorial at Hyde Park Corner (right), on which the names of 49,000 war dead are incised.*
*London's monuments (map below) The greatest single concentration of monuments is in Westminster, especially close to Whitehall, Pall Mall and St James's Park, which formed the 'heart of the empire' in Victorian and Edwardian times. Other impressive clusters are in Chelsea, South Kensington, the City, along the Victoria Embankment and at Greenwich. The discreet Holocaust memorial garden is in Hyde Park.*

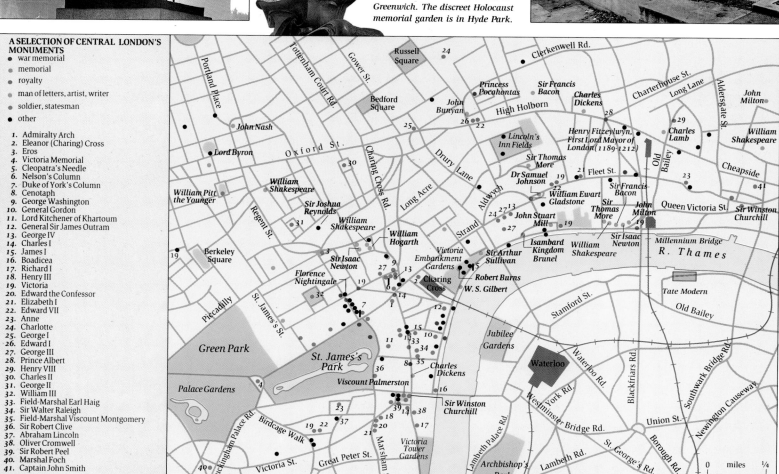

## A SELECTION OF CENTRAL LONDON'S MONUMENTS

- war memorial
- memorial
- royalty
- man of letters, artist, writer
- soldier, statesman
- other

1. Admiralty Arch
2. Eleanor (Charing) Cross
3. Eros
4. Victoria Memorial
5. Cleopatra's Needle
6. Nelson's Column
7. Duke of York's Column
8. Cenotaph
9. George Washington
10. General Gordon
11. Lord Kitchener of Khartoum
12. General Sir James Outram
13. George IV
14. Charles I
15. James I
16. Boadicea
17. Richard I
18. Henry III
19. Victoria
20. Edward the Confessor
21. Elizabeth I
22. Edward VII
23. Anne
24. Charlotte
25. George I
26. Edward I
27. George III
28. Prince Albert
29. Henry VIII
30. Charles II
31. George II
32. William III
33. Field-Marshal Earl Haig
34. Sir Walter Raleigh
35. Field-Marshal Viscount Montgomery
36. Sir Robert Clive
37. Abraham Lincoln
38. Oliver Cromwell
39. Sir Robert Peel
40. Marshal Foch
41. Captain John Smith

167

# LONDON THAT NEVER WAS

London's architectural history includes countless designs for projects that were never realised. Some were prepared after urban disasters – especially fires – others responded to the quest for grandeur, the need to provide new facilities, or the desire to make use of new technology. Many were speculative designs, others were commissioned by distinguished patrons. Some were works of vision and genius, others were simply banal. All shared a common fate – they never became reality.

The most famous item in this catalogue of urban imagination is Christopher Wren's reconstruction scheme following the Great Fire (1666) which envisaged a radically new approach to the remnants of the medieval City (*below*).

*Grandiose visions An artist's impression (below) of Christopher Wren's plan for rebuilding London after the Great Fire, drawn up within a week of the flames being controlled. Narrow streets and cramped courtyards were to be replaced by broad avenues radiating from piazzas and lined with buildings worthy of a great trading capital. Francis Goodwin designed a Grand National Cemetery (right) in 1824. Inspired by the architecture of Classical Greece, it was to occupy 150 acres and contain buildings modelled on ancient Athens. Distinguished citizens would be buried at its centre, the wealthy in a middle zone, and humbler folk on its margins.*

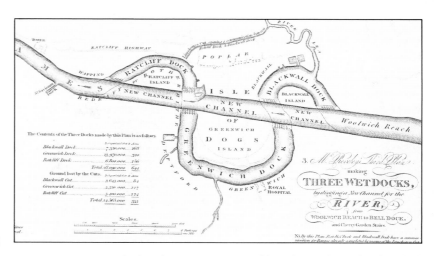

Rival projects were proposed by John Evelyn, who sketched a dozen interconnecting squares for his imaginary city and Robert Hooke, who designed a grid system of roads. Valentine Knight's plan included a canal running from the River Fleet to Billingsgate that would be lined with profit-making quays. Richard Newcourt wanted London greatly enlarged. Each scheme would have been costly and slow to implement. London had to recover fast as it needed to continue competing with its Dutch trading rivals. So the medieval street pattern re-surfaced, simply adorned with new buildings. It was almost three hundred years before the widespread devastation of the Second World War encouraged architectural imagination and inspiration to flourish once again on a vast scale in London.

Urban disasters offered the opportunity for enhancing as well as restoring the capital. Following the terrible fire of 1834 (*page 155*), almost a hundred projects were submitted for the new Houses of Parliament. Numerous speculative designs had been prepared long before then, including projects by Wren, William Kent (1733) and Sir John Soane (1779). Inigo Jones's scheme (1638) for reconstructing and enlarging Whitehall Palace would have given Charles I a grander residence than those of his rivals Philip IV in Madrid and Louis XIV in Paris, while Sir John Soane (1753-1837), designed a great palace for George IV in Green Park.

During the Victorian era, elegant but unrealised projects for churches, museums, exhibition halls, opera houses and parks proliferated, as did more mundane but arguably more essential schemes for cemeteries, hospitals, railways, sewers and much else besides. Together they make up the fascinating story of the London that never was.

# LONDON NOW

Cities throughout the world commemorated the Millennium in their own ways. London was the centre of the United Kingdom's year-long celebrations. Over £4 million were invested in the capital's leisure industry, with 50 new hotels opened for 2000. The Millennium Commission, funded from the National Lottery, worked on schemes throughout the country. After fierce competition between cities, Greenwich, in south-east London, was chosen to house the Millennium Experience, the national focus of celebration. The choice was a logical one as Greenwich contained the Royal Observatory, through the meridian (north-south line) was aligned, and from which longitude was measured since 1675. In 1884 leading nations decided on a single prime meridian, passing through Greenwich. Greenwich Mean Time became the global standard for measuring time. A brass bar in the courtyard of the old Royal Observatory marked 0' longitude; satellite technology has redefined the prime meridian 100 yards to the east.

In 1996 a 300-acre site on the Greenwich peninsula, outside the LDDC zone of regeneration, was selected for the Millennium Experience. Sir Richard Rogers designed a vast Millennium Dome. The unique structure contained an open arena surrounded by fifteen segments. These accommodated exhibits depicting life, work, recreation, and faith in the UK, the diversity and challenges of the nation's environment, and how the UK interacts with the rest of the world. A massive station at North Greenwich on the new Jubilee Line provided the main form of public transport to the Dome. Early in 2000 the Dockland Light Railway was extended under the Thames to the historic town centre of Greenwich, whose Observatory, Royal Park and National Maritime Museum attracted large numbers of visitors. Some land around the Dome was developed for housing, retailing and other functions. Following the closure of the Millennium Experience, a two-fold challenge remained: to find a purchaser for the Dome, and to develop its immediate surroundings.

Millennium funds helped finance other commemorative schemes in the capital. The Tate Gallery of Modern Art, partly funded by the Millennium Commission, occupies the vast remodelled interior of Bankside power station opposite St. Paul's Cathedral, and houses the Tate's collection of 20th-century art. It has proved a great success, attracting enormous numbers of visitors (5 million in its first year) and making a major contribution to the regeneration of the southern waterfront of central London. The old building on Millbank has been renamed the Tate Gallery of British Art. A new pedestrian bridge across the Thames, between St. Paul's and Tate Modern, gained notoriety for its vibration that has been rectified. In Bloomsbury, the Great Court of the British Museum has been covered with a vast translucent roof. The round Reading Room, formerly the heart of the British Library (now relocated to the Euston Road) houses an information centre on the Museum's collections, a bookshop and other facilities. Millennium funds also helped construct an education

Battersea Power Station (above), *designed by Sir Giles Gilbert Scott. With a sumptuous Art Deco control room, Italian marble turbine hall, polished parquet floors, wrought iron staircases and the four characteristic white smokestacks, it provided London with electricity between 1937 and 1980. Today, now derelict and a shadow of its past, the building awaits its future fate but the four majestic chimneys of Battersea Power Station remain as one of the best loved landmarks for Londoners.*

The Swiss Reinsurance Tower or 30 St Mary Axe (above), *is the second tallest building to grace the Square Mile. Designed by world renowned architect Sir Norman Foster, this post-modern creation occupies the plot of land that was the site of the famous Baltic Exchange, which in 1996 was damaged beyond repair by an IRA bomb. Londoners love or loathe the building, which they have dubbed the 'Erotic Gherkin'; certainly it adds a striking new feature to the City's ever-changing skyline.*

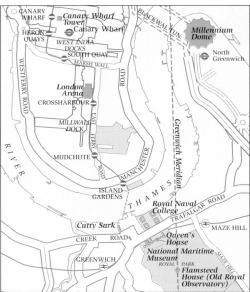

## Greenwich and the Millennium Dome
⊖ Docklands Light Railway Station
⊖ Underground station

*Greenwich has a distinguished history as a royal residence and maritime base (map above). At the heart of the National Maritime Museum is the Queen's House (1635) designed by Inigo Jones. To the south lie the Royal Observatory and Park, while the historic tea clipper – the Cutty Sark lies close to the Thames. The former Royal Naval College now houses part of the University of Greenwich. The controversial Millennium Dome is in the midst of a Thames meander. The extension of the Jubilee Line and the southern extension of the Docklands Light Railway have enhanced access to Greenwich from central London, Canary Wharf and the eastern suburbs. The Dome will be redeveloped for hosting major events and surrounding land is being used for housing and retail activities.*

The new Paternoster Square, with its dramatic views of St Paul's Cathedral (opposite, top). *It was intended by the architects to create an appropriate setting for St Paul's with the Cathedral as its chief point of reference reflecting the traditional texture of the City. The development involves the construction of three buildings totalling some 70,000 square metres of office and rental space, and known as Warwick, King Edward and St. Martin's Courts. The scope also includes a paved public square, complete with a monument, and surrounded on the north and west sides by a stone loggia. The site now presents a dense city-centre appearance, rather than the wind-swept development that replaced the bomb sites of World War II.*

*Rising 1016 ft into the air, Renzo Piano's spire at London Bridge (right) is set to become an instantly recognisable symbol for London. On the banks of the Thames, the London Bridge Tower will soar above London and become Europe's tallest building. It will house offices, hotels, homes, shops and restaurants adjacent to London Bridge station and was approved by the government in November 2003. Heritage groups, however, have objected to the skyscraper saying it would spoil views of historic City buildings, including St Paul's Cathedral. The proposed tower will appear as a slender spire of glass with steeply sloping faces made of large shards of 'extra white glass'. This combination will make the tower seem partly to disappear into the sky and it is likely to change its character and appearance with seasonal variations of light and weather.*

centre at London Zoo, concentrating on the themes of conserving biological resources throughout the world. A giant Ferris wheel, known as the 'London Eye', rises 400 ft from the South Bank almost opposite the Houses of Parliament. Its 32 enclosed capsules afford views not only of London but also as far afield as Tunbridge Wells, Windsor, Luton, Stansted and Rochester. The wheel has proved hugely popular among Londoners and visitors alike.

The year 2000 also saw the election of a mayor by voters in the area covered by the new Greater London Authority (identical to the area managed by the former GLC). The GLA now occupies a striking new building opposite the Tower of London. The Mayor's responsibilities include preparing a strategic plan for London (discussed overleaf). In the present era of globalisation, London's main advantage continues to lie with the vast experience of its bankers, traders and financiers. However, the capital needs to modernise its facilities, both to satisfy international business and to serve the millions of ordinary Londoners who service its

daily activities. In many respects London's historical legacy may be seen as something of a handicap for a prosperous future, since so much needs to be restored, renewed or replaced.

As London's economy has changed over the past century, so 'brownfield' sites have become available for redevelopment. Redundant railway land opened new opportunities at King's Cross, Stratford and other locations. As factories, riverside docks and power stations closed, the challenge of re-using the banks of the Thames in imaginative ways has had to be confronted. The upstream docks and the Isle of Dogs have already changed beyond recognition, but parts of the Royal Docks and land further downstream await regeneration. In the city centre, riverside redevelopment

continues to pose social and architectural challenges. A master plan seeks to transform the 70-acre site of the South Bank Centre into a user-friendly cultural environment.

Important investments are being made in mass transit but much more is needed to improve London's Underground and surface stations, and to provide new lines beneath the crowded centre of the city. The Jubilee Line extension facilitates links eastwards to Bermondsey, Docklands and Stratford. Direct rail links from Paddington, Victoria and Liverpool Street serve Heathrow, Gatwick and Stansted airports. (Further proposals are discussed overleaf). Waterloo International is the present terminal for Eurostar trains from Paris and Brussels, and a restored St. Pancras station will accommodate these services from 2007 onwards when the fast rail link to the Channel Tunnel is fully operational. About 100 million passengers use five international airports around London, with over a half passing through Heathrow and a quarter through Gatwick. A fifth terminal at Heathrow will increase annual capacity to 80 million passengers by 2015, and major enlargement at Stansted has been proposed. London's roads are woefully inadequate to cope with the current volume of traffic and pose serious challenges for London's economy in the future. Road-building schemes have been shelved because of high costs and environmental disruption. Arguments to control the use of private cars in central London have found favour with the elected Mayor whose controversial vehicle-pricing scheme is in place. Without doubt, existing roads need to be managed better and public transport to be greatly enhanced, not only for London's residents and workforce, but also for the 30 million tourists who visit London each year.

171

# LONDON OF THE FUTURE

London's history has been chequered by phases of growth interspersed with periods of decline. At the start of the new millennium, the capital faces major challenges. Profound deindustrialisation has been accompanied by heavy reliance on providing a great variety of services, from administration, higher education and tourism to high-level banking and commerce. London is a 'world city', comparable in strength with New York and Tokyo, but its role in the European Union is being challenged by Paris and Frankfurt. Central London heads the league of European regions in terms of wealth generation, but its ring of Victorian suburbs and areas in the East End are among the most deprived localities in Britain, with high unemployment, low average incomes, and worrying levels of educational achievement. The very rich and the very poor are co-existing, almost side by side.

At the start of the 21st century, London has many impressive projects underway. A major office complex (nicknamed the 'erotic gherkin' after its shape and glass dome) is being built on the site of the Baltic Exchange destroyed in 1992 by an IRA bomb. On the southern bank of the Thames, a remarkable project has been launched for a 66-storey London Bridge Tower (to rise 1015 ft, or more than twice as high as the wheel of the 'London Eye'), to comprise financial activities, apartments and a hotel. Some 60 acres of former railway land at King's Cross are being developed for commercial activities and housing, with the local Underground station being enlarged to cope with greatly increased numbers of passenger when Eurostar trains arrive at St. Pancras Station in 2007. A massive redevelopment project has been proposed for offices, over 5,500 new homes and other activities on 140 acres of former railway land at the site of the Stratford Eurostar station. Eleven acres of former goods years at Paddington Basin on the Grand Union Canal have been developed for corporate headquarters offices, housing and shops. Planning permission has been granted for the half-demolished giant power station at Battersea, set in 36 acres of land, to form the heart of a scheme comprising business premises, hotels, a theatre, residential units and shops. Fast transport links to Victoria and a new pedestrian bridge spanning the Tames have been proposed for this ambitious project.

In June 2002, the elected Mayor of London announced his 15-year master plan for the capital as a whole. This offers strategic guidance for planners in the 32 London Boroughs and the City of London. The plan argues that available space in London should be used more intensively through increasing densities of new housing and employment, while defending the green belt. Its ambitions include making London a better place to live in, promoting strong and diverse economic growth, tackling deprivation and discrimination, improving public transport, promoting sustainable development, and enhancing London's appearance and ecology.

Since 1990, London's population has grown steadily to 7.5 millions in 2000 and is likely to

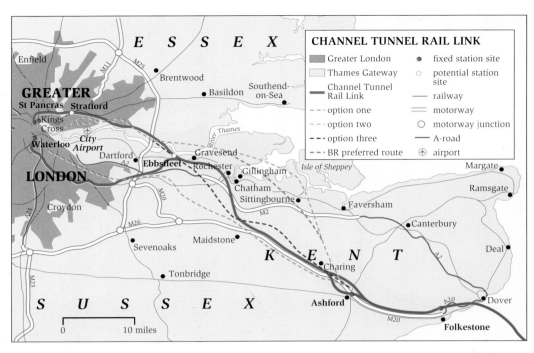

**CHANNEL TUNNEL RAIL LINK**

The Channel Tunnel Rail Link *The map (above) shows alternative routes that were proposed for the fast rail link. These options gave rise to much controversy among environmentalists and the residents of Kent. The chosen route will cross the Thames at Ebbsfleet, have a station at Stratford and terminate at St Pancras, where special platforms are being built for Eurostar trains. It is hoped that regeneration in the economically depressed Thames Gateway area to the east of London will be boosted by these new connections. Work on the 70 miles of track, one sixth of which will be underground will take an estimated six years to complete. Some Channel Tunnel services will continue to use the new terminal at Waterloo International*

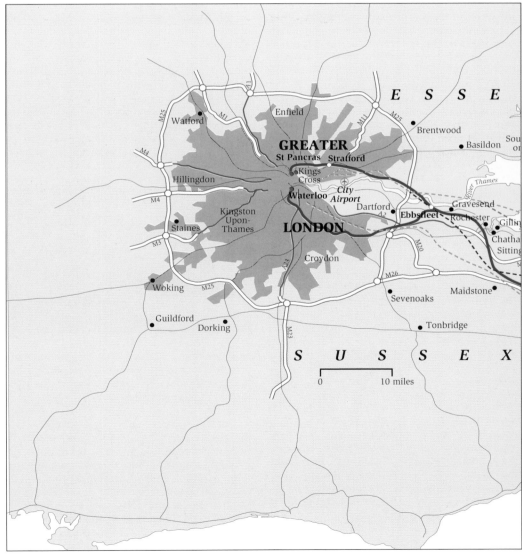

The area administered *by the Greater London Authority (above) stands at the centre of a vast 'metro region' bound together by railways and roads, and with vast* numbers of commuters travelling in from cities such as Brighton, Cambridge and Oxford each day.

**The London Authority HQ** *After long consultation it was decided to construct a new building to house the chamber and offices of London's future elected authority (left). Both the design and site of the new headquarters are controversial. The design has been compared with a giant eye or a massive headlamp. The site comprises vacant land immediately across the Thames from the Tower of London and close to London Bridge. This choice expresses faith in the future of London, while recognising the tremendous importance of its historic legacy.*

**Congestion Charge Zone** *Introduced in autumn 2002, the £5 congestion charge operates during working hours, Monday to Friday. Despite initial difficulties with equipment identifying vehicles entering the zone, by the end of the first year of operation the quantity of traffic in central London had dropped by 50,000 cars (down 16%), making central zone journeys 14% quicker; however some roads just outside the zone have become more congested as drivers seek alternative routes to avoid paying the charge. The Mayor proposes that the zone be almost doubled by extending it westward.*

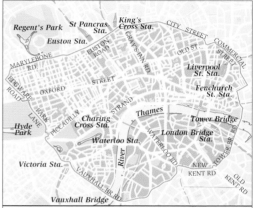

**CENTRAL LONDON CONGESTION CHARGE**
▨ Boundary of congestion charge

**The Mayor's Plan for London** *incorporates a number of massively expensive tunnelling schemes that will require major investment from the private sector as well as from the State. The aim of these schemes that have been considered for some years is to link sections of the existing rail system by new tunnels underneath the centre of the capital, emulating what has been achieved in Paris. Light transit/ tramway routes for certain suburban and inner-city areas are also proposed.*

reach 8.1 millions by 2016. Much more housing will be needed in the immediate future, and the plan urges that half of all new-build homes should be 'affordable'. The residents of almost every London Borough increased in the 1990s, with notable growth of numbers of young people, members of black, ethnic and other minority communities, and many newcomers from across Europe. New jobs were especially numerous in the service sector and especially in central and north-west districts. Deindustrialisation released many 'brownfield' sites for regeneration. London's wealth increased dramatically during the last decade, but so did disparities between rich and poor. Health care, education facilities and public transport need to be improved, the latter especially so since a traffic charge has been introduced on private vehicles entering central London on weekdays. Perhaps not surprisingly, the capital is running out of burial space, but its legacy of cemeteries, together with parks and other open spaces, offers a great ecological resource. This is paralleled by London's 'blue ribbon network' of waterways and lakes.

The Thames Gateway area downstream of the City offers enormous potential for housing and employment, but rail improvements must be introduced first to make it accessible to central London where most office-based employment is still likely to occur. The Crossrail project, providing a deep tunnel to link lines at Paddington with those in east London and Essex, has a 2011 completion target set, having first been mooted in the late 1970s. Improvements to the north/south Thameslink 2000 system are due for 2008. The tunnel for Crossrail 2, from Dalston to Victoria, is hoped to be ready by 2016. Each of these massively expensive rapid-transit tunnels will be served by a limited number of intermediate stations; for example, at Bond Street, Tottenham Court Road, Farringdon, and Liverpool Street on the east/west Crossrail. These are intended to be mega-stations that will convey a genuine sense of volume and space very different from the cramped Tube stations on lines constructed before the recent Jubilee Line Extension.

The capital's link with its surrounding metropolitan region (totalling 18 million inhabitants) and with other parts of the world call for improved roads to ports and airports, and increased capacity at Heathrow and Stansted. Economic opportunities will be great, while environmental costs will be enormous. One idea involved building a new international airport on the Cliffe marshes on the southern side of the Thames estuary. Within the GLA, the Mayor emphasises the need to protect and enhance biodiversity. His plan favour light transit systems (tramways), encourages more cycling and walking routes, and emphasises the need to recycle urban waste. In fact, many of the ideas in the plan are not new; most are costly and controversial. The balancing act between stimulating economic growth, promoting social justice, and guaranteeing biodiversity will be difficult to achieve. Nonetheless, the plan offers a long-awaited scrutiny of London's strengths and weaknesses, while offering a vision of urban renaissance to which many will subscribe.

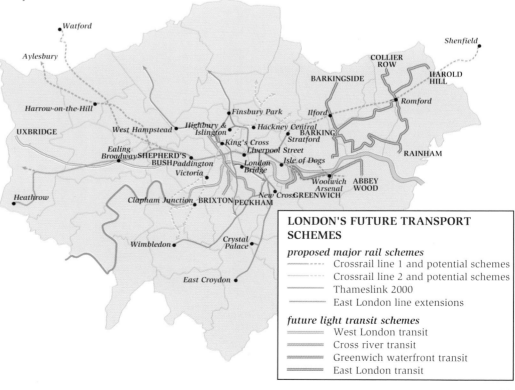

**LONDON'S FUTURE TRANSPORT SCHEMES**

*proposed major rail schemes*
----- Crossrail line 1 and potential schemes
----- Crossrail line 2 and potential schemes
——— Thameslink 2000
——— East London line extensions

*future light transit schemes*
═══ West London transit
═══ Cross river transit
═══ Greenwich waterfront transit
═══ East London transit

# ETYMOLOGY OF LONDON PLACE NAMES

Not all London place-names are mysterious – **Highgate** actually does refer to a 'high gate' (probably a *toll-gate*) – but many are. London place-names have histories of different lengths. New ones are created from time to time; **Highgate's** history goes back to 1354; **Hendon's** ('high hill') to 959; **London's** to 115. Many changes can take place in the course of time: *Londinium* has become **London**; *Tidwulf's tree* has become **Elstree**; *St. Vedast's Lane* has become **Foster Lane**. In some cases, the cumulation of changes of form has led to amazing changes of meaning: today's **Cannon Street** began life as, in effect, 'candlemaker street'. Fortunately, the written records of these changes are copious enough to allow us to parade before you an ordered sequence of well-preserved fossils that preceded the place-name's latest form, like the well-attested evolution of the horse from *Eohippus* to *Red Rum*.

For reasons of space this appendix concentrates on the names of London's rivers and districts (or 'villages'), and the names of streets in its old City. They are listed in alphabetical order; after each map name comes its history given as clearly and succinctly as necessary. Each such history has one or more of the following parts in the following order:

**Name** /pronunciation (where noteworthy)/ : 'meaning of the name as it might have appeared to those who coined it' [history of the forms of the name : analysis of the parts of the name (with their individual meanings) ; additional information] *cross-references to other relevant* **Names**.

Off-putting conventions have been avoided; **bold-face** means 'name listed in this appendix'; ? means 'perhaps'; ‹ means 'from'. The analysed parts of each name come from Old English (in use till about 1100) unless otherwise specified. Pronunciations are given in the version of the International Phonetic Alphabet used in the *Collins English Dictionary*; a key to these symbols is provided below.

The symbols used in the pronunciation transcriptions are those of the International Phonetic Alphabet. The following consonant symbols have their usual English values: *b, d, f, h, k, l, m, n, p, r, s, t, v, w, z*. The remaining symbols and their interpretations are listed in the tables below.

**English Sounds**

ɑ: as in *father* ('fɑ:ðə), alms (ɑ:mz), *clerk* (klɑ:k), *heart* (hɑ:t), *sergeant* ('sɑ:dʒənt)
æ as in *act* (ækt), *Cædmon* ('kædmən), *plait* (plæt)
aɪ as in *dive* (daɪv), *aisle* (aɪl), *guy* (gaɪ), *might* (maɪt), *rye* (raɪ)
aɪə as in *fire* ('faɪə), *buyer* ('baɪə), *liar* ('lɪə), *tyre* ('taɪə)
aʊ as in *out* (aʊt), *bough* (baʊ), *crowd* (kraʊd), *slouch* (slaʊtʃ)
aʊə as in *flour* ('flaʊə), *cower* ('kaʊə), *flower* ('flaʊə), *sour* ('saʊə)
ɛ as in *bet* (bɛt), *ate* (ɛt), *bury* ('bɛrɪ), *heifer* ('hɛfə), *said* (sɛd), *says* (sɛz)
eɪ as in *paid* (peɪd), *day* (deɪ), *deign* (deɪn), *gauge* (geɪdʒ), *grey* (greɪ), *neigh* (neɪ)
ɛə as in *bear* (bɛə), *dare* (dɛə), *prayer* (prɛə), *stairs* (stɛəz), *where* (wɛə)
g as in *get* (gɛt), *give* (gɪv), *ghoul* (gu:l), *guard* (gɑ:d), *examine* (ɪg'zæmɪn)
ɪ as in *pretty* ('prɪtɪ), *build* (bɪld), *busy* ('bɪzɪ), *nymph* (nɪmf), *pocket* ('pɒkɪt), *sieve* (sɪv), *women* ('wɪmɪn)
i: as in *see* (si:), *aesthete* ('i:sθi:t), *evil* ('i:vᵊl), *magazine* (ˌmægə'zi:n), *receive* (rɪ'si:v), *siege* (si:dʒ)
ɪə as in *fear* (fɪə), *beer* (bɪə), *mere* (mɪə), *tier* (tɪə)
j as in *yes* (jɛs), *onion* ('ʌnjən), *vignette* (vɪ'njɛt)
ɒ as in *pot* (pɒt), *botch* (bɒtʃ), *sorry* ('sɒrɪ)
əʊ as in *note* (nəʊt), *beau* (bəʊ), *dough* (dəʊ), *hoe* (həʊ), *slow* (sləʊ), *yeoman* (jəʊmən)
ɔ: as in *thaw* (θɔ:), *broad* (brɔ:d), *drawer* ('drɔ:ə), *fault* (fɔ:lt), *organ* ('ɔ:gən)
ɔɪ as in *void* (vɔɪd), *boy* (bɔɪ), *destroy* (dɪ'strɔɪ)
ʊ as in *pull* (pʊl), *good* (gʊd), *woman* ('wʊmən)
u: as in *zoo* (zu:), *do* (du:), *queue* (kju:), *shoe* (ʃu:), *spew* (spju:) *true* (tru:), *you* (ju:)
ʊə as in *poor* (pʊə), *skewer* ('skjʊə), *sure* (ʃʊə)
ə as in *potter* ('pɒtə), *alone* (ə'ləʊn), *furious* (fjʊərɪəs), *nation* ('neɪʃən), *the* (ðə)
ɜ: as in *fern* (fɜ:n), *burn* (bɜ:n), *fir* (fɜ:), *learn* (lɜ:n), *term* (tɜ:m), *worm* (wɜ:m)
ʌ as in *cut* (kʌt), *flood* (flʌd), *rough* (rʌf), *son* (sʌn)
ʃ as in *ship* (ʃɪp), *election* (ɪ'lɛkʃən), *machine* (mə'ʃi:n), *mission* ('mɪʃən), *pressure* ('prɛʃə), *schedule* ('ʃɛdju:l), *sugar* ('ʃʊgə)
ʒ as in *treasure* ('trɛʒə), *azure* ('æʒə), *closure* ('kləʊʒə), *evasion* (ɪ'veɪʒən)
tʃ as in *chew* (tʃu:), *nature* ('neɪtʃə)
dʒ as in *jaw* (dʒɔ:), *adjective* ('ædʒɪktɪv), *lodge* (lɒdʒ), *soldier* ('səʊldʒə), *usage* ('ju:sɪdʒ)
θ as in *thin* (θɪn), *strength* (strɛŋθ), *three* (θri:)
ð as in *these* (ði:z), *bathe* (beɪð), *lather* ('lɑ:ðə)
ŋ as in *sing* (sɪŋ), *finger* ('fɪŋgə), *sling* (slɪŋ)
ᵊ indicates that the following consonant (*l* or *n*) is syllabic, as in *bundle* ('bʌndᵊl) and *button* ('bʌtᵊn)
x as in Scottish *loch* (lɒx).
əɪ as in Scottish *aye* (əɪ), *bile* (bəɪl), *byke* (bəɪk).

**Length**
The symbol : denotes length and is shown together with certain vowel symbols when the vowels are typically long.

**Stress**
Three grades of stress are shown in the transcription by the presence or absence of marks placed immediately *before* the affected syllable. Primary or strong stress is shown by ', while secondary or weak stress is shown by ˌ. Unstressed syllables are not marked. In *photographic* (ˌfəʊtə'græfɪk), for example, the first syllable carries secondary stress and the third primary stress, while the second and fourth are unstressed.

[In addition, the following special letters are used in the transcription of old manuscripts: *ǣ/Ǣ* (as above), *ð* (as above), þ (pronounced like *ð* or *θ* above), ʒ (like ʒ above in shape, but pronounced like *j* or *x* above or like the voiced equivalent of *x*). In earlier forms of a place name, ' at the end of a word shows that the scribe has omitted one or more letters; a bar over a letter (*ā*) shows that *m* or *n* has been omitted. In the analysis of place-name elements, such a bar over a vowel functions like ':' in the pronunciations: it shows that the vowel is pronounced long.]

# A

**Abchurch Lane** [1291-92 (*Abbechirchelane*); by the church of *St. Mary Abchurch*]

**Acton:** 'oak-tree estate' [1181 (*Acton(e)*): *āc* 'oak' + *tūn* 'estate, home farm']

**Acton Common** ‹ **Acton**

**Aldermanbury:** 'alderman's manor; aldermen's manor' [c. 1130 (*Aldremanesburi*), 1336 (*Aldermannebury*): *(e)aldermann* 'elder, chief; alderman' + *burh* 'stronghold, fortified manor']

**Aldersgate** *see* **Aldersgate Street**

**Aldersgate Street:** 'street of Ealdred's gate' [1303 (*Aldresgatestrete*): *Ealdre(d)* (name) + *geat* 'gap; gate' + *strǣt* 'paved) road, street' (‹ Latin)]

**Aldgate:** 'ale gate' [c. 1095 (*Ealsegate*), 1275 (*Alegate*): *ealu* 'ale' + *geat* 'gap; gate'; City gate previously called *Ǣst Geat* 'east gate']

**Aldgate Street:** 'ale-gate street' [13th C. (*Alegatestrat*), c.1600 (*Aldgate street*); now **Aldgate**] ‹ **Aldgate**

**The Artillery Ground** [named officially in 1746; the 'Old Artillery Ground' near Spitalfields is mentioned in the diary of Samuel Pepys (1633-1703)]

**Ashford:** 'Eccel's ford' [1042-66 (*Echelsford*), 1062 (*Exforde*), 1488 (*Assheford*): *? Ecceles* (from name) + *ford* '(river-) ford']

# B

**The Bailey** [c.1166 (*Bali*), 1298 (*le Bail*), 1431-32 (*la Baillye*), 1444-45 (*Old Bailey*): Middle English *bail, bailey* 'outermost wall or court (as of a castle), bailey' (‹ Old French); sited just west of the City wall; now *Old Bailey*]

**Baker Street** [after William *Baker*, 18th-century property-developer of land here that he acquired from W.H. Portman]

**Balham** /'bæləm/: 'Bælga's village; Bælga's river-bend land' [957 (*Bælgenham*), 1472 (*Balam*): *?Bælgen* (from name ?‹ *bealg* 'rounded') + *hām* 'settlement, village' or *hamm* 'river-bend land']

**Banstead:** 'bean-place' [675 (*Benstede*), 1062 (*Bænstede*), 1198 (*Banstede*): bēan 'bean' + *stede* 'place, stead']

**Barbican Street** [1348-49 (*Barbecanstret*), 1377 (*Barbycanstret*): Middle English *barbican* 'outer fortification, typically with a tower' (‹ Middle French ‹ Medieval Latin ‹ Persian) + *strǣt* '(paved) road, street' (‹ Latin)]

**Barking:** 'Berca's folk' [c.730 (*Bercingum*), 1086 (*Berchinges*): *Berc(a) (name)* + *-ing(as)* 'followers of']

**Barnes:** 'barns' [1086 (*Berne*), 1222 (*Bernes*), 1387 (*Barnes*): *bern* 'barn' (‹ *bere* 'barley' + *ærn* 'building for the stated purpose')]

**Barnet** /'bɑ:nɪt/: 'burnt (site)' [c. 1070 (*Barneto*): *bærnet* 'burnt'; area cleared for settlement by burning part of the former Middlesex and Hertfordshire woodland]

**Basinger Lane, Basing Lane:** 'Basing('s) lane' [1279-80 (*Basingelane*), 1324 (*Basingeslane*), 1544 (*Basinglane*): *Basing* (attested local surname, perhaps originally from *Basing* in Hampshire) + *lane* 'lane'; now part of **Cannon Street**] *compare* **Bassishaw Street**

**Bassishaw Street:** 'the Bas(s)ings' manor street; Bassishaw-ward street' [1279 ((the street of) *Basingeshawe*), c.1600 (*Bassings hall streete*): *Bas(s)ing(a)s* 'followers of Bas(sa)' (perhaps as in *Basing*stoke in Hampshire) + *haga* 'hedge; enclosure, property; town house' + *strǣt* '(paved) road, street' (‹ Latin); *Bassishaw* was also the name of a ward of the City of London; now *Basinghall Street*] *compare* **Basinger Lane**

**Battersea:** 'Beadurīc's (high) ground' [c.1050 (*Batrices ege*): *Batric* (name) + *ēg* 'high ground']

**Battersea Park** ‹ **Battersea**

**Bayswater Road** ‹ **Bayswater:** 'Bayard's watering place' [1380 (*Bayards Watering Place*): *?Baynardus*, henchman of William the Conqueror]

**Bearward Lane, Berewards Lane:** 'bear-keeper's lane' [1285 (*Berewardeslane*), 1417 (*Berwardeslane*): Middle English *bereward*e 'bearward, bear-keeper' (‹ *?beraweard*) + *lane* 'lane']

**Beckenham:** 'Biohha's village' [862 (*Biohhahema mearc*), 1086 (*Bacheham*): *Biohha* (name) + *hām* 'settlement, village' (+ *mearc* 'boundary, landmark')]

**Beddington:** 'Beadda's folk's estate' [675 (*Bedintone*), c. 905 (*Beaddinctun*), 1229 (*Bedington*): *Bead(da)* (name) + *-ing* '-follower of' + *tūn* 'estate, home farm']

**Bedfont:** 'hollow spring' [1086 (*Bedefunt, Bedefunde*): *?byde(n), bede(n)* 'hollow (place), depression' + *funta* 'spring' (‹ Celtic ‹ Latin)]

**Belleyetteres Lane:** 'bell-maker's lane' [1306 (*Belleyetterslane*), 1421 (*Belleterlane*), 1667 (*Billiter Lane*); mainly *Billiter Lane* till the 19th century, but now **Billiter Street**] *see* **Billiter Street**

**Bercher's Lane:** 'barber's lane' [1193-95 (*Bercheuere lane*), 1260 (*Bercherevereslane*), 1300 (*Berchenereslane*), 1372-73 *Berchereslane, Bercherlane*), 1386 (*Birchenlane*), 1493-94 (*Birchinlane*): ?Middle English *berdcherver(e)* 'barber' (‹ *?beardceorfere* ‹ *beard* 'beard' + *ceorfere* 'carver') + *lane* 'lane'; now *Birchin Lane*]

**Bermondsey:** 'Beornmund's (high) ground' [1086 (*Bermundeseye*): *Beornmund* (name) + *ēg* 'high ground']

**Bethnal Green:** 'Blitha's-corner green' [13th C. (*Blithehale*), 1443 (*Blethenalegreene*): *Blithe(n)* (from name) + *halh* 'corner/nook of land' + *grēne* '(village) green']

**Beverley Brook** ‹ **Beverley:** 'beaver rivulet' [693 (*Beferiþi*): *beofor* 'beaver' + *rīð* 'stream' + *-ig* (diminutive)]

**Bexley:** 'box(-tree) lea/grove' [c.780 (*Bixle*): *?byxe* (variant of *box* 'box-tree') + *lēah* 'grove; meadow, lea']

**Bexleyheath** ‹ **Bexley**

**Billingsgate:** 'Belling's gate' [c.1205 (*Bælʒesʒate*), c.1250 (*Bellinges-ʒate*): *Belling* (name) + *geat* 'gap; gate'; the *gate* presumably gave access to the Thames]

**Billiter Street:** 'bell-maker street' [1298 *Belʒeterslane*), 1349 *Belleʒeterestret*): Middle English *belleyetere* 'bell-founder' + *strǣt* '(paved) road, street' (‹ Latin)] *see also* **Belleyetteres Lane**

**Bishopsgate** *see* **Bishopsgate Street**

**Bishopsgate Street:** 'street of the bishop's gate' [1275 (*Bis(s)hopesgatestrete*): *biscop* 'bishop' (‹ Late Latin ‹ Greek *episcopos*) + *geat* 'gap; gate' + *strǣt* '(paved) road, street' (‹ Latin); a gate in the north-eastern part of the City wall was built by order of Erkenwald, Bishop of London 675-693]

**Blackheath** [1166 (*Blachedefeld*); from the dark colour of the peat thereon]

**Blackheath Common** ‹ **Blackheath**

**Borough Road** [*burh* 'stronghold, fortified manor'; from (the) *Borough* (of *Southwark*)] *see* **Southwark**

**Bowyer Row** [1359 (*Bowiarresrowe*): Middle English *bowiar* 'bowyer, (archery) bow-maker' + *rǣw* 'row' (of trees or houses); now *Ludgate Street* east of **Ludgate**]

**Bread Street** [1163-70 (*Bredstrate*): *brēad* 'bread' + *strǣt* '(paved) road, street' (‹ Latin); from the baking and selling of *bread* here]

**Brent:** 'Holy One' [c.974 (*Brægentan*): Latin *brigantiā* 'holy one' (‹ Celtic)]

**Brentford:** *(River) Brent ford'* [705 (*Bregunt ford*), 1222 (*Brainford*): **Brent** + *ford* '(river-) ford'] ‹ **Brent**

**Bridge Street** [1193-1212 (*vicus de ponte*), 1226-27 (*Brygestrate*); after **London Bridge;** later *Fish Street*; now *Fish Street Hill*]

**Brixton:** 'Brihtsige's stone' (1062 (*Brixges stane*), 1279 (*Brixistane*): *Brihtsige* (? name) + *stān* 'stone']

**Broad Street** [c. 1212 (*Bradestrate*), 1513 (*Brodestrete*):*brād* broad, wide' + *strǣt* '(paved) road, street' (‹ Latin)]

**Bromley:** 'broom (-plant) lea/grove' [862 (*Bromleag*): *brōm* 'broom' + *lēah* 'grove; meadow, lea']

**Brompton:** 'broom (-plant) estate' [1294 (*Brompton*): *brōm* 'broom' + *tūn* 'estate, home farm']

**Buckingham Palace** [?1825: originally *Buckingham House*; built 1703 for John Sheffield, Duke of *Buckingham*; remodelled about 1825 by Nash for George IV]

**Bucklersbury:** 'Bukerel's manor' [1343 (*Bokerellesbury*), 1477 (*Bokelersbury*): *Bukerel, Bucherel(l)* (attested surname) + *burh* 'stronghold, fortified manor']

**Budget Row, Budge Row:** 'budge-fur row' [1342 (*Bogerowe*), 1383-84 (*Bugerowe*), 1553-54 (*Bouge Rowe*), 1591 (*Budgerowe*): Middle English *bugee, boge* 'fur of lamb, rabbit or kid' (?‹ French) + Middle English *rowe* ‹ *rǣw* 'row' (of trees or houses); near the skinners' district]

**Bull's Cross, Bulls Cross** [1540 (*Bellyscrosse*), 16th C. (*Bulls Cross*): ?(Gilbert) *Bolle* (name attested locally in 1235) + *cros* 'cross' (‹ Old Irish ‹ Latin)]

**Bunhill Fields:** 'bone-hill fields' [1544 (*Bonhilles*), 1567 (*Bonhill Field*), 1799 (*Bunhill Fields Burying Ground*): *bān* 'bone' + *hyll* 'hill' + *feldas* 'fields'; perhaps from the transfer here of *bones* from St. Paul's charnel house for burial; also *Tindals Burying Ground* (1746)]

**Bushy Park, Bushey Park** (Middlesex) [1650 (*Bushie Park*), 1667 (*Bushey Park*): ?*busc* 'bush, shrub' + (ge)*hæg* 'enclosure']

**Butchery** [1349 (*Bocherie*)] *see* **Shambles**

# C

**Camberwell:** [1086 (*Cambrewelle*): ? + *well(a)* 'well; spring']

**Camden** ‹ **Camden Town**

**Camden Town** [1795; after Charles Pratt, Earl *Camden* of *Camden* Place in Kent, local landowner]

**Candlewick Street** [1241 (*Kandelwiccestrate*), 14th C. (*Candelwikstrete*, etc.): ‹ *Candelwrichstrete* 'candlemaker street' (by folk etymology); now **Cannon Street**] *see* **Cannon Street**

**Cannon Street:** 'candlemaker street' [c. 1185 (*Candelwrichstrete*), 1480 (*Canyngesstrete*), 1664 (*Cannon-street*): ?*Candelwyrhta* 'candle-wright, chandler' + *strǣt* '(paved) road, street' (‹ Latin)] *compare* **Candlewick Street**

**Canonbury:** 'canon's manor' [1373 (*Canonesbury*): Middle English *canoun* 'canon' (‹ Old Northern French ‹ Latin) + *burh* 'stronghold, fortified manor'; after the *canons* of St. Bartholomew's in **Smithfield**, granted land here in 1253]

**Carshalton** /kɑːˈʃɔːltᵊn; formerly keɪsˈhɔːtᵊn/: 'cress well-spring farm' [1086 (*Aultone*), 1235 (*Cresaulton*), 1279 (*Carshaulton*): *cærse* '(water-) cress' + *ǣwell, ǣwiell* 'spring; well-spring, (stream-) source' (‹ *éa* 'stream' + *well(a), wiell(a)* 'well, spring') + *tūn* 'estate, home farm']

**Carter Lane** [1295 (*Carterestrate*), 1349 (*Cartereslane*): Middle English *carter(e)* (‹ *crǣt* + *-ere*) + *strǣt* '(paved) road, street' (‹ Latin) or *lane* 'lane']

**Caterham** /ˈkeɪtərəm; formerly ˈkætərəm/: 'hill-fort village' [1179 (*Catheham*), 1200 (*Katerham*), 1372 (*Caterham*): ?Celtic *cater* 'hill-fort' (‹ Latin) + *hām* 'settlement, village']

**Chancellor's Lane** [1227 (*Newestrate*), 1278-79 (*Converslane*), 1338 (*Chauncellereslane*), 1454 (*Chauncerylane*): *Newestrate* 'new street'; *Converslane* 'converts' lane' (after the *Domus Conversorum* founded here in 1231-32 by Henry III for Jewish *converts* to Christianity); *Chauncellereslane, Chauncerylane* (from the subsequent use of the *Domus* as seat of the *Chancery* and perhaps office of the *Chancellor*); now *Chancery Lane*]

**Charing Cross:** 'turning-point cross' [c.1000 (*Cyrringe*), 1360 (*La Charryngcross*): *cierring* 'bend' (in a river or road) + *cros* 'cross' (‹ Old Irish ‹ Latin); from the *cross* put here in 1291 by Edward I to mark the last stage in the funeral procession of his first Queen, Eleanor of Castile, from Harby in Nottinghamshire to Westminster Abbey] *compare* **Waltham Cross**

**Charlton:** 'peasants' farmstead; peasants' (part of) estate' [1086 (*Cerletun*): *ceorla* '(free) peasants'' + *tūn* 'estate, home farm']

**Charlton** (Middlesex): 'Cēolrēd's folk's estate' [1086 (*Cerdentone*), 1550 (*Charleton*), 1594 (*Charleton al. Chertington*): ?*Cēolrēd* (name, with *d/l* confusion) + *-ing* '-follower of' + *tūn* 'estate, home farm']

**Cheam** /tʃiːm/: '(tree-) stump village; (tree-) stump river-bend land' [675 (*Cegeham*), 933 (*Cheham*): ?*cege* '(tree-) stump; underbrush' + *hām* 'settlement, village' or *hamm* 'river-bend land']

**Cheapside:** 'market-side' [1436 (*Chapeside*): *cēap* 'market; trade' + *sīde* 'side'; formerly *Westcheap*] *see also* **West Cheap**

**Chelsea:** 'chalk landing-place' [789 (*Celchyth*), 1214 (*Chelchee*): *cealc* 'chalk, lime; limestone' (‹ Latin) + *hȳð* 'landing place, harbour']

**Chessington:** 'Cissa's folk's hill' [1086 (*Cisendone*), 1279 (*Chessingdone*): *Cis(sa)* (name) + *-ing* '-follower of' + *dūn* 'hill']

**Chicken Lane, Chick Lane** [1181-89 (*Chikenslane*), 1540-41 (*Cheke Lane*): *cicen* 'chicken' + *lane* 'lane'; where *chickens* were reared and sold]

**Chigwell:** 'Cicca's folk's spring/well' [1086 (*Cingheuuella*), 1158 (*Chigwell*, etc.): *Cicc(a)* (name) + *-ing* '-follower of' + *wella, wiella* 'well; spring']

**Chigwell Row** ‹ **Chigwell**

**Chingford:** 'shingle-ford' [1086 (*Cingefort*): ?*cinge(l)* 'shingle' + *ford* '(river-) ford']

**Chipping Barnet:** 'market Barnet' [1329 (*Chepyng Barnet*), 1628 (*Chipping Barnet al. High Barnet*): *cēping, cī(e)ping* 'market' + **Barnet**; also *High Barnet*] ‹ **Barnet**

**Chislehurst:** 'gravel hill' [973 (*Cyselhyrst*), 1159 (*Chiselherst*): *cisel, ceosel* 'gravel; flint; pebble' + *hyrst, herst* 'hill(ock); copse']

**Chiswell** /ˈtʃɪzwɛl, -wəl/ **Street:** 'gravel street' [13th C. (*Chysel strate*), 1458 (*Cheselstrete*), late 16th C. (*Chiswell Street*): *cisel, ceosol* 'gravel; flint; pebble' + *strǣt* '(paved) road, street' (‹ Latin); perhaps from the character of the local soil]

**Chiswick** /ˈtʃɪzɪk/: 'cheese farm' [c.1000 (*Ceswican*): *ciese* 'cheese' + *wīc* 'farm or harbour of the stated kind']

**City Road** ‹ the City (of **London**)

**Clapham:** 'hill village' [c.880 (*Cloppaham*): ?*clop* (perhaps from a Germanic word cognate with *hill* and *culminate*) + *hām* 'settlement, village']

**Clapham Common** ‹ **Clapham**

**Clapton:** 'hill estate' [1339 (*Clopton*), 1593 (*Clapton*): ?*clop* (*see* **Clapham**) + *tūn* 'estate, home farm']

**Clarence House** [built 1825 for William IV when Duke of *Clarence*]

**Clay Hill** [1524 (*Clayhyll*): ?*Clay, Cleye* (local surnames) + *hyll* 'hill']

**Clerkenwell** /ˈklɑːkənwɛl/: 'clerics' well; scholars' well [c. 1150 (*Clerkenwell*): Middle English *clerken(e)* 'clerics', scholars' (‹ *clerc* ‹ Latin ‹ Greek) + *well(a)* 'well, spring']

**Cock Lane** [c.1200 (*Cockeslane*), 1543 (*Coklane*): *cocc* 'cock' + *lane* 'lane'; perhaps from *cock*fighting here]

**Coleman Street:** 'Coleman's street' [1181-83 (*Colemanestrate*): ?(St. Stephen) *Coleman* (variant name, recorded in 1276, of the former church of St. Stephen here) + *strǣt* '(paved) road, street' (‹ Latin)]

**Cordwainer Street** [1216-17 (*Corueiserestrate*), 1230 (*Cordwanere-strete*): Middle English *corviser, cordwaner* 'cordwainer: leather-merchant; shoemaker' (‹ Old French ‹ Old Spanish *cordovano* 'cordovan'); now *Bow Lane* and *Garlick Hill*]

**Cornhill:** 'hill where corn is grown; hill where corn is sold' [1055 (*Cornehulle*): *corn* 'corn' + *hyll* 'hill']

**Counter's Creek:** 'countess's creek' [after the *Countess* of Oxford, wife of the Earl of Oxford (after whom *Earl's Court* was named)]

**Cowley:** 'Cofa's lea/grove' [959 (*Cofenlea*), 1086 (*Covelie*), 1294 (*Cowelee*): *Cofen* (from name) + *lēah* 'grove; meadow, lea']

**Cranford:** 'crane-ford; heron-ford' [1086 (*Cranforde*): *cran* 'crane; heron' + *ford* '(river-) ford']

**Crayford:** '(River) Cray ford' [1322 (*Crainford*): Celtic *crai* ?'fresh, new; clean, pure' + *ford* '(river-) ford']

**Cricklewood:** 'crinkled wood' [1294 (*le Crikeldwode*), 1509 (*Crykyll Wood*): ?dialectal *crickled* 'bent' (perhaps related to *crinkled*) + *wudu* 'wood']

**Cripplegate:** 'low gate' [991-1002 (*Cripelesgate*): *crypel* (as in *cripple*, ‹ *crēopan* 'creep') + *geat* 'gap; gate'; in some dialects *cripplegate* still has a similar meaning]

**Crooked Lane** [1278 (*la Crokedelane*)]

**Croydon:** 'saffron valley' [809 (*Crogedene*): *croh* 'saffron + *denu* 'valley']

**Crudrun Lane, Godrun Lane:** 'Gōdrūn('s) lane' [1180-92 (*Godrun lane*), c. 1206-7 (*Godruneslane*), 1349 (*Gother lane*), 1472 (*Gutterlane*): *Gōdrūn, Guðrún* (woman's name) + *lane* 'lane'; now *Gutter Lane* (by folk etymology)]

**Crutched Friars**: 'be-crossed friars' [1405 (*le Crouchedfrerestrate*): Middle English *crutched* 'crossed' (‹ Latin) + Middle English *freres* 'friars' (‹ Old French ‹ Latin *fratres* 'brothers') (+ *strǣt* '(paved) road, street' ‹ Latin); after the insignia of the Augustinian *Friars* of the Holy *Cross*, whose house here was founded in 1298]

# D

**Dagenham** /ˈdægənəm/: 'Dæcca's village' [695 (*Dæccenham*), 1499 (*Dagnham*): *Dæccen* (from name) + *hām* 'settlement, village']

**Dalston** /ˈdɔːlstən/: 'Dēorla's estate' [1294 (*Derleston*), 1581 (*Darleston*): *Dēorla* (name) + *tūn* 'estate, home farm']

**Dartford:** '(River) Darent ford' [1086 (*Tarenteford*), 1089 (*Darenteford*), c. 1100 (*Derteford*): Celtic *Darent* 'oak river' + ford '(river-) ford']

**Deptford** /ˈdɛtfəd/: 'deep ford' [14th C. (*Depeford*): *deop* 'deep' + *ford* '(river-) ford']

**Dicer's Lane, Dicer Lane:** 'ditcher's lane' [1275 (*Dicereslane, Dikereslane*), 1411-12 (*Diserlane*): *dīc* 'ditch; dyke' + *-ere* '-er: - maker; -worker' + *lane* 'lane'; spellings with *Dicer-* and *Diser-* may show Norman-French influence; later *Rose Street*]

**Dollis Brook** ‹ **Dollis Farm** (Hendon): 'share of land' [? Middle English *dol* ‹ *dāl* 'share']

**Dowgate:** 'dove-gate' [1244 (*Douegat*), c. 1600 (*Dowgate*): ?*dūfe* 'dove, pigeon' + *geat* 'gap; gate'; a former water*gate* and wharf that gave its name to a street now called *Dowgate Hill*]

**Down, Downe:** 'hill' [1316 (*Doune*): *dūn* 'hill']

**Dulwich** /ˈdʌlɪdʒ, -ɪtʃ/: 'dill-marsh' [967 (*Dilwihs*), 1210-12 (*Dilewisse*): *dile* 'dill' (the herb) + *wisce* 'marshland' (not *wīc* as in **Greenwich**)]

**Dulwich Common** ‹ **Dulwich**

# E

**Ealing:** 'Gilla's folk' [c. 700 (*Gillingas*), c. 1170 (*Yllinges*), 1553 (*Elyng*): *Gill(a)* (name) + *-ingas* '-followers of, -people of']

**Earl's Sluice** [after the first *Earl* of Gloucester, bastard son of Henry I (1086-1135) and lord of the manor of **Camberwell** and **Peckham**]

**East Acton** [1294 (*Estacton*): *ēast* 'east' + **Acton**] ‹ **Acton**

**East Barnet** [c. 1275 (*Est Barnet*): *ēast* 'east' + **Barnet**] ‹ **Barnet**

**East Dulwich** [1340 (*Est Dilewissh*): *ēast* 'east' + **Dulwich**] ‹ **Dulwich**

**East Molesey** ‹ **Molesey**

**East Smithfield** [1229 (*Estsmethefeld*), 1272 (*Est Smythefeld*): *ēast* 'east' + **Smithfield**] ‹ **Smithfield**

**Eastcheap, East Cheap:** 'east market' [c.1100 (*eastceape*): *ēast* 'east' + *cēap* 'market; trade'; former site of a meat-market]

**Ebbgate:** 'ebb-tide gate' [c. 1190 (*Ebbegate*): *ebb(a)* 'ebb, low tide' + *geat* 'gap; gate'; a former water*gate*; now *Swan Lane*]

**Edgware:** 'Ecgi's weir' [c. 975 (*Ǽcges Wer*): *Ǽcge* (name) + *wer* 'weir']

**Edgware Road** [1574 (*Edgware High Waie*)] ‹ **Edgware**

**Edmonton:** 'Ēadhelm('s) (folk's) estate' [1086 (*Adelmetone*), 1211 (*Edelmintone*), 1214 (*Edelmeston*), 1369 (*Edmenton*): *Ēadhelm* (name) (+ *-ing* '-follower of' or *-es* '-'s') + *tūn* 'estate, home farm']

**Elbow Lane:** 'old Bow Lane' [1343 (*Eldebowelane*), c. 1600 (*Elbow lane*): *eald* 'old' + *boga* '(archery) bow; arch, arched bridge' + *lane* 'lane'; *Elbow(e)* ‹ *Eldebowe* (by folk etymology, as the lane has a bend); now *College Street*]

**Elstree:** 'Tidwulf's tree' [785 (Tiðulfes treow), 1188 (*Tidulvestre*), 13th C. (*Idulfestre*), 1320 (*Idelstre*), 1487 (*Illestre*), 1598 (*Elstre*): *Tidwulf* (name) + *treow* 'tree']

**Eltham** /ˈɛltəm/: 'Elta's village' [1086 (*Elteham*): *Elte* (from name) + *hām* 'settlement; village']

**Enfield:** 'Ē(a)na's field' [1086 (*Enefelde*), 13th C. (*Enesfeud*), 1293 (*Enfeld*): *Ē(a)na* (name) + *feld* 'field']

**Enfield Highway** [14th C. (*Alta Via*), 1610 (*the kings highe way leading from Waltham Cross toward London*)] ‹ **Enfield**

**Epsom:** 'Ebbi's village; Ebbi's river-bend land' [933 (*Ebesham*), 973 (*Ebbesham*), 1086 (*Evesham*), 1404 (*Epsam*): *Eb(bi)* + *hām* 'settlement, village' or *ham(m)* 'river-bend land']

**Erith** /ˈɪərɪθ/: 'gravel landing' [695 (*Earhyð*), 1610 (*Eryth*): *ēar* 'gravel; mud, earth' + *hyð* 'landing-place, harbour']

**Esher** /ˈiːʃə; formerly ˈɛʃə/: 'ash (-tree) district' [1005 ((to) *Ǽscæron*), 1062 (*Esshere*): *æsc* 'ash(-tree) ' + *scearu* 'share, district; boundary']

**Euston** [after *Euston* in Suffolk, seat of the Duke of Grafton, lord of the manor of **Tottenham Court** when the *Euston* Road was built (1756-75)]

**Ewell** /ˈjuːəl/: 'well-spring' [675 (*Euuelle*), 1066 (*Ǽwelle*): *ǣwell, ǣwiell* 'spring; well-spring, (stream-) source' (‹ *ēa* 'stream' + *well(a), wiell(a)* 'well, spring')]

# F

**Faitour Lane:** 'layabouts' lane' [1292 (*Faytureslane*), 1568 (*Feter Lane*): Middle English *faitour* 'vagrant; beggar' (‹ Anglo-French ‹ Old French ‹ Latin) + *lane* 'lane'; now *Fetter Lane*]

**Falcon** [(*Falcon Brook*): after the *Falcon* Inn, near Clapham Junction]

**Farnborough:** 'fern hill' [1180 (*Ferenberga*), 1242 (*Farnberg*): *fearn* 'fern, bracken' + *beorg* 'hill, mound; barrow']

**Feltham** /ˈfɛltəm/: 'field village; mullein (-plant) village' [969 (*Feltham*), 1086 (*Feltehā*): *feld* 'field' or *felte* (name of various plants, such as *mullein, marjoram, couch grass*) + *hām* 'settlement, village']

**Fenchurch Street** [1377-78 (*Fancherchestret*), 1510 (*Fanchurche Strete*)] ‹ **Fenchurch:** 'fen church' [1337 (*Fanchurche*): *fenn* 'fen, marsh' + *cirice* 'church' (‹ Late Greek)]

**Finameur Lane, Finamour Lane** [1316 (*Fynamoureslane*), c. 1600 (*Finimore lane or fiue foote lane*): *Finamour* (attested local surname, of French origin) + *lane* 'lane'; later *Fye Foot Lane*]

**Finchley:** 'finch lea/grove' [c. 1208 (*Finchelee*): *finc* 'finch' + *lēah* 'grove; meadow, lea']

**Finks Lane** [1231-45 (*Finkeslane*), 1305-6 (*Fynghis Lane*), 1326 (*Fyncheslane*): *Fink* (attested local surname ‹ *finc* 'finch') + *lane* 'lane'; by the church of *St. Benet Fink* (same surname); now *Finch Lane*]

**Finsbury:** 'Fin's stronghold' [1231 (*Vinisbir*), 1535 (*Fynnesbury*): *Fin* (‹ *Vin* name, perhaps Scandinavian) + *burh* 'stronghold, fortified manor']

**Finsbury Fields** ‹ **Finsbury**

**Fleet Lane** [1544 (*Fletelane*): *Flete* (name of river or person) + *lane* 'lane'] ‹ **River Fleet**

**Fleet Street** [1271-72 (*Fletestrete*): (River) *Flete* + *strǣt* '(paved) road, street' (‹ Latin)] ‹ **River Fleet**

**Foot's Cray:** 'Fot's (property by the River) Cray' [c. 1100 (*Fotescræi*), 1210 (*Fotescraye*): Fot *(name)* + *Cray* (river-name)] *see* **Crayford**

**Foster (Vedast) Lane:** 'St. Vedast's Lane' [1271 (*Seint uastes lane*), 1321 (*Seint Fastes lane*), 1337 (*Fasteslane*), 1359 (*Fasterslane*), 1428 (*Foster lane*); by the church of *St. Vedast*]

**Friday Street** [1138-60 (*Fridaiestraite*): *Frīgdæg* 'Friday' + *strǣt* '(paved) road, street' (‹ Latin); from a fish-market there on *Fridays* or a person called *Friday*]

**Friern Barnet** /ˌfraɪən ˈbɑːnɪt, ˌfriːən ˈbɑːnɪt/: 'friars' burnt (site)' [1235 (*le Bernet, la Barnate*), 1274 (*Frerennebarnethe, Frerebarnet*, etc.): Middle English *freren* 'friars'' (‹ Old French ‹ Latin) + *bærnet* 'burnt'; formerly held by the monastic order of Knights of St. John of Jerusalem] *see* **Barnet**

**Fulham:** 'Fulla's river-bend land' [c. 705 (*Fulanham*), c. 895 (*Fullanhamme*): *Ful(l)an* (from name) + *hamm* 'river-bend land']

# G

**Giltspur Street** [1547 (*Gyltesporestrete*); the *gilt spur(s)* were made there or displayed on a local signboard; also *Knyghtryders Strete* (1547)]

**Godliman Street** [? after *Godalming* (in Surrey, formerly a leather-tanning centre); the Cordwainers' Hall was near this street] *compare* **Cordwainer Street.**

**Golden Lane:** 'Golda's lane' [1291-92 (*Goldinelane*), 1317 (*Goldenlane*): ? *Goldine* (from woman's name *Golda*, attested nearby in 1245) + *lane* 'lane']

**Golders Green:** 'Le Godere's green; Godyer's green' [1612 (*Golders Greene*), 1790 (*Groles or Godders Green*): (John le) *Godere* or (John) *Godyer* (names in 14th C. records) + *grēne* '(village) green'; the surname *Golder* is not attested]

**Gracechurch Street:** 'grass-church street' [1284 (*Garscherchestrate*), 1437 (*Gracechirche strete alias Graschirche strete*): *græs* 'grass' + *cirice* 'church' (‹ Late Greek) + *strǣt* '(paved) road, street' (‹ Latin); after the nearby church of *St. Benet Gracechurch*, perhaps thatch-roofed or grass-surrounded]

**Gray's Inn Fields** ‹ **Gray's Inn:** 'Gray's dwelling-place' [1396 (*Grays Inn in Holborne*): (Reginald de) *Gray* (died 1308; owner of the property) + *inn* 'dwelling, lodging'; formerly called *Portpoole Manor*]

**Great Stanmore:** 'great stony pool' [793 (*Stanmere*), 1392 (*Great(e) Stanmare*): Middle English *grēat* 'big' (‹ Old English *grēat* 'thick, bulky') + *stān* 'stone' + *mere* 'pool'; *Great* by contrast with *Little Stanmore* (*Whitchurch*)]

**Green Hill Green, Greenhill Green** (Middlesex, near Harrow) ‹ **Greenhill** [1334 (*Grenehulle*), 1563 (*Grenehill*), 1675 (*Green Hill*); ? after the local family *de Grenehulle, de Grenhulle* or *de Grenehill*]

**The Green Park** [because embellished with *green*ery (lawns and trees) rather than flowers]

**Greenford:** 'green (river-)ford' [845 (*Grenan Forda*): *grēne* 'green' + *ford* '(river-) ford']

**Greenwich** /ˈgrɪnɪdʒ, ˈgrɛnɪtʃ/: 'green harbour' [964 (*Grenewic*): *grēne* 'green' + *wīc* 'farm or harbour of the stated kind']

**Gresham Street** [1845; after the nearby *Gresham* College (founded 1579 by Sir Thomas Gresham); previously *Lad Lane* and *Cateaton Street*]

# H

**Hackney:** 'Haca's (high) ground' [1198 (*Hakeneia*): *Hacan* (from name) + *ēg* 'high ground']

**Hackney Marsh** [1397 (*Hackenemershe*)] ‹ **Hackney**

**Hackney Wick:** 'Hackney farm' [1294 (*...atte Wyk in Hakeney*): **Hackney** + *wīc* 'farm or harbour of the stated kind'] ‹ **Hackney**

**Hammersmith:** 'hammer smithy' [1294 (*Hamersmyth'*): *hamor* 'hammer' + *smiððe* 'smithy']

**Hampstead:** 'settlement, homestead' [959 (*Hemstede*): *hām* 'settlement, village, home' + *stede* 'place, stead']

**Hampstead Heath** [1543 (*Hampstede Heth*)] ‹ **Hampstead**

**Hampton:** 'river-bend estate' [1086 (*Hammtone*): *hamm* 'river-bend land' + *tūn* 'estate, home farm']

**Hampton Court:** 'Hampton manor' [1476 (*Hampton Courte*): **Hampton** + Middle English *court(e)* 'manor' (‹ Old French)] ‹ **Hampton**

**Hampton Court Park** ‹ **Hampton Court**

**Hanwell Common** ‹ **Hanwell:** 'cock well' [959 (*Hanewelle*): *hana* 'cock(erel)' + *well(a)* 'well, spring']

**Hanworth:** 'cock's ward' [1086 (*Haneworde*), 1254 (*Hanesworth*): *hana* 'cock(erel)' (perhaps used as a personal name) + *worð* 'ward, enclosure']

**Harefield** /formerly ˈhɑːvəl/: 'army field' [1086 (*Herefelle*), 1206 *Herefeld*), 1223 (*Harefeld*): *here* 'army' + *feld* 'field']

**Haringey:** 'Haering's enclosure' [1201 (*Haringeie*)] *see* **Hornsey**

**Harlington:** 'Hygered's folk's estate' [831 (*Hygereding tun*), 1362 (*Herlyngdon*), 1521 (*Harlyngton*), 1535 (*Hardington al. Harlington*): *Hygered* (name, with *d/l* confusion) + *-ing* '-follower of' + *tun* 'estate, home farm']

**Harmondsworth** /formerly ˈhɑːmzwəːθ/: 'Heremōd's ward' [1086 (*Hermodesworde*), 1408 (*Hermesworth*): *Heremōd* (name) + *worð* 'ward, enclosure']

**Harrow:** 'heathen shrine' [767 (*Gumeninga Hergae*), 825 (*Hearge*), 1234 (*Herewes*), 1347 (*Harwo*), 1369 (*Harowe*), 1398 (*Harowe atte Hille*): (*Gumeninga* 'Guma's folk('s)'+) *hearg* 'heathen sacred place or temple' (+ *hyll* 'hill')]

**Harrow on the Hill** [1426 (*Harrowe on the Hill*)] ‹ **Harrow**

**Hatton:** 'heath estate' [1086 (*Hatone, Haitone*): *hǣð* 'heath' + *tūn* 'estate, home farm'; near **Hounslow** Heath]

**Havering** /ˈheɪvərɪŋ/: 'Hæfer's folk' [1086 (*Haueringas*): *Hæfer* (name) + *-ingas* '-followers of, -people of']

**Haverstock** /ˌhævəstɒk/ **Hill** ‹ **Haverstock:** 'cattle (live)stock; Stock's cattle' [1627 (*Haverstocke*): ?*aver(ia)* 'cattle' (which may have grazed there) (‹ Late Latin) + *stocc* 'livestock' or *Stock* (name of local family originally from *Stock* in Essex)]

**Hayes:** 'brushwood' [1177 (*Hesa*), 1610 (*Heys*): ?*hæse* 'brushwood(-land)']

**Heathrow:** 'heath-side row' [c.1410 (*La Hetherewe*): *hǣð* 'heath' + *rǣw* 'row' (of trees or houses)]

**Hendon:** 'high hill' [959 (*Hendun*): *hēan* (‹ *hēah* 'high') + *dūn* 'hill']

**Heston** /nonstandardly ˈhɛsən/: 'brushwood farm' [1123-33 (*Heston(e)*): ?*hæse* 'brushwood(-land)'+ *tūn* 'home farm, estate']

**High Holborn:** 'high (part of the River) Holborn' ‹ **Holborn**

**Highbury:** 'high stronghold' [1274 (*Neweton Barrewe*), c. 1375 (*Heybury*), 1548 (*Newington Barowe al. the manor of Highbury*): *Neweton/Newington* (as in **Stoke Newington**) + *Barrewe/Barowe* (after the landholder Thomas de *Barewe*) + *hēah* 'high' + *burh* 'stronghold, fortified manor'; called *high* because higher than **Canonbury** or *Barnsbury*]

**Highgate:** 'high (toll-)gate' [1354 (*Le Heighgate*): *hēah* 'high' + *geat* 'gap; gate']

**Hillingdon:** 'Hilda's hill' [c.1080 (*Hildendune*), 1086 (*Hillendone*), 1274 (*Hylingdon*): *Hilden* (from name, probably short for *Hild*(rīc), *Hild*(wulf), etc.) + *dūn* 'hill']

**Hogsmill River:** 'Hogs' mill river' [1638] ‹ **Hogs Mill** [1535 (*Hoggs Myll*), 1564 (*Hoggesmyll*): after (the family of John) *Hog* (attested 1179 in **Merton**)]

**Holborn** /ˈhəʊbən/: 'valley stream' [959 (*Holeborne*): *holh* 'valley, hollow' + *burna* 'stream, brook'; former name of (the upper part of) the **River Fleet**]

**Holloway:** 'valley way' [1307 (*Le Holeweye...*), 1553 (*Holowaye...*): *holh* 'valley, hollow' + *weg* 'road, way']

**Homerton** /ˈhɒmətən/: 'Hūnburh('s) estate' [1343 (*Humburton*), 1581 (*Hummerton*): *Hūnburh* (woman's name ? ‹ *hūne* 'horehound' + *burh* 'stronghold') + *tūn* 'estate, home farm']

**Honey Lane** [c.1200 (*Hunilane*), 1274-75 (*Honylane*): Middle English *hony* (‹ *hunig* 'honey') + *lane* 'lane'; from bee-keeping here]

**Hook:** 'hook (of land)' [1227 (*Hoke*), 1680 (*Hook*): *hōc* 'hook, bend, spit' (of land, as by a river)]

**Hornsey:** 'Haering's enclosure' [1201 (*Haringeie*), 1243 (*Haringesheye*), 1524 (*Harnesey*), 1564 (*Hornsey*): *Haering* (name) + (ge)*hæg* 'enclosure'; **Haringey** and *Harringay* have the same origin]

**Hosier Lane** [1328 (*Hosiereslane*), 1338 (*Hosierlane*)]

**Houndsditch:** 'dog's ditch' [1502 (*Hundesdich*), 1550 (*Houndesdyche*): *hund* 'dog, hound' (probably not a personal name as in **Hounslow**) + *dīc* 'ditch; dyke'; after the City of London ditch *Houndsditch* (1275 *Hondesdich*), into which dead dogs and rubbish were discarded]

**Hounslow:** 'Hund's mound; Hund's barrow' (1217 (*Hundeslawe*), 1341 (*Houndeslowe*): *Hund* (name) + *hlaw* 'mound, mount; burial mound']

**Hoxton:** 'Hoc's estate' [1086 (*Hochestone*): *Hoc* (name) + *tūn* 'estate, home farm']

**Hubbard Lane** [1231 (*vicus Sancti Andreæ*), 1252-65 (*venella Sancti Andree Hubert*); by the church of *St. Andrew Hubbard*; now **Philpot Lane**] *see* **Philpot Lane**

**Hyde** (Middlesex, near Hendon): 'hide of land' [1281 (*la Hyde*): *hīd* 'enough land to support a family' (generally believed to have been 120 acres)]

**Hyde Park:** 'park at Hyde (in the manor of Ebury)' [1204 (*Hida*), 1543 (*Hide Park*): *hīd* (as in **Hyde**) + Middle English *park* 'park' (‹ Old French)] *compare* **Hyde**

# I

**Ickenham:** 'Ticca's village' [1086 (*Tichehā*), 1176 (*Tikeham*), 1203 (*Tikenham, Ikeham*), 1236 (*Ikenham*): *Ticcan* (from name, with loss of initial *T* through merger with final *t* of preceding *æt* 'at') + *hām* 'settlement, village']

**Ilford:** '(River) Hyle ford' [1086 (*Ilefort*), 1300 (*Hyleford*): *Hyle* '? trickling stream; ? still stream' (former name of the **River Roding**) + *ford* '(river-)ford'] *see also* **River Roding**

**Isle of Dogs** [1365 (*marsh of Stebenhithe*), 1593 (*Isle of doges ferm*), 1799 (*Poplar Marshes or Isle of Dogs*); of unknown origin, the present name is probably derogatory]

**Isleworth** /ˈaɪzᵊlwəːθ/: 'Gīslhere's ward' [695 (*Gislheresuuyrth*), 1231 (*Istleworth*): '*Gīslhere* (name) + *worð* 'ward, enclosure']

**Islington:** 'Gisla's hill' [c.1000 (*Gislandune*): *Gislan* (from name) + *dūn* 'hill']

**Ivy Lane** [13th C. (*Yvi lane*), 1280 (*Ivilane*); perhaps from *ivy* on nearby houses; previously *Alsies Lane*]

# J

**Jewry Street:** 'street where Jews live' [1366 (*la Porejewerie*); also *Jewry*; previously **Poor Jewry**]

# K

**Kennington:** 'Cæna's folk's estate' [1086 (*Chenintune*), 1263 (*Kenyngton*): *Cæn(a)* (name) + *-ing* '-follower of' + *tūn* 'estate, home farm']

**Kensal Green:** 'king's-wood green' [1253 (*Kingisholte*), 1367 (*Kyngesholt*), 1550 (*Kynsale Grene*): *cyning* 'king' + *holt* 'wood, holt; thicket' + *grēne* '(village) green']

**Kensington:** 'Cynesige's folk's estate' [1086 (*Chenist'*), 1235 (*Kensington*): *Cynes(ige)* (name) + *-ing* '-follower of' + *tūn* 'estate, home farm']

**Kensington Gardens** ‹ **Kensington Palace**

**Kensington High Street** ‹ **Kensington**

**Kensington Palace** ‹ **Kensington**

**Kentish Town:** 'Kentish estate; Le Kentiss(h)'s estate' [1208 (*Kentisston*), 1278 (*Le Kentesseton*), 1294 (*La Kentishton*), 1488 (*Kentisshtown*): *Kentish* (‹ *Kent* (place-name) or *Le Kentiss(h)* (name or nickname)) + *tūn* 'estate, home farm']

**Keston:** 'Cyssi('s) stone('s folk's boundary)' [862 (*Cystaninga mearc*), 1086 (*Chestan*), 1205 (*Kestan*): *Cyssi* (name) + *stān* 'stone' (+ *-inga* '-followers' of' + *mearc* 'boundary, boundary marker')]

**Kew:** 'quay on a neck of land' [1327 (*Cayho*): Middle English *kai* 'quay' (‹ Old French ‹ Celtic) + *hōh* 'neck/spur of land']

**Kew Gardens** ‹ **Kew**

**Kidbrook:** 'kite brook' [1202 (*Ketebroc*): *cēta* ‹ *cȳta* 'kite (bird)' + *brōc* 'brook']

**Kilburn:** 'royal stream; cows' stream; kiln stream' [c.1130 (*Cuneburna*), 1181 (*Keleburne*): *cyne-* 'royal' or *cȳna* 'cows' or *cyln* 'kiln' + *burna* 'stream, brook']

**King Edward Street** [1843: after *King Edward* (VI) (1537-53), who endowed Christ's Hospital school here; previously **Stinking Lane**] *see* **Stinking Lane**

**King William Street** [built 1829: after *King William* (IV) (1765-1837), who opened it]

**Kings Cross:** 'the King's cross-roads' [from a statue of *King* George IV at a cross-roads here from 1830 to 1845; formerly *Bradford (bridge), Battlebridge*]

**Kings End** [1550 (*Kings End*): owned then by *King's* College Cambridge, but perhaps already so called after the *King* family prominent locally since at least 1296]

**Kingsbury:** 'the King's stronghold' [1044 (*Kynges Byrig*): *cyning* 'king' + *burh* 'stronghold, fortified manor']

**Kingsland:** 'the King's land' [1395 (*Kyngeslond*)]

**Kingston:** 'the King's demesne' [838 (*Cyninges tun*): *cyning* 'king' + *tūn* 'estate, home farm']

**Kingston Hill** ‹ Kingston

**Kingston upon Thames** ‹ **Kingston, River Thames**

**Knightrider Street:** 'knight's street' [1322 (*Knyghtridestrete*): *cniht* 'youth; servant, soldier; knight' + *ridere* 'knight; rider' + *strǣt* '(paved) road, street' (‹ Latin); *knight* and *rider* overlapped in meaning for a time]

**Kyroun Lane:** 'Cynrūn('s) lane' [1259 (*Kyrunelane*), 1275 (*Kyroneslane*): ?*Cynrūn* (woman's name) + *lane* 'lane'; later *Maiden Lane*]

# L

**La Riole** [1331 (*la Ryole, la Riole*), 1455-56 (*le Royall*): *La Ryole* (name of house here ‹ *La Réole* wine-exporting town in Bordeaux); later *Royal Street* (*Royal* ‹ *Réole* by folk etymology); now *College Hill*]

**Ladle Lane** [c.1300 (*Ladelane*): Middle English *ladel* 'ladle' (‹ *hlædel*) + *lane* 'lane'; *ladles* may well have been made here]

**Laleham:** 'withe village; withe river-bend land' [1042-66 (*Læleham*): *lǣl* 'twig, withe' + *hām* 'settlement, village' or *hamm* 'river-bend land']

**Lambard's Hill:** 'Lambert's rise' [1283 (*Lamberdeshul, Lambardeshull*), 1645 (*Lambert-Hill*), 1659-60 (*Lambeth Hill*): *Lambert, Lamberd* (surname) + *hyll* 'hill'; hill in such London street names means 'steep street'; now *Lambeth Hill* (*Lambeth* ‹ *Lambert* by folk etymology)]

**Lambeth:** 'lambs' landing-place' [1088 (*Lamhytha*), 1312 (*Lambhehithe*): *lamb* 'lamb' + *hȳð* 'landing-place, harbour']

**Lambs Conduit Fields** ‹ **Lamb's Conduit** [?1577: (William) *Lamb(e)* (name of the conduit's builder) + Middle English *conduit* 'aqueduct' ( ‹ Anglo-French ‹ Old French ‹ Medieval Latin]

**Lampton:** 'lamb farm' [1376 (*Lampton feld*), 1438 (*Lamtonfeld*), 1611 (*Lambton*), 1633 (*Lampton*): *lamb* 'lamb' (with *b* as *p* before *t*) + *tūn* 'estate, home farm' (+ *feld* 'field')]

**Leadenhall Street:** 'street of the lead(-roofed) hall' [1605 (*Leaden Hall Street*): after *Leadenhall* (a large local house)]

**Lee:** 'lea/grove' [1086 (*Lee*): *lēah* 'grove; meadow, lea']

**Les(s)nes(s) Heath** ‹ **Les(s)nes(s):** 'pasture promontory' [1086 (*Lesneis*): *lǣs* 'pasture; meadow' + *nǣs* 'headland, promontory, cape'; from its projection into the **Erith** Marshes]

**Leveroune Lane:** 'Lēofrūn's lane' [1233 (*Le Vrunelane*), 1331 (*Lyveroneslane*), 1353 (*Leverounelane*), 1604 (*Lither lane al. Liver lane*), 1682 (*Leather Lane*):? *Lēofrūn* (woman's name) + *lane* 'lane'; now *Leather Lane*]

**Lewisham:** 'Liof's village' [862 (*Liofshema mearc*), c.1060 (*Liofesham*): *Liof* (name) + *hām* 'settlement, village' (+ *mearc* 'boundary, landmark')]

**Leyton:** '(River) Lea demesne' [c.1050 (*Lugetune*): **Lea** + *tūn* 'estate, home farm'] ‹ **River Lea**

**Leytonstone:** 'Leyton (at the) stone' [1370 (*Leyton atte Stone*), 1426 (*Leyton Stone*): **Leyton** + *stān* 'stone' (from the reputed site here of a Roman milestone)] *see* **Leyton**

**Lime Street:** 'street where (quick)lime was burnt and sold' [1170-87 (*Limstrate*): *līm* '(quick)lime' + *strǣt* '(paved)road, street' ‹ Latin)]

**Limehouse:** '(quick)lime-kilns' [1367 (*Le Lymhostes*), 1547 (*Lymehouse*): *līm* '(quick)lime' + *āst* 'oast, kiln']

**Lincoln's Inn Fields** ‹ **Lincolns Inn:** 'Lincoln's dwelling-place' [1399 (*Lincolnesynne*): *Lincoln* (name) + *inn* 'dwelling, lodging'; after Thomas de *Lincoln*, owner of related property elsewhere, and Henry de Lacy, Earl of *Lincoln* (died 1311), lawyers' patron]

**Little Britain** [1329 (*Brettonstrete*), 1547 (*Britten Strete*), c. 1600 (*little Brittain streete*): after (Robert le) *Bretoun*, local landowner (attested 1274) (+ Middle English *strete* ‹ *strǣt* '(paved) road, street' ‹ Latin)]

**Little Chelsea** [1655 (*Little Chelcy*)] ‹ **Chelsea**

**Liverpool Street** [after R.B. Jenkinson, 2nd Earl of *Liverpool*, Prime Minister 1812-27]

**Lombard Street** [1318 (*Lumbardstret*): *Lumbard* 'Lombard' + *strǣt* '(paved) road, street' (‹ Latin); after the *Lombards* (north Italians, often early bankers) there]

**London** [115 (*Londinium*), 150 (*Londinion*), c.380 (*Lundinium*), 962 (*Lundene*), 12th C. (*Lundres*), 1205 (*Lundin*); origin unknown]

**London Bridge** [10th C. (*Lundene brigc*): *Lundene* 'London' + *brycg* 'bridge'] ‹ **London**

**London Wall** [1547 (*London Walle*); after the former city *wall;* previously also called *Babeloyne* 'Babylon' (1385-86)] ‹**London**

**Long Ditton:** 'long ditch estate' [1086 (*Ditune*), 1233 (*Ditton*), 1242 (*Longa Dittone*): *lang* 'long' + *dīc* 'ditch; dyke' + *tūn* 'estate, home farm']

**Long Lane** [1530 (*Long Lane*)]

**Lothbury** /ˈləʊθbərɪ, -brɪ/: 'Lotha's manor' [1293 (*Lotheberi*): *Hloþa* (name) + *burh* 'stronghold, fortified manor']

**Loughton** /ˈlaʊtᵊn/:'Luh(h)a's folk's estate' [1062 (*Lukintone*), 1200 (*Lucheton'*), 1331 (*Lughton*), 1338 (*Loughton*): *Luh(ha)* (name) + *-ing* '-follower of' + *tūn* 'estate, home farm']

**Lower Clapton** ‹ **Clapton**

**Lower Norwood** ‹ **Norwood**

**Lower Sydenham** ‹ **Sydenham**

**Lower Tooting** ‹ **Tooting**

**Ludgate:** 'postern gate; low gate' [1164-79 (*Ludgate*): *ludgeat* 'back gate' or 'low gate' (?‹ *lud-* ‹ *lūtan* 'bow (head), lower' + *geat* 'gap; gate')]

# M

**Malden** /ˈmɔːldən/: 'cross hill' [1086 (*Meldon(e)*), 1225 (*Maldon*): *mǣl* 'sign; cross' + *dūn* 'hill']

**Mark Lane:** 'Martha's lane' [c.1200 (*Marthe-lane*), 1481 (*Markelane*): ?*Marthe* 'Martha' + *lane* 'lane'; formerly also *Mart Lane*]

**Marlborough** /ˌmɑːlbərə,-brə, îmɔːl-/ **House** [built 1709-11 by Wren for John Churchill (1650-1722), first Duke of *Marlborough*]

**Mart Lane** ‹ **Mark Lane**

**Marylebone** /ˈmærələbən, ˈmærlə-/: '(St.) Mary's stream; (St.) Mary('s) by the stream' [1453 (*Maryburne*): *Mary* (name) + French *le* 'the' (17th-C. insertion) + *burna* 'brook, stream'] *see also* **Tyburn Street**

**Mayes Brook** [after (Richard le) *May* (attested 1314) or his family]

**Merton:** 'pool(-side) estate' [967 (*Mertone*): *mere* 'pool' + *tūn* 'estate, home farm']

**Mile End:** 'mile's end' [1288 (*La Mile Ende*): *mīl* 'mile' (‹ Latin) + *ende* 'end, edge; district'; from its being a *mile* from **Aldgate**]

**Milk Street** [c.1140 (*Melecstrate*), 1153-67 (*Milkstrete*): *meoluc, milc* 'milk' + *strǣt* '(paved) road, street' (‹ Latin); from the selling of *milk*, and perhaps also the *milk*ing of cows, here]

**Mill Hill** [1547 (*Myllehill*): *myln* 'mill' (‹ Latin) + *hyll* 'hill']

**Minchen Lane** [1360 (*Mynchenelane*)] *see* **Mincing Lane**

**Mincing Lane:** 'nuns' lane' [12th C. (*M(e)ngenelane*): *mynecenu* 'nuns'' + *lane* 'lane'; formerly also **Minchen Lane**] *see also* **Minchen Lane**

**Mitcham:** 'big village' [1086 (*Michelham*), c.1150 (*Micham*): *micel* 'big, large, great' + *hām* 'settlement, village']

**Molesey:** 'Mūl's (high) ground' [675 (*Muleseg*), 967 (*Muleseye*): *Mūl* (name) + *ēg* 'high ground']

**Monument Street** [after its *Monument* (built 1671-7) commemorating the Great Fire of London (1666)]

**Moor Fields:** 'marsh fields' [*mōr* 'marsh, moor' + *feld* 'field; now *Moorfields*]

**Moorgate:** 'marsh gate' [*mōr* 'marsh, moor' + *geat* 'gap; gate']

**Morden:** 'marsh hill' [969 (*Mordune*), 1204 (*Moreden*): *mōr* 'marsh, moor' + *dūn* 'hill']

**Moselle** /məʊˈsɛl, -ˈzɛl (both according to the National Rivers Authority)/, **Moselle Brook** [previously *Campsborne* (1608)] ‹ **Muswell Hill**

**Mottingham:** 'Mod(da)'s folk's river-bend land' [973 (*Modinga hammes gemǣro*), 987 (*Modinga hæma mearc*), 1044 (*Modingeham*), 1206 (*Modingh'*): ?*Mod(da)* (name) + *-inge-, -inga-* '-followers' of' + *hamm* 'river-bend land']

**Mugwell Street:** 'Muc(c)a's well street' [c. 1200 (*Mukewellstrete*), 1279 (*Mogewelstrete*), 1544 (*Mugwellstrete*), c. 1600 (*Monkeswell Streete*): ?*Muc(c)a* (name) + *well(a)* 'well; spring' + *strǣt* '(paved) road, street' (‹ Latin); later called *Monkwell Street*, probably through folk etymology]

**Muswell** /îmʌzwəl; formerly îmʌzəl/ **Hill:** 'moss-spring hill' [c.1155 (*Mosewella*), 1535 (*Muswell*), 1631 (*Mussell Hill*): *mēos* 'moss' + *wella* 'well; spring' + *hyll* 'hill']

**Mutton Brook:** 'Mordin's brook' [1574 (*Mordins Brook*), 1819 (*Mutton Brook*): ?*Mordin* (name) + *brōc* 'brook']

# N

**Necklinger, Neckinger:** 'noose; bend' [from (the Devil's) *Neckercher* 'the Devil's neckerchief' (former slang name for 'hangman's noose') or from the stream's sinuosity]

**Needler Lane, Needler's Lane** [1400-01 (*Nedlerslane*), 1403 (*Nedelerslane*), c. 1600 (*Needlers lane, Needlars lane*): Middle English *nedlere* 'needler: needle-maker; needle-seller' + *lane* 'lane'; now *Pancras Lane*]

**New Bond Street** [1732 (*New Bond Street*): after Sir Thomas *Bond*, developer of land in the area]

**New Cross:** 'new cross-roads' [? from the junction of the Old Kent Road with a road leading to **Dartford** in Kent]

**New River** [1625 (*the Newe River*); engineered 1609-13]

**Newham** [London borough comprising west **Barking**, **West Ham**, *East Ham* and **Woolwich** north of the Thames]

**Newington** (Middlesex): 'new estate' [1086 (*Neutone*), 1255 (*Newinthon*); another name for **Stoke Newington**] *see* **Stoke Newington**

**Newington** (Surrey): 'new estate' [c. 1200 (*Neuton*), 1258 (*Newenton*): *nīwe* 'new' + *tūn* 'estate, home farm'; *-ing-* probably from the *-an* of Old English "æt þæm nīwan tūne" ('at the new estate')]

**Newington Green** [1480 (*Newyngtongrene*): **Newington** + *grēne* '(village) green'] ‹ **Newington** (Middlesex)

**North End** (Hampstead): 'the north end of Hampstead' [1741-45: *nor* 'north' + *ende* 'end, edge; district']

**Northolt** /ˈnɔːθəʊlt/: 'north corner' [960 (*(æt) norð healum*), 1086 (*Northala*), 1610 (*Northolt*): *norð* 'north' + *halh, healh* 'corner/nook of land'; contrasted with **Southall**]

**Northwood** [1435 (*Northwode*): *norð* 'north' + *wudu* 'wood'; north of **Ruislip**]

**Norwood:** 'north wood' [1176 (*Norwude*): *norð* 'north + *wudu* 'wood'; north of **Croydon**]

**Norwood Common** ‹ **Norwood**

# O

**Old Broad Street** [eastern part of the former **Broad Street**; contrasted with the later *New Broad Street*] ‹ **Broad Street**

**Old Change:** 'old trading-place' [1297-98 (*Chaunge*), 1316-17 (*Eldechaunge*), 1393 (*Oldechaunge*): *eald* 'old' + ?Middle English *chaunge* 'change; merchants' meeting place' (‹ Anglo-French ‹ Old French ‹ Latin ‹ Celtic); this *change* may have been the royal mint formerly here]

**Old Dean's Lane** [1257 (*Eldedeneslane*), 1513 (*Eldens lane* alias *Warwik lane*): *eald* 'old' + Middle English *deen* 'dean' (‹ Middle French ‹ Late Latin) + *lane* 'lane'; after a former *Dean* of St. Paul's; now **Warwick Lane**]

**Old Fish Street** [1230-40 (*Westfihistrate*), 1272-73 (*Fihstrate*), 1293-94 (*Old Fistrete*); probably from a *fish*-market there; now **Knightrider Street**] *see also* **Knightrider Street**

**Old Fish Street, Old Fish Street Hill** [c. 1600 *Old Fishstreete Hill*); *hill* in such London street-names means 'steep street']

**Old Ford:** 'old (river-)ford' [1230 (*Eldefordmelne*), 1313 (*Oldeforde*): *eald* 'old' + *ford* 'river-ford' (+ *meln, myln* 'mill' ‹ Latin)]

**Old Jewry:** 'former Jewish quarter' [1327-28 (*la Oldeiuwerie*), 1336 (*la Elde Jurie*): (French *la* 'the' +) *eald* 'old' + Middle English *giwerie, juerie* 'Jews' territory, Jews' district' (‹ Anglo-French ‹ Old French); formerly *Colechurch Lane*]

**Old Oak Common:** 'old-grove common' [1380 (*Eldeholt*), c.1415 (*Oldeholte*), 1650 (*Common called Old Oake*): *eald* 'old' + *oak* (by folk etymology ‹ *holt* 'holt, grove, copse') + English *common* 'common land' (‹ Latin *commūnia*)]

**Old Street:** 'old road' [c.1200 (*Ealdestrate*): *eald* 'old' + *strǣt* '(paved) road, street' (‹ Latin)]

**Orpington:** 'Orped's folk's estate' [1042 (*Orpedingtun*), 1086 (*Orpinton*), 1207 (*Orpington'*): *Orped* (name) + *-ing* '-follower of' + *tūn* 'estate, home farm']

**Osterley Park** ‹ **Osterley:** 'sheep-fold lea/grove' [1274 (*Osterle*): *eowestre* 'sheep-fold' (‹ *eowu* 'ewe') + *lēah* 'grove; meadow, lea']

**Oxford Street** [1720; previously called *Tyburn Road, Road to Worcester, Road to Oxford*, etc.]

**Oystergate** [1259 (*Oystregate*); a former water*gate* where *oyster*s may have been sold]

# P

**Paddington:** 'Pad(d)a's folk's estate' [c. 1045 (*Padington*): *Pad(da)* (name) + *-ing* '-follower of' + *tūn* 'estate, home farm']

**Pall Mall** /ˈpælˈmæl/: 'mall or alley used for playing pall-mall' [1650 (*Pall Mall Walk*): *pall-mall* 'alley for pall-mall, a game of getting a ball through a raised ring by hitting it with a mallet' (‹ Middle French ‹ Italian)]

**Pancras** ‹ **St. Pancras**

**Paternoster Row:** 'rosary-makers' row' [1307 (*Paternosterstrete*), 1320-21 (*Paternoster Lane*), 1344 (*Paternosterowe*), 1374 (*Paternostererowe*): *paternostrere* 'pater-nosterer, rosary-maker (‹ Latin) + *rǣw* 'row' (of trees or houses)]

**Peckham:** 'peak village' [1086 (*Pecheham*), 1241 (*Peckham*): ?*pēac* 'peak, hill' + *hām* 'settlement, village']

**Penge** /pɛn(d)ʒ/: 'head wood, chief wood' [1067 (*Penceat*), 1206 (*Penge*), 1472 (*Pengewode*): ?Celtic *pen* 'head, top; chief' (as in *Pen(zance)*) + ?Celtic *cēt* 'wood']

**Pentecost Lane** [1280 (*Pentecostelane*), 1290 (*Pentecostes lane*): Middle English *Pentecoste* (Christian festival or man's Christian name) (‹ *pentecosten* ‹ Late Latin ‹ Greek) + *lane* 'lane']

**Petersham Road** ‹ **Petersham:** 'Peohtric's river-bend land' [675 (*Piterichesham*): *Peotric* (name) + *hamm* 'river-bend land']

**Petty Wales:** 'little Wales' [1298-99 (*petit Walles*), 1349 (*Pety Wales*): French *petit* 'little' + *Wal(l)es* 'Wales'; perhaps from Welsh people resident here]

**Philpot Lane** [1480-81 (*Philpot Lane*): after Sir John *Philpot*, Lord Mayor 1378-79; formerly probably **Hubbard Lane**] *see* **Hubbard Lane**

**Piccadilly** [? after *Pickadilly* (Hall) (a 17th-C. tailor's house nearby) ‹ *piccadil* 'border with a cut-out pattern, ornamenting especially the edge of a collar or ruff' (‹ French ?‹ Spanish)]

**Pimlico** [1630 (*Pimplico*), c.1743 (*Pimlico*): ? after *Pimlico* (Walk) in **Hoxton**, named after Ben *Pimlico*, 16th-C. innkeeper there]

**Pinkwell** [1754 (*Pinkwell*)]

**Pinner:** 'pin(-shaped) (river-)bank; Pinn(a's) river-bank' [1232 (*Pinnora*), 1332 (*Pinnere*): *pinn* 'pin, peg' or *Pinn* (name) + *ōra* 'bank, edge; slope' (‹ Latin)]

**Pinner Green** ‹ **Pinner**

**Plaistow** /'plɑ:stəʊ, 'plæst-/: 'playing/sporting ground' [1278 (*Pleystowe*): *pleg* 'play' + *stōw* 'place']

**Plaistow Levels:** '? Plaistow level ground' ‹ **Plaistow**

**Plumstead:** 'plum(-tree) place' [c.965 (*Plumstede*): *plume* 'plum; plum-tree' + *stede* 'place, stead']

**Ponders End** [1593 (*Ponders ende*): *Ponder* (surname of local family) + *ende* 'end, edge; district'; on the **Enfield/Edmonton** border]

**Pool River** ‹ **Pool:** 'Pool of London' [1258 (*La Pole*): *pōl* 'pool']

**Poor Jewry** [1366 (*la Porejewerie*)] *see* **Jewry Street**

**Poplar:** 'poplar(-tree)' [1327 (*Popler*): Middle English *poplere* 'poplar' (‹ Middle French)]

**Potter's Bar:** 'Potter's Gate (to Enfield Chase)' [1509 (*Potterys Barre*), 1548 (*Potters Barre*): (*le*) *Pottere* (attested surname) + Middle English *barre* 'rod, bar; gate, barrier' (‹ Old French)]

**Poultry:** 'poultry-market' [1301 (*Poletria*), 1422 (*Pulterye*): Middle English *pultrie* 'poultry; poultry-market' (‹ Old French)]

**Primrose Hill** [1586 (*Prymrose Hill*); allegedly from the former profusion of *primrose(s)* there]

**Pudding Lane** (near Billingsgate): 'guts lane' [1360 (*Puddynglane*): Middle English *pudding* 'guts, entrails' + *lane* 'lane'; perhaps whence "the Butchers of Eastcheape" got rid of such parts of their animals]

**Purley:** 'pear-tree lea/grove' [1200 (*Pirlee*), 1220 (*Purle*): *pirige* 'pear-tree' (‹ *peru, pere* 'pear' ‹ Latin) + *lēah* 'grove; meadow, lea']

**Putney:** 'Put(t)a's landing' [1086 (*Putelei*), 1279 (*Puttenhuthe*): *Putten* (from name) + *hȳð* 'landing-place, harbour']

**Putney Heath** ‹ **Putney**

**Pyl Brook** ‹ **Pylford Bridge** [1548 (*Pillefordebrudge*)]

**Pymme's Brook** [after the family of Reginald *Pymme* of Edelmetone (**Edmonton**), attested locally since the 14th C.; formerly *Medeseye* (c. 1200)]

# Q

**Quaggy River:** 'quagmire river; boggy river' [from its sluggish flow]

**Queen Street** [after Catherine of Braganza (1638-1705), *Queen* as wife of King Charles II; includes the former **Soper Lane**] *see* **Soper Lane**

**Queen Victoria Street** [opened 1871]

**Queenhithe:** 'Queen('s) dock' [898 (*Æðeredes hyd*): *Æðered* '?Ethelred, Alderman of Mercia' + *hȳð* 'landing-place, harbour'; now *Queenhithe Dock* perhaps because formerly owned by Isabella of Angoulême]

# R

**Radlett:** 'cross-roads' [1453 (*Radelett*): *?rād-(ge)lǣt(e)* 'road-junction' (‹ *rād* 'riding; road' + *(ge)lǣt(e)* 'junction of roads, cross-roads')]

**Rainham** (Essex): 'top-people's settlement' [1086 (*Renaham, Raineham*): *?roeginga-ham* (as attested for *Rainham* in Kent) ‹ *roegingas* 'dominant folk' + *hām* 'settlement, village']

**Red Cross Street** [1275 (*Redecrochestrete*), 1341 (*Redecrouchestrete*), 1502 (*Redcrosse strete*): *rēad* 'red' + Middle English *crouche* 'cross' (‹ Latin) or *cros* 'cross' (‹ Old Irish ‹ Latin) + *strǣt* '(paved) road, street' (‹ Latin); perhaps after a local house or a boundary *cross*]

**Redbridge** [after a *red bridge* across the **River Roding** between **Wanstead** and **Ilford**]

**Regent's Park** [1817 (*The Regents Park*): after the Prince *Regent*, later George IV]

**Richmond** [1502 (*Richemont*): after Henry VII, Earl of *Richmond* in Yorkshire; formerly (*West*) *Sheen*]

**Richmond Park** ‹ **Richmond**

**Richmond upon Thames** ‹ **Richmond, River Thames**

**River Brent** ‹ **Brent**

**River Ching** [1562 (*the Boorne*), 1585 (*the Brook*): *burna* 'stream, brook'; *Ching* is a later back-formation from **Chingford**] *see* **Chingford**

**River Colne** ‹ **Colne** /kəʊn/: 'water stream' [1301 (*Collee*), 1351 (*Colne*): ? Celtic *colūn* 'water' + *ēa* 'stream'; found elsewhere too as a river-name]

**River Crane** [1825 (*Cran Brook*); formerly *Fishbourne*] ‹ **Cranford**

**River Effra** ‹ **Effra:** 'river-bank' [? *efre* 'bank' (of river); cognate with German *Ufer* 'bank, shore']

**River Fleet** ‹ **Fleet:** 'stream' [c. 1012 (*Fleta*): *fleot* 'inlet, stream']

**River Gade** ‹ **Gade:** 'Gǣte's stream' [1242 (*Gatesee*), 1349-96 (*Gateseye*), 1728 (*river Gade*): *?Gǣtesēa* 'Gǣte's stream' (‹ *Gǣte* (name or nickname ‹ *gat* 'goat') + *ēa* 'stream')]

**River Graveney:** 'river by Tooting Graveney' [1272 (*Thoting Gravenel*): after (Richard de) *Gravenel*, lord of the manor of Lower/South **Tooting** in 1215 (whose family were perhaps from *Graveney* in Kent)]

**River Lea** **Lea:** 'bright' [895 (*Lygan*); perhaps related to *lēah* 'lea, meadow as light-filled place' (‹ Indo-European base ? *leuk, louk* 'light, brightness')]

**River Mole** [1214 (*aqua de Mulesia*), 1595 (*Moulsey River*)] ‹ **Molesey**

**River Pinn** [from **Pinner**] *see* **Pinner**

**River Ravensbourne** ‹ **Ravensbourne:** 'raven's stream' [1575 (*Ravensburn*): *hrǣfn* 'raven' + *burna* 'stream, brook']

**River Roding** [1576 (*Rodon*), 1622 (*Roding*); formerly *Hyle*] ‹ **Roding** (Essex): 'Rod(da)'s folk' [c. 1050 (*Rodinges*): *Rod(da)* (name) + *-ingas, -inges* '-followers of']

**River Thames** ‹ **Thames** /'tɛmz/: 'dark water' [?‹ Celtic base cognate with Sanskrit *tamasa-* 'dark']

**River Wandle** [from the *Wa(e)nd(e)l* of **Wandsworth**] *see* **Wandsworth**

**River Wey** ‹ **Wey:** 'flowing' [675 (*Waie*): ?‹ Indo-European *wegh* -(referring to motion, as in *wǣg* 'wave')]

**Romford:** 'ample ford' [1177 (*Romfort*), 1199 (*Rumford*): *rūm* 'roomy, spacious' + *ford* '(river-)ford']

**Roper Lane:** 'rope-maker's lane; Roper's lane' [1313 (*Roperesiane*): Middle English *roper* 'rope-maker' or *Roper(e)* (attested local surname) + *lane* 'lane'; now *Love Lane*]

**The Ropery, Roper Street** [1271 (*Roperestrete*), 1307 (*la Roperie*); after the *rope*-makers there; now **Thames Street**]

**Rotherhithe:** 'cattle landing-place' [c. 1105 (*Rederheia*), 1301 (*Rotherhethe*): *hrīðer* 'horned beast, ox; cattle' + *hȳð* 'landing-place, harbour']

**Royal Botanic Gardens** *see* **Kew Gardens**

**Ruislip** /'raɪslɪp/: 'rush(y) leap' [1086 (*Rislepe*), 1341 (*Ruysshlep*): *rysc* 'rush(-plant)' + *?hlype* 'leap'; ? from a nearby crossing place of the **River Pinn**]

# S

**St. Botolph's Lane** [1348-49 (*Seyntbotulfeslane*), 1432 (*Botulpheslane*), 1544 (*Botulphe Lane*); after the church of *St. Botulph Billingsgate*; now *Botolph Lane*]

**St. Bride Street** [? after *St. Bride*'s churchyard nearby]

**St. Clement's Lane** [1348 (*Seint Clementeslane*); by the church of *St. Clement Eastcheap*; now *Clement's Lane*]

**St. Dunstans Lane** [1329 (*Donstoneslane*), 1363 (*Seint Dunstoneslone*); by the church of *St. Dunstan in the East*; now *St. Dunstan's Hill*]

**St. James** ‹ **St. James's Palace**

**St. James's Palace** [built on the site of a leprosy hospital dedicated to *St.James* the Less]

**St. James's Park** ‹ **St. James's Palace**

**St. Katharine's Dock** [1422 (*Katerines Dokke*): *St. Katherine's* (from the name of a former local hospital founded 1148) + Middle English *dok* 'dock; wharf' (? ‹ Middle Dutch ‹ Latin)]

**St. Laurence Lane** [1320 (*Seint Laurencelane*), c. 1600 (*Poultney lane*); after the church of *St. Laurence Pountney*; now *Laurence Pountney Lane*]

**St. Margaret Patten's Lane** [1577 (*Rood Lane*): Middle English *rood* 'cross' (‹ *rōd*) + *lane* 'lane'; from a *rood* put before 1538 in the churchyard of *St. Margaret Pattens*, from which church comes the previous name of this lane now called *Rood Lane*]

**St. Mary Axe:** 'St. Mary at/of the Axe' [1275 (*strata Sancte Marie atte Ax*); after the church of *St. Mary Axe* (demolished 1561), housing the *axe* with which St. Ursula was said to have been martyred]

**St. Mary (Axe) Street** [now **St. Mary Axe**] *see* **St. Mary Axe**

**St. Mary Cray:** 'St. Mary('s church by the River) Cray' [1257 (*Creye Sancte Marie*)] *see* **Crayford**

**St. Mary at Hill Lane** [1275 (*venella Sancte Marie de la Hulle*), 1520-21 (*seint mary hill lane*); after the church of *St. Mary at Hill*]

**St. Marylebone** ‹ **Marylebone**

**St. Martin Orgar Lane** [1236-37 (*venella Sancti Martini*), c.1600 (*Saint Martins Orgar Lane*); after the church of *St. Martin Orgar*; now *Martin Lane*]

**St. Martin's Le Grand:** 'St. Martin the Great's' [1265 (*St. Martin le Grand*); after the former local church of *St. Martin le Grand*]

**St. Michael's Lane** [1303 (*Seint Micheleslane*); by the church of *St. Michael Crooked Lane*; later *Miles's Lane* (*Miles* ‹ *Michael*)]

**St. Nicholas Lane** [1381 (*Seint Nicholaslane*); by the church of *St Nicholas Acon*; now *Nicholas Lane*]

**St. Pancras** [1086 (*Sanctum Pancratiū*), 1588 (*Pankeridge al. St Pancras*); after *St. Pancras*, martyred under Diocletian (Roman emperor 284-305)]

**St. Paul's Cathedral** [built 1675-1710; replacing old *St. Paul's* (burnt 1666)]

**St. Paul's Churchyard** [after **St. Paul's Cathedral** or old *St. Paul's*]

**St. Peter's Hill** [1263 (*Venella sancti Petri*), 1378 (*Seint Petrelane*), 1564 (*Peter Lane*) c. 1600 (*Saint Peters Hill, Peter hill lane*); *hill* in such London street-names means 'steep street'; by the church of *St. Peter (the Little) Paul's Wharf*; formerly *Peter Lane*]

**Salmon's Brook** [1754: after (the family of John) *Salmon* (attested 1274 at **Edmonton**)]

**Sanderstead** /'sɑ:ndəstɛd/: 'sandy place' [c. 880 (*Sandenstede*), 1086 (*Sandestede*), 1221 (*Sanderstede*): *?sanden* 'sandy' + *stede* 'place, stead']

**Seacoal Lane**: 'coal lane' [1253 (*sacolelane*), c. 1600 (*Seacole lane*): *sǣcol* 'coal, not charcoal' (delivered by *sea* or mined by the *sea*) + *lane* 'lane'; *coal* may have been delivered here from the **River Fleet**]

**Sewardstone:** 'Sigeweard's estate' [1176-90 (*Siwardeston'*): *Sigeweard* (name) + *tūn* 'estate, home farm']

**Shambles, Butchery:** 'meat-market; slaughterhouse' [1349 (*Bocherie*), 1425-26 (*Shameles*), 1530 (*le Fleshambles*): (*flǣsc* 'flesh, meat'+) Middle English *shambles* 'meat-market; slaughterhouse' (‹ Middle English *shamble* 'meat-seller's table' ‹ *sceamel* 'stool' ‹ Late Latin) or Middle English *butchery* 'slaughterhouse' (‹ Old French); now *Newgate Street*]

**Shepherds Bush** [1635 (*Sheppards Bush Green*), 1675 (*Shepperds Bush*)]

**Shepperton:** 'shepherd farm' [959 (*Scepertune*): *?sceaphir(de), sceaphier(de)* 'shepherd' + *tūn* 'estate, home farm']

**Shepperton Green** [1754] ‹ **Shepperton**

**Shitbourn Lane**: 'shithouse lane' [1272-73 (*Shitteboruelane*), 1321 (*Shiteburghlane*), 1313 (*Shitebournelane*), 1467 (*Shirbouruelane* alias *Shetbouruelane*), 1540 (*Shirborne lane*), c. 1600 (*Sherborne lane*): Middle English *Shitebourne* 'shit stream' (by scribal error ‹ Middle English ? *shiteburgh* 'shithouse, privy' ‹ *scite* 'shit' + *burh, burg* 'stronghold, fortified manor') + *lane* 'lane'; now *Sherborne Lane* (by euphemism)]

**Shoe Lane:** 'shoe(-shaped) land; shelter-land' [1187-1216 (*Solande*), 1272 (*Sholand*), 1279 (*Sholane*): *scōh* 'shoe' or *?scēo* 'shelter' + *land 'land'*]

**Shooters Hill:** 'archer's slope' [1292 (*Shetereshelde*): Middle English *sheter* 'shooter, archer' (‹ ? *scēotere*) + *helde* 'slope']

**Shoreditch:** 'slope-ditch' [c. 1148 (*Soredich*): ? *scora* 'shore, bank; slope' + *dīc* 'ditch, trench; dyke'; the name's referent is obscure]

**Sidcup:** 'flat-top; camp-site top' [1254 (*Cetecopp'*), 1332 (*Sedecoppe*): *?set* 'seat-shaped, flattened; camp' + *copp* 'hill-top']

**Silk Stream:** 'gully stream' [957 (*Sulh, Sulue, Sulc*), 13th C. (*Solke, Selke*): *?sulh* 'plough; ?furrow' ( ? with *h* changed to *c* or *k* before *stream*)]

**Sipson:** 'Sibwine's estate' [13th C. (*Sibwineston*), 1391 (*Sibston*), 1638 (*Sipson*): *Sibwine* (name) + *tūn* 'estate, home farm']

**Smallbury:** 'narrow mound' [1436 (*Smalborow*), 1680 (*Smallbury Green*): *smæl* 'thin, narrow; small' + *beorg* 'hill, mound; barrow']

**Smithfield:** 'level field' [*smēðe* 'smooth, level' + *feld* 'field']

**Soper Lane, Soper's Lane:** 'soaper's lane' [c. 1246 (*Soperesiane*), 1282 (*Soperlane*), 1600 (*Sopers lane*): Middle English *sopere* 'soaper: soap-maker; soap-seller' (‹ *sāpe* + *-ere*) + *lane* 'lane'; now part of **Queen Street**] *see* **Queen Street**

**South Mimms** [1086 (*Mimes*), 1211 (*Mimmes*), 1253 (*Suthmimes*): "*South* in contrast to North Mimms in Hertfordshire....The name must remain an unsolved problem." – *The Place-Names of Middlesex*, p.76]

**Southend** [*sūð* 'south' + *ende* 'end, edge; district']

**Southgate** [1370 (*Suthgate, Southgate*): *sūð* 'south' + *geat* 'gap; gate'; by the *south gate* to **Enfield** Chase]

**Southall:** /'saʊθɔ:l/: 'south corner' [1198 (*Suhaut*), 1204 (*Sudhale*), 1261 (*Suthall(e)*): *suð* 'south' + *halh* 'corner/nook of land'; contrasted with **Northolt**]

**Southwark** /'sʌðək/: 'south fortress' [1086 (*Sudwearca*): *sūð* 'south' + (ge)*weorc* 'construction, fortification']

**Spittlefields:** 'hospital fields' [1561 (*Spyttlefeildes*): Middle English *spitel* 'hospital' (here, of St. Mary *Spital*, ‹ Medieval Latin) + *feld* 'field'; now *Spitalfields*]

**Staines:** 'stone(s)' [969 (*Stána*), 1086 (*Stanes*): *stān(as)* 'stone(s)'; probably after a nearby Roman milestone]

**Stamford Brook:** 'stony ford brook' [1650 (*Stamford Brooke*) ‹ **Stamford:** 'stony ford' [1274 (*Staunford*): Middle English *stoon, ston, stan* ‹ *stān* 'stone' + *ford* '(river-)ford']

**Stamford Hill:** 'sand-ford hill' [1225 (*Sanford*), 1294 (*Saundfordhull*), 1675 (*Stamford Hill*)]

**Stanmore** [793 (*Stanmere*)] *see* **Great Stanmore**

**Stanwell:** 'stony spring' [1086 (*Stanwelle*): *stān* 'stone' + *well(a) 'well; spring'*]

**Stepney:** 'Stybba's landing' [c. 1000 (*Stybbanhyþe*), 1542 (*Stebenheth al. Stepney*): *Stybban* (from name) + *hȳð* 'landing-place, harbour']

**Stinking Lane** [1228 (*Styngkynglane*); presumably from the *stink* of the nearby **Shambles**; now **King Edward Street**] *see* **King Edward Street**

**Stockwell:** 'tree-stump well' [1197 (*Stokewell*): *stocc* 'tree-trunk, stump, log' + *well(a)* 'well; spring]

**Stoke Newington:** 'log new estate' [1086 (*Neutone*), 1255 (*Newinthon*), 1274 (*Neweton Stoken, Stokeneweton*): *stocc* 'tree-trunk, stump, log' + *nīwe* 'new' + *-ing-* (perhaps as in **Newington** in Surrey) + *tūn* 'estate, home farm'] *see* **Newington** (Surrey)

**The Strand:** 'the bank (of the Thames)' [1185 (*Stronde*): *strand* 'shore, bank'; the Thames used to be wider]

**Stratford:** '(Roman-)road ford' [1066 (*Stratforde*): *strǣt* '(paved)road, street' (‹ Latin) + *ford* '(river-)ford'; where the old London-Colchester road crossed the **River Lea**]

**Stratford-le-Bow:** '(Roman-)road ford (at) the arched bridge' [1177 (*Stratford*), 1279 (*Stratford atte Bowe*), c. 1560 (*Stratford le Bow(e)*): *strǣt* '(paved) road, street' (‹ Latin) + *ford* '(river-) ford' (across the **River Lea**) + French *le* 'the' + *boga* '(archery) bow; arch, arched bridge'; now *Bow*]

**Streatham** /ˈstrɛtəm/: '(Roman-)road village' [1086 (*Estreham*), 1175 (*Stratham*): *strǣt* '(paved) road, street' (‹ Latin) + *hām* 'settlement, village']

**Sudbury:** 'south stronghold' [1292 (*Suthbery*): *sūð* 'south' + *burh* 'stronghold, fortified manor']

**Sunbury:** 'Sunna's stronghold' [959 (*Sunnabyri*): *Sunn(a)* (name) + *burh* 'stronghold, fortified manor']

**Surbiton:** 'south grain-farm, south grange' [1179 (*Suberton*): *sū(ð)* 'south' + *bertūn* 'grain-farm; lord's grange' (‹ *bere* 'barley' + *tūn* 'estate, home farm')]

**Sutton:** 'south estate' [1181 (*Suthtona*): *sūð* 'south' + *tūn* 'estate, home farm']

**Swithin Lane** [1269-70 (*vicus Sancti Swithuni*), 1410-11 (*Seint Swithoneslane*), 1532 (*St. Swithens Lane*); after the church of *St. Swithin* in **Cannon Street**; now *St. Swithin's Lane*]

**Sydenham** /ˈsɪdᵊnəm/: 'Chippa's village' [1206 (*Chipenham*), 1315 (*Shippenham*), 1690 (*Sidenham*): *Syden* (from name ‹ *Shippen* ‹ *Chipen*) + *hām* 'settlement, village'; similar to *Chippenham* (Camb, Wilts), *Cippenham* (Bucks)]

**Syvethe Lane, Syvthe Lane:** 'chaff lane' [1258-59 (*Syvidlane*), 1322 (*Syvthelane*), 1533 (*Sedyng Lane*): *sifeða* 'siftings, chaff' + *lane* 'lane'; perhaps from threshing done nearby; now *Seething Lane*]

# T

**Teddington:** 'Tuda's folk's estate' [969 (*Tudinton*), 1274 (*Tedinton*): *Tud(a)* (name) + *-ing* '-follower of' + *tūn* 'estate, home farm']

**Thames Ditton:** 'Thames ditch estate' [1005 (*Dictun*), 1235 (*Temes Ditton*): (**River**) **Thames** + *dīc* 'ditch; dyke' + *tūn* 'estate, home farm']

**Thames Street** [1222 (*vicus super Ripam Tamis*), 13th C. (*la rue de Thamise*), 1275 (*Tamisestrete*), 1308 (*Temestret*)] ‹ **River Thames**

**Threadneedle Street:** 'three-needle street; street where *threadneedle* is played' [1598 (*Three needle street*), 1616 (*Thred-needle-street*); ? from a local signboard or coat of arms displaying *three needles*, or from the children's game *threadneedle*]

**Tilbury:** 'Til(la's) stronghold' [c. 735 (*Tilaburg*), 1066-87 (*Tillabyri*), 1218 (*Tylleber, Tyllebery*): *Til(la)* (name) + *burh* 'stronghold, fortified manor']

**Tooting:** 'Tota's folk' [675 (*Totinge*): *Tot-* (from name) + *-ing* '-follower of']

**Tooting Common** ‹ **Tooting**

**Tottenham:** 'Tota's village' [1086 (*Toteham*), 1189 (*Totenham*), 1254 (*Tottenham*): *Tote(n)* (from name) + *hām* 'settlement, village']

**Tottenham Court:** 'Totta's-corner manor' [c. 1000 (*þottanheale*), 1083 (*Totenhala*), 1487 (*Totenhalecourt*), 1593 (*Totten Court*), 1741-45 (*Tottenham Court*): *Totten* (from name) + *halh, healh* 'corner/nook of land' (to *ham* influenced by **Tottenham**) + Middle English *court* 'manor' (‹ Old French)] *compare* **Tottenham**

**Tottenham Court Road** [1708 (*Tottenham Court Row*)] ‹ **Tottenham Court**

**Tower Hamlets:** 'hamlets near the Tower (of London)'

**Tower Hill** [after the adjacent *Tower* of London]

**Turnagain Lane:** 'blind alley' [1415 (*Turneageyne lane*): Middle English *turne-agayne lane* 'blind alley, cul-de-sac'; formerly *Wendageyneslane* (from 1293)]

**Turnbaston Lane** [1328 (*Tornebastonlane, Tornebastones-lane*), 1436 (*Turnebastlane*), 1568 (*Turnebaslane, Turnesbas-lane*): Middle English ?*turnebaston* '?tollgate' (‹ Middle French) + *lane* 'lane'; now part of **Cannon Street**]

**Turnham Green:** 'round-village green; river-bend-land green' [c. 1235 (*Turneham*), 1396 (*Turnhamgrene*): ?*trun, turn* 'circular, round' + *hām* 'settlement, village' or *hamm* 'river-bend land' + *grēne* '(village-) green'; near a big bend in the Thames]

**Twickenham** /formerly ˈtwɪtnəm/: 'Tuic(c)a's river-bend land' [704 (*Tuican hom, Tuiccanham*): *Tuic(c)an* (from name) + *hamm* 'river-bend land']

**Twickenham Common** ‹ **Twickenham**

**Tyburn Street** ‹ **Tyburn** /ˈtaɪbən/: 'boundary brook' [959 (*Teobernan*), 1222 (*Tyburn'*): ?*tēo* 'boundary' + *burna* 'stream, brook'; formerly marking the boundary of **Westminster** Abbey lands; sometimes also called *Marybourn*] *see also* **Marylebone**

# U

**Upminster:** '(high-)up monastery' [1062 (*Upmynstre*): *upp* 'up' + *mynster* 'monastery, church']

**Upper Clapton** ‹ **Clapton**

**Upper Norwood** ‹ **Norwood**

**Upper Sydenham** ‹ **Sydenham**

**Upper Tooting** ‹ **Tooting**

**Uxbridge:** 'the Wixans' bridge' [c. 1145 (*Oxebruge, Wixebrug'*): *Wixan* (from tribal name) + *brycg* 'bridge' (over the **River Colne**)]

# V

**Vedast Lane** *see* **Foster Lane**

**Victoria** [after Queen *Victoria* (1819-1901), reigned 1837-1901]

# W

**Walbrook:** '(Celtic) Britons' brook' [1104 (*Walebroch*): *wal(h)* '(Celtic) stranger' + *brōc* 'brook']

**Walham** /ˈwɔːlhəm/ **Green:** 'de Wenden's Green' [1386 (*Wendenegrene*), 1615 (*Wandon's Green*), 1710 (*Wallam Green*), 1819 (*Walham Green*): *de Wenden(e), de Wanden(e)* (name of local family, perhaps originally from *Wendens* in Essex) + *grēne* '(village) green']

**Waltham Abbey** ‹ **Waltham** /ˈwɔːlθəm; formerly ˈwɔːltəm/: 'wood-land village; wood-land river-bend land' [1062 (*Waltham*): *wald, weald* 'wood-land, forest' + *hām* 'settlement, village' or *hamm* 'river-bend land']

**Waltham Cross** [**Waltham** + *cros* 'cross' (‹ Old Irish ‹ Latin); from the (Eleanor) *Cross* put here in 1291 by Edward I to mark the penultimate stage in the funeral procession of Eleanor of Castile] *see* **Waltham Abbey**; *compare* **Charing Cross**

**Waltham Forest** [London borough comprising **Walthamstow, Chingford** and **Leyton**]

**Walthamstow** /ˈwɔːlθəmstəʊ; formerly ˈwɔː(l)təmstəʊ/ 'welcome place; Celts' place' [c. 1076 (*Wilcumestowe*), 1446 (*Walthamstowe*): *wilcume* 'welcome' or *walh* '(Celtic) stranger' + *stōw* 'place']

**Walthamstow Mead:** 'Walthamstow meadow' [**Walthamstow** + *mǣd* 'meadow'] ‹ **Walthamstow**

**Walworth** /ˈwɔːlwəθ/: 'Celts' ward' [1006 (*Wealawyrð*), 1086 (*Waleorde*), 1196 (*Wallewurd*), 1354 (*Walworth*): *wealh, walh* '(Celtic) stranger' + *worð* 'ward, enclosure']

**Wandsworth:** 'Wændel's ward' [c. 1000 (*Wendleswurðe*): *Wænd(e)l* (name) + *worð* 'ward, enclosure']

**Wanstead:** '(wen-like) mound site' [c.1050 (*Wænstede*): *wænn* 'wen' + *stede* 'place, stead']

**Wapping Dock** ‹ **Wapping:** 'Wæppa's folk' [c.1220 (*Wapping'*), 1231 (*Wappinges*): *Wæpp(a)* (name) + *-ingas* '-followers of']

**Warwick** /ˌwɒrɪk/ **Lane** [1474-75 (*Werwyk Lane*); after the Earls of *Warwick*, who held property locally; formerly **Old Dean's Lane**]

**Waterloo** [after *Waterloo* in Belgium, site of the famous defeat of Napoleon in 1815]

**Watford:** 'hunters' ford' [944-46 (*Watford*), c. 1180 (*Wathford, Wathforda*): *wað* 'chase, hunting' + *ford* '(river-) ford']

**Watling Street:** 'prince's street' [c. 1213 (*Aphelingestrate*), 1289 (*Athelingstrate*), 1307 (*Watlingstrate*): *æðeling* 'prince; nobleman' (becoming *Watling* perhaps by folk etymology through similarity of sound to the Roman road *Watling* Street) + *strǣt* '(paved) road, street' (‹ Latin)]

**Wealdstone Brook** [1453 (*le Weldebroke*), 1548 (*Weyldbrooke*); also *Kenton Brook*; formerly *Lyddying (Water)*] ‹ **Wealdstone:** 'woodland (boundary-)stone' ‹ **Harrow Weald:** 'Harrow woodland' [1282 (*Weldewode*), 1388 (*Harewewelde*), 1603 (*Harrow weale*): **Harrow** + *weald* 'woodland, forest'] *see* **Harrow**

**Weir** /ˈwɪə/ **Hall** [1086 (*Winehel(l)e*), 1198 (*Wylehale*), 1207-8 (*Wirhale, Wilehal'*), 1593 (*Wirehall, Wyerhall*): *Wylehale, Wyrhale* (attested surname)]

**Welling** [1362 (*Wellyngs*): *Welling* (surname of 14th-C. local landowners)]

**Wembley:** 'Wemba's lea/grove' [825 (*Wemba Lea*): *Wemba* (name) + *lēah* 'grove; meadow, lea']

**West Bedfont** [1086 (*Westbedefund*)] ‹ **Bedfont**

**West Cheap:** 'west market' [1304 (*Chepe*), 1249 (*Westchepe*): *west* 'west' (by contrast with **Eastcheap**) + *cēap* 'market; trade'; also *Cheap*; now **Cheapside**] *see* **Cheapside, Eastcheap**

**West Drayton:** 'west portage farm' [939 (*Drægton*), 1086 (*Draitone*), 1465 (*Westdrayton*): *west* 'west' (added perhaps to contrast with Ealing's *Drayton* (Green) + *dræg* 'drag; portage, slipway' (perhaps in reference to the adjacent **River Colne**) + *tūn* 'estate, home farm']

**West End** (Middlesex, near Northolt) [1274 (*(atte) Westende*), 1660 (*West End*)]

**West End** (Middlesex, near Pinner) [1448 (*le Westhend*)]

**West Ham:** 'west river-bend land' [958 (*Hamme*), 1186 (*Westhamma*): *west* 'west' + *hamm* 'river-bend land']

**West Molesey** [1200 (*Westmoleseie*)] ‹ **Molesey**

**West Smithfield** [*west* 'west' + **Smithfield**] ‹ **Smithfield**

**West Thurrock** [1219 (*West Turroc*, etc.): *west* 'west' + **Thurrock**] ‹ **Thurrock**: 'bilge; muck-heap' [1086 (*Turoc*): *þurruc* 'bilge; ship's bottom; muck-heap']

**West Wickham:** 'west farm village; west Romano-British-site village' [973 (*Wichamm*), 1086 (*Wicheham*), 1284 (*Westwycham*): *west* 'west' + *wīc-hām* 'farm village; village on Romano-British site']

**West Wood Common** [c. 1350 (*Westwode*)]

**Westbourne** [formerly *Knightsbridge Brook, Bayswater Rivulet*; flows into the Serpentine in Hyde Park] ‹ **Westbourne Green:** 'west-stream green; green west of the stream' [1222 (*Westeburne*), 1294 (*Westbourne*), 1548 (*Westborne Grene*): *west* 'west' + Middle English *bourne, burne* ‹ *burna* 'stream, brook' + *grēne* '(village) green']

**Westminster:** 'west monastery' [c.975 (*Westmynster*): *west* 'west' + *mynster* 'monastery, church'; previously *Thorney* (969)]

**Whetstone** [1417 (*Wheston*), 1437 (*Whetestonesstret*), 1492 (*Whetstone*): *hwetstān* 'whetstone']

**White Chapel** [1282 (*St Mary de Mattefelon*), 1340 (*Whitechapele by Algate*): *hwīt* 'white' + Middle English *chapel* 'chapel' (‹ Old French ‹ Late Latin); now *Whitechapel*]

**White Cross Street** [1226 (*Whitecruchestrete*), 1309-10 (*Whitecrouchestrate*), 1502 (*Whitecrosse Strete*): *hwīt* 'white' + Middle English *crouche* 'cross' (‹ Latin) or *cros* 'cross' (‹ Old Irish ‹ Latin) + *strǣt* '(paved) road, street (‹ Latin); after a local *white cross*]

**Whitehall** ‹ **Whitehall Palace** [1530 (*Whytehale*); from the name of the Lords' Chamber in the old Parliament; previously called *York Place* when the London residence of the Archbishops of York]

**Willesden** /ˈwɪlzdən/: 'spring's hill' [939 (*Wellesdune, Willesdone*), 1290 (*Willesden*): *well(a), wiell(a)* 'well; spring' + *dūn* 'hill']

**Wimbledon:** 'Wynman('s) hill; Winebeald('s) hill' [c. 950 (*Wunemannedune*), 1202 (*Wimeldon*), 13th C. (*Wymendon*), 1211 (*Wimbeldon, Wimbeldona*): *Wunemanne* (name) or *Winebeald* (name) + *dūn* 'hill']

**Wimbledon Common** ‹ **Wimbledon**

**Winchmore Hill:** 'Wynsige('s) boundary hill' [1319 (*Wynsemerhull*), 1543 (*Wynsmore hill*), 1586 (*Winchmore Hill*): *Winsige* (name) + (ge)*mǣre* 'boundary, border' + *hyll* 'hill'; near the southern boundary of **Edmonton** parish]

**Wood End** [1531 (*Wodehende*): *wudu* 'wood' + *ende* 'end, edge; district']

**Wood Green** [1502 (*Wodegrene*): *wudu* 'wood' + *grēne* '(village) green']

**Wood Hall** [1271 (*Wodehalle*), 1349 (*Wodhall*): *wudu* 'wood' + *hall* 'hall, manor']

**Wood Street:** 'street where wood was sold' [1156-57 (*Wodestrata*): *wudu* 'wood' + Latin *strāta* (source of *street*)]

**Woodford:** 'wood(-side) ford' [1062 (*Wodeforda*), 1225 (*Wudeforde*): *wudu* 'wood' + *ford* '(river-)ford']

**Woodford Bridge** [1238 ((Thomas de) *ponte de Wodeford*), 1429 (*Woodfordbrigge*): **Woodford** + *brycg* 'bridge'; name of **Woodford** east of the **River Roding**] ‹ **Woodford**

**Woodford Wells** [1285 ((William de) *fonte de Wodeford*)] ‹ **Woodford**

**Woodruff Lane, Woodroffe Lane** [1260 (*Woderouelane*), c. 1600 (*Woodroffe lane*): Middle English *woderove* 'woodruff (plant)' (‹ *wudurōfe*) + *lane* 'lane'; now probably *Cooper's Row*]

**Woodside** [1686 (*Woodside*): *wudu* 'wood' + *sīde* 'side']

**Woolwich** /ˈwʊlɪdʒ, -ɪtʃ/: 'wool harbour' [918 (*Uuluuich*): *wull* 'wool' + *wīc* 'farm or harbour of the stated kind']

# Y

**Yeading Brook** ‹ **Yedding**

**Yedding, Yeading** /ˈjɛdɪŋ/: 'Geddi's folk' [757 (*Geddinges*), 1325 (*Yedding(g)s*), 1331 (*Yeddyng*): *Gedd(i)* (name) + *-(i)ngas* '-followers of']

# BIBLIOGRAPHY

**GENERAL AND 20TH CENTURY LONDON**

The London Journal *is a scholarly periodical devoted to the history and contemporary life of London and its inhabitants.*

**Abercrombie, P:** Greater London Plan 1944, *HMSO 1945*
**Abercrombie, P & Forshaw, JH:** County of London Plan *London County Council 1943*
**Ackroyd, P:** Dickens' London: an imaginative vision *Headline 1987*
**Ackroyd, P:** London: the biography *Chatto and Windus 2000*
**Aldous, T:** Book of London's Villages *Secker & Warburg 1980*
**Amery, C:** Wren's London *Lennard, Luton 1988*
**Anon:** Report: improvements and town planning committee on the preliminary draft proposals for post-war reconstruction in the City of London *Batsford 1944*
**Banks, FR:** The Penguin Guide to London Penguin 1958
**Barker, F:** Edwardian London *Laurence King 1995*
**Barker, F & Gay, J:** Highgate Cemetery: Victorian Valhalla *John Murray 1984*
**Barker, F & Hyde, R:** London as it might have been *John Murray 1982*
**Barker, F & Jackson, P:** The History of London in Maps *Barrie & Jenkins 1990*
**Barker, F & Jackson, P:** London: 2000 years of a city and its people *Macmillan 1983*
**Barker, TC & Robbins, LM:** A History of London Transport *George Allen & Unwin 1975-6*
**Barson, S & Saint, A:** A Farewell to Fleet Street *Historic Buildings and Monuments Commission for England 1988*
**Barton, NJ:** The Lost Rivers of London *Phoenix House & Leicester University Press 1962*
**Bell, WG:** The Great Fire of London in 1666 *Lane 1920*
**Betjeman, J:** London's Historic Railway Stations *John Murray 1972*
**Birdle, M & Hudson, D:** The Future of London's Past *Rescue, Worcester 1973*
**Bird, J:** The Geography of the Port of London *Hutchinson 1957*
**Bird, J:** The Major Seaports of the United Kingdom *Hutchinson 1963*
**Bolsterli, MJ:** The Early Community at Bedford Park *Routledge & Kegan Paul 1977*
**Breheny, MJ &Congdon, P:** Growth and change in a core region: the case of South-East England *Pion, London 1989*
**Brimblecome, P:** The Big Smoke: a history of air pollution in London since medieval times *Methuen 1987*
**Brownhill, S:** Developing London's Docklands *Paul Chapman 1990*
**Butler, T & Rustin, M (eds):** Rising in the East? The Regeneration of East London *Lawrence & Wishart 1996*
**Byron, A:** London's Statues: a guide to London's outdoor statues and sculpture *Constable 1981*
**Cady, M:** The Book of London *Automobile Association, Basingstoke 1979*
**Centre for Urban Studies:** London, Aspects of Change *MacGibbon & Kee 1964*
**Chandler, TJ:** The Climate of London *Hutchinson 1965*
**Charlton, J:** The Tower of London: its buildings and institutions *HMSO 1978*
**Clayton, A:** Subterranean City: beneath the streets of London *Historical Publications 2000*
**Clayton, KM [ed]:** Guide to London Excursion: Twentieth International Geographical Congress *London school of Economics 1964*
**Clayton, R [ed]:** The Geography of Greater London *Philip 1964*
**Clout, H [ed]:** Changing London *University Tutorial Press, Cambridge 1978*
**Clout, H & Wood PA [eds]:** London: problems of change *Longman 1986*
**Coppock, JT & Prince HC [eds]:** Greater London *Faber 1964*
**Corporation of the City of London:** Reconstruction of the City of London *Batsford 1944*
**Corporation of the City of London:** The City of London: a record of destruction and survival *Architectural Press 1951*
**Cox, J:** London's East End: Life and Tradition *Weidenfeld & Nicolson 1994*
**Creaton, H (ed):** Bibliography of Printed Works on London History *Library Association 1994*
**Croad, S:** London's Bridges *Royal Commission on Historical Monuments England & HMSO 1983*
**Crowe, A:** The Parks and Woodlands of London *Fourth Estate 1987*
**Dalzell, WR:** The Shell Guide to the History of London *Michael Joseph 1981*
**Darlington, I & Howgego, J:** Printed Maps of London 1553-1850 *Philip 1964*
**Davies, A:** Literary London *Macmillan 1988*
**Davis, T:** John Nash: the Prince Regent's Architect *Country Life 1966*
**Day, B:** This Wooden 'O': Shakespeare's Globe Reborn *Oberon 1996*
**Department of the Environment:** Strategic Plan for the South East: review, government statement *HMSO 1978*
**Department of the Environment:** Thames Strategy *HMSO 1995*
**Dolphin, P, Grant, E & Lewis, E:** The London Region: an annotated geographical bibliography *Mansell 1981*
**Donnison, D & Eversley DEC [eds]:** London: urban patterns, problems and policies *Heinemann 1973*
**Downes, K:** Hawksmoor *Thames & Hudson 1970*
**Dugdale, GS:** Whitehall through the Centuries *Phoenix House 1950*
**Dunning, JH & Morgan EV:** An Ecomonic Study of the City of London *George Allen & Unwin 1971*
**Dyson, T:** The Medieval London Waterfront *Museum of London 1989*
**Edwards, D & Pigram R:** The Romance of Metroland *Midas, Tunbridge Wells 1979*
**Edwards, D & Pigram R:** London's Underground Suburbs *Boston Transport 1986*
**Edwards, D & Pigram R:** The Golden Years of the Metropolitan Railway and the Metro-land Dream *Bloomsbury Books 1988*
**Feldman, D & Stedman Jones, G (eds):** Metropolis London: Histories and Representations since 1800 *Routledge 1989*
**Fiddes, A:** The City of London: the historic square mile *Pevensey Press, Cambridge 1984*
**Fishman, WJ, Breach, N & Hall, JM:** East End and the Docklands *Duckworth 1990*
**Fitter, RSR:** London's Natural History *Collins 1945*
**Fitzgibbon, C:** The Blitz *MacDonald 1970*
**Forman, C:** Spitalfields: a battle for land *Hilary Shipman 1989*
**Forshaw, A & Bergström, T:** The Markets of London *Penguin 1983*
**Forshaw, A & Bergström, T:** The open spaces of London *Alison & Busby 1986*
**Forshaw, A & Bergström, T:** Smithfield: past and present *Hale 1990*
**Foster, J:** Docklands: cultures in conflict, worlds in collision *UCL Press 1999*
**Fox, C (ed):** London – World City 1800-1940 *Yale University Press, New Haven & London 1992*
**Galinou, M [ed]:** London's Pride: the glorious history of the capital's gardens *Anaya 1990*
**Girouard, M:** Sweetness and Light: the 'Queen Anne' Movement 1860-1900 *Clarendon Press, Oxford 1977*
**Glanville, P:** London in Maps *Connoisseur 1974*
**Glanville, P:** Tudor London *Museum of London 1979*
**Gleichen:** London's Open-air Statuary *Cedric Chivers Bath 1973*
**Goode, D:** Wild in Lodon *Michael Joseph 1986*
**Grant, N:** Village London: past and present *Pyramid Books 1990*
**Grant, I & Maddren, N:** The City at war *Jupiter 1975*
**Gray, R:** A History of London *Hutchinson 1978*
**Green, DR:** People of the Rookery: a pauper community in Victorian London *King's College, London 1986*
**Greeves, IS:** London Docks 1800-1900: a civil engineering history *Thomas Telford 1980*
**Grimes, WF et al:** Time on our side? *A survey of the archaeological needs of Greater London Department of Environment 1976*
**Gwynn, RD:** Huguenot Heritage: the history and contribution of the Huguenots in Britain *Routledge & Kegan Paul 1985*
**Hall, JM:** London: metropolis and region *Oxford University Press 1976*
**Hall, PG:** The Industries of London since 1861 *Hutchinson 1962*
**Hall, PG:** London 2000 *Faber 1963*
**Hall, PG:** Cities of Tomorrow *Basil Blackwell, Oxford 1988*
**Hall, PG:** London, 2001 *Unwin Hyman 1989*
**Hamnett, C:** Unequal City: London in the global arena *Routledge 2003*
**Harrison, P:** Inside the Inner City *Penguin 1983*
**Harte, N:** The University of London 1836-1986: an illustrated history *Athlone Press 1986*
**Hawkins, R:** Green London: a handbook *Sidgwick & Jackson 1987*
**Hearsey, JEN:** London and the Great Fire *John Murray 1965*
**Hebbert, M:** London: more by fortune than design *Wiley 1998*
**Henrey, R:** London under fire 1940-45 *Dent 1969*
**Hibbert, C:** London : the biography of a city *Penguin 1980*
**Hobhouse, H & Saunders A [eds]:** Good and Proper Materials: the fabric of London since the Great Fire *London Topographical Society 1989*
**Hobley, B:** Roman and Saxon London: a reappraisal *Museum of London 1986*
**Hoggart, K & Green, DR [eds]:** London, a new metropolitan geography *Edward Arnold 1991*
**Holden, CH & Holford, WG:** The City of London: A Record of Destruction and Survival *Architectural Press 1951*
**Humphries, S & Taylor J:** The Making of Modern London 1945-1985 *Sidgwick & Hackson 1986*
**Hunter, M & Thorne, R:** Change at King's Cross: From 1800 to the Present *Historical Publications 1990*
**Hyde, R:** The A to Z of Georgian London *Harry Margary, Lympne Castle 1981*
**Inwood, S:** A History of London *Macmillan 1998*
**Jackson, AA:** London's Termini *David & Charles, Newton Abbot 1969*
**Jackson, JA:** Semi-detached London *George Allen & Unwin 1973*
**Jenkins S:** Landlords to London: the story of a capital and its growth *Constable 1975*
**Jenner, M:** London Heritage. The Changing Style of a City *Michael Joseph, 1988*
**Johnson, D:** The City ablaze: the second great fire of London 29 December 1940 *William Kimber 1980*
**Jones, E & Sinclair DJ [eds]:** Atlas of London and the London Region *Pergamon, Oxford 1968*
**Jones, LR:** The Geography of London River *Methuen 1931*
**Kiek, J:** Everybody's Historic London *Quiller Press 1984*
**King, AD:** Global cities: post-imperialism and the internationalization of London *Routledge 1990*
**Leapman, M [ed]:** The Book Of London *Weidenfeld & Nicolson 1989*
**Lloyd, D [ed]:** Save the City: a conservation study of the City of London *Society for the Protection of Ancient Buildings 1976*
**Lobel, M [ed]:** The British Atlas of Historic Towns Volume III. The City of London from prehistoric times to c.1520 *Oxford Univeristy Press and Historic Towns Trust 1989*
**London County Council:** County of London Plan *Macmillan 1943*
**London County Council:** The Administrative County of London Development Plan, 3 volumes *LCC 1951*
**London County Council:** The Youngest County *LCC 1951*
**London County Council:** The County Planning Report *LCC 1960*
**London Transport:** Planning London's Transport *London Transport 1995*
**Luckin, B:** Pollution and Control: a social history of the Thames in the nineteenth century *Adam Hilger, Bristol 1986*
**Mack, J & Humpries S:** The Making of Modern london 1939-1945: London at war *Sidgwick & Jackson 1985*
**Mander, R & Mitchenson, J:** The Theatres of London *Rupert Hart-Davis 1961*
**Maré, E de:** London's River: past, present and future *Reinhardt 1958*
**Martin, JE:** Greater London: an industrial geography *Bell 1966*
**Matheson, J & Holding, A (eds):** Focus on London 99 *The Stationery Office 1999*
**McAuley, I:** Guide to Ethnic London *Immel 1993*
**McRae, H & Cairncross, F:** Capital City: London as a financial centre *Methuen 1991*
**Meller, H:** London Cemeteries *Avebury, Aldershot 1981*
**Merrifield, R:** The Archaeology of London *Heinemann 1975*
**Merriman, N (ed):** The Peopling of London *Museum of London 1993*
**Milne, G:** The Great Fire of London *Historial Publications 1986*
**Ministry of Housing and Local Government:** The South East Study *HMSO 1964*
**Ministry of Town and Country Planning:** The Greater London Plan *HMSO 1945*
**Morris, J:** Londinium: London in the Roman Empire *Weidenfeld & Nicolson 1982*
**Munby, DL:** Industry and Planning in Stepney *Oxford university Press 1951*
**Munton, RJC:** London's Green Belt: containment in practice *Allen & Unwin 1983*
**Naib, Al SK:** London's Dockland: past, present and future *Thames & Hudson 1990*
**Olding, S:** Exploring Museums: London *HMSO 1989*
**Olsen, DJ:** Town Planning in London *Yale University Press 1964*
**Olsen, DJ:** The Growth of Victorian London *Batsford 1976*
**Ormsby, H:** London and the Thames *Sifton Praed 1924*
**Phillips, H:** Mid-Georgian London *Collins 1964*
**Phillips, H:** The Thames about 1750 *Collins 1951*
**Piper, D:** London: an illustrated companion guide *Collins 1980*
**Plummer, B & Shewan, D:** City Gardens. An Open Spaces Survey in the City of London *Belhaven 1992*
**Porter, R:** London: A Social History *Hamish Hamilton 1994*
**Porter, S:** The Great Fire of London *Sutton, Stroud 1996*
**Power, MJ:** John Stow and his London *Journal of Historical Geography, 11, 1985, 1-20*
**Prockter, A & Taylor, R:** The A to Z of Elizabethan London *Harry Margary, Lympne Castle 1979*
**Pudney, J:** Crossing London's river *Dent 1972*
**Pudney, J:** London's Docks *Thames & Hudson 1975*
**Rasmussen, SE:** London: the unique city *Jonathan Cape 1937*
**Robinson, E:** London, illustrated geological walks 2 volumes *Scottish Academic Press, Edinburgh 1984-5*
**Saint, A (ed):** Politics and th People of London: The London County Council, 1889-1965 *Hambledon Press 1989*
**Saint, A & Darley, G:** The Chronicles of London *Weidenfeld & Nicolson 1994*
**Saunders, A:** Regent's Park *David & Charles, Newton Abbot 1969*
**Schofield, J & Dyson, T:** Archaeology of the City of London *City of London Archaeological Trust 1980*
**Schubert, D & Sutcliffe, A:** The 'Haussmannization' of London?: The Planning and Construction of Kingsway-Aldwych *Planning Perspectives, 11, 1996, pp115-144*
**Seaborne, M:** Photographers' London 1839-1994 *Museum of London 1995*

Shepherd, J, Westway, J & Lee, T: A Social Atlas of London *Oxford University Press 1974*

Sheppard, F: London, a History *Oxford University Press 1998*

Simmie, J (ed): Planning London *UCL Press 1994*

Smith, DH: The Industries of Greater London *PS King 1933*

South East Economic Planning Council: A Strategy for the South East *HMSO 1967*

South East Joint Planning Team: Strategic Plan for the South East *HMSO 1970*

South East Joint Planning Team: Strategic Plan for the South East 1976 Review *HMSO 1976*

Stamp, G: The changing metropolis: earliest photographs of London 1839-79 *Penguin 1986*

Stedman Jones, G: Outcast London: a study in the relationship between classes in Victorian society *Oxford University Press 1971*

Tames, R: City of London Past *Historical Publications, New Barnet 1995*

Thomas, D: London's Green Belt *Faber 1970*

Thompson, FML: Hampstead: building a borough 1650-1964 *Routledge & Kegan Paul 1974*

Thompson, FML [ed]: The Rise of Suburbia *Leicester University Press 1982*

Thompson, FML [ed]: the University of London and the World of Learning 1836-1986 *Hambledon Press 1990*

Thorold, P: The London Rich: the creation of a great city, from 1666 to the present *Viking 1999*

Thurston, H: Royal Parks for the People *David & Charles, Newton Abbot 1974*

Tindall, G: The Fields Beneath *Temple Smith 1980*

Tindall, G: The Man who drew London: Wenceslaus Hollar in reality and imagination *Chatto and Windus 2002*

Townsend, P: Poverty and Labour in London *Low Pay Unit 1987*

Trench, R & Hillman, E: London under London: a subterranean guide *John Murray 1984*

Wales, HRH Prince of: A Vision of Britain: a personal view of architecture *Doubleday 1989*

Wallace, D: London: the Circle Line Guide *Penguin 1990*

Wallmann, S: Living in South London: perspectives on Battersea 1871-1981 *Gower, Farnborough 1982*

Warner, M: The Image of London: views by travellers and emigrés 1550-1920 *Trefoil 1987*

Webb, E: Literary London *Spellmount, Tunbridge Wells 1990*

Weightman, G: Bright Lights, Big City: London Entertainment, 1830-1950 *Collins & Brown, 1992*

Weightman, G: London River: the Thames story *Collins & Brown 1990*

Weightman, G & Humphries, S: The Making of Modern London 1914-1939 *Sidgwick & Jackson 1984*

Weinreb, B & Hibbert, C [eds]: The London Encyclopaedia *Macmillan 1983*

Wheeler, A: The Tidal Thames: the history of a river and its fishes *Routledge & Kegan Paul 1979*

White, HP: A Regional History of the Railways of great Britain Volume III Greater London *David & Charles, Newton Abbot 1963*

White, J: London in the 20th Century: a city and its people *Penguin 2001*

Williamson, E. & Pevsner, N: London Docklands, An architectural guide *Penguin 1998*

Wilmott, P & Young, M: Family and Class in a London Suburb *Routledge & Kegan Paul 1960*

Wilson, D: The Tower of London *Constable 1978*

Yelling, JA: Slums and Redevelopment: Policy and Practice in England, 1918-45, with Particular Reference to London *UCL Press 1992*

Young, K & Garside, P: Metropolitan London: politics and urban change 1837-1981 *Edward Arnold 1982*

Young, K & Wilmott, P: Family and Kinship in East London *Routledge & Kegan Paul 1957*

Ziegler, P: London at War 1935-45 *Sinclair Stevenson 1995*


**HISTORICAL LONDON**

**CHAPTER 1:** LAND UNDER LONDON

Merriman, N: Prehistoric London *HMSO 1990*

**CHAPTER 2:** ROMAN LONDON

Chapman, H, Hall, J & Marsh, G: The London Wall Walk *Museum of London 1985*

Hall, J & Merrifield, R: Roman London *HMSO 1986*

Marsden, P: Roman London *Thames & Hudson 1980*

Merrifield, R: London – City of the Romans *Batsford 1983*

Milne, G (ed): From Roman Basilica to Medieval London *HMSO 1992*

Milne, G: The Port of Roman London *Batsford 1985*

Milne, G: Londinium – Map and Guide to Roman London *Ordnance Survey 1983*

Milne, G: Roman London *Batsford 1995*

**CHAPTER 3:** SAXON AND NORMAN LONDON

Bailey K: "The Middle Saxons" in S Bassett [ed] The Origins of Anglo-Saxon Kingdoms *Leicester University Press, London 1989*

Brooke, C & Keir, G: London 800-1216: the shaping of a city *Secker & Warburg, London 1975*

Clark, J: Saxon and Norman London *HMSO, London 1989*

Cowie, R & Whytehead, R: Lundenwic: the archaeological evidence for middle Saxon London *Antiquity 63 1989-706-18*

Darby, HC & Campbell, EMJ [eds]: The Domesday Geography of South-East England *Cambridge University Press 1962*

Horsman, V, Milne, C & Milne, G: Aspects of Saxo-Norman London: 1 Building and Street Development *London & Middlesex Archaeological Society Special Paper 11 1988*

Vince, A: Saxon London: an archaeological investigation *Batsford 1990*

Yorke, B: Kings and Kingdoms of Early Anglo-Saxon England *BA Seaby, London 1990*

**CHAPTER 4:** MEDIEVAL LONDON

Barron, CM: Richard Whittington, in Studies in London History: Essays presented to PE Jones [eds] A Hollaender and W Kellaway *Hodder & Stoughton 1969*

Bolton, JL: The medieval English economy 1150-1500 *Dent, Rowman & Littlefield 1980*

Holt, R & Rosser, G [eds]: The medieval town, a reader in English urban history *Longman, Harlow 1990*

Reynolds, S: An introduction to the history of English medieval towns *Clarendon Press, Oxford 1977*

Rosser, AG: Medieval Westminster 1200-1540 *Clarendon Press, Oxford, 1989*

Schofield, J: Medieval London Houses *Yale University Press, New Haven & London 1995*

Sharpe, RR: London and the Kingdom *Longmans, Green & Co 1895*

Thomson, JAF [ed]: Towns and townspeople in the fifteenth century *Alan Sutton 1988*

Thrupp, SL: The Merchant Class of Medieval London *University of Michigan, Ann Arbor 1948*

Unwin, G: The Guilds and Companies of London *Methuen 1908*

Victoria County History of London: ed W Page: Ecclesiastical history and religious houses *Archibald Constable 1908*

Williams, G: London: from Commune to Capital *Athlone Press, University of London 1963*

**CHAPTER 5:** TUDOR AND STUART LONDON

Baker, TMM: London: rebuilding the City *Phillimore 2000*

Beier, AL & Finlay R [eds]: London 1500-1700: The Making of the Metropolis *Longman 1986*

Brett-James, NG: The growth of Stuart London *Allen & Unwin 1935*

Brigden, S: London and the Reformation *Clarendon Press, Oxford 1989*

Coates, B: The Impact of the Civil War on the Economy of London *Ashgate 2001*

Cobb, G: London City Churches *Batsford 1977*

Griffiths, P and Jenner, M (eds): Londinopolis: essays in the cultural and social history of early modern London *Manchester University Press 2000*

Hanson, N: The Dreadful Judgement: the true story of the Great Fire of London *Corgi 2001*

Harding, VA: The Population of London 1550-1700: A Review of the Published Evidence *London Journal, 15, 1990, pp111-128*

McKellar, E: The Birth of Modern London: the development and design of the city 1660-1720 *Manchester University Press 1999*

Reddaway, TF: The Rebuilding of London after the Great Fire *Edward Arnold 1940*

Saunders, A & Schofield, J (eds.): Tudor London: a map and a view *Museum of London and London Topographical Society, 2001*

Schofield, J: The building of London from the Conquest to the Great Fire *Colonnade 1984*

Thurley, S: Whitehall Palace: an architectural history of the royal apartments 1240-1690 *Yale University Press 1999*

Ward, JP: Metropolitan Communities: trade guilds, identity, and change in early modern London *Stanford University Press 1997*

Weinstein, S: Tudor London *HMSO 1994*

**CHAPTER 6:** GEORGIAN LONDON

Arnold, D (ed.): The Metropolis and its Image: constructing identities for London, c.1750-1950 *Blackwell 1999*

Beattie, JM: Policing and Punishment in London 1660-1720: urban crime and the limits of terror *Oxford University Press 2001*

Bull, GBG: Thomas Milne's land utilization map of the London area in 1800 *Geographical Journal, 122, 1956*

Clark, P and Gillespie, R (eds): Two Capitals: London and Dublin 1500-1840 *British Academy and Oxford University Press 2001*

George, D: London, Life in the Eighteenth Century *Routledge & Kegan Paul 1951*

Johnson, N: Eighteenth-Century London *HMSO 1991*

Laxton, P: The A to Z of Regency London *London Topographical Society and Harry Margary, Lympne Castle 1985*

Longstaffe Gowan, T: The London Town Garden 1700-1840 *Yale University Press 2001*

Ogburn, M: Spaces of Modernity. London's Geographies 1680–1780 *Guilford Press 1999*

Rendell, J: The Pursuit of Pleasure: gender, space and architecture in Regency London *Athlone Press 2001*

Rocque, J: A plan of the cities of London and Westminster from an actual survey in 1746 *London Topographical Society and Harry Margary, Lympne Castle 1971*

Rudé, G: Hanoverian London 1714-1808 *Secker & Warburg 1971*

Schwarz, L: London in the Age of Industrialisation: Entrepreneurs,
Labour Force and Living Conditions, 1700-1850 *Cambridge University Press 1992*

Spate, OHK: The growth of London, AD 1660-1800, in [ed] Darby, HC, An Historical Geography of England before 1800 *Cambridge University Press 1936*

Summerson, J: Georgian London *Barrie & Jenkins 1978*

Summerson, J: The Life and Work of John Nash *George Allen & Unwin 1980*

Wedd, K: Creative Quarters: the art world in London 1700-2000 *Merrell 2001*

**CHAPTER 7:** VICTORIAN LONDON

Adburgham, A: Shopping in style: London from the Restoration to Edwardian elegance *Thames & Hudson 1979*

Allen, R: The Moving Pageant: a literary sourcebook on London street life 1700-1914 *Routledge 1998*

Arnold, D: Re-presenting the Metropolis: architecture, urban experience and social life in London 1800-1840 *Ashgate 2000*

Barker, T: Moving millions: a pictorial history of London Transport *London Transport Museum 1990*

Bennett, A: Riceyman Steps *1923*

Davis, J: Reforming London: The London Government Problem, 1855-1900 *Clarendon Press, Oxford 1988*

Dyos, HJ: Victorian suburb: a study of the growth of Camberwell *Leicester University Press 1961*

Dyos, HJ & Wolff, M [eds]: The Victorian city: images and realities *Routledge & Kegan Paul 1973*

Fishman, WJ: East End 1888 *Duckworth 1988*

Fried, A & Elman, R [eds]: Charles Booth's London *Hutchinson 1969*

Gissing, George: The Nether World *1889*

Green, DR: From Artisans to Paupers: Economic Change and Poverty in London, 1790-1870 *Scolar Press 1995*

Grossmith, G & W: The Diary of a Nobody *1892*

Halliday, S: The Great Stink of London *Sutton 1999*

Hollingshead, J: Ragged London in 1861 *Dent Everyman reprinted in 1986*

Horrall, A: Popular Culture in London c.1890-1918: the transformation of entertainment *Manchester University Press 2001*

Hyde, R [ed]: The A to Z of Victorian London *London Topographical Society and Harry Margary, Lympne Castle 1987*

Keating, P [ed]: Into Unknown England 1866-1913: selections from the social explorers *Fontana 1976*

Kynaston, D: The City of London, vol. 1: A World of its Own, 1815-90 *Chatto & Windus 1994*

Kynaston, D: The City of London, vol. 2: Golden Years, 1890-1914 *Chatto & Windus 1995*

Kynaston, D: The City of London, vol. 3 *Chatto and Windus 1999*

Kynaston, D: The City of London, vol. 4 *Chatto and Windus 2001*

Mayhew, H: London Labour and the London Poor *Penguin 1985*

Morrison, Arthur: A Child of the Jago *1896*

Nead, L: Victorian Babylon: people, streets and images in 19th-century London *Yale University Press 2000*

Olsen, DJ: The growth of Victorian London *Penguin 1979*

Olsen, DJ: Town planning in London: the eighteenth and nineteenth centuries *Yale University Press 1982*

Port, MH: Imperial London: Civil Government Building in London, 1851-1915 *Yale University Press, New Haven & London, 1995*

Purbick, L: The Great Exhibition of 1851 *Manchester University Press 2001*

Kynaston, D: The City of London, vol. 1: A World of its Own, 1815-90 *Chatto & Windus 1994*

Rappaport, E: Shopping for Pleasure: women in the making of London's West End *Princeton University Press 2000*

Schneer, J: London 1900. The Imperial Metropolis *Yale University Press 1999*

Sheppard, F: London 1808-1870: The Infernal Wen *Secker & Warburg 1971*

Stedman Jones, G: Outcast London *Penguin 1984*

Walkowitz, JR: City of Dreadful Delight: Narratives of Sexual Danger in Late Victorian London *Virago 1992*

Weightman, G & Humphries, S: The making of modern London 1815-1914 *Sidgwick & Jackson 1983*

White, J: Rothschild Buildings: life in an East End tenement block 1887-1920 *Routledge & Kegan Paul 1980*

Winter, J: London's Teeming Streets, 1830-1914 *Routledge 1993*

Wohl, AS: The eternal slum: housing and social policy in Victorian London *Edward Arnold 1977*

Yelling, JA: Slums and slum clearance in Victorian London *Allen & Unwin 1986*

**PLACE NAME HISTORIES**

Ekwall, E: Street names of the City of London *Clarendon Press, Oxford 1954*

English Place Name Society: Middlesex, Essex, Hertfordshire, Surrey, English Place name Elements *Cambridge University Press*

Field, J: Place names of Greater London *Batsford 1986*

Pointon, GE [ed]: BBC Pronouncing Dictionary of British Names *Oxford University Press 1990*

Wallenberg, JK: Kentish Place Names *Uppsala 1931*

Wallenberg, JK: Place names of Kent *Uppsala 1934*

Wells, JC: Longman Pronunciation Dictionary *Harlow 1934*

Wittich, J: Discovering London Street Names *Shire Publications Ltd. Princes Risborough 1990*

THE TIMES LONDON HISTORY ATLAS

# PICTURE ACKNOWLEDGEMENTS

All the illustrations in this book are the work of Ralph Orme, Swanston Graphics. The publishers would like to thank the following museums, publishers and picture agencies for permission to base illustrations on their photographs or to reproduce them. Where there is no such acknowledgement, we have been unable to trace the source or the illustration is a composition by our illustrators and contributors.

cover — (far left) Ancient Art & Architecture Collection/R. Sheridan; (centre right) Corbis

p.14 — (centre top and background to page) Guildhall Library, Corporation of London

p.15 — (centre top) Guildhall Library, Corporation of London/Bridgeman Art Library, London; (centre right) Science & Society Photo Library; (bottom right) National Remote Sensing Centre Ltd

p.20 — (top) Museum of London Archaeology Service; (centre) The British Museum; (bottom left) The Museum of London

p.21 — (top) The Museum of London; (bottom) Dr Pamela Greenwood & Newham Museum Service

p.23 — (centre right) Times Newspapers; (bottom right) The Museum of London.

p.24 — The Museum of London

p.25 — The Museum of London

p.26 — The Museum of London

p.27 — The Museum of London

p.32 — The Museum of London

p.34 — The Museum of London

p.35 — The Museum of London

p.36 — The Museum of London

p.37 — The British Library

pp.38-9 — Michael Holford

p.40 — The Museum of London

p.41 — The Museum of London

p.42 — (centre) Michael Holford; (bottom left) The Museum of London

p.44 — Guildhall Library, Corporation of London/ Bridgeman Art Library, London

p.45 — The Museum of London

p.46 — The British Library

p.47 — The Museum of London

p.48 — (top) Greater London Records Office; (centre) The British Museum

p.50 — The British Museum

p.51 — (inset) Rector and Churchwardens of the United Parishes of SS Magnus-the-Martyr, St Margaret, New Fish Street and St Michael, Crooked Lane (right) Bridgeman Art Library, London

pp.54-5 — Society of Antiquaries

p.55 — (top) The Mansell Collection

p.56 — The Museum of London

p.58-9 — The Mansell Collection

p.64 — The Museum of London

p.65 — The Museum of London

p.66 — (top and centre) The Museum of London;

pp.66-7 — (centre) National Monuments Record; (bottom) The Museum of London

p.67 — (right) The Museum of London

p.68 — The Museum of London

p.69 — (top) The Museum of London/National Monuments Record; (centre) Guildhall Library, Corporation of London; (bottom right) The Museum of London

pp.70-1 — Reproduced by Gracious Permission of Her Majesty the Queen

p.72 — The Museum of London

p.73 — The Mansell Collection

pp.74-5 — The British Library

p.75 — Guildhall Library, Corporation of London

p.76 — The Museum of London

p.77 — (left, top right and bottom right) The Museum of London; (centre) The Governor and Company of the Bank of England;

p.79 — (top) Guildhall Library, Corporation of London; (centre right) The Museum of London

p.80 — The Museum of London

p.81 — The Museum of London

p.82 — (bottom) Guildhall Library, Corporation of London/Bridgeman Art Library, London

pp.82-3 — Guildhall Library, Corporation of London/Bridgeman Art Library, London

p.83 — (right) Guildhall Library, Corporation of London; (right) National Maritime Museum, Greenwich

p.84 — The Museum of London

p.85 — The Dickens House, London

pp.86-7 — London Transport Museum

pp.88-9 — The Museum of London

p.89 — (centre) Royal Institute of British Architects; (right) Private Collection (Mark Girouard)

p.90 — (top) The Museum of London; (bottom) Courtauld Institute Galleries, London (Courtauld Collection)

p.91 — (centre right) Vestry House Museum; (bottom right) The Museum of London

p.92 — (right) Bancroft Road L.H. Library

pp.92-3 — Museum in Docklands project

p.94 — (top) The Museum of London; (left) Architectural Review/A. Acland; (centre) Illustrated London News; (bottom right) Courtesy of the Trustees of the V&A

p.95 — (top right) The Museum of London; (top left) The Mansell Collection, courtesy of the Trustees of the V&A

p.97 — (centre) The Salvation Army; (right) Andres Press Agency; (bottom left) Punch

p.98 — (top) Illustrated London News; (bottom left) The British Library

p.99 — Illustrated London News

p.100 — (top) The Museum of London; (top right) Kensington and Chelsea Public Libraries; (left) Hulton-Deutsch Collection; (bottom left) Guildhall Library, Corporation of London

p.101 — (top right and right) Greater London Records Office; (bottom left) Guildhall Library, Corporation of London

p.102 — (bottom left) Punch; (bottom right) Southwark Arts Libraries

p.104 — (left) Guildhall Library, Corporation of London; (bottom) Illustrated London News

p.105 — (left) Guildhall Library, Corporation of London/Bridgeman Art Library, London; (right) Illustrated London News

p.106 — Private Collection

p.107 — (top) Selfridge's; (bottom left) Marks & Spencer

p.108 — London Transport Museum

p.109 — Royal Institute of British Architects

p.110 — Popperfoto

p.112 — London Borough of Camden Local History Library

p.113 — London Transport Museum

p.114 — (right and bottom right) Hulton-Deutsch Collection; (bottom left) Greater London Records Office

p.115 — (top left and bottom left) London Transport Museum; (right) Hulton-Deutsch Collection; (bottom right) Greater London Records Office

p.117 — (top right) C.E.G.B.; (centre right and below right) Gunnersbury Park Museum

p.118 — (left) Popperfoto; (bottom centre) London Topographical Society; (above right and bottom right) The Times

p.119 — London Transport Museum

p.120 — Associated Press

p.121 — Tony Stone Worldwide

p.122 — Aerofilms

p.124 — The Times

p.125 — Alan J. Millard

p.126 — (centre) Hulton-Deutsch Collection

pp.126-7 — Hulton-Deutsch Collection

p.127 — (centre) The London Journal Trust; (right) National Magazine Company Ltd.

p.129 — Aerofilms

p.132 — (centre) New Zealand House

pp.132-3 — (above) National Westminster Bank; (bottom) Architectural Association/Valerie Bennett

p.133 — (top right) Architectural Association/Valerie Bennett; (right and centre right) Architectural Association/Jane Beckett

p.134 — (right) Punch; (bottom left) The Museum of London

p.135 — (left) Punch; (top right) The Times

p.136 — (centre) Illustrated London News; (bottom right) The Museum of London

p.137 — (bottom left) East London Mosque; (bottom centre) Michael Nicholson/Corbis; (right) Popperfoto

p.138 — (centre top and bottom left) The Museum of London; (centre below) Nick Daley

p.139 — (top right and left) The Museum of London; (bottom right) Guildhall Library, Corporation of London

p.140 — (top) Westminster City Libraries; (centre, bottom left and bottom right) The Museum of London; (bottom centre) Illustrated London News

p.141 — London Transport Museum

p.142 — (top left) Guildhall Library, Corporation of London/Bridgeman Art Library, London; (top centre and below left) The Museum of London

p.143 — (top right) Aerofilms; (below right) London Transport Museum

pp.144-5 — The Dickens House, London

p.146 — (centre, bottom left and bottom right) Richard Kalina/The International Shakespeare Globe Centre Ltd; (top right) Guildhall Library, Corporation of London

p.147 — (top left and top centre) The Museum of London; (top right) Victoria and Albert Museum; (centre left) Diana Howard: London Theatres and Musical Halls 1850-1950; (bottom right) National Theatre

p.148 — John Topham Picture Library

p.149 — (top left and top right) The Museum of London; (below right) Harrods

pp.152-3 — Telegraph Colour Library

p.155 — (top right and bottom) The Museum of London; (centre right) Westminster City Libraries

p.157 — (top, centre right and bottom) The Museum of London; (centre left) Paul Mellon Collection

p.159 — Canary Wharf

p.160 — (top) London Transport Museum; (bottom right) Architectural Association/Canon Parsons

p.161 — (top left) Bridgeman Art Library, London; (top right and bottom left) London Transport Museum; (bottom right) The Post Office

p.162 — Hulton-Deutsch Collection

p.163 — (top) By Gracious Permission of Her Majesty the Queen; (centre and bottom centre) The Museum of London

p.164 — (bottom left) Illustrated London News

p.165 — (top left) London Transport Museum; (top right) Architectural Association/E. Hurwicz; (centre right) The Museum of London; (below right) Keith Wynn/Photocraft Hampstead; (bottom left) Aerofilms

p.166 — (bottom) Westminster City Libraries; (above right) John Gay

p.167 — (left and right) The Times; (centre) Royal Festival Hall

pp.168-9 — (top) Guildhall Library, Corporation of London; (bottom) Paul Draper/Sunday Times

p.169 — Guildhall Library, Corporation of London

p.170 — (top) PA Photos; (bottom) Londonstills.com

p.171 — (top) Mitsubishi Estate Company / Miller Hare Limited; (bottom) Hayes Davidson and John Maclean

p.172 — PA Photos

Endpapers — The Mansell Collection

Holborn WC Medieval London 49; Tudor London 58, 60 market 79; shops 106; Underground station 113, 161
Holborn (borough) WC crime 98; local government district in 1855 104; population decline 112; industry 116; employment 117; bombing 118, 119; Irish population 137
Holborn Bar and Street see Holborn
Holborn Hill WC market 79
Holborn Theatre Royal WC 147
Holborn Viaduct Station CITY 91, 105; commuter traffic 126; 153
Holborn, The stream of NW London 58, 60, 61
Holland Estate W 75
Holland Park W 141; Underground station 160
Holloway N on coaching road 82; growth 88; trams 91; comparative poverty 103; railway station 113; bombing 118; gentrification 127; Greater London Development Plan 128; village in 1800 156
Holloway Gate N tollgate 82
Holloway Prison N 99
Holsdon Green NW village in 1800 156
Holy Trinity SE † 77
Holy Trinity Church Clapham † 157
Holy Trinity the Little CITY † Medieval church 50
Holy Trinity Priory CITY 43, 51, 58, 59; Great Fire 69
Holywell Priory NE 43
Home Office SW 95
Homerton E agriculture 79; comparative poverty 103
Honey Lane CITY Medieval London 53; market 79
Honorable Artillery Company EC museum 165
Hook Surrey village in 1800 156
Hoop, The Golders Green coaching inn 82
Hoop Lane Cemetery NW 166
Hope Estate NW 75
Hope Theatre SE 146
Horley Surrey growth 112
Horn Coffee House CITY Dickens 144
Hornsey N village in 1800 156
Hornsey Wood House N pleasure gardens 142
Horse Guards SW 76, 95, 154
Horse Guards Avenue SW 95
Horse Guards Parade SW 154
Horseferry SW 64
Horsemonger Lane Jail SE Dickens 145
Hospital for Consumption and Diseases of the Chest SW 96
Hospital for Sick Children WC 96
Hospital for Women WC 96
Hospital for Women and Children SW 96
Hospital Hill Wood Essex 141
hospitals 96
Hounslow Middlesex geology 18; agriculture 78; Greater London Development Plan 128; immigrant population 137; village in 1800 156
Hounslow Heath Middlesex 141
House of Commons prison 99
House of Correction EC 99
Houses of Parliament SW 155
housing Tudor London 61, 63; Victorian London 100-101; inter-war 112-13; gentrification 1961-71 127
Hoxton E market 78, 148; comparative poverty 103; industry 116; village in 1800 156
Hrofescaestir see Rochester
Hubbard Lane CITY Medieval London 53
Hulks, The Woolwich prison 99
Hulviz see Woolwich
Hungerford Bridge WC 163; South Bank 124
Hungerford Market WC 79; Dickens 144
Hungerford Stairs WC 23; Dickens 145
Hungerford Street WC 17th century 64
Hungerford Wharf WC 95
Hunterian Museum WC 165
Hutchins Estates E and SW 75
Hyde NW village in 1800 156
Hyde Park W Crown estates 75, 78, 138, 139, 141
Hyde Park Corner SW Civil War fort 66; Underground station 161; underpass 161

Iceland trade with London 42
Ickenham Middlesex village in 1800 156
Ilefort see Ilford
Ilford Essex geology 19; Domesday Book Ilefort 43; growth 89, 112; railway station 91, 113; bombing 119; Greater London Development Plan 128; brickworks 133; village in 1800 156
IMAX cinema 173
immigration 136-7
Imperial College SW 164
Imperial Institute SW 164
Imperial Theatre SW 147
Imperial War Museum (formerly Bethlehem Royal Hospital – Bedlam) SE 77, 165
Inderwick Estate SW 75
India Office SW 95
India Office Library and Records SE 165
Indian Museum SW 95
Indian population 137
industry Tudor London 60, 61; Victorian London 92-3; tailoring 92; furniture 92; 1947-8 116-17
Ingrebourne, River Essex 19
Inner Temple CITY 152
Inner Temple Gateway CITY Tudor London 58
Innholders' Hall CITY 62
Inns of Court 99

Inns of Court and City Yeomanry Museum WC 165
Insolvent Court WC Dickens 144
Institute of Advanced Legal Studies WC 164
Institute of Archaeology WC 164
Institute of Classical Studies WC 164
Institute of Commonwealth Studies WC 164
Institute of Education WC 164
Institute of Germanic Studies WC 164
Institute of Historical Research WC 164
Institute of Latin American Studies WC 164
Institute of U.S. Studies WC 164
Inverness Street NW market 148
Ipswich (OE Gipeswic) Essex Anglo-Saxon trade 41; growth 128
Irish population 137
Ironmonger Lane CITY Medieval London 49
Ironmongers Estate N 75
Ironmongers' Hall CITY 62, 152
Insendone see Islington
Island Barn Reservoir Surrey 141
Island Dock SE 158
Island Gardens E railway station 158
Isle of Dogs E comparative poverty 103; pumping station 104; development 158, 170, 172
Isleworth Middlesex village in 1800 156
Islington N Domesday Book Isendone 43; estates 75; market 79; tollgates 82; growth 88; factories 93; cholera epidemics 96; crime 98; housing 100, 101; local government district 1855 104; market 106; decline in population 112; industry 116; employment 117; bombing 118, 119; gentrification 127; Jewish settlement 136; immigrant population 137; open spaces 141; village in 1800 156
Islington Spa N pleasure gardens 142
Islington Tunnel N canal tunnel 161
Italian Hospital WC 96
Italy trade with London 52
Iver Buckinghamshire shopping centre 126
Ivy Lane WC Medieval London 52; 17th century 64

Jacob's Island (a/c Folly Ditch) SE Dickens 145
Jamaica Road SE develoment 158
Jenny's Whim SW pleasure gardens 142
Jesus College (Oxford) Estate SW 75
Jewish Museum WC 164
Jewish population 136
Jews' College NW 165
Jew's Harp House NW pleasure gardens 142
John Wesley's House EC 165
Johnson's Beef House WC Dickens 144
Joiners' Hall CITY 62
Jubilee Gardens SE 167
Jubilee Line extension 171, 173
Jubilee Market WC 148

Kaupang S Norway trade with London 42
Keats House NW 165
Kelvedon Hatch Essex geology 19
Ken Wood NW 141
Kennington SE factories 93; comparative poverty 103; Underground station 113, 161; bombing 118; village in 1800 156
Kennington Park SE 141
Kennington Park Road SE bombing 118
Kensal Green NW village in 1800 156; Underground station 160; cemetery 166
Kensington SW agriculture 78; cholera epidemics 96; crime 98; housing 101; comparative poverty 102; local government district 1855 104; decline in population 112; industry 116; bombing 118, 119; gentrification 127; village in 1800 156; Hanwell cemetery 166
Kensington Gardens W 139, 141
Kensington Gore Estate SW 75
Kensington High Street W shops 106; Underground station 113, 160
Kensington Olympia W Underground station 160
Kensington Palace W 139, 164
Kent (OE Cantware) 40; Domesday Book Chenth 43; suburban expansion 114; Green Belt 126; commuting population 126; main roads into London 127; South-East Regional Plan 128
Kent Street SE market 106
Kentish Town NW on coaching road 82; comparative poverty 103; village in 1800 156
Kentish Town Road NW shops 106
Kent's Treasury SW 95
Keston Surrey Roman buildings 28; village in 1800 156
Kew Bridge SW trams 91; 162, 163
Kew Gardens Surrey Royal Gardens 78, 138, 139, 141, 143
Kew Palace Middlesex 143
Kew Railway Bridge SW 162, 163
Kilburn NW railway station 91; comparative poverty 102; Greater London Development Plan 128; Jewish settlement 136; village in 1800 156
Kilburn Park NW trams 91; Underground station 160
Kilburn Priory Estate NW 75
Kilburn Square NW market 148
Kilburn Wells NW pleasure gardens 142
King George V Dock E 93, 158, 159
King George VI Reservoir Middlesex 141
King William Street CITY WW2 deep shelter 161
King's Bench Debtors' Prison Dickens 144
King's Bridge SW Medieval London 48
King's College WC and SW 165
King's College Hospital WC 96

Kings Cross trams 91; industry 116
Kings Cross Station N 91, 113; commuter traffic 126; Underground 91, 113, 161
King's Lane 50
King's Langley Hertfordshire geology 18
Kings Scholars Pond W sewer 104
King's Street SW market 79, 148
Kingsbury NW Domesday Book Chingesberie 43; agriculture 78; village in 1800 156
Kingsbury Road Cemetery N 166
Kingsdown Kent geology 19
Kingsland N agriculture 79; Greater London Development Plan 128
Kingsland Road CITY Civil War fort 66; 83; bombing 118
Kingsland Waste E market 148
Kingston Bypass SW open spaces 139
Kingston (upon Thames) Surrey geology 18; flooding risk 23; Domesday Book Chingestune 43; growth 88; railway station 113; Greater London Development Plan 128; open spaces 141; village in 1800 156; cemetery 166
Kingsway Theatre WC 147
Kinnaird House WC 132
Knightrider Street CITY Medieval London 49, 52
Knights Templar, House of CITY 50
Knightsbridge SW 83; market 106; Underground station 161
Kyroun Lane CITY Medieval London 53

La Patente E Huguenot church 136
La Patente, Soho W Huguenot church 136
La Riole CITY Medieval London 53
La Rochelle W France trade with London 52
Ladbroke Grove W Underground station 160
Ladbroke Estate W 75
Ladle Lane CITY Medieval London 53
Lady Dock (f/c Lady Pond) SE 92, 158
Laleham W Middlesex village in 1800 156
Lambard's Hill CITY Medieval London 53
Lambeth SE flooding risk 23; growth 74; estates 75; cholera epidemics 96; crime 98; police and county court 99; housing 101; comparative poverty 103; licensed premises 103; local government district 1855 104; decline in population 112; industry 116; employment 117; bombing 118, 119; gentrification 127; immigrant population 137; open spaces 141; village in 1800 156; cemetery 166
Lambeth Bridge SE 163
Lambeth Infirmary SE 96
Lambeth North SE Underground station 161
Lambeth Palace (f/c Lambeth House) SE 43; 17th century 64; 136
Lambeth Road SE market 79; bombing 118
Lambeth Stairs SE 64
Lambeth Walk SE market 106, 148
Lambeth Wells SE pleasure gardens 142
Lambeth Wick Estate SE 75
Lamb's Conduit Fields WC 17th century 64; 79
Lambs Farm Estate E 75
Lampton W Middlesex village in 1800 156
Lancaster Gate W underground station 161
Lancaster House SW 76, 139
land use 78
Langbourn CITY ward of Medieval City 52
Lansbury Estate E planning 124
Latimer Road W Underground station 160
Lauriston Road Cemetery E 166
Lavender Dock (f/c Lavender Pond) SE 92, 158
law courts 99
Le Carré W Huguenot church 136
Lea, River E 17, 19, 40, 81, 92; industrial complex 93
Lea Bridge N trams 91
Lea Valley Park E 139
Leadenhall CITY Tudor London 59; market 79; Dickens 144; 148
Leamouth E railway station 159
Leather Lane (f/c Leveroune Lane) CITY Medieval London 49; market 106, 148
Leatherhead Surrey geology 18; growth 122
Leathersellers' Hall CITY 62
Leaves Green Kent village in 1800 156
Lee SE village in 1800 156; cemetery 166
Leicester Estate W 75
Leicester Fields WC Huguenot church 136
Leicester Square WC Underground station 161
Leighton House W 164
Lesnes Heath Kent village in 1800 156
Leveroune Lane see Leather Lane
Levesham see Lewisham
Lewisham SE Domesday Book Leveshham 43; agriculture 79; trams 91; cholera epidemic 96; churches 97; housing 101; comparative poverty 103; licensed premises 103; local government district 1855 104; increase in population 112; industry 116; employment 117; bombing 119; gentrification 127; Greater London Development Plan 129; Irish population 137; open spaces 141; village in 1800 156
Lewisham Road SE shops 107
Leybourne Kent new community 126
Leyton E agriculture 79; railway station 91; growth 112; bombing 119; village in 1800 156
Leytonstone E trams 91; village in 1800 156
L'Hôpital E Huguenot church 136
licensed premises 103
Lime Street CITY Medieval London 49, 53; ward of Medieval city 52
Limehouse E comparative poverty 103; local government district 1855 104; market 106; industry 116; railway station 158

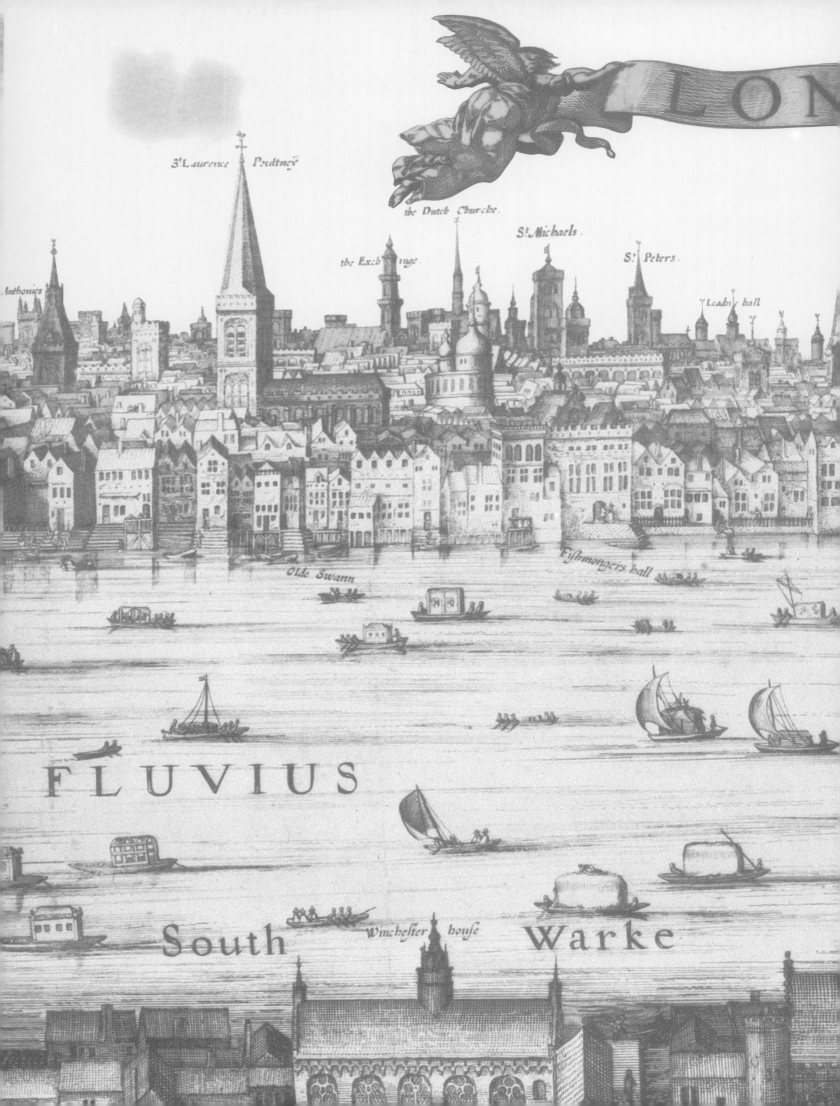